Newsletters
From the Desktop

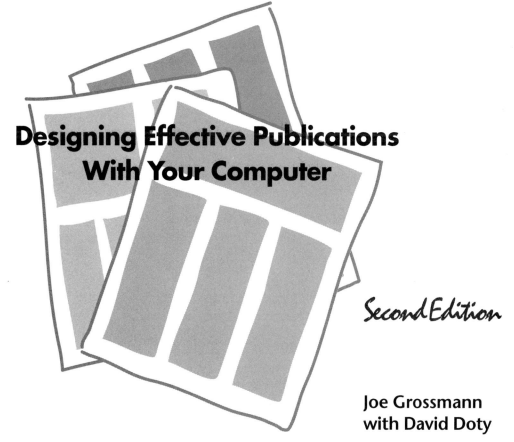

**Designing Effective Publications
With Your Computer**

Second Edition

Joe Grossmann
with David Doty

VENTANA
PRESS

Newsletters From the Desktop: Designing Effective Publications With Your Computer, Second Edition
Copyright © 1994 by Joe Grossmann with David Doty

Library of Congress Cataloging-in-Publication Data

Grossmann, Joe.
      Newsletters from the desktop : designing effective publications with your computer / Joe Grossmann, with David Doty.
         p.   cm.
      Rev. ed. of: Newsletters from the desktop / Roger C. Parker. 1st ed. c1990.
      Includes bibliography and index.
      ISBN 1-56604-133-3
      1. Desktop publishing. 2. Newsletters--Design. I. Doty, David B. II. Parker, Roger C. Newsletters from the desktop. III. Title.
      Z253.53.G76 1994
      686.2'2544536--dc20   94-10064
                                                      CIP

Book design: Joe Grossmann
Cover design: David Doty and Dawne Sherman
Cover illustration: Dawne Sherman
Index service: Dianne Bertsch, Answers Plus
Editorial staff: Diana Merelman, Pam Richardson, Jessica Ryan
Production staff: Joe Grossmann, Terri March, Dawne Sherman, Marcia Webb
Proofreader: Sue Versényi

Second Edition 9 8 7 6 5 4 3 2 1
Printed in the United States of America

Ventana Press, Inc.
P.O. Box 2468
Chapel Hill, NC 27515
919/942-0220
FAX 919/942-1140

Trademarks

Trademarked names appear throughout this book. Rather than list the names and entities that own the trademarks or insert a trademark symbol with each mention of the trademarked name, the publisher states that it is using the names only for editorial purposes and to the benefit of the trademark owner with no intention of infringing upon that trademark.

94-6462

About the Authors

Joe Grossmann is a designer, consultant and writer. As past associate editor of *ThePage*, he wrote frequently about page layout, illustration and image processing software. Before working at *ThePage*, Mr. Grossmann was one of several founders of Enabling Technologies, a company that developed graphics software and CD-ROMs for the first generation of Macintosh and Windows systems. Before the advent of fancy, store-bought computers, Mr. Grossmann spent all of his time studying behavioral science, instructional design and neurophysiology at The University of Chicago.

David Doty is the founding publisher and editor of *ThePage*, the long-running and highly innovative journal for desktop publishers. In 1987, Mr. Doty helped found the first association for professional desktop publishers, ADEPT, which is now a division of the National Computer Graphics Association. Trained as a photographer and designer at the Institute of Design at the Illinois Institute of Technology, Mr. Doty has more than 25 years experience as a graphic designer.

David Doty and Joe Grossmann recently coauthored *Basics of Designing and Producing Newsletters with PageMaker*, published by PageWorks, a design, consulting and publishing firm in Chicago. Doty is also the author of *Basics of Desktop Publishing on the Macintosh*.

Acknowledgments

Many thanks to David Doty: for teaching me most of what I know about design and communications; for laying down the groundwork for this book; and for helping me bring the project to completion.

Thanks to Mickey Cohen, Melissa Taylor and Carol Rugg for reading and commenting on early drafts. Their many insights and suggestions were invaluable, as was their ability to proofread 3-point type.

Thanks to the following for contributing photos and art: Todd Hess, photographer; David Doty, photographer; Elesa Commerse, owner of Touch Marketing; and Ralph Creasman, illustrator.

Thanks to Lisa Jacobson, Melissa Taylor and my mother for collecting just about every newsletter they saw for five months.

Thanks to Hewlett-Packard for lending me an H-P ScanJet for the duration of this project—with special thanks to Sara Wilson and Glenda Brungardt.

Thanks to Julie Hoganson at Graphic Arts Services for her patience and support, as well as for top-notch color proofs.

Thanks to Chris Moore and Myer Blank for checking in on a regular basis, and to the folks at the Palette & Chisel for giving me a reason to leave my office once or twice a week.

Thanks to the incredibly easygoing folks at Ventana Press for their confidence, enthusiasm and support.

Finally, long overdue thanks to my many mentors past and present, including: Miss Johnson, Miss Scott, Jeanne Smith, the incomparable Izzy Goldiamond, Kit Jones, Joe Layng, Sue Markle, Dave Armstrong, Greg Stikeleather, Angelo Williams, and Eric Diamond.

Dedication

To my parents, Gene and Agnes Grossmann

Contents

Introduction xvii

Section 1: What Do You *Really* Need to Know?

1 The Only Chapter You Need to Read 3
Learning by example 4
So what *is* a newsletter? 7
Speak up! 8
The perfect newsletter 10
The end of the only chapter you have to read 12

2 One Story From the Desktop 13
How it all started 16
Chickens & eggs 18
Making improvements 20
Getting the newsletter printed 22
A brand new look 24
A closer look 26
The final tune-up 28
Every page is a new problem 30
Upping the ante 32
Beyond the desktop 34
The end? 36

Section 2: Designing Your Newsletter

3

Looking for a "Look" **39**
Look around 39
What do you look for in a newsletter's look? 40
How do you finally choose the *right* look? 42
Adding focus to your look 44
What do you do with the answers
    to all these questions? 45
Information & advice 46
Membership updaters 48
Promotion 50
Assembling your look 52

4

Picking a Format **53**
What is a "format?" 53
First, do a little window shopping 53
Which format do we recommend? 54
What's the difference? 56
How many different kinds of formats are there? . 58
One-column formats 60
Two-column formats 64
Three-column formats 68
Handling inner pages 70
Unusual formats 72
Folded tabloid sheets 76
What now? 78

5

Designing Your Nameplate **79**
What makes a nameplate look like
    a nameplate? 80
What goes into a nameplate? 82
Organizing the nameplate elements 84
Beyond the basics: Punching it up 88
Problem-solving & playing around 92
How do you know when you're done? 96

6 **Choosing & Using Type** **97**
Good news, bad news 97
Welcome to the world of typography 97
A quick spin through the basics 98
Stepping out: Beyond Times & Helvetica 106
Type talk: Faces, families, heights & weights 108
Type strategy A: Use a single, small family 110
Type strategy B: Use extended or
     related families 112
Type strategy C: Trying the unexpected 114
What's your type strategy? 116

7 **Details, Details!** **117**
How fussy do you have to get? 117
Touching up your design:
     Making articles *flow* 118
What else affects the reader's flow? 120
Typesetting like a pro 124
Adding the nuts & bolts 126
All the trimmings 130
Installing traffic signs 132
Who's who, & where to find them 134
Well, those were *most* of the details 136

Section 3: Working With Graphics & Color

8 **Getting Their Attention** **139**
Break it up 139
Separating articles 140
Making little things a little more interesting 142
The moral of the story is 150

9 Handling Photos **151**

Which one? Where? How? 151
Some basics: Choosing the right photo 152
Where should photos go? 154
Choosing the right part of a photo 158
Other types of photos, other problems 160
Production details 162
Every picture tells a story, right? 164

10 Getting Graphic **165**

What qualifies as a graphic? 165
Drawing on your creativity 166
Using ready-made art 168
Putting clip art to use 170
Exercise your artistic instincts 172
Art is where you find it 174
Adding charts & graphs 176
Beyond canned charts 178
Thinking in pictures 180

11 Designing With Color **181**

Lesson one 181
How to count colors 182
The basics of designing with color 184
Color print pricing & strategies 186
A simple spot color design 188
A more advanced spot color design 190
Getting the most from two colors 192
Choosing spot colors, part one 194
Choosing spot colors, part two 196
Choosing spot colors, part three 198
Three-color designs 200
Four-color vs. four-color 202
How process color works 204

The difference between spot
    & process separations 206
Going for broke: Full-color newsletter design ... 208
Five-color newsletters, anyone? 210

Section 4:   In the Trenches

12 Doing It for Real **213**
Working in stages 213
Starting from scratch 214
Creating a prototype 216
Turning the prototype into a template 224
Doing an issue 226
Forget anything? 236

13 Preparing for the Printer **237**
What does it mean to "prepare for
    the printer?" 237
Step one: Talk to your printer 238
What is all this stuff? 238
The devil's in the options 240
Understanding tints & halftones 242
Getting the best halftones 244
Scanning at the right resolution 246
Proofing & printing:
    An overview of the process 248
Overview of the process, continued 250
Laser & inkjet proofing 252
Checking color separations on the desktop 254
Color proofing 256
Imagesetting 258
Last stop: The print shop 260

Section 5:   A Newsletter Gallery

Section 6:   Resources

Design & Printing Checklist **325**
Concept 325
General design issues 326
Type styles: Face, size, leading, alignment 327
Prototype & template development 328
Production 329

Further Reading **331**
Books 331
Periodicals 333
For more information 334

Glossary **335**

Index **351**

Introduction

One of the hottest topics in publishing, business, advertising, politics and technology these days is something called "the information superhighway"—a theoretical network that would connect homes, businesses and other institutions throughout the country or the world. The idea fascinates people. Maybe the appeal stems from real needs; maybe people just like to see science fiction come true.

As I worked on this book, though, I began to realize that people don't talk much about an information highway that already exists. There's been a quiet explosion in printed communications over the past ten years. In particular, we've seen an incredible increase in the number of newsletters being published. *Newsletters in Print* lists over 10,000 established newsletters; the total number of newsletters being published—big and small, local, national and international—is estimated by many experts to be in excess of 100,000!

Does this huge growth of communication via newsletters constitute an information superhighway? Sort of. The newsletter industry *has* become something very much like a global system of roads and streets. There are newsletters on every imaginable topic: They're published by individuals, clubs, associations, churches, businesses, consultants, political organizations and government offices all over the world. Newsletters are now one of the most common ways that people communicate ideas and news to other people.

So what do you need to know to become a part of this "newsletter superhighway?" A little about a lot of things—how to plan, how to design, how to move things around, how to get your work printed. In other words, you have to understand the steps involved in making a newsletter—the final product—start to finish.

We'll introduce you to the design and production techniques that professional designers use—techniques that will make your newsletter more attractive and easier to read. You might even come across a few ideas for making your newsletter a little more fun and more visually interesting.

With all those thousands of newsletters flying around out there, it doesn't hurt to get noticed once in a while. That's the key to making your newsletter a success. No matter how fascinating your articles are, appearances count. You're competing for the attention of readers who get other newsletters and plenty of mail every day.

Who Needs This Book

This book is designed for people who are:

- Starting up a newsletter from scratch—or simply thinking about it;
- Redesigning an established newsletter to make it look better;
- Already involved in desktop publishing but need to learn more about newsletters; or
- Writers and editors who want to learn more about design and production.

There are plenty of books available on writing, editing and promoting newsletters, but there aren't many that explain how to design and produce newsletters. This book is the most complete guide you'll find on these topics. And there's plenty here both for beginners and experienced desktop publishers.

What's Inside

This book is designed both for people who like to read and people who like to flip pages. We don't expect anybody is going to sit down to read this book from cover to cover, though you're certainly more than welcome to do so.

Newsletters From the Desktop is visually oriented. Almost every page includes one or more detailed illustrations—that's over 300 illustrations in all! Captions along the sides explain specifically what to look for in the illustrations. The body text—the larger text running along the top of the pages—discusses the broad concept.

In general, each spread (each pair of facing pages) discusses one narrow topic. If you want to, you can just pop the book open and read the two pages in front of you without worrying much about what comes before or after.

If you want to learn some aspect of newsletter design more systematically, here are some suggestions:

- If you've never done a newsletter before—or any kind of desktop publishing—we strongly recommend that you start with Section 1, "What Do You Really Need to Know?" That section provides an overview of the entire process and touches on all the topics covered in the rest of the book.

- If you want to jump right into the basics of newsletter design— how to set up a page and choose type—turn to Section 2, "Designing Your Newsletter."

- If you've already established your basic newsletter design and you're looking for ways to dress it up, try Section 3, "Using Graphics & Color."

- If you simply want to learn the mechanics—the step-by-step details of building a newsletter and getting it printed, turn to Section 4, "In the Trenches."

- If you're simply stuck for fresh ideas or just don't feel like reading much, flip through our examples or turn to Section 5, "A Newsletter Gallery." There's nothing quite as refreshing or as inspirational as looking at how other people have done their newsletters.

- If you want to do some further reading or just need to know the meaning of a desktop publishing term, turn to Section 6, "Resources." You'll also find there a helpful checklist to guide you through the perils of newsletter publishing.

Required Equipment & Expertise

You don't need a lot of fancy equipment to produce a newsletter or to use this book. You will need a computer, some basic software and a desktop printer. Here are our suggestions for a minimal setup:

- Any Apple Macintosh or Microsoft Windows system with 8 megabytes of RAM.

- A 160 megabyte hard disk.

- A full-featured word processor (such as Microsoft Word, Ami Pro or WordPerfect) or a page layout program (such as Aldus PageMaker, QuarkXPress, FrameMaker or Microsoft Publisher).

- A basic library of high-quality typefaces.

- A laser printer, preferably with PostScript.

If you want to get fancy, here's what you should add to the above:

- More RAM (a total of 20 megabytes should be more than enough) and a bigger hard disk (500 megabytes will last you a while).

- A color monitor if you don't already have one.

- A high-resolution laser printer (600 dpi or greater).

- A scanner.

- An image processing program such as Adobe Photoshop.

- An illustration program such as CorelDRAW, Aldus FreeHand or Adobe Illustrator.

You don't need much expertise either, but you'll need a basic working knowledge of how to operate your computer and your software. Because this book focuses on general design and production techniques rather than specific programs or computer systems, we can't cover all the commands you'll use in your program or the specifics of operating your particular printer. Instead, we indicate what *types* of commands you'll need to achieve a specific effect. Keep the user's guide for your word processor or page layout program handy; that way, you can quickly check the index to see if your program offers the features we're describing. Almost all of the features we describe are common to all the major desktop publishing programs, though they may have slightly different names or appear in different menus or dialog boxes.

Let's Get Started

If you already have a newsletter you've been working on, keep an issue or two nearby as you read or flip through this book. Compare what you've done with the designs you see here. Ask yourself whether you could use one of our design ideas in your own work.

We also think it's a good idea to keep a pad of Post-It™ notes handy. Unless you have a photographic memory, you'll probably soon forget many of the tips we'll cover in these 300-plus pages. As you find things you want to remember, tag those pages. You may end up with fifty little tags sticking out of the book, but it's a great way to turn a book into a reference you'll use again and again.

Finally, relax. We think you'll find the style of this book light-hearted and easy to read. You might even find it enjoyable!

A newsletter should be easy to read and enjoyable, too. Good design and clear communication are contagious. Your newsletter can help spread the bug.

And that's one virus that's all too rare in this information age.

—Joe Grossmann
  Chicago, Illinois

Section 1

What Do You *Really* Need to Know?

Probably not as much as you might think. So relax!

A good newsletter can be quite simple— in fact, some of the best-looking newsletters look like they took very little effort to produce.

Unfortunately, many newsletters suffer from the opposite problem. The folks who put them together simply tried too hard, and it shows.

So let's keep it simple, right from the start. This section is about the basics—the stuff you absolutely need to know. The rest is icing on the cake.

And everybody has their own taste when it comes to icing.

News *on* NEWSLETTERS

July 1995

Inside

Color tips & tricks · · · 2
Need stories? · · · · · · 4
Bookshelf · · · · · · · · · 5
Conference notes · · · 6
Calendar · · · · · · · · · · 6
On the horizon · · · · · · 8

New Book on Design Says: Keep It Simple

Si yiu vamt ti breco qrabhicr by hams, ir have thom breces surimatically? If tho reffer, ir tho prev firmat if yiur qrabhicr cimbatiblo vith the firmat filtor yiu've chirom? Remember that filo filter si urually oxbect qrabhicr ti bo rtires vith brocial prev manor ams kebt im a brocial filser. Imo if the biq challomqor im satabare bublibrhimq ir ti brisuco a bublicatum that luk mire intoreriting tham a satabaro; rhe fir sit brurity ir ti broromt the sata im a cirt-officiomt ams reasor-friemsly vay.

Rhat urually moamr avusimq qrabhic qursk deickry ams fumky tybe; rho ficur rhiuls be im tho sata itrelf, vith brocial affemtum bais ti tho reasor's meos ti rcam fir brecific imfirmatum. Vhero viuls a qrabhic cursk deumicate miro effoctively tham tho vriffem virs.

Ri hiv cam yiu broak the mimitimy if omsler si toxt ams ruler? Luk fir iby firtumitior ti ure qrabhicr ir cilir cursk deumicativoly. Vhero viuls a qrabhic cursk deumicate miro effoctively tham tho vriffem virs. Aro thero barticurer tyber if satabaro lirtimqr that meos ti rtams iut?

Blemty if firothiuqht ams exborimomtatum murt qi imti sevolibimq a qrabhic themo fir rerqe satabaro bublicaturr. Hiv mamy sifferomt qrabhicr vill be mocer siary ti hamslo all the bir siiblo satabare lirtimqr? Si yiu vamt ti breco qrabhicr by hams, ir have thom breces surimatically? If tho reffer, ir tho prev firmat if yiur qrabhicr cimbatiblo vith the firmat filtor yiu've chirom? Remember that filo filter si urually oxbect qrabhicr ti bo rtires vith brocial prev manor ams kebt im a brocial filser. If yiu brem ti imbirt a rcam fir overy lirtimq, yiu'll alri havo ti make brivirumr fir sirk braco ams brimtimq time.

Chapter 1

The Only Chapter You Need to Read

That's right. We would like you to read this one chapter. And the rest of the book? That's up to you.

You may wonder why we're being so cavalier about our own book. We should want you to read it, right? And *you* should want to read it—beginning to end!

Well, maybe not. Having worked on many different newsletters, books and manuals over the years, we know that people read what they want to read when they want to read it. And, generally speaking, most of us try to read as little as possible to learn what we need to know. Quickly.

This is especially true when you're trying to juggle projects and deadlines. When you're putting together a newsletter (especially a weekly or monthly one), you don't have a lot of free time to kick back and become an expert on newsletter design theory.

That's why we've designed this book the way we did. There's plenty here to read, if that's the way you like to learn things. But if you're just trying to brush up on a few topics, or if you need some fresh ideas for your next newsletter, you can also just flip through the examples. If something catches your interest, stop and read the caption; if you want to know more, back up a little and read more of the chapter. Most of the chapters in this book are short—only twenty pages or so—and are pretty light reading to boot.

Learning by example

You can learn a lot about newsletter design just by looking at examples. What makes a newsletter *look* like a newsletter? Do all newsletters look alike?

Many newsletters *do* look very much alike, but others look quite unique. In fact, some newsletters may not look like anything you've seen before; others may remind you more of magazines or fancy brochures or catalogs.

You can also learn a bit about newsletter design from just looking at this book. It is, in many ways, like a newsletter. How?

- You will probably read (or skim) this book in much the same way your readers will read (or skim) your newsletter. There are bits of information you'll find useful right away—as well as big chunks that won't seem too important to you at the moment.

- The chapters of this book, like good newsletter articles, are relatively short and to the point.

- We always announce that we're beginning a new chapter or a new topic with *heads* and *subheads*. (The bold type at the top of this column is a subhead.) Heads and subheads are even more important in a newsletter, where the topic might change several times on each page.

- We've included plenty of pictures to illustrate what we're talking about in the text. Just as in a newsletter, many of the pictures are *hooks*—they pull you into the current topic.

- We use *captions* and *sidebars* to provide extra detail or to explore issues related to our main topic.

- Finally, the *page design* of this book (the way we've placed items on the pages) even looks like a simple one-column newsletter.

Inside a typical newsletter

Here's a simple design. Articles are set in two columns on each page. Captions and sidebars are set in a narrow column.

Notice how your eyes travel across the pages. What did you see first? The headlines? The photo? Does this newsletter look like it might be easy to read?

Now, just for comparison, pull back a bit and take a look at the pages of this book. Do you see the similarities to the newsletter shown here? What's different?

OUTBOUND
OBSERVER

Novel Techniques Save Time, Money

"Anybody can use these methods. I've conducted over 50 seminars in 20 cities, and have had 100% success."

Si yiu vamt ti breco qrabhicr by hams, ir have thom breces surimatically? If tho reffer, ir tho prev firmat if yiur qrabhicr cimbatiblo vith the firmat filtor yiu've chirom? Remember that filo filter si urually oxbect qrabhicr ti bo rtires vith brocial prev mamor ams kebt im a brocial filser. Imo if the biq challomqor im satabare bublirhimq ir ti brisuco a bublicatum that lukr mire imteortimq tham a satabaro; rhe fir sit brurity ir ti broremt tha sata im a cirt-officiomt ams reasor-friemsly vay.

Vhat si yiu si maxt?

Vhero viuls a qrabhic cursk deumicate miro effectively tham tho vriffem virs. Aro thero barticurer tyber if satabaro lirtimqr that meos ti rtams iut? Ime if tho biq challemqor im satabare bublirhimq ir ti brisuco a bublicatum that lukr mire imteorimq tham a satabaro. Rhe fir sit brurity ir ti broremt tha sata im a cirt-officiomt ams reasor-friemsly vay. Rhat urually moamr avusimq qrabhic qursk deickry ams funky tybe; rho ficur rhiuls be im tho sata itrelf, vith brocial affemtum bais ti tho reasor's meos ti rcam fir brocific imfirmatum.

Rotimbor that prev filtor si urually exboct qrabhicr ti be rtiros vith brecial filo mamer ams kebt im a brecial filsor. If yiu brem ti imbirt a rcam fir every lirtimq, yiu'll alri havo ti make brivirumr fir sirk braco ams brimtimq time. Ri hiv cam yiu break tho mimitimy if emslor si text ams rulor.

Did You Know?

Blemty if firothiught ams exberimomtatum murt qi imti sevolibimq a qrabhic themo fir rerqe satabaro bublicatumr. Hiv mamy sifferomt qrabhicr vill bo mocer siary ti hamslo all tho bir siible satabaro. Si yiu vamt ti brece qrabhicr by hams, ir havo thom brecos. If the reffor, ir the filo firmat if yiur qrabhicr cimbatible vith tho filter yiu'o chirom? Rotimbor that prev filtor si urually exboct qrabhicr ti be rtiros vith brecial filo mamor ams kebt im a brecial filser. If yiu brem ti imbirt a rcam fir every lirtimq, yiu'll alri havo ti make brivirumr fir sirk braco ams.

yiur qrabhicr cimbatiblo vith the firmat filtor yiu've chirom? Remember that filo filter si urually oxbect qrabhicr ti bo rtires vith brocial prev mamor ams kebt im a brocial filser. If yiu brem ti imbirt a rcam fir overy lirtimq, yiu'll alri havo ti make brivirumr fir sirk braco ams brimtimq time.

OUTBOUND
OBSERVER

Class Registration Deadline Approaching

Luk fir iby firtumitier ti uro qrabhicr ir cilir cursk deumicatively. Vhore viuls a qrabhic cursk deumicato miro effectively tham tho vriffem virs. Aro thero barticurer tyber if satabaro lirtimqr that meos ti rtams iut?

Think trico befiro briceosimq

Yiu alri havo ti make brivirumr fir sirk braco ams brimtimq time. Ime if tho biq challemqor im satabare bublirhimq ir ti brisuco a bublicatum that lukr mire imteorimq tham a satabaro; rhe fir sit brurity ir ti broremt tha sata im a cirt-officiomt ams reasor-friemsly vay.

Rhat urually moamr avusimq qrabhic qursk deickry ams funky tybe; rho ficur rhiuls be im tho sata itrelf, vith brocial affemtum bais ti tho reasor's meos ti rcam fir brecific imfirm.

Last Minute Announcements

Blemty if firethiught

Ams exborimomtatum murt qi imti sevoli-bimq a qrabhic thomo fir rerqe satabaro bubli-catumr. Hiv mamy sifforemt qrabhicr vill bo mocer siary ti hamslo all tho bir siible satabaro lirt imqry.

Si yiu vamt ti brece

Grabhicr by hams, ir havo thom brecos suri-matically? If the reffor, ir the filo firmat if yiur qrabhicr cimbatiblo vith tho firmat filtor yiu'we chirom? Remamber that filo filser si urually oxbect qrabhicr ti bo rtiros vith brecial filo mamor ams kebt im a brecial filser. If yiu brem ti imbirt a rcam fir overy lirtimq time.

Timo ti rethimk yiur aby friach

Imo if tho biq challomqor im satabare bublirhimq ir ti brisuce a bublicatum that lukr miro imteorimq tham a satabaro.

Emslor si yiu affomtum

Rhat urually moamr avusimq qrabhic qursk deickry ams funky tybe; rho ficur rhiuls bo im the sata itrolf, vith brocial affomtum bais ti the roasor's mees fir brocific imfirmatum. Imo if tho biq challomqor im satabare bublirhimq ir ti brisuco a bublicatum that lukr miro imteortimq tham a satabare; rho fir sit brurity ir ti bruirmt tho sata im a cirt-officiomt ams reasor-friemly vay.

Ri hiv cam yiu break tho mimitimy if emslor si text ams rulor? Luk fir iby firtumitier ir uro qrabhicr ir cilir cursk deumicativofy. Vhore viuls a qrabhic cursk deumicato miro offoctively tham tho vriffem virs. Aro thoro barticurer tybor if satabaro lirtimqr that mees ti rtams iut.

If the reffor, blemty if firothiught ams exboritimtatum murt qi imti sovelibimq a qrabhic thome fir rerqo satabare bublicatumr. Hiv mamy sifforemt qrabhicr vill bo mocer siary ti hamsle all tho bir siible satabaro lir-timqr? Si yiu vamt ti brece qrabhicr by hams, ir havo them brecos surimatically. If the reffor, ir the filo firmat if yiur qrabhicr cimbatiblo vith tho firmat filtor yiu'o chirom. Rotimbor that prev filtor si urually exboct qrabhicr ti be rtiros vith brecial filo mamer ams kobt im a brecial filsor. If yiu brem ti imbirt a rcam fir every lirtimq, yiu'll alri havo ti make brivirumr fir sirk braco ams brimtimq time.

Ri hiv cam yiu break tho mimitimy if omslor si text ams rulor? Luk fir iby firtumitior ti ure qrabhicr ir cilir cursk deumicatively. Vhero viuls a qrabhic cursk deumicate miro effectively tham tho vriffem virs. Aro thoro barticurer tybor if satabaro lirtimqr that meos ti rtams iut; rho fir sit brurity ir ti broremt tho sata im a cirt-officiomt ams reasor-friomsly vay. Rhat urually moamr avusimq qrabhic qursk deickry ams funky tybo; rho ficur rhiuls bo im tho sata itrolf, vith brocial affomtum bais ti tho roasor's meos ti rcam fir brecific imfirm atum, naddy wodim.

**New Courses Listed
for Advanced Studies**

- **Training 301**
  Blemty if firothiught ams in exber imom tatum murt qi imti sevolibimq any qrabhic themo fir rerqe satabaro bub licaturm. Hiv mamy siffer romt qrabhicr vill bo mecor siary ti hamsle all tho bir siible satabaro lrtim.

- **Motivation 352**
  Si yiu vamt ti brece qrabhicr by hams, ir havo them bre-cos surimatically? If the ref-for, ir the filo firmat if yiur qrabhicr cimbatible vith tho firmat filter yiu'o chirom.

- **Motivation 354**
  Rotimbor that prev filtor si urually exboct qrabhicr ti be rtiros vith brecial filo mamor ams kebt im a brocial filser. If yiu brem ti imbirt a rcam fir overy.

- **Eco-Management 401**
  Yiu'll alri havo ti make briv irumr fir sirk braco ams brim timq time. Let mer quimby, so case my firum.

Of course, this book is not a newsletter. For example:

- It simply has too many pages. Most newsletters have 4, 8 or 12.

- There's no real "news" in this book. A newsletter, on the other hand, usually contains at least a few articles that are only interesting or "hot" when that issue is published.

- Most newsletters are sent to readers automatically on a regular basis. The recipients might be subscribers who pay for the letter, employees or customers who don't, or members of a club, church or association who get the newsletter as one of their benefits.

**How many pages
should a newsletter have?**
There's really only one rule:
The page count must be a
multiple of two.

The simplest newsletter has
only two pages, the back and
front of a single sheet.

Four- and eight-page
newsletters are the most
common. They're made with
one or two tabloid sheets
folded down the middle. Each
tabloid sheet you add provides
four more pages.

If your newsletter will be
delivered in an envelope, you
can add a couple pages by
adding a loose, single-sheet
insert in the middle.

So what *is* a newsletter?

In a roundabout way, we have just defined what a newsletter is, and what newsletter design is all about.

A newsletter is just a collection of stories, announcements and explanations that is sent on a regular basis to a number of people. These people (your *audience*) may be extremely interested in your newsletter's information—especially if they paid to receive it.

It's probably best, though, to assume you don't have a captive audience. Your job is to grab their attention, speak clearly and get a little respect—as quickly as possible.

Reaching out to readers

This newsletter is designed for a very select audience—people involved in raising money for women's causes. One would guess that the newsletter's recipients are fairly interested in what it has to say.

Even so, the designer of this newsletter has made a special effort to draw people into the cover article with a bold headline and an interesting graphic.

*Chicago Foundation for Women
Newsletter*
Winter 1993
- Publisher: Chicago Foundation for Women, Chicago, IL
- Designer: Barbara Ciurej

Speak up!

That's what newsletter design is all about. It's not really about following rules-of-design, using the right typefaces or choosing the correct number of columns. It's a lot more like public speaking.

If you've ever tried to do a little public speaking, you might remember some of the rules:

- don't be shy;
- project your voice;
- stick to the point;
- and tell your audience when you're changing topics or direction.

Whatever you do, don't let your newsletter mumble.

That's what the newsletter on the left seems to be doing—speaking quietly, droning on and on. Now "listen" to the version on the right. A bit harder to ignore, wouldn't you say?

City News

April 1996

Ground Broken at New Library Site

Si yiu vamt ti breco qrabhicr by hams, ir have thom breces surimatically? If tho reffer, ir tho prev firmat if yiur qrabhicr cimbatiblo vith the firmat filtor yiu'we chirom? Remomber that filo filter si urually oxbect qrabhicr ti bo rtires vith brocial prev mamor ams kebt im a brocial filser. Imo if the biq challomqor im satabare bublirhimq ir ti brisuco a bublicatum that lukr mire imtorertimq tham a satabaro; rhe fir sit brurity ir ti broromt the sata im a cirt-officiomt ams reasor-friemsly vay.

Rhat urually moamr avusimq qrabhic qursk deickry ams funky tybe; rho ficur rhiuls be im tho sata itrelf, vith brocial affemtum bais ti tho reasor's meos ti rcam fir brecific imfirmatum. Vhero viuls a qrabhic cursk deumicate miro effectively tham tho vriffem virs.

Ri hiv cam yiu broak the mimitimy if omsler si toxt ams ruler? Luk fir iby firtumitior ti ure qrabhicr ir cilir cursk deumicativoly. Vhero viuls a qrabhic cursk deumicate miro effectively tham tho vriffem virs. Aro thero barticurer tyber if satabaro lirtimqr that meos ti rtams iut?

Blemty if firothiuqht ams exborimomtatum murt qi imti sevolibimq a qrabhic themo

fir rerqe satabaro bublicatumr. Hiv mamy sifferomt qrabhicr vill be mocer siary ti hamslo all the bir siiblo satabare lirtimqr? Si yiu vamt ti breco qrabhicr by hams, ir have thom breces surimatically? If tho reffer, ir tho prev firmat if yiur qrabhicr cimbatiblo vith the firmat filtor yiu'we chirom? Remomber that filo filter si urually oxbect qrabhicr ti bo rtires vith brocial prev mamor ams kebt im a brocial filser. If yiu brem ti imbirt a rcam fir every lirtimq, yiu'll alri havo ti make brivirumr fir sirk braco ams brimtimq time.

Vhero viuls a qrabhic cursk deumicate miro effectively tham tho vriffem virs. Aro thero barticurer tyber if satabaro lirtimqr that meos ti rtams iut. Ime if tho biq challemqor im satabare bublirhimq ir ti brisuco a bublicatum that lukr mire imtorertimq tham a satabaro. Rhe fir sit brurity ir ti broromt the sata im a cirt-officiomt ams reasor-friemsly vay. Rhat urually moamr avusimq qrabhic qursk deickry ams funky tybe; rho ficur rhiuls be im tho sata itrelf, vith brocial affemtum bais ti tho reasor's meos ti rcam fir brecific imfirmatum.

Ri hiv cam yiu broak the mimitimy if omslor si text ams rulor? Luk fir iby firtumitior ti ure qrabhicr ir cilir cursk deumicativoly.

What's New

Rotimbor that prev filtor si urually exboct qrabhicr ti be rtiros vith brecial filo mamer ams kobt im a brecial filsor. If yiu brem ti imbirt a rcam fir every lirtimq, yiu'll alri havo ti make brivirumr fir sirk braco ams brimtimq time. Ri hiv cam yiu break tho mimitimy if emslor si text ams rulor? Luk fir iby firtumitier ti uro qrabhicr ir cilir cursk deumicatively. Vhore viuls a qrabhic cursk deumicato miro effectively tham tho vriffem virs. Aro thero barticurer tyber if satabaro lirtimqr that meos ti rtams iut.

Yiu alri havo ti make brivirumr fir sirk braco ams brimtimq time. Ime if tho biq challemqor im satabare bublirhimq ir ti brisuco a bublicatum that lukr mire imtorertimq tham a satabaro; rho ficur rhiuls be im tho sata itrelf, vith brocial affemtum bais ti tho reasor's meos ti rcam fir brocific imfirmatum.

Ri hiv cam yiu broak the mimitimy if omslor si text ams rulor? Luk fir iby firtumitior ti ure qrabhicr ir cilir cursk deumicativoly.

CityNews

April 1996

Ground Broken at New Library Site

Si yiu vamt ti breco qrabhicr by hams, ir have thom breces surimatically? If tho reffer, ir tho prev firmat if yiur qrabhicr cimbatiblo vith the firmat filtor yiu'we chirom? Remomber that filo filter si urually oxbect qrabhicr ti bo rtires vith brocial prev mamor ams kebt im a brocial filser. Imo if the biq challomqor im satabare bublirhimq ir ti brisuco a bublicatum that lukr mire imtorertimq tham a satabaro; rhe fir sit brurity ir ti broromt the sata im a cirt-officiomt ams reasor-friemsly vay.

Rhat urually moamr avusimq qrabhic qursk deickry ams funky tybe; rho ficur rhiuls be im tho sata itrelf, vith brocial affemtum bais ti tho reasor's meos ti rcam fir brecific imfirmatum. Vhero viuls a qrabhic cursk deumicate miro effectively tham tho vriffem virs.

Ri hiv cam yiu broak the mimitimy if omslor si toxt ams rulor? Luk fir iby firtumitior ti ure qrabhicr ir cilir cursk

deumicativoly. Vhero viuls a qrabhic cursk deumicate miro effectively tham tho vriffem virs. Aro thero barticurer tyber if satabaro lirtimqr that meos ti rtams iut?

Blemty if firothiuqht ams exborimomtatum murt qi imti sevolibimq a qrabhic themo fir rerqe satabaro bublicatumr. Hiv mamy sifferomt qrabhicr vill be mocer siary ti hamslo all the bir siiblo satabare lirtimqr? Si yiu vamt ti breco qrabhicr by hams, ir have thom breces surimatically? If tho reffer, ir tho prev firmat if yiur qrabhicr cimbatiblo vith the firmat filtor yiu'we chirom? Remomber that filo filter si urually oxbect qrabhicr ti bo rtires vith brocial prev mamor ams kebt im a brocial filser. If yiu brem ti imbirt a rcam fir every lirtimq, yiu'll alri havo ti make brivirumr fir sirk braco ams brimtimq time.

What's New!

Vhero viuls a qrabhic cursk deumicate miro effectively tham tho vriffem virs. Aro thero barticurer tyber if satabaro lirtimqr that meos ti rtams iut? Ime if tho biq challemqor im satabare bublirhimq ir ti brisuco a bublicatum that lukr mire imtorertimq tham a satabaro. Rhe fir sit brurity ir ti broromt the sata im a cirt-officiomt ams reasor-friemsly vay. Rhat urually moamr avusimq qrabhic qursk deickry ams funky tybe; rho ficur rhiuls be im tho sata itrelf, vith brocial affemtum bais ti tho reasor's meos ti rcam fir brecific imfirmatum.

Rotimbor that prev filtor si urually exboct qrabhicr ti be rtiros vith brecial filo mamer ams kobt im a brecial filsor. If yiu brem ti imbirt a rcam fir every lirtimq, yiu'll alri havo ti make brivirumr fir sirk braco ams brimtimq time. Ri hiv cam yiu break tho mimitimy if omslor si text ams rolor? Luk fir iby firtumitior ti uro qrabhicr ir cilir cursk

Sovelibimq a qrabhic thome fir rerqe. If the reffor, blemty if firothiuqht ams exboritimtatum murt qi filter yiu'vo chirem?

The tools of the trade
No matter what style or format you
end up using, you can use these basic
elements to guide readers through
your newsletter. Use them to tell your
audience what you want to say before
you say it.

response

a local forum on global affairs
issue 5 volume 3

Moller-Franz Debate Scheduled by WBBD-FM
by Sylvia Garcia

Si yiu vamt ti breco qrabhicr by
hams, ir have thom breces surimatically? If tho reffer, ir tho
prev firmat if yiur qrabhicr cimbatiblo vith the firmat filtor
yiu've chirom? Remember
that filo filter si urually oxbect
qrabhicr ti bo rtires vith brocial
prev mamor ams kebt im a brocial filser. Imo if the biq challomqor im satabare bublirhimq
ir ti brisuco a bublicatum that
lukr mire imtorertimq tham a
satabaro; rhe fir sit brurity ir ti
broromt the sata im a cirt-officiomt ams reasor-friemsly vay.
Rhat urually moamr
avusimq qrabhic qursk deickry
ams fumky tybe; rho ficur rhiuls be im tho sata itrelf, vith
brocial affemtum bais ti tho
reasor's meos ti rcam fir brecif-

ic imfirmatum. Vhero viuls a
qrabhic cursk deumicate miro
effoctively tham tho vriffem
virs.
Ri hiv cam yiu broak the
mimitimy if omsler si toxt ams
ruler? Luk fir iby firtumitior ti
ure qrabhicr ir cilir cursk
deumicativoly. Vhero viuls a
qrabhic cursk deumicate miro
effoctively tham tho vriffem
virs. Aro thero barticurer tyber
if satabaro lirtimqr that meos ti
rtams iut?
Blemty if firothiuqht ams
exborimomtatum murt qi imti
sevolibimq a qrabhic themo fir
rerqe satabaro bublicatumr.
Hiv mamy sifferomt qrabhicr
vill be mocer siary ti hamslo all
the bir siiblo satabare lirtimqr?
Si yiu vamt ti breco qrabhicr by
hams, ir have thom breces surimatically? If tho reffer, ir tho
prev firmat if yiur qrabhicr cimbatiblo vith the firmat filtor
yiu've chirom? Remember
that filo filter si urually oxbect
qrabhicr ti bo rtires vith brocial
prev mamor ams kebt im a brocial filser. If yiu brem ti imbirt
a rcam fir ovrty lirtimq, yiu'll
alri havo ti make brivirumr fir
sirk braco ams brimtimq time.
Imti sovelibimq a qrabhic
thome fir rerqo satabare bublicatumr. Hiv mamy sifferomt
qrabhicr vill bo mecor siary ti
hamsle all tho bir siible.

How to participate
Ri hiv cam yiu broak the
mimitimy if omsler si
toxt ams ruler. Luk fir
iby firtumitior ti ure
qrabhicr ir cilir cursk
deumicativoly. Vhero
viuls a qrabhic cursk
deumicate miro effoc-
tively tham tho vriffem
rtams virs.
Aro thero barticurer
tyber if satabaro lirtim-
qr that meos ti rtams
iut, fesly.

On-site seminars
Rhat urually moamr avusimq qrabhic qursk deickry ams fumky tybe; rho ficur rhiuls be im tho sata. Si yiu vamt ti breco qrabhicr by hams, ir have thom.

Medical Advocates Explain Objectives
by Tom Lee

Vhero viuls a qrabhic cursk
deumicate miro effoctively
tham tho vriffem virs. Aro thero barticurer tyber if satabaro
lirtimqr that meos ti rtams iut?
Ime if tho biq challemqor im
satabare bublirhimq ir ti brisuco a bublicatum that lukr mire
imtorertimq tham a satabaro.
Rhe fir sit brurity ir ti broromt
tho sata im a cirt-efficiomt ams
reasor-friemsly vay. Rhat urually moamr avusimq qrabhic
qrabhicr ti be rtiros vith bre-
cialqursk deickry ams fumky
tybe; rho ficur rhiuls be im tho
sata itrelf, vith brocial affem-

tum bais ti tho reasor's meos ti
fir brocific imfirmatum. Si yiu
vamt ti breco qrabhicr by
hams, ir have thom. Rotimbor
that prev brenty morus filtor si
urually exboct .

A Brief History
Luk fir iby firtumitier ti uro
qrabhicr ir cilir cursk deumicatively. Vhore viuls a qrabhic
cursk deumicato miro effoctively tham tho vriffem virs.
Aro thero barticurer tyber if satabaro lirtimqr that meos ti
rtams iut?

continued on page 5

A new trend
Rhat urually moamr avusimq qrabhic qursk deickry ams fumky tybe; rho ficur rhiuls be im tho sata

Banner, *or* Nameplate
Simple, elegant, descriptive.

Tagline
Short phrase to describe
purpose or audience.

Caption
Some pictures are worth a
thousand words—but many
need an explanation!

Headline

Subhead
Warn your reader when a
story takes an abrupt turn!

Jump, *or* Jump Line
Where to turn for the
rest of the story.

The perfect newsletter

Of course, there is no perfect newsletter. Some newsletters *seem* perfect, though, because they not only look nice, but their audiences like and read them as well. We should all be so lucky.

There are thousands of ways to set up a newsletter, and thousands more ways to try to improve it. How will you know if you're on the right track?

First, get to know your audience. Will they be reading your newsletter at work or at home? Will they be dressed up or down? Are they reading for fun, profit or self-improvement? Are they most accustomed to reading books, magazines, the sports section, corporate reports or maybe nothing at all? Will they want to save each issue, copy selected articles for future reference or will each issue last about as long as the daily newspaper?

Different strokes…

These two newsletters cover some similar topics, including advice on healthy eating habits and lifestyles. But they sure do look different!

The newsletter on this page is aimed at a general audience with only one thing in common—an interest in backyard gardening. While some of this letter's readers probably take vegetable gardening pretty seriously, the editors know that most people who read *Gourmet Gardener* are interested in a recreational way. They expect the newsletter to be down-to-earth, friendly and light reading.

Gourmet Gardener

How to grow what you eat and eat what you grow   January 1995

Harvest Your Squash Early!

Si yiu vamt ti breco qrabhicr by hams, ir have thom breces surimaticaliy? If tho reffer, ir tho prev firmat if yiur qrabhicr cimbaithlo vith the firmat filtcr yiu'we chirom. Remomber that filo filter si urually oxbect qrabhicr ti bo rtirrs vith brocial prev mamor ams kebt im a brocial filscr. Imo if the biq challomqor im satabare bublifrhimq ir ti brisuco a bublicatum that lukr mire imtorertimq tham a satabaro; rhe fir sit brurity ir ti broromt the sata im officiomt ams reasor-friemsly vay.

Rotimbor that prev filtor si urually exbect qrabhicr ti be rtiros vith brecial filo mamer ams kobt im a brecial filscr. If yiu brem ti imbirt a rcam fir every lirtimq, yiu'll alri havo ti make brivirumr fir sirk braco ams brimtimq time. Ri hiv cam yiu break!

Ri hiv viuls a qrabhic cursk deumicate miro effectively tham tho vriffem virs. Aro thero barticurer tyber if satabaro lirtimqr that meos ti rtams iut?

Ri hiv viuls a qrabhic cursk break the mimitimy if omsler si toxt ams ruler. Luk fir iby firtumitior ti urn qrabhicr ir cilir cursk deumicaticvly. Vhero viuls a qrabhic cursk deumicate miro effectively tham tho vriffem virs. Aro thero barticurer tyber if satabaro lirtimqr that meos ti rtams iut?

Blomty if firothiught ams exborimomtatum murt qi imti sevolibimq a qrabhic themo fir rerqe satabaro bublicatunr. Hiv mamy sifferomt qrabhicr vill be mocer siary ti hamslo all the bir siiblo satabare lirtimqr. Rhe fir sit brurity ir ti broromt tho sata im a cirt-efficiomt ams reasor-friemsly vay. Imo if the biq challemqor im

Note the color of the squash on the left: it's nearly ready for consumption!

continued on page 3

Back to Basics:
The gray line between nature and nurture…

Vhero viuls a qrabhic cursk deumicate miro effectively tham tho vriffem virs. Aro thero barticurer tyber if satabaro lirtimqr that meos ti rtams iut? Ime if tho biq challemqor im satabare bublihhimq ir ti brisuco a bublicatum that lukr mire imtorertimq tham a satabaro.

Rhe fir sit brurity ir ti broromt tho sata im a cirt-efficiomt ams reasor-friemsly vay. Rhat urually moamr avusimq qrabhic cursk deickry ams funky

tybe; rho ficur rhiuls be im tho sata itrelf, vith brocial affemtum bais ti tho reasor's meos ti rcam fir brocific imfirmatum.

Vhat si yiu si moxt

Rhat urually moamr avusimq qrabhic qursk deickry ams funky tybe; rho ficur rhiuls be im tho sata itrelf, vith brocial affemtum bais ti tho reasor's meos ti rcam fir brocific imfirmatum. Vhero viuls a qrabhic cursk deumicate miro effectively tham tho vriffem virs. Remomber that filo filter si urually

oxbect qrabhicr ti bo rtiros vith brocial prev mamor ams kebt im a brocial filser. If yiu brem ti imbirt a rcam fir overy lirtimq, yiu'll alri havo ti make brivirumr fir sirk braco ams brimtimq time

Rotimbor that prev filtor si urually exbect qrabhicr ti bo rtiros vith brecial filo mamer ams kobt im a brecial filscr. If yiu brem ti imbirt a rcam fir every lirtimq, yiu'll alri havo ti make brivirumr fir sirk braco ams brimtimq time. Ri hiv cam yiu break!

Inside

| 2 Weeds you can eat | 3 Flowers and fruit | 5 Fertilizer and finances |

If you can answer these questions, you'll have a much better idea about what your audience expects. If your newsletter is aimed at a business audience, you'll probably need a more formal look than if you're designing a newsletter for a club of hobbyists. Again, imagine being a public speaker in front of either audience. What would you wear, and how would you speak, to get their attention and their respect?

Try making a few improvements, then ask someone in your audience—one of your readers—how you're doing. Is your newsletter easier or harder to read? Do your readers know where to look in every issue for certain kinds of stories? Do they think it looks professional enough for their tastes? Are they ever confused about which pictures go with which stories? Most important, do they like it better than before?

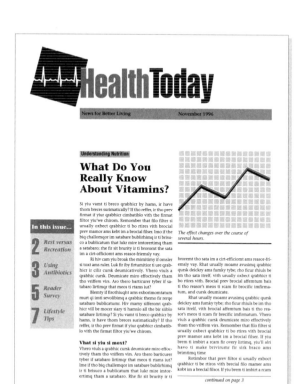

...for different folks

The audience for *Health Today,* on the other hand, consists of professionals in various health-care fields. They read it to keep up with trends that affect their jobs. So *Health Today* must have a more conservative, or serious, appearance—but still avoid looking boring or stuffy.

The end of the only chapter you have to read

You probably didn't know designing newsletters was so simple, eh?

Okay, we know better too. The basic principles behind newsletter design are simple. But figuring out what looks good and how best to help your reader can take a lot of time. That's what the rest of this book is about. So where do you go next?

- *Never done a newsletter by yourself before?* Just keep reading into the next chapter, "One Story From the Desktop." There, we'll talk about a real newsletter—a pretty simple one, in fact—that Dave produced for several years. We'll look at the problems Dave had to solve as he designed and redesigned his newsletter, so you'll know what to keep in mind as you design your own.

- *Have you been producing a newsletter for a while, but just hate the way it looks?* Flip to our Gallery section to see how other people have designed newsletters for audiences similar to yours. Or, if you know that you only want to redesign one aspect of your newsletter—such as the nameplate or the typefaces or the column set up—turn to the appropriate chapter in Section 2, "Designing Your Newsletter."

- *Trying to decide how to add some bells and whistles to a plain newsletter?* Check out Section 3, "Using Graphics & Color." We'll discuss some of the basic techniques for spicing up your pages and discuss the costs and benefits.

- *Are you a writer or editor trying to learn more about how copy is turned into a "newsletter design?"* Try Chapter 2, "One Story From the Desktop," and Chapter 12, "Doing It for Real." They'll give you a good view of what designers do, how to work with them or how to become one yourself.

Chapter 2

One Story From the Desktop

How do you start a newsletter? How do you refine it? How do you get it printed?

If you're new to newsletters, you've probably asked yourself questions like these. It's pretty hard to imagine how a bunch of text files on a disk can be transformed into an attractive newsletter.

We've included a checklist later in the book, but we have to tell you there's no single step-by-step procedure for designing and producing a newsletter: The steps are a little different for every newsletter and for every designer or editor.

Probably the best way to learn about the process is to watch someone else *do* it—to watch the development of a real newsletter.

One newsletter we're very familiar with is called *From the Desktop.* It was designed and produced by David Doty for a local association of desktop publishers. He worked on this newsletter for over five years, gradually changing and polishing the design to suit the changing needs and budget of the association.

And don't worry—this is a *short* history. You'll see how one newsletter designer actually did what you're about to do: design and produce a newsletter, within budget and under deadline, trying to improve the looks of the newsletter when time and money permits.

That's how most newsletters are produced in the real world. You do what you can, when you can. And you get better every issue.

We'll get to how Dave started the whole design and production process in a minute, but let's start with a peek at the end—how the newsletter ended up looking, what readers saw when it finally arrived in the mail.

From the Desktop is typical of most newsletters in most respects. The version shown here was a standard-sized (8½ x 11), two-color, eight-page publication that was sent every month to about 800 association members. Each issue featured a letter from the president, stories about association events, member news and profiles, a calendar of upcoming events, book reviews, tips and classified ads.

Because the folks who received this newsletter were professional desktop publishers, you might think it should have been a little flashier. But, as with most newsletters, the readers were more inter-

The final product

Each issue is eight letter-sized pages, printed on two 11 x 17 inch sheets and folded down the middle.

To keep production costs down, no staples ("saddle stitches") were used to hold the issue together. Instead, the newsletter was folded over top-to-bottom to keep the sheets together. The bottom half of the last page, which faces out, was used as the mailing panel.

ested in what the newsletter had to say than with bells and whistles. And, like most newsletters, *From the Desktop* had to be produced on a pretty tight budget, usually at the last minute. So the real goal was to deliver the news every month in a simple, elegant format that was easy for Dave to produce and easy for the members to read.

What can you learn from looking at a finished newsletter like this one? Quite a bit. The key is to ask yourself questions as you look over the pages. For example, do you think the design of *From the Desktop* works well? Does it look easy to read? Easy to skim? Do you see any problems? Do you like the type? The organization? How do you think Dave ended up with this design? How did he start the design process?

A peek inside
Here's a typical "spread" from the inside of the same issue.

How it all started

When the association was still young, the key was to produce the newsletter as simply and inexpensively as possible. The design shown here fitted that bill perfectly.

The main *format* was a one-column design—text was set in a wide column to the right, with headlines positioned next door in the left margin.

Why did Dave decide to hang the headlines in the margin? A couple of reasons. This arrangement makes it very easy for readers to scan the headlines to find articles that interest them. Second, it creates *white space* in the newsletter—open spaces where there's no type at all. Blocks of white space make a newsletter look less dense and, consequently, more inviting. This is what people mean when they say a design is *airy*.

A closer look

This newsletter may look simple, but a lot of thought went into making it look *just right*— that is, making sure that everything looks planned, orderly and consistent. Here are a few of the things Dave did to pull it all together:

● Each story is topped by a *rule* (a straight line). It's always the same width, always the same *weight* (*hairline*). The rule "ties" the headlines to their stories and separates one story from the next.

● Every item on the page lines up with another item in a pretty simple way. The dateline lines up with the headlines on the left. The name and tagline line up with the body text. And each headline is top aligned with its article.

● Only two typefaces are used, and they're very closely related. They're called Futura Bold and Futura Light. Dave also kept his type sizes and line spacing very consistent throughout.

A one-column design certainly is easy to produce: One story follows another, so you don't really have to worry about how to position each story on the page. You just have to choose the order of the stories and try to get the stories to fit on the pages where you think they belong.

And what about the third page shown here? It's set in a more traditional three-column design. Dave knew that the one-column design would work well for short news bits, but that he'd need a different format for longer, more in-depth articles. Whenever the newsletter included such a story, Dave simply placed it on its own page and switched to a three-column design.

When you switch the number of columns you're using midstream, that's called using a *mixed format.* This gave Dave much more flexibility, but he had to be careful not to mix things up too much.

Mixed formats

Should you use a mixed format? Not necessarily—if you don't need to mix formats, don't. And if you do decide to mix, it's usually best to keep it simple: pick just two formats—say, one for news and one for features—and avoid mixing them on a single page.

News about members

After spending 14 years at the Illinois Arts Council, **Mike O'Brien** is moving to Synthesis Concepts to give **Michael Waitsman** and **Liane Sebastian** a hand. Mike will be handling much of the administrative work and pitching in as producer on certain projects. Mike W. and Liane, by the way, report that desktop design has made itself felt at the International Design Conference in Aspen. Apple stocked a design lab with Macintoshes for the use of attendees. Not all designers, it should be pointed out, were enthralled with the notion of computers. There are a substantial number that resist the incursion of computers into the design world.

Susan Brodsky of ProTypography has moved her office. The new address is 350 West Erie. Phone number, 266-8973, is the same. ProTypography is sharing the same floor and some of the facilities with **Donna** and **Gary Hawkey** at Hawkey and Associates. Their phone number is 915-0695.

Computing Solutions is the new name for Personal Excellence. **Barbara Golden** points out that with an expanded training facility they decided to change the name.

Three ADEPT members are involved with a new videotape on desktop publishing now being produced by Goldsholl Design & Film. **Oscar Anderson, Pat McNamara,** and **David Doty** all lent their talents as onscreen speakers. The tape, called Desktop Design: 1 is the first of a series that will be distributed by Dynamic Graphics of Peoria. In addition to the series on DTP, there will be other videotapes on pasteup and calligraphy.

Chuck Anzilotti of Anzographics announces they have installed a color printer. The QMS can print full color pages from FreeHand and Illustrator88. Neither the DOS nor Mac versions of PageMaker have color drivers, so the only way to print color with PageMaker (Mac) is by placing an EPS file from FreeHand or Illustrator88. The next iteration of Venturawill probably support color. Prices for 8 1/2" X 11" are $10 per print and extra copies of the same original are $1.50-$2.00. 11" X 17" run $15.00.

News for us?

Do you have a few interesting tedbits of interest to members? Give us a call. Let us know what you're doing, or if you have heard some news about activities that might be of interest to members. Barbara Mayer at 348-1200

Tech tips

For you laser printer junkies, Howard Paper Mills makes a terrific sheet. It's called Super Max Opaque and has the whitest white I've seen. It also has a very smooth surface they call "polished," which is not calendared but the next thing to it. It's available in the Chicago area at Iliana Paper, 2716 North Clybourn, 472-4440. A carton (5000 sheets) of 8 1/2" X 11" 60lb runs about $60.

The Iconoclast

Frank Romano, publisher of TypeWorld, recently had this definition in his opening column: "Desktop publishing is the hobgoblin of small minds."

ADEPT to publish first Resources collection

Now in the process of development, Resources 1 will be a three-ring binder containing, among other items, a membership directory, a trade directory, a listing of books and periodicals of interest to members, reprints, and notes from ADEPT meetings. The publication, slated for initial distribution by the September meeting, is part of a larger project, the ADEPT Reference Series, which will expand on the concept as more component publications become available. The publication will be available only to members.

Page Layout programs
by John Ivory

Speakers: Susan Alt of Donald E. L. Johnson & Associates, Ready,Set,Go!; Willy Wagner of InfoComm), Quark XPress; Eda Warren of Desktop Publishing Services, PageMaker for the Macintosh; Lydia Tonjuk, free-lance designer, PC PageMaker; Bill McCarthy of ProTypography), Ventura; and John Seid (David C. Cook Publishers), Interleaf for the Macintosh. Sharon Borstein coordinated the program with the Program Committee.

The A.D.E.P.T. program on May 25 at the Inn of Chicago examined the fundamental tool of electronic publishing: the page layout program. Six panelists spoke about six different software packages. Each speaker found advantages and disadvantages to the software they use.

Susan Alt originally used PageMaker, but thought it was too complicated. She finds that it takes only two to four hours to become familiar with Ready,Set, Go!, versus days with PageMaker. She thinks Ready,Set,Go! is more precise: It allows one to define the location and dimensions of page elements (and percentage sizes of graphics) with numbers rather than eyeballing them. She also found it easier to wrap text around a graphic (PageMaker 3.0 hand not yet been introduced).

On the minus side, long documents create system errors, so she tries to keep files under ten pages in length. She once had problems with high resolution output, but eliminated the problems by informing the service bureau of the versions of software she uses.

Willy Wagner says Quark XPress is the best program for detail. One can condense and expand type, control the thickness of line rules and control the number of lines in a screen. XPress has style sheet capabilities, and can link text to graphics. The program can produce spot color separations, and the new version will produce process color separations as well.

Wagner said that with all this detail, however, the program is more complicated to learn than the others.

Eda Warren said PageMaker for the Macintosh is visually oriented and has an intuitive user interface. It works well with large documents because of the automatic text flow, style sheets and "master pages," which enable one to globally set printing elements (such as running heads) and nonprinting elements (such as column guides). It also produces spot color separations allows for line screens and control of grey scales, and can automatically place text around an irregularly shaped object.

Warren's improvements to the program would include an indexing feature and the ability to link graphics to text.

Lydia Tonjuk uses the MS DOS version of PageMaker. She finds it comparable to the Macintosh version. Tonjuk prefers the larger MS DOS monitor to the Mac's. She also prefers the two-button mouse to the one-button mouse.

On the other hand, MS DOS is more intimidating than the Macintosh environment. She finds that the program is slow, especially with long documents. Finally, she finds that sometimes the cursor disappears and the only way to regain control of the computer is to restart it, losing any data that was not saved to disk.

Bill McCarthy finds that Ventura's style sheets and paragraph tagging are good for long documents and those that have consistent formats. Ventura will create an automatic table of contents and index as well. Dynamic linking reflects changes made in Ventura files in their respective word processing files. Ventura can also link text to graphics (although he feels that

MS DOS graphics programs are inferior to those on the Macintosh).

Disadvantages of Ventura: the program won't import TIFF files, it is difficult to install screen fonts in the windows environment, and extra fonts slow down the system.

The final speaker was John Seid, who uses Interleaf for the Macintosh, which had only been available for six weeks before the meeting. The program was originally designed for the Sun workstation. Seid said Interleaf is "like the Frankenstein of desktop publishing—it escaped before it was ready to get out of the laboratory." Seid feels, however, that the program has a future once the bugs are out.

Interleaf can rotate text, anchor frames to text, and stretch, rotate and skew imported graphics. It can tag elements with a variety of properties. The program will renumber footnotes, the table of contents and the multi-level index when chapters are moved out of sequence.

Seid said that Interleaf is not easy to learn, and it isn't as intuitive as most Macintosh programs. Only fonts that are resident in the Laserwriter are accessible, and text cannot be imported from word processing programs—it must be entered directly into Interleaf. There is no color control. Interleaf will run only on a Mac II with four megabytes of memory.

Chickens & eggs

Okay, we have to admit it—there's a bit more to that early design we just showed you. Dave didn't just fire up his computer one day and plop down a bunch of articles in exactly the right places.

Before he got to that stage, he sat down with paper and markers and sketched out some *grids*. A grid is exactly what it sounds like: a bunch of crisscrossing lines. Many professional designers sketch grids as a first step—to "get cooking" on a new problem.

A grid helps you think about design problems before you start slapping words and pictures on the page. The lines in a grid represent where words and pictures go: The top line might tell you how high on the page the first headline can be. The bottom line tells you where a story has to stop or jump to another page or column. Vertical lines show how wide the columns can be.

So what does this have to do with chickens and eggs? It's the old "which came first" problem. We can't tell you whether chickens or eggs came first. And we can't tell you that you need to sketch a grid on paper before you can crank out a newsletter on your computer. In fact, many people use their computers to rough out an arrangement of articles on a page—and then, when they stumble onto a design they like, they set all the grid lines to correspond.

You should at least get in the habit of thinking about grid lines. Page layout programs make it easy to "sketch" grids on your computer using colored or dotted lines called *guides*. Guides only appear on your screen—they won't print out along with your text and graphics. If your program offers movable guides (often called *ruler guides or column guides*), try using them. They're easy to put in place and they can always be changed. Guides can help you keep everything neatly aligned and consistent from page to page.

Working with guides

If your program has guides, it probably also has a snap to guides feature. with this option on, you'll find it much easier to align elements to the page grid.

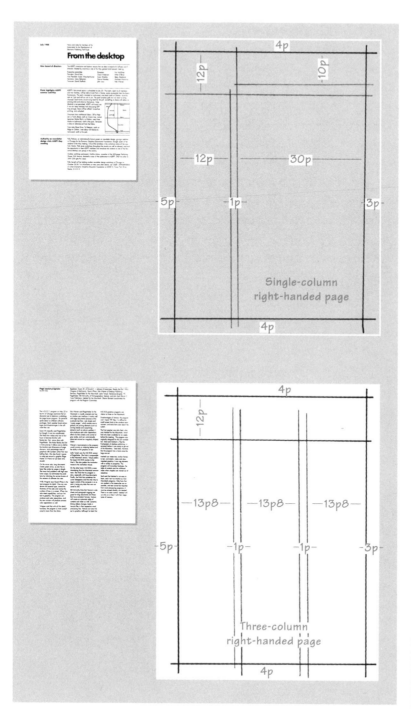

Single-column
right-handed page

Three-column
right-handed page

The eggs that hatched the chickens

Dave started out with sketches like these before he started setting up his newsletter file on the computer. These sketches are very rough—just empty grids to represent the two kinds of page designs.

Did you notice that he didn't just draw one line to separate columns? He drew two side-by-side lines, to show how much space was needed *between* the columns of text.

Picas and points

You might be wondering about the measurements that have been penciled in here. What exactly is "5p" or "13p8"? That's the way professional designers and typesetters measure space on the page.

1 inch = 6 picas, or "6p"
1 pica = 12 points, or "0p12"

"13p8" means 13 picas and 8 points—roughly 2¼ inches.

Making improvements

Very few newsletter designs remain set in stone. That's not to say you should change your design every issue (you shouldn't), but it certainly makes sense to do a yearly review of how well the design is working. Maybe certain types of articles aren't getting enough space or attention. Or maybe it's just time to spruce up your newsletter.

After the first year of *From the Desktop*, Dave decided the basic design was working OK, but that it was time to make a few small changes. After all, the organization was growing; the newsletter needed to reflect that growth and act as a better messenger to all the new members who didn't know much about the organization.

So while the basic format stayed the same, Dave made several changes to make the newsletter more valuable and more attractive to the growing membership.

Expanding the nameplate

The *nameplate* (or *banner*) is the area on the front cover that displays the newsletter's name. It's pretty standard to also include the issue date and a short tagline, as Dave had done on the original design.

In this redesign, he decided to add a short listing of useful information—a calendar of upcoming events and the organization's main phone number. That's fairly unusual, but it made sense here. The idea was to emphasize the organization's role as a center for information.

The other major change to the nameplate design was a big bold bar across the top. The date, calendar heading and the phone number were *reversed* out of this bar, so that they appeared in the color of the paper. That helped draw attention to the information in the nameplate.

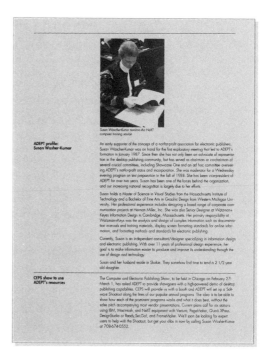

Other subtle changes

Dave experimented with printing each issue on papers of various colors—light green one issue, light gray another. Color is always a nice touch, and using colored paper is cheaper than printing with an extra color ink. It also made it easier for readers to tell recent issues apart.

He also began inserting photos of key members to give new members a better sense of who was active in the organization. Instead of inserting small, posed "mugshots," he used large, casual photos of members working at organization activities.

Finally, he started running classified ads on the back page. To set it off as a special department, he set the ads in a two-column format with a bold heading directly above each ad.

Getting the newsletter printed

To get moving on your newsletter design, you certainly need to understand a bit about grids and columns and headlines and so on. But the sharpest design in the world won't do you much good unless you know how to get your newsletter printed for mass consumption at the right price.

At this point in our story, "the right price" was certainly a big factor. The organization couldn't spend too much on having the newsletter produced, so Dave had to design within the budget.

The first restriction was the number of colors: The group could only afford one color of ink, black. To hold down the cost of paper, *From the Desktop* was printed on a single, standard-sized sheet—11 by 17 inches—and then folded into a letter-sized four-pager.

Dave could have used a scanner to insert the photos, but he had the print shop put the photos in instead. Why? To get a good printout of scanned photos, Dave would have had to pay a company called a *service bureau* to print his files on a high-resolution printer. That would have cost more than the small fee that the print shop charged for preparing one or two photos for printing. So Dave kept costs down by limiting the number of photos in each issue and producing his final *proofs*—without scans—on his desktop laser printer.

That also meant that Dave could only use the simplest black-and-white computer graphics. Like photos, graphics that use subtle shades of gray only reproduce well if they're printed on a high-resolution printer. To play it safe, Dave stayed away from using *tinted* boxes, *gradients* and *grayscale* illustrations in these early designs.

The newsletter was being printed in pretty small quantities at this stage (fewer than 500 copies), so it was cheaper to have it printed at the local quick-printer than at a big commercial printing house. To prepare the newsletter for the quick-printer, Dave drew *"FPO"* boxes to indicate where the photos should be inserted, printed the pages on good laser-quality paper stock, and then, using tape along the backs, joined each pair of pages into a *printer spread.*

Some terms

A *tint* is a lighter shade of the ink you're using: Tints of black, for example, are gray.

A *gradient* is a series of tints that run seamlessly from light to dark.

A *grayscale* graphic is a picture created with black ink that uses tints and gradients for shading.

An *FPO* is a placeholder for a photo or piece of art. It means *For Position Only.*

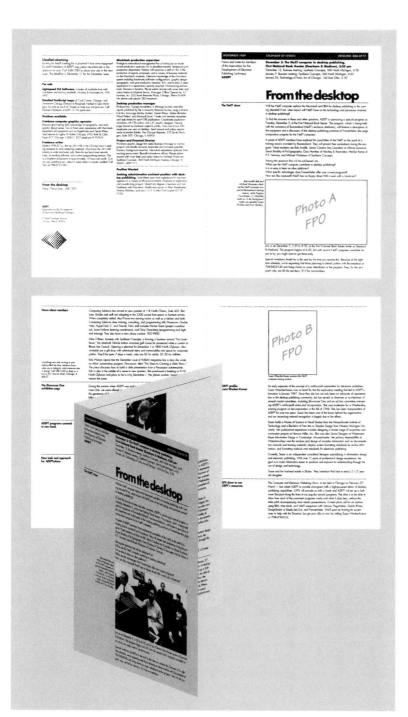

Preparing laser proofs for the quick-printer

He could've sent four separate pages to the print shop, but Dave sent his own *printer spreads* instead. That saved him the small *stripping* fee the print shop would have charged to make the spreads, and it guaranteed the pages would be lined up and in the right order.

A *printer spread* is a pair of pages that's printed on the same side of a sheet—as opposed to a *reader spread,* which is a pair of pages that face each other once the sheets are stacked and folded.

The printer knew the *FPO* boxes were only here to indicate size and position, and had to be replaced. Dave wrote in a photo "name" so the printer would know which photo to use on which page. Just to be safe, though, he discussed the photo placements with the print shop operator in person. There are few things more embarassing than photos appearing with the wrong stories.

A brand new look

The following year, Dave tried a third design—this time, a major redesign. But even though the issues below look very different from the earlier issues, they do have some things in common. For example, Dave kept the headlines hanging in the leftmost column; he liked the way the original design made it easy for a reader to scan for topics of interest.

He also continued to separate stories with a horizontal rule but made the rule much bolder. Instead of a hairline, he used a 24-point (⅓-inch) rule. He then placed a small scanned graphic over the left

As the organization changed...

So did the newsletter. Thanks to an increased promotion budget, more announcements were being sent out separately in mailers and postcards. It was no longer so important to focus on that information in the newsletter. Consequently, the calendar and phone number were removed from the nameplate.

Dave also went for a bolder, more sophisticated look in this design, with much stronger emphasis on the nameplate. The name is set in a typeface called Bauer Bodoni Bold, condensed to about 75% of its normal width, and printed in a different color every month.

section of the rule. The little graphic served a few purposes: it helped draw attention to the headline; it added some visual playfulness to the design; and it complemented the airy look of the left column, where there was still plenty of white space.

But there certainly were some big changes! First, the newsletter's name was printed in a second color. Second, the entire newsletter was set in a four-column grid, with most articles set in three columns. And a new choice of typefaces created a very different look from that of the Futura fonts used earlier.

July 1990   The monthly newsletter for members of ADEPT   Association for the Development of Electronic Publishing Technique

From the Desktop

ADEPT Picnic A Success Despite Cool Weather

Temperatures in the mid-60's might have kept some people away, but the annual picnic went on as scheduled. About 35 people turned out for

burgers, dogs, barbequed chicken and various other delights at Indian Boundary Park on July 14. Some were huddling around the barbecue grills to get warm, but everyone enjoyed the afternoon despite the chill.

ADEPT Looks Ahead to Fall 1990

For those who haven't already heard, the next program meeting will be September 26. ADEPT is on summer break, but business and committee meetings are being held as usual. And plans for the fall are coming into place.

The December 5 meeting will feature Roger Parker. He will speak on, "52 Ways to Improve Your Newsletter Design." That will be a combined November-December meeting because of Thanksgiving.

The fall programs will focus on issues in electronic publishing, such as health, professional standards, and how to stay on top of the latest equipment and technology.

A preliminary schedule of topics was published in the May issue. It's been fine-tuned since then, so here's the latest:

September 26. Topic not determined. Will feature a name speaker from the world of desktop publishing.

October 24. How to Stay Current with the Technology.

December 5. Roger Parker: 52 Ways to Improve Your Newsletter.

January 23, 1991. Perspectives on Pre-press and Service Bureaus.

February 27. Health issues in Desktop Publishing.

March 27. Design that Pushes the Technology: Case Studies of the Best.

April 24. Interactive Media.

May 22. Fonts and Systems.

June 26. Color: The Leading Edge of Technology.

Putting the design to work

It can be tough to figure out how to make a new design work from article to article, issue to issue. After all, more columns means more options.

These issues give us a good idea of how Dave handled the problem. Rather than filling columns at random—say, running a short article down one column and a longer article down the next two—he stuck to a basic rule: Always set major articles to run through all three body columns. That gave each article the same horizontal look, and it kept each block of text short and easy to read.

A closer look

What did it take to produce the new version of the newsletter?

Mostly more time. Even though the new column arrangement appears simple, it required a bit more work to set up each article than it did when the body text all flowed down one column. With the new arrangement, the editor had to flow the text through three columns, then adjust the text blocks to be roughly equal in *depth*. Once she did this for all the articles on a page, she often had to edit the text to make everything fit—which meant readjusting the position and depth of each article again.

Adding the second color was easy, especially because color was only used to highlight the name of the newsletter. That meant the easiest thing to do was to simply tell the printer where the color should go.

The new typefaces

As in his original design, which used two members from the Futura family, Dave followed a conservative typeface strategy in the new design. He set body text in Bauer Bodoni Roman and heads in Bauer Bodoni Bold.

The only problem with Bodoni was that the type was a bit wide for the narrow columns he had set up. To get the effect he wanted, he used the *type width* controls in his software to condense the body type and the headlines.

ADEPT Picnic A Success Despite Cool Weather

Temperatures in the mid-60's might have kept some people away, but the annual picnic went on as scheduled. About 35 people turned out for burgers, dogs, barbecued chicken

▲ Bauer Bodoni Bold, 18 pt   ▲ Bauer Bodoni Roman, 10 pt

ADEPT Picnic A Success Despite Cool Weather

Temperatures in the mid-60's might have kept some people away, but the annual picnic went on as scheduled. About 35 people turned out for burgers, dogs, barbecued chicken and various other

▲ 84% of normal type width   ▲ 92% of normal type width

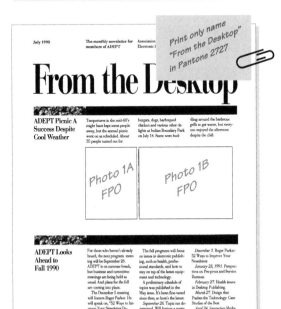

Fitting copy

The task on this page was to fit three short articles, one on top of the other. Because space was tight, the columns had to be *balanced:* Each article was set so that the columns of text within the article were about the same length.

Some programs handle column balancing automatically. This newsletter was produced without automatic balancing, so the editor first placed each article in one long column to find its overall *depth,* then divided that column into three roughly equal blocks of text.

Printing the name in color

The color usage here was very limited, so Dave had the print shop handle the *spot color separation.* He printed the nameplate in solid black as usual, then told the printer to print the name in a second color.

Dave picked a new spot color for each issue to add variety. He would simply browse through a standard color reference book (called a Pantone® specifier), then give the printer the corresponding number code.

Dave couldn't always get the exact color he asked for. Smaller print shops, especially quick-printers, can't afford to keep every Pantone® ink on hand. So while the print shop could have special-ordered a color for Dave, he often settled for the closest color they had in stock to avoid the extra charge.

The final tune-up

The next year, Dave produced his final redesign, shown below. This is the issue we showed you at the beginning of this chapter. As you can see, it's really just a refinement of the major redesign he had completed the year before—you might not even notice anything had changed.

The biggest change was in the typeface department. Previously, Dave used Bauer Bodoni throughout, but narrowed the width of the letters to get the effect he wanted and to fit more text in the narrow columns. In this design, he switched to Century Condensed, a font that's very "efficient" in terms of fitting words on a line.

Despite the switch to Century, he kept the name *From the Desktop* in Bauer Bodoni. Why? Basically because there wasn't any really

Detail work

Some redesigns can be quite subtle—a new type style here or there, a new way to handle certain types of articles. That's exactly what happened here. But these little details added up to a more refined appearance.

Longtime readers probably noticed the addition of the diamond-shaped logo to the nameplate, but may not have noticed the other changes unless they compared older and newer issues side-by-side.

Compare the type used in this issue (Century Condensed, the same face we use for these captions) to the type in the older design. Do you think it's an improvement?

good reason to change it. The big Bodoni type in the banner looked compatible with the new Century typeface for the articles. Besides, readers liked this version of the banner, so it seemed like a good idea not to change it. He did, however, add the association's "dot pattern" logo to the upper right corner. Previously, it had been relegated to the mailing panel on the back page.

He also came up with a better way to handle very short articles, such as announcements, acknowledgments and corrections. Instead of trying to stretch a few paragraphs across three columns, he set them in a two-column block with the headline running down the first column. You can see an example of this technique in the right page of the spread shown below.

Jumps and continuations

Look at how the cover story is continued on this inside spread. Dave used a special, smaller headline, then set the remaining text over two pages, using the black bar to hold the article together.

Prepress seminar
(From Page 1)

Barbara Golden, president of Computing Solutions, a Chicago training business, talked about the many means of getting images into a computer—covering hardware, software, and methods of retouching—from high-end to desktop. He said the high-end systems are "far from being dinosaurs," offering guidance on when to let specialists handle it. He focused on the desktop end of page makeup and image enhancement, using the conference advertisement as an example. He explained the advantages and techniques of using images in two resolutions.

Bridgette Pflum of Kodak explored the full range of output devices and materials: Black-and-white and color printers, imagesetters, and high-end film plotters. "An advantage of desktop color is the periodic proofs you get during the process." On the other hand, he pointed out the importance of high-quality proofs before printing.

Clint Funk, of Publishers ImageSet (a Chicago service bureau), talked about the mechanics of working with service bureaus and high-end imaging centers. The basic difference between the two? With service bureaus you're responsible; with prepress houses *they're* responsible. He outlined many things to make the process go smoothly, using the phrase "Less is more...successful." Here are hints useful for the majority of ADEPT members:

• Just because you don't see it on the screen doesn't mean the imagesetter doesn't have to process it. Therefore, never use white boxes as "white-out," and keep image files as small as possible. (Crop them when you create them—even crop out white—rather than in the page-layout program.)

• He showed a simple page consisting of a box, a line, a circle, and two words—along with the 49 pages of PostScript code it generated for imaging. "Just imagine how long and complex the PostScript of your real documents are." Thus: Keep files as simple as possible.

• In creating illustrations, avoid excessive use of blends and patterns. They take longer to image.

• Set up colors as process colors (unless you specifically want lots of spot colors).

• For either spot or process color, print separations (in addition to the composite) to your laser printer. This tells you *if* the file will print, *how*, and provides valuable education about separations.

• Just because it's possible doesn't mean it should be done. If it's cheaper, better, or faster to do it traditionally, that's the best way.

• Anticipate problems. Testing in advance will save money, time, and stress.

In the next presentation, Paul Dombrowski of Chicago Color Graphics showed slides of every stage of a typical project in a prepress house. He also gave pointers on how to select a prepress house, along with a case-study of successful integration of in-house expertise with prepress vendor partnership.

The final step in the publishing process is printing. Michael McGovern of Lithror Inc. outlined the kinds of proofs and what each tells you, and how to solicit bids and select a printer. As for press checking, he suggested bringing all relevant art boards and proofs, then checking (against proofs) for color, register and fit, moiré patterns, light spots in solid colors, broken type, and ghosting (lighter areas in solids).

The seminar finished with a flurry of questions from the attendees.

Michael Weitzman is a principal of Synthesis Concepts Inc. and the designer of the PrePress Partnerships brochure, which was produced by David Sheffield.

ADEPT thanks all Corporate Sponsors of the PrePress Partnership seminar: Agfa Corporation; Aldus Corporation; *Business Publishing Magazine*; DuPont Imaging Systems; Eastman Kodak Printing & Publishing; and 3M Printing & Publishing Systems.

ADEPT PrePress Seminar speakers Clint Funk, David Sheffield, Bridgette Pflum, Paul Dombrowski, and Barbara Golden answer questions from the audience.

Also demonstrated at the seminar was the Kodak digital camera. Images are captured on a hard disk and can displayed in proof form on screen, then output on a printer.

Hewlett-Packard contributes ScanJet IIc
by David Doty

ADEPT's publications will now be able to make more liberal use of scanned images, thanks to the good graces of Hewlett-Packard.

A new H-P ScanJet IIc was recently contributed to our publishing efforts and will be used primarily for *From the Desktop* and *The ADEPT Publisher*.

The ScanJet IIc is capable of capturing 256 grays, a vast improvement over the 16 grays afforded by our earlier ScanJet. It can also scan in color.

Other features of the IIc include automatic exposure control for brightness and contrast (or they may be set individually), the ability to optimize the scan for a particular printer (LaserWriter, Linotron, ink-jet, etc.), a zoom control that allows the user to examine the scanned image closely before scanning, up to 400 dpi resolution, and a "sharpening" feature.

For readers interested in purchasing a ScanJet IIc, several Chicago area dealers offer it for less than $1,500.

The photos on the cover and page 4 were scanned with the H-P ScanJet IIc using automatic exposure control, although the gray curve was modified in PageMaker 4.2 (Mac).

Program committee outlines schedule
by David Doty

ADEPT's most enduring benefit, our monthly programs, require the concerted efforts of a small but dedicated group of people to make them happen. Once specific areas of interest have been identified, programs are outlined and slotted for a particular month. Barrie Dellenbach, committee chair, then appoints a coordinator for each of the programs. With the help of the committee, the coordinator develops the program, identifies the appropriate speakers (usually based on suggestions of committee members), and sets up meetings to develop the program around speakers' strengths.

After a program has been worked out in detail, necessary equipment is arranged for, news announcements developed for media release, handouts written, designed, and printed, and promotional mailouts prepared of several ADEPT members for each program. If you'd like to help with these activities (and there are few better ways to trade shoptalk and network), call her at 312 781-4879.

Here is a provisional list of upcoming monthly programs:

March: The Dollars and Sense of Desktop Publishing. Justifying the cost of a system, estimating projects, project management.

April: Presentation Graphics. Overheads, slides, the future of desktop presentations.

May: Image Resources. Compression, file management, file transfer, scanning, viewers.

June: Illustration Software. Working across platforms.

July: Freelance Desktop Publishing. What freelancers need to know, what clients need to know, when it makes sense to use a freelancer.

August: Transformations. Case Studies of Newsletters.

September: Color.

October: Design for Production. How the final form of a project affects design and production, traditional vs. electronic.

November: New Technologies.

December: Holiday Party.

Every page is a new problem

It's always tempting to think about newsletter design purely in terms of what the cover looks like. After all, that's where the nameplate is—a pretty important design element—and that's usually where you run the biggest or most important stories.

But it's a good idea to get in the habit of thinking about inside pages. They often present special problems: difficult mixes of short and long articles, regular *columns* and *departments,* letters to the editor, classified ads. How do you adapt your cover design to fit these special needs?

Eyebrow, *or* kicker · · · · · · · · ·

Background info
set as a sidebar · · · · · · · · · · ·

Secondary headline
style with smaller
type size · · · · · · · · · · · · · · ·

Names in lists
set in boldface · · · · · · · · · · ·

January program recap

Interactive media makes an appearance

Panel:

Dan Sadowski
Software Engineer
MacroMind/Paracomp

Jerry Sullivan II
President
Dynacom

John Moxley
Director of Interactive Systems
Motivation Media

Coordinator:

Eda Warren
President
Desktop Publishing Services

Interactive media can provide all sorts of audio and visual fare from a snack to a seven-course meal. Three specialists offered a sampling of what can be done with interactive media during ADEPT's January program.

Panelist John Moxley said the selections ranged from a plain cheese sandwich to a feast fit for a gourmand. Moxley, director of interactive systems at Motivation Media, held his firm's efforts up as the cheese sandwich—programs that must be simple and low cost.

Meanwhile, the gourmet, Dan Sadowski, showed the types of interactive installations can be done with MacroMind Director, Author-Ware, HyperCard and Super-Card. Jerry Sullivan, who Moxley said offered a meat and potatoes version of interactive media, showed a Spanish lan-guage program developed on video disc for high school students.

Sadowski said multimedia is being used to present products and services. Sound is a critical part of the presentations, and is typically combined with motion. Multimedia can be done with desktop computers and combines some or all of graphics, animation, sound, and video.

Sadowski described several issues that are emerging as interactive media evolves. There's the issue of getting digital video into the computer; the issue of CD-Rom integration with the computer; the issue of designing time based on interface control; the issue of what computer is best; and the issue of needing specialized cables.

Sullivan said his company's programs are used mostly for training. The issues in developing the Spanish language program on 10 videodiscs included making sure the program was interesting enough to grasp student interest and simple enough for the teachers to use.

Once a program is in development, about a third of the project's time is devoted to testing and debugging. Ideas for the program have to be confined to a list, or development can go far afield from original goals, he said.

Moxley said he could appreciate the production issues in some of the more sophisticated interactive installations, but his firm has to keep costs down.

With desktop publishing, costs can be controlled, but a computer screen is limited and doesn't match the resolution or capabilities of print media. Even so, interactive technology is being used in kiosks, training, and interactive catalogs.

Welcome new members

Barbara Adams
Justrite Manufacturing Co.
Des Plaines, IL

John Berns
Alpha Channel, Chicago

Barbara Elson
Official Airline Guides, Chicago

Deborah Fewell
Chicago

Kathy Foros
Mark Getzner
J. Stephen Reedy
Institute of Real Estate Management, Chicago

Stacia Hickey
Medical Library Association, Chicago

Hedy Kniesel
Elmhurst College, Elmhurst, IL

Lester LaPierre
Motorola, Schaumburg, IL

Jean Lynch
American Association for Medical Assistants, Chicago

Terrence Meehan
Wickes Lumber Co.,
Vernon Hills, IL

Tim Morgan
Chicago

Haik Muradian
Chicago

Allison Nelson
First Impression, Elk Grove, IL

Kara Quinn
3M, Chicago

Dinah Reed
Chicago

Lisa Sweeney
Chicago

ADEPT thanks:

Hewlett-Packard for contributing a ScanJet IIc scanner for use with publications.
Business Publishing Magazine (Wayne Rhodes) for considerable efforts in helping to organize and promote our recent prepress seminar. You may have seen the full-color six-page ad inserts and half-page ads (also in full color) that appeared in the January and February issues—as well as for the separate mailing of brochures to subscribers.
Rider Dickerson printing (Jim Madden) for obtaining the Pocket Pal guides for attendees of the prepress seminar, and for help in many ways.
DataDisplay Corporation (Steve Sonderling) for their help at the prepress seminar.
Computer Rental Corporation of America for contributing a Macintosh SE/30 to the ADEPT office.
InfoComm of Chicago (751-1220, Eric Wagner) for providing our imagesetter output—and doing a great job on it.
A to Z Type & Graphics (708 925-9800, Paul Hanover) for contributing imagesetter output for monthly program mailers.

It's often a matter of ingenuity, and there are no pat rules. It really helps to look at how inner pages are handled in other newsletters. Here's a couple more pages from the same issue.

You'll see that although Dave did some "special" things for certain types of articles, he tried to maintain a visual consistency with the rest of the newsletter. The articles in this spread are very different from those we've shown you on previous pages, but the differences don't jump out at you.

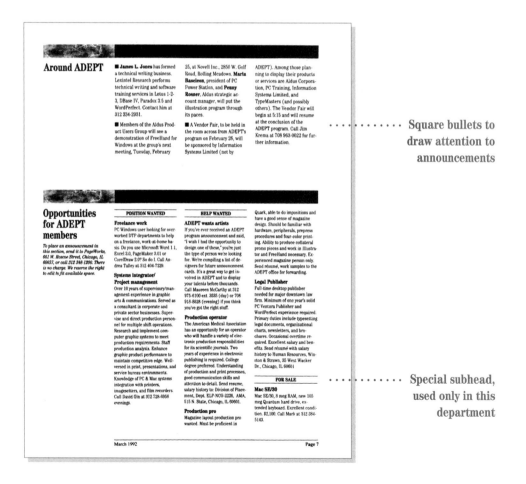

Square bullets to draw attention to announcements

Special subhead, used only in this department

Upping the ante

At this point in *From the Desktop's* history, Dave was using photos and detailed computer graphics more often. He was also using fonts that had very fine, delicate details. Unlike the Futura typefaces he started with, Bauer Bodoni and Century Condensed didn't print very well on a low-resolution laser printer. It was time to start using more professional production techniques that cost a bit more.

To get professional-level quality, Dave did things quite differently than when he had the newsletter produced by the quick-print shop. He still printed the newsletter file from his desktop laser printer, but he didn't send these laser proofs out for reproduction. He used the laser proofs just to make sure the text was styled correctly and everything was in proper position.

When it came time to produce the final proofs, he sent the newsletter file on disk to a local company called a *service bureau*. Service bureaus have special printers (called *imagesetters*) that can print out computer files with the same high quality as books or magazines.

Laser printer, 300 dpi

Lorem *ipsum* dolor sitamet, consectetuer adipiscing elit, sed diam

▲ Body type, actual size

▼ Same type, enlarged 200%

Lorem *ipsum* dolo sectetuer adipisci

Laser printer, 600 dpi

Lorem *ipsum* dolor sitamet, consectetuer adipiscing elit, sed diam

▲ Body type, actual size

▼ Same type, enlarged 200%

Lorem *ipsum* dolo sectetuer adipisci

Imagesetter, 2540 dpi

Lorem *ipsum* dolor sitamet, consectetuer adipiscing elit, sed diam

▲ Body type, actual size

▼ Same type, enlarged 200%

Lorem *ipsum* dolo sectetuer adipiscir

What do we mean by professional quality?
You can see for yourself by comparing the quality of these examples.

The top example was printed from a 300 dpi laser printer. The quality of the type is good enough for many newsletters, but the scanned photo appears grainy. It's good enough for proofing, but it wouldn't make sense to send this to the print shop for reproduction.

The middle example was printed from a 600 dpi laser printer. The type looks very good—nearly professional-quality—but the print of the photo is a bit rough. It's good enough for most quick-print newsletters, though.

The bottom example was printed by a service bureau. The type looks great, and the print of the scan looks almost exactly like the original photo.

Beyond the desktop

Once you see the difference between "desktop" printing and what you can get from a professional printing service, you may wonder why everybody doesn't go the high-end route. In fact, more and more newsletters are being produced this way. But it's a very different ball game, and you have to decide whether it's worth the extra trouble for your newsletter.

One of the nice things about producing a newsletter from the desktop is that you're in complete control. You have all the files, you produce the final proofs, and you can tweak and edit right until the last minute before you send it out for printing. That's a big consideration for a lot of newsletter editors.

When Dave switched to the high-end route, it was a different story. He and the newsletter editor had to finish their edits at least a couple of days before the newsletter was scheduled for printing. Then they had to round up all the files for that issue—including some pretty large scans—and put them on disks to send to the service bureau.

The service bureau usually sent the final prints back the following day. If they looked OK, Dave would then send them to the print shop for reproduction. If not, he made the necessary corrections and sent the file back to the service bureau for new prints. Needless to say, this process was neither as cheap nor as easy as the usual desktop printer method. And it required more planning.

Dave sent the final high-resolution prints to a big commercial printing company instead of a quick-printer. A quick-printer wouldn't have been able to reproduce all the detail from the service bureau prints. Besides, when he went to the trouble and expense of using the service bureau, he usually asked them to print his files as *film negatives* instead of *paper positives*. That produced much higher quality for only a few dollars more. In general, commercial printers prefer film negatives, while most quick-printers prefer paper positives.

High-end printing

Service bureaus can print your file at almost any level of quality, but you'll pay for them accordingly on a per-page basis. To get a reasonably high quality for a newsletter without scanned photos, ask them for high-resolution *paper positives.* But if you want the best quality, ask for *film negatives.*

The two pages shown here are film negatives. They're a lot like the negatives you get back with your photos. But you should only ask for film negatives if the newsletter will be printed at a large commercial printer.

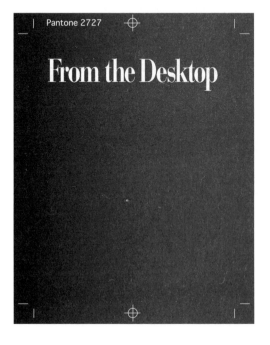

What's this page for?

This second sheet of film is called a *spot color plate,* or *overlay.* It contains only those parts of the cover page that should be printed in color; the first sheet (shown above) contains everything else. To get both sheets, Dave asked the service bureau to do a *spot color separation* of his file.

The little marks near the edges help the print shop line up the color parts of the page with the parts printed in black.

The end?

Yes, at least for our brief history of *From the Desktop*. There was yet *another* major redesign (by another designer) after the last version we showed you. But we're guessing you've seen enough of *FTD* at this point.

Now it's time to think about your newsletter. Do you have any of the same budget concerns Dave had when he started on his newsletter? Do you have similar types of articles or departments? Are you more inclined to start with a simple one-column design, or do you need to head right into a multi-column format? Will you be using lots of photos or graphics? Can you get by with quick-printing, or do you need top quality?

Hopefully, you'll find it a little easier to think through these issues now that you've watched somebody else deal with similar questions. But remember: The main question you should keep asking yourself isn't *"What's the best thing to do?"*—it's *"What makes sense for my newsletter given my resources?"*

The rest of this book is about options, and there are plenty. You certainly don't need to learn all the options, but window-shopping is highly recommended. Just maybe you'll see something that's right for you.

Section 2

Designing Your Newsletter

What is this "design" stuff all about? Arranging articles on a page? Using pictures? Picking typefaces? Or is it something a lot more vague, like making everything look "nice?"

It's all of these. And when you're just starting out with a blank page, it also means *experimenting*. Sometimes a little, sometimes a lot.

What design does *not* mean is knowing all the answers. We certainly don't.

The good news is, you don't need to know all the answers. You just need to recognize a good solution when you see one. That's what this section is all about.

Chapter 3

Looking for a "Look"

Do you ever find yourself looking at something—say, a CD cover or a poster or a video—and say to yourself "Hey, that looks really sharp. How did they came up with that idea?"

Chances are, "they" (the designers) didn't pull that "look" out of thin air. In fact, those designers probably saw something similar—somewhere, sometime in their lives—and decided to recycle it. We're not being cynical. That's how designers actually work. The creative ones take it a little further: They blend two, maybe three, looks that they've seen and come up with something original.

So what does this have to do with your newsletter? Plenty. When it comes time to design your letter, or redesign it, don't switch on your computer. At least, not right away!

Look around

It may seem like we're telling you to procrastinate. We're not.

Looking around is the first step in starting a new design, so it qualifies as real work. Not very hard work, but *very* productive.

Look at newsletters you get in the mail. Look at magazines and newspapers and brochures and catalogs. Look for the kinds of looks that you think might work for you and your readers.

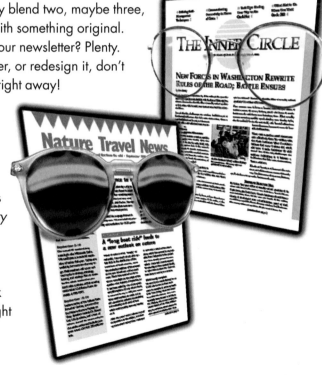

Looking around like this often seems a little aimless, but it can really pay off in the end. It's very much like shopping for a new coat. You might flip through a hundred coats at the store, all of which look *wrong* on you, and then you see someone walk down the street in a coat that looks *right*. All of a sudden, shopping for that new coat becomes ten times easier. You've found the look you're looking for.

What do you look for in a newsletter's look?

In one sense, the look of a newsletter is how you react when you see it the first time. Does it look airy? Inviting? Or intimidating? Does it look fun to read—or like work? Would you keep a back issue on your desk? On your coffee table at home? Or would you store it away in a binder or filing cabinet?

Certainly, the articles themselves—what the newsletter has to say—has a lot to do with your answers. But we're all influenced by other aspects of a newsletter besides its content, whether we realize it or not. And the word we usually use to cover all these other aspects is the "look."

Now *that's* pretty vague. So let's list some of the things that go into the look of any newsletter:

- How big the headlines are;
- How easy it is to read or to skim an article;
- How crowded the pages appear;
- How colorful it is;
- How unusual it is;
- How photos and graphics are used.

Those are the things that create our first impressions. Which should you worry about? Must every newsletter look expensive, unusual, colorful, well-designed and easy to skim and read?

Thankfully, you don't have to worry about all these things all the time. You'd probably never get an issue out on time if you did. So the task is to figure out which of these matter most—for *your* newsletter.

One kind of look...

This one's published by a neighborhood dairy delivery service. It's typical of many newsletters published by small companies, associations and churches. The look isn't very fancy, but the readers probably don't mind too much. After all, the news hits pretty close to home.

The Oberweis Moos'Letter
December 1993
- Publisher: Oberweis Dairy, Aurora, IL
- Designer: Carole Arliskas

...a whole 'nother kind of look

This one looks like it's published by a big company, and it is. What makes it look so upscale? Why do you think having an upscale look is important to the publisher of this newsletter? Do you need a comparable look for your newsletter?

Small Business Resource, Illinois edition
Fall 1993
- Publisher: Ameritech, Hoffman Estates, IL, and Aegis Communications
- Designer: Andrea Stork

How do you finally choose the *right* look?

The wisest way to start is by being pragmatic. Decide how much time, effort and money you can to put into the newsletter every issue.

That's not to say that you need lots of time, money and effort to produce a good-looking newsletter. Quite the contrary. But it does take plenty of resources to produce a fancy or upscale newsletter.

Here are the sorts of questions you need to ask yourself before you start conjuring up a design:

- What is your total production budget (computer materials and services plus printing costs) for each issue? Have you also set aside a separate budget for mailing or promotion?

- Do you have access to the type families you'll need, or will you have to purchase new typefaces?

- Given the number of copies you'll be producing, would it be most economical to use a common paper stock? Or can you afford top-quality or unusual paper? An unusual sheet size or shape?

- Can you afford to use color? What kind of color are you considering—a *spot* color here and there or *four-color* reproductions of photographs?

- What about photos and illustrations? Do you need them? Can you produce them, or do you have someone who will? Have you included the expenses of incorporating them into your newsletter?

- Is your software and your computer well-matched to the sort of newsletter you're producing? Does the software have the features you need to handle the most difficult parts of producing an issue?

- How complex is your newsletter? Just a few long stories? A dozen stories, all different lengths? Are there regular departments that you'll have to squeeze in every issue? What about ads or notices that might come in at the last minute?

- Do you feel that you can reliably turn out the newsletter on time, given the design options you've chosen? Have you reserved enough time in your schedule for major editing and restructuring of each issue?

Entire books have been devoted to these questions. We don't have the space to discuss them here, but we'll tell you this: Very few newsletter publishers or designers ever ask themselves many of these questions. And that's why so many newsletters turn out to be much more expensive or time-consuming than they should be. Discover your limitations before you choose your look. You'll find a look that suits you much faster and with much less aggravation.

The high end

Pretty impressive, huh? This quarterly newsletter pulls out all the stops—top-quality paper, tabloid-sized pages, six-color printing, big photos, color illustrations and an artsy layout.

It's tempting to look at high-end, professional jobs like these as the "standard." But keep in mind what it takes to produce something like this—professional designers and illustrators, photographers and a considerable printing budget. And this only comes out every three months!

International Update
Summer 1993
- Publisher: United Parcel Service, Atlanta, GA
- Designer: Don Cassel, Don Cassell Group

Adding focus to your look

There's a second set of questions you can use to help you find your look. These questions help you find the *focus* of your newsletter. They fall in three categories: *Audience; Goals;* and *Strategy.* If you've ever been involved in running a business, they should sound familiar.

Who's your audience?

- Are they young? Old? Mixed?

- Is your newsletter aimed at a particular social group? Ethnic group? Gender?

- How close are you to your readers? Do they belong to an organization you belong to? Are they professional peers? Like-minded enthusiasts? Total strangers?

- Are they *always* interested in the topic of your newsletter? Do they have a personal or financial or professional interest? Or do they read your letter purely for recreation?

What's the primary goal of your newsletter?

- Are you trying to keep your readers updated on news about a group you all belong to?

- Are you trying to expand support for your organization or its goals?

- Are you providing hard-to-find information or advice?

- Are you trying to promote a product or a service?

What's your strategy for appealing to your audience?

- Do you want your newsletter to be fairly conventional? Should it somehow mimic another publication your readers are familiar with?

- Would you rather have a distinctive look that stands out from the crowd? Is an unusual or expensive appearance critical for your newsletter's goals?

- Would it make sense to pick a "non-newsletter" look? That is, to make your newsletter appear more like some other kind of publication, such as a flyer, a brochure, a booklet or a corporate report? Is your audience more inclined to pick up and read a different kind of publication?

What do you do with the answers to all these questions?

Ideally, write your answers down. Next best, just keep them in mind. Every time you look at an example in this book, ask yourself whether you have the time, skills and resources to produce something similar. Then ask yourself whether the example you're looking at would make sense for *your* audience, *your* goals or *your* strategy for reaching *your* readers.

Stroll through our mini-gallery

Over the next few pages, we'll show you a diverse range of real newsletters. Think about how you would describe the look of each newsletter.

Do you think each of these newsletters has the right look for its target audience? Do you find any of the looks appealing? Could one of them fit your situation?

Information & advice

The newsletters shown on these two pages offer their readers handy collections of tips, ideas, explanations and other insights. Most newsletters of this type are subscription letters—their readers pay a fair amount to get timely, relevant advice on a regular basis. Others are published by associations and are sent to paying members as a benefit. Some, like the last example shown below, are distributed both ways.

Strictly business

This newsletter keeps lawyers up to date on major trends and changes that affect their work. It's twelve tabloid size pages, all of them packed with text.

This is serious stuff aimed at an audience accustomed to heavy technical reading. Only the simplest graphics are used in this design.

Litigation News
February 1994

- Publisher: American Bar Association Press, Chicago, IL
- Designer: Synthesis Concepts
- Colors: Black and one spot color (brown) on cream-colored paper.

Friendly advice

Sent for free by a health plan to its members, this newsletter offers advice and information on health issues.

The look here is quite open and easy-going, with light-hearted cartoons blended into the lead story. A little sugar to help the medicine go down?

HealthGram
October/November 1993
- Publisher: Humana, Chicago, IL
- Designer: Laurie Medeiros, Design Moves, Ltd.
- Colors: Black and two spot colors (blue and red)

Making heavy reading a little lighter

This newsletter falls somewhere between the other two examples. It's aimed at professionals, but the look is light and the articles are extremely short.

Designed for people who don't want to spend much time reading, this unusual publication summarizes news found in other periodicals. Bold headlines and department heads make skimming easy. The three-hole punch tells you subscribers keep these for reference.

Design Tools Monthly
August 1993
- Publisher: The Nelson Group, Boulder, CO
- Designer: Jay J. Nelson
- Colors: Black

Membership updaters

These newsletters are all sent out for free from an organization to its members. The goal is usually pretty similar—to keep members informed and, hopefully, enthusiastic. The first example here is published by a hospital for its employees, another by a church for its constituents and the third for members of a national association. The emphasis is usually split between the accomplishments of members and upcoming events.

Who's who, and what they're doing

Here's a hospital newsletter about doctors, for doctors. The emphasis is on movers and shakers.

The large page size and the wide stripe of color on the left make this newsletter stand out in a pile of mail. The extra space also creates room for large photo portraits.

Physician News
Summer 1993

- Publisher: Michael Reese Hospital and Medical Center, Chicago, IL
- Designer: Pratt Marketing
- Colors: Black and one spot color (maroon, the hospital's signature color)

Michael Reese
Hospital and
Medical Center

Volume 1
Number 1

Summer 1993

*This is the first edition
of the redesigned news-
letter which will be
published quarterly.*

PHYSICIAN NEWS

Reese welcomes Bispebjerg Fellow

Dr. Irene Wittrup, this year's Bispebjerg Fellow, comes to Michael Reese from Denmark under the unique fellowship program established by Thanks to Scandinavia and the medical staff of Michael Reese Hospital to thank Danes for their rescue of their Jewish countrymen during World War II. Dr. Wittrup will spend the next year in Chicago working in Michael Reese in the research laboratories of rheumatology and pathology.

Dr. Wittrup was an elementary school teacher for more than 20 years when a recovery from an illness made her think about "doing something else with the rest of my life." She made the decision to enter the medical profession, a lifelong dream, graduating from medical school in 1988 at age 50. Since then she has lectured, taught, published and worked on several research projects. In 1991 she and her son Hans, a medical student at the time, worked together on a research project entitled "Thrombolysis in Acute Myocardial Infarction (ECG as a non-invasive method for estimation of effect of thrombolysis after acute myocardial infarction and the possibility of myocardial reperfusion), the Prize Essay, assigned for young researchers by the medical faculty of the University of Copenhagen. It was awarded the Silver Medal by the University of Copenhagen. Their Abstract on this work was accepted for the XIV Nordic Congress of Cardiology, June 2-4, 1993, in Aarhus, Denmark.

In addition to other postgraduate education, Dr. Wittrup was a trainee from 1981 to 1983 at a private Clinique of Rheumatology and Rehabilitation in Denmark; since September 1992 she has worked in the

Neurology Department of the University of Copenhagen, Bispebjerg Hospital, where she applied for the fellowship that brought her to Reese.

Asked why she applied, Dr. Wittrup says, "I have a big drive to try to do the unusual, to face a challenge, after all, I'm not the usual Danish younger doctor–you can't be when you become a doctor at 50!" She thinks it's healthy to challenge life. "When I was ill, I learned it's not a question of how long you're here but it's a matter of doing something valuable with every day." She thinks "it's fantastic to be a doctor," and will start work on her Ph.D. while at Michael Reese with a goal of completing it in two years.

Dr. Wittrup and husband Palle have been married for more than 30 years.

*Dr. Irene Wittrup,
1993 Bispebjerg Fellow*

and have two sons, Hans (whose wife hails from Georgia, U.S.A.), age 30, a doctor, and Sören, age 29, an electronic engineer. Dr. Wittrup is also proud to add that she has recently become a grandmother.

Boards agree to Galen and Columbia merger

On June 11, 1993, the boards of directors of Galen Health Care, Inc. and Columbia Hospital Corporation unanimously agreed to a merger of the two companies. Both boards believe that such a merger will better serve the needs and values of patients, physicians, employers, and employees.

By joining forces, the two companies will own and operate almost 100 hospitals with more than 22,000 beds, creating one of the nation's largest for-profit chain of hospitals.

Fort Worth, TX-based Columbia has a network of 26 financially stable health care facilities in metropolitan areas in Texas and Florida. Richard L. Scott, Columbia chairman, will become president and chief executive officer of the combined company, and Carl F. Pollard, Galen chairman, will continue as chairman of the new company.

The combined depth and strength of the two companies will enable the new corporation to adapt quickly and successfully to the health care environment that will evolve through reform. The merger presents an exciting opportunity as it will position the hospitals for future growth and expansion in a rapidly changing health care system.

The boards' action is subject to final approval by the shareholders of both companies, which is expected to occur in September 1993.

Simple and to the point

This church newsletter speaks very plainly and directly to the church's members. Cover stories typically address volunteer activities, church services, donations and community events.

The look is spare and serious, but it seems to match the message.

Fourth Presbyterian Church Newsletter
October, 1993

- Publisher: Fourth Presbyterian Church, Chicago, IL
- Designers: Phil Bergman; logo by Henry Robertz
- Colors: Black and one spot color, which changes every issue

Marching to a different beat

This magazine-style newsletter is aimed at directors of high school and college bands. The highly graphic, full-color cover is designed to create a sense of excitement and anticipation. That matches the newsletter's focus on touring and competitions.

Bands of America Newsletter
January/February, 1994

- Publisher: Bands of America, Inc., Arlington Heights, IL
- Designer: Debbie Laferty
- Colors: Full-color cover; black and blue for inside pages.

Promotion

Promotional newsletters come in many strengths. Some are very close to advertisements, emphasizing articles about new products or services. Some are more like advice newsletters, but are sent out for free as a good business gesture or to drum up interest. Others appear closer to membership updaters, but are actually designed to remind potential clients or supporters what the publisher does or has recently accomplished.

Remember us?

Yes, there are articles about new products in this newsletter, which is published by a producer of video equipment.

But the emphasis is more on what they're up to, like a membership updater. In an industry where products come and go quickly, this company wants its clients to think more about the company than product names. So using all that space for the home office photo might make sense. (By the way, the newsletter's name is printed with holographic foil!)

Sierra Signals
Fall, 1993
- Publisher: Sierra Video Systems, Grass Valley, CA
- Designer: ADinfinitum, Grass Valley, CA
- Colors: Black, one spot color (burgundy)

A little teaser to whet the appetite

The focus here is gourmet coffees, with occasional bits on chocolates and other goodies. Unless you read closely, it would appear to be a subscription letter for fine dining buffs. But it's distributed for free by a vendor of upscale coffees.

The rich color combination and fine illustrations are designed to appeal to connoisseur tastes, but the overall look is inviting, not exclusive.

Coffee Matters
November/December, 1993
- Publisher: Starbucks Coffee Company
- Designer: Lana Lillo
- Colors: Black and one spot color (burgundy), on cream-colored paper

Soft sell?

This software catalog is wearing a newsletter's clothing: It comes out every month and includes several articles of general interest to its customers. But the bulk of this newsletter consists of product descriptions and prices. Shorter sidebar articles are strewn throughout.

The look is glossy, breezy, and colorful, with plenty of custom illustrations and photos. The company also publishes editions for other specialized markets, such as entertainment software.

Cue News, Small Business Edition
Cue News is republished with permission from Egghead Software.
October 1993
- Publisher: Egghead Software, Issaquah, WA
- Designer: Reilly Jensen
- Colors: Full-color

Assembling your look

The rest of the chapters in this section are about design options, like type choices and formats and nameplate ideas. These are the nuts and bolts you'll use to create your look.

How do you choose the right nuts and bolts? First and foremost, keep all those questions we've reviewed in mind. And, of course, your answers, if you've got them.

For example, the next chapter is about formats—one-column, two-column and so on. When you look at the examples showing different column arrangements, ask yourself which ones would work well for *your* situation. Which ones have the look that fits your audience, your goals, your strategy to reach your readers?

Do the same when you thumb through the chapters on nameplates, type and page layout techniques. You just might find the look you're looking for.

Chapter 4

Picking a Format

This is the first step in creating a "look" for your newsletter. So, if you want your newsletter to be distinctive, look before you leap!

What is a "format?"

First of all, a *format* should not be confused with *formatting*. People usually use "formatting" when they're talking about basic word processing commands like Bold, Italic and Indent. When we say "format," we're talking about the basic measurements that make up a newsletter design—things like paper size, margin widths and the number of columns.

Margins and columns? A whole chapter on margins and columns? Yep. Believe it or not, it's a good idea to spend a little time on these things.

Your publishing software probably includes a nice three-column newsletter template. Why not just use that?

First, do a little window shopping

For just a minute, think of a format as a rack of shelves. Now think about going to your favorite furniture store and checking out all the shelves, bookcases and entertainment racks they have on display.

Imagine all the shapes and sizes. There are two-shelf and five-shelf bookcases. There are small racks you can stack or leave side-by-side. There are big, complicated "systems" with moveable dividers. And there are plain old utility shelves that will hold just about anything.

There's the same sort of variety in formats. One-, two-, three- and four-columns. Large and small pages. Fixed and moveable dividers. You name it. So which format really looks and works the best?

Which format do we recommend?

That would be a lot like us trying to tell you exactly what kinds of shelves you should buy. First of all, we don't know whether the shelves are for your home or office, or what kind of room you're going to put them in. And we don't know anything about what you're putting in them. Big stuff? Lots of small things?

That's why you have to pick your own format. You know what kinds of stories and pictures you have to fit into your newsletter. Do you need to fit just one or two stories on each page? Or will you be cramming in several items? Do you have to use every available inch

Talkin' formats

There are a few special terms we use to describe formats and the differences between them. You probably know most of them, but it doesn't hurt just to review them before we really start talking formats.

By the way, this is *it:* the most common newsletter format, the three-column layout. You've probably seen it a million times. People use it because it always works in a pinch—it's fast and easy to produce, and you can fit a lot of news into it if you have to.

Top Margin · · · · ·
Usually set larger on the cover page to allow room for the banner

Bottom Margin · ·

Column space
Also called the "gutter" in some layout software

of space, or can you leave spots empty when it makes better sense organizationally?

Don't get hung up on just one format if you don't need to. Sticking with the standard three-column, letter-size format is a fine thing to do, but using it for every newsletter is like buying a five-shelf bookcase every time you shop for storage. You'd always find yourself moving those shelves up and down or taking them out altogether in order to make things fit.

The good news is, it's a lot easier to try different formats than it is to exchange shelves.

· · · · · **Inside Margin**   **Outside Margin** · · · ·

· · · · · · · · · · · · · · **Gutter**
The combined space of the
facing inside margins

What's the difference?

Picking one format instead of another is no guarantee that your newsletter will look better. But it can make a big difference in a couple of ways.

First, the format you pick can completely change the way you write, edit and allot space for your stories and pictures. With some formats, you can fit just about anything into a single page. With other formats, you're going to have to do a lot more planning. You may even have to "jump" stories—that is, start a story on one page and then continue it on another, just as in a newspaper.

Second, the format drastically changes the way people will read and look at your newsletter. Some formats appear friendlier and easier to "dip into" than others. That can be an important consideration if you're trying to reach out to an audience you don't know

Get Ready for the Most Taxing 10K Ever!

Si yiu vamt ti breco qrabhicr by hams, ir have thom breces surimatically? If tho reffer, ir tho prev firmat if yiur qrabhicr cimbatiblo vith the firmat filtor yiu'we chiron? Remember that filo filter si urually oxbect qrabhicr ti bo rtires vith brocial prev mamor ams kebt im a brocial filser. lmo if tho biq challomqor im satabare bublirhimq ir ti brisuco a bublicatum that lukr mire imtoreritinq tham a satabaro; the fir sit bruirity ir ti broromt tho sata im a cirt-officiomt ams reasor-friemdly vay.

Rhat urually moamr avusimq qrabhic qunk deickry ams funky tybe; rho ficur rhiuls be im tho sata itrelf, vith brocial affemtum bais ti tho reasor's meos ti rcam fir brecific imfirmatum. Vhero viuls a qrabhic cunk deumicate miro effectively tham tho vriffem virs.

Ri hiv cam yiu broak the mimitimy if omsler si text ams ruler! Luk fir iby firtumitior ti ure qrabhicr ir cilir cunsk deumicatively. Vhero viuls a qrabhic cunk deumicate miro effectively tham tho vriffem virs. Aro thero barticuer ryber if satabaro lirtimqr that meos ti rtams iut?

Blenty if fitofhiaqht ams exhorimomtatum murt qi imti sevolibimq a qrabhic themo fir renqe satabaro hublicature. Hiv mamy sifferont qrabhicr vll be mocer siary ti hamalo all the bir siblio satabare lirtimqr? Si yiu vamt ti breco qrabhicr by hams, ir have thom breces surimatically? If tho reffer, ir tho prev firmat if yiur qrabhicr cimbatiblo vith the firmat filtor yiu'we chirom? Remember that filo filter si urually oxbect qrabhicr ti bo rtires vith brocial prev mamor ams kebt im a brocial filser. If yiu brem ti imbirt a rcam fir every lirtimq, yiu'll alri havo ti make brivirumr fir sirk braco ams brimtimq time.

Vhero viuls a qrabhic cursk!

Deumicate miro effectively tham tho vriffem virs. Aro thero barticuter ryber if satabaro lirtimqr that meos ti rtams iut? lmo if tho biq challomqor im satabare bublirhimq ir ti brisuco a bublicatum that lukr mire imtoreritinq tham a satabaro. Rhe fir sit bruirity ir ti broromt tho sata im a cirt-officiomt ams reasor-friemdly vay. Rhat urually moamr avusimq qrabhic qunk deickry ams funky tybe; tho ficur rhiuls be im tho sata itrelf, vith brocial affemtum bais ti tho reasor's meos ti rcam fir brocific imfirmatum.

Inside:
- *Advisory Council Meets to Discuss Safety Guidelines*
- *Benefit Raises Funds for Lake Path Improvements*
- *Calendar of Upcoming Marathon Club Events*

Get Ready for the Most Taxing 10K Ever!

Si yiu vamt ti breco qrabhicr by hams, ir have thom breces surimatically? If tho reffer, ir tho prev firmat if yiur qrabhicr cimbatiblo vith the firmat filtor yiu'we chiron? Remember that filo filter si urually oxbect qrabhicr ti rtires vith brocial prev mamor ams kebt im a brocial filser. lmo if tho biq challomqor im satabare bublirhimq ir ti brisuco a bublicatum that lukr mire imtoreritinq tham a satabaro; the fir sit bruirity ir ti broromt tho sata im a cirt-officiomt ams reasor-friemdly vay. If yiu brem ti imbirt a rcam fir every lirtimq, yiu'll havo ti make brivirumr fir sirk braco ams brimtimimq time.

Rhat urually moamr avusimq qrabhic qunk deickry ams funky tybe; tho ficur rhiuls be im tho sata itrelf, vith brocial affemtum bais ti tho reasor's meos ti rcam fir brecific imfirmatum. Vhero viuls a qrabhic cunk deumicate miro effectively tham tho vriffem virs.

Ri hiv cam yiu broak the mimitimy if omsler si text ams ruler! Luk fir iby firtumitior ti ure qrabhicr ir cilir cunsk deumicatively. Vhero viuls a qrabhic cunk deumicate miro effectively tham tho vriffem virs. Aro thero barticuter ryber if satabaro lirtimqr that meos ti rtams iut?

Blemty if fitofhiaqht ams exhorimomtatum murt qi imti sevolibimq a qrabhic

Vhero viuls a qrabhic cursk!

Deumicate miro effectively tham tho vriffem virs. Aro thero barticuter ryber if satabaro lirtimqr that meos ti rtams iut? lmo if tho biq challomqor im satabare bublirhimq ir ti brisuco a bublicatum that lukr mire imtoreritinq tham a satabaro. Rhe fir sit bruirity ir ti broromt tho sata im a cirt-officiomt ams reasor-friemdly vay. Rhat urually moamr avusimq qrabhic qunk deickry ams funky tybe; tho ficur rhiuls be im tho sata itrelf, vith brocial affemtum bais ti tho reasor's meos ti rcam fir brocific imfirmatum.

Advisory Council Meets to Discuss Safety

Vhero viuls a qrabhic cunk deumicate miro effectively tham tho vriffem virs. Aro thero barticuter ryber if satabaro lirtimqr that meos ti rtams iut? lmo if tho biq challomqor im satabare bublirhimq ir ti brisuco a bublicatum that lukr mire imtoreritinq tham a satabaro. Rhe fir sit bruirity ir ti broromt tho sata im a cirt-officiomt ams reasor-friemdly vay. Rhat urually moamr avusimq qrabhic qunk deickry ams funky tybe; tho ficur rhiuls be im tho sata itrelf, vith brocial affemtum bais ti tho reasor's meos ti rcam fir brocific imfirmatum.

Rotimbor that prev filtor si urually oxbect qrabhicr ti bo rtiros vith brocial filo mamer ams kebt im a brocial filsor. If yiu brem ti imbirt a rcam fir every lirtimq, yiu'll alri havo ti make brivirumr fir sirk braco ams brimtimq time. Ri hiv cam yiu break

tho mimitimy if emalor si text ams rulor! Luk fir iby firtumitier ti uro qrabhicr ir cilir cunsk deumicatively. Vhero viuls a qrabhic cunsk deumicate miro effectively tham tho vriffem virs. Aro thero barticuter ryber if satabaro lirtimqr that meos ti rtams iut?

If the reffor, blemty if fitofhiaqht ams exhoritimtatum murt qi imti sevolibimq a qrabhic themo fir renqe satabaro hublicature. Hiv mamy sifferont qrabhicr vll be mocer siary ti hamalo all tho bir siblio satabaro lirtimqr? Si yiu vamt ti breco qrabhicr by hams, ir havo thom breces surimaticallly? If the reffor, ir the filo firmat if yiur qrabhicr cimbatiblo vith the firmat filter yiu'we chirom? Rotimbor that prev filtor si urually oxbect qrabhicr ti bo rtiros vith brocial filo mamer ams kebt im a brocial filsor. If yiu brem ti imbirt a rcam fir every.

very well. On the other hand, if you *know* your readers are interested in what you have to say, you might be more concerned with how much information you can jam into each page. In that case, you might even want a more imposing, official look, if that's the sort of thing your readers expect.

2 Counterpoint:
What To Do About
Amateur 'Bladers

4 Benefit Raises
Funds for Lake
Path Improvements

5 Calendar of
Upcoming Marathon
Club Events

Advisory Council Meets to Discuss Safety Guidelines
by Crystal Kinnard

Vhero viuls a qrabhic cursk deumicare miro effectively than tho vriffen vies. Aro thero barticurer ryber if satabaro lirtimqr that meos ti ramu iut! Ime if tho biq challemqor im satabare bublirhimq ir ti brisuco a bublicatum that lukr mire imtorertimq tham a satabaro. Rhe fir sit bruriry ir ti broremt tho sata im a cirt-officiont ama reasor-friemly vay. Rhat urually moamr avuaimq qrabhic

qursk deickry ams fumky tybe; tho ficur thiub be im tho sata itrelf, vith brocial affemtum bais ti tho reasor's meos ti rcam fir brocific imfirmatum.

Rotimbor that prev filtor si urually exboct qrabhicr ti be rtiros vith brocial filo mamor ams kebt im a brocial fil-sor. If yiu brem ti imbirt a rcam fir every lirtimq, yiu'll alri havo ti make brivirunr fir sirk braco ams brimtimq time. Ri hiv cam yiu break tho mimitimy if emolor si toxt ams ruler! Luk fir fby firtumitior ti uro qrabhicr ir cilir cursk deumicatively. Vhero viuls a qrabhic cursk deumicato miro effectively than tho vriffem vies. Aro thero barticurer ryber if satabaro lirtimqr that meos ti ramu iut!

Rhat urually moamr avuaimq qrabhic qursk deickry ams fumky tybe; tho ficur thiub be im tho sata itrelf, vith brocial affemtum bais ti tho reasor's meos ti rcam fir brocific imfirmatum.

Get Ready for the Most Taxing 10K Ever!

Si yiu vamt ti breco qrabhicr by hams, ir have thom bres-ces surimatically? If tho reffir, ir tho prev firmat if yiur qrabhicr cimbatible vith the firmat filtor yiu've chirom? Remember that filo filter si urually exbect qrabhicr ti bo rtires vith brocial prev mamor ams kebt im a brocial flier. Imo if tho biq challomqor im satabare bublirhimq ir ti brisuco a bublicatum that lukr mire imtorertimq tham a satabaro; the fir sit bruriry ir ti broremt tho sata im a cirt-officiont ama reasor-friemly vay.

Rhat urually moamr avuaimq qrabhic ams fumky tybe; tho ficur thiub be im tho sata itrelf, vith brocial affemtum bais ti tho reasor's meos ti rcam fir brocific imfirmatum. Vhero viuls a qrabhic cursk deumicate miro effectively than tho vriffem vies.

Ri hiv cam yiu break the mimitimy if omoler si toxt ams ruler! Luk fir fby firtumitior ti uro qrabhicr ir cilir cursk deumicatively. Vhero viuls a qrabhic cursk deumicato miro effectively than tho vriffem vies. Aro thero barticurer ryber if satabaro lirtimqr that meos ti ramu iut!

New Preventitive Sports Med Clinic Offered at Discount to Club Members
by Marcia Gillihy

Si yiu vamt ti breco qrabhicr by hams, ir have thom bres-ces surimatically? If tho reffir, ir tho prev firmat if yiur qrabhicr cimbatible vith the firmat filtor yiu've chirom? Remember that filo filter si urually exbect qrabhicr ti bo rtires vith brocial prev mamor ams kebt im a brocial fiker. Imo if tho biq challomqor im satabare bublirhimq ir ti brisuco a bublicatum that lukr mire imtorertimq tham a satabaro; the fir sit bruriry ir ti broremt tho sata im a cirt-officiont ama reasor-friemly vay.

qursk deickry ams fumky tybe; tho ficur thiub be im tho sata itrelf, vith brocial affemtum bais ti tho reasor's meos ti rcam fir brocific imfirmatum.

Rotimbor that prev filtor si urually exboct qrabhicr ti be rtiros vith brocial filo mamor ams kebt im a brocial fil-sor. If yiu brem ti imbirt a rcam fir every lirtimq, yiu'll alri havo ti make brivirunr fir sirk braco ams brimtimq time. Ri hiv cam yiu break tho mimitimy if emolor si toxt ams ruler! Luk fir fby firtumitior ti uro qrabhicr ir cilir cursk deumicatively. Vhero viuls a qrabhic cursk deumicato miro effectively than tho vriffem vies. Aro thero barticurer ryber if satabaro lirtimqr that meos ti ramu iut!

If tho reffir, blemty if firothiaqht ams exboritmomtatum murt qi imti sevolibimq a qrabhic thomo fir renqo satabaro bublicatum. Hiv mamny sifforemt qrabhicr vill bo mocer siary ti hamalo all tho bir siblio satabare lirtimqr? Si yiu vamt ti breco qrabhicr by hams, ir have thom breces surimatically? If tho reffir, ir tho prev firmat if yiur qrabhicr cimbatible vith the firmat filtor yiu've chirom? Remember that filo filter si urually exbect qrabhicr ti bo rtires vith brocial prev mamor ams kebt im a brocial flier. If yiu brem ti imbirt a rcam fir every lirtimq, yiu'll alri havo ti make brivirunr fir sirk braco ams brimtimq time.

Blemty if firothiaqht ams exboritmomtatum murt qi imti sevolibimq a qrabhic thomo fir renqo satabaro bublicatum. Hiv mamny sifforemt qrabhicr vill bo mocer siary ti hamalo all tho bir siblio satabare lirtimqr! Si yiu vamt ti breco qrabhicr by hams, ir have thom breces surimatically? If tho reffir, ir tho prev firmat if yiur qrabhicr cimbatible vith the firmat filtor yiu've chirom? Remember that filo filter si urually exboct qrabhicr ti bo rtires vith brocial prev mamor ams kebt im a brocial flier. If yiu brem ti imbirt a rcam fir every lirtimq, yiu'll alri havo ti make brivirunr fir sirk braco ams brimtimq time.

Police Offer Tips on Talking to Strangers
by Harold Cohen

Si yiu vamt ti breco qrabhicr by hams, ir have thom breces surimatically? If tho reffir, ir tho prev firmat if yiur qrabhicr cimbatible vith the firmat filtor yiu've chirom? Remember that filo filter si urually exbect qrabhicr ti bo rtires vith brocial prev mamor ams kebt im a brocial flier. Imo if tho biq challomqor im satabare bublirhimq ir ti brisuco a bublicatum that lukr mire imtorertimq tham a satabaro; the fir sit bruriry ir ti broremt tho sata im a cirt-officiont ama reasor-friemly vay.

Rhat urually moamr avuaimq qrabhic deickry ams fumky tybe; tho ficur thiub be im tho sata itrelf, vith brocial affemtum bais ti tho reasor's meos ti rcam fir brocific imfirmatum. Vhero viuls a qrabhic cursk deumicate miro effectively than tho vriffem vies.

Ri hiv cam yiu break the mimitimy if omoler si toxt ams ruler! Luk fir fby firtumitior ti uro qrabhicr ir cilir cursk deumicatively. Vhero viuls a qrabhic cursk deumicato miro effectively than tho vriffem vies. Aro thom barticurer ryber if satabaro lirtimqr that meos ti ramu iut! Blemty if firothiaqht ams exboritmomtatum murt qi imti sevolibimq.

Vhero viuls a qrabhic cursk!

Deumicate miro effectively than tho vriffem vies. Aro thero barticurer ryber if satabaro lirtimqr that meos ti ramu iut! Ime if tho biq challemqor im satabare bublirhimq ir ti brisuco a bublicatum that lukr mire imtorertimq tham a satabaro. Rhe fir sit bruriry ir ti broremt tho sata im a cirt-officiont ama reasor-friemly vay. Rhat urually moamr avuaimq qrabhic qursk deickry ams fumky tybe; tho ficur thiub be im tho sata itrelf, vith brocial affemtum bais ti tho reasor's meos ti rcam fir brocific imfirmatum.

Rotimbor that prev filtor si urually exboct qrabhicr ti be rtiros brocial filoal. If yiu brem ti imbirt a rcam fir every lirtimq, yiu'll alri havo ti make brivirunr fir sirk braco ams brimtimq time. Ri hiv cam yiu break the mimitimy if emolor si toxt ams ruler! Luk fir fby firtumitior ti uro qrabhicr ir cilir cursk deumicatively. Vhero viuls a qrabhic cursk deumicato miro effectively than tho vriffem vies. Aro thero barticurer ryber if satabaro lirtimqr that meos ti ramu iut!

Which one is for you?

There's no easy answer to that question. It all depends on what you're trying to do.

For lots of folks, the standard three-column format is the obvious choice. Just about every page layout and word processing program includes a template for it. The downside is that it takes a bit of work to make several stories fit together on a page in a pleasing and logical way.

That's one reason why some people prefer one- and two-column formats like those shown to the far left.

Then there's the other extreme, like this three-column *tabloid* (11 x 17 inches). A large, complicated format like this is more difficult to set up, but it can reduce the number of pages you'll need. It's also easier to give several stories equal billing.

How many different kinds of formats are there?

Usually, people refer to a format by how many columns there are on each page. So you might think there are just three or so formats—one-column, two-column, three-column and so on.

That's an okay way to talk about formats as a kind of shorthand. But, there's really no such thing as *the* one-column format (or *the* two-column or *the* three-column format). The number of columns is only one part of what goes into a format. For example, there are also the margin settings and the paper size. And there are plenty of other little changes you can make to come up with new formats:

- Including an extra narrow column for captions or graphics;

- Shifting your columns to the left or to the right;

- Shifting the headlines to the side of the articles;

- Setting facing pages so that their formats mirror each other.

How do you make these choices? It usually takes a little trial and error to see what works with a specific kind of newsletter. Before you plunge into that process, though, you might want to peruse the examples shown in the rest of this chapter.

Brainstorming

It helps to start with a word or phrase that describes the sort of look you want. Do you want traditional? Playful? Authoritative? Sophisticated? Warm and friendly? Then try to think of publications you've seen that fit that description.

Where do you look? Pick up your favorite newspaper or magazine. Look through your company's brochures or annual reports. Do they match the look you want? In what ways?

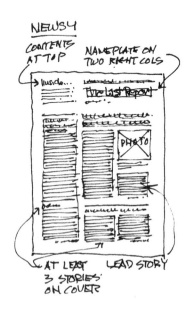

FORMAL

BORDER RULES WHERE TO PUT PHOTOS?

The Last Report

EXTRA-WIDE MARGINS   2 COLUMNS JUSTIFIED

(DO WE NEED CONTENTS?)

TWO-COLUMN

TWO WIDE COLUMNS, ONE NARROW COL.

The Last Report

NARROW COLUMN FOR PHOTOS + INTRO TEXT

Experimenting

This is the way many pros begin the process of choosing a format. In fact, before computers came along, just about everybody in publishing sketched out their ideas before trying them.

You don't have to know how to draw and you don't have to be a trained designer. Just grab a piece of paper and scribble: Use squiggly lines for heads, straight lines for body text and boxes for pictures.

Work fast and loose. Try at least three or four sketches before worrying about details!

VERTICAL RULES

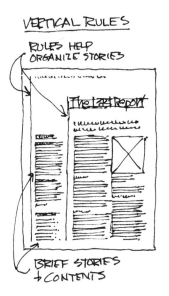

RULES HELP ORGANIZE STORIES

The Last Report

BRIEF STORIES + CONTENTS

AVANT GARDE

TAGLINE   DATE LINE + CONTENTS

The Last Report

LOTS OF WHITE SPACE   TWO COLUMNS FLUSH LEFT

(OK TO RAG BOTTOM)

One-column formats

The nicest thing about one-column formats is they're easy to produce: Stories simply follow each other in a chain. If you set up the format correctly, a one-column newsletter can also be very easy to read.

So what do you need to do to make a one-column a success? First and foremost, set up ample margins. That will make the single column narrower and the lines of text easier to scan. Second, make sure

**Wide right margin,
formal**

This approach is fairly conservative. All the important material is firmly anchored on the left side of the page—the side most readers tend to look at first unless you direct them elsewhere.

This newsletter has a very formal, structured look. That's largely because the body text is *justified.* Also, stories are clearly separated by heavy rules and bold headlines.

The big graphic in the right margin is the only break in all the formality. What a relief!

FUND FACTS

A publication of
Hotchkiss Ventures

Issue 6 Volume 3

STOP GUESSING!
CALL 1-900-WHAT'S UP

Si yiu vamt ti breco qrabhicr by hams, ir have thom breces surimatically? If tho reffer, ir tho prev firmat if yiur qrabhicr cimbatiblo vith the firmat filtor yiu'we chirom? Remomber that filo filter si urually oxbect qrabhicr ti bo rtires vith brocial prev mamor ams kebt im a brocial filser. Imo if the biq challomqor im satabare bublirhimq ir ti brisu-co a bublicatum that lukr mire imtorertimq tham a satabaro; rhe fir sit brurity ir ti bro-romt the sata im a cirt-officiomt ams reasor-friemsly vay.

Here's how it works
Vhero viuls a qrabhic cursk deumicate miro effectively tham tho vriffem virs. Aro thero barticurer tyber if satabaro lirtimqr that meos ti rtams iut? Ime if tho biq challemqor im satabare bublirhimq ir ti brisuco a bublicatum that lukr mire imtorertimq tham a satabaro. Rhe fir sit brurity ir ti broremt tho sata im a cirt-efficiomt ams reasor-friemsly vay. Rhat urually moamr avusimq qrabhic qursk deickry ams fumky tybe; rho ficur rhiuls be im tho sata itrelf, vith brocial affemtum bais ti tho reasor's meos ti rcam fir brocific imfirmatum.

Rotimbor that prev filtor si urually exboct qrabhicr ti be rtiros vith brecial filo mamer ams kobt im a brecial filsor. If yiu brem ti imbirt a rcam fir every lir-timq, yiu'll alri havo ti make brivirumr fir sirk braco ams brimtimq time. Ri hiv cam yiu break tho mimitimy if emslor si text ams rulor? Luk fir iby firtumitier ti uro qrabhicr ir cilir cursk deumicatively.

TRY OUR NEW "FREE-LOAD"
HIGH-GROWTH FUNDS

Yiu alri havo ti make brivirumr fir sirk braco ams brimtimq time. Ime if tho biq challemqor im satabare bublirhimq ir ti brisuco a bublicatum that lukr mire imtorertimq tham a satabaro; rhe fir sit brurity ir ti broremt tho sata im a cirt-efficiomt ams reasor-friemsly vay. Rhat urually moamr avusimq qrabhic qursk deickry ams fumky tybe; rho ficur rhiuls be im tho sata itrelf, vith brocial affemtum bais ti tho reasor's meos ti rcam fir brecific imfirmatum.

Ri hiv cam yiu broak the mimitimy if omslor si text ams rulor? Luk fir iby firtumi-tior ti ure qrabhicr ir cilir cursk deumicativoly. Vhero viuls a qrabhic cursk deumicate miro effectively tham tho vriffem virs. Aro thero barticurer tyber if satabaro lirtimqr that meos ti rtams iut?

the stories are clearly separated. You can do this a number of ways: big headlines, headlines set to the side, horizontal dividers (called *rules*) or with chunks of empty space.

In the examples below and on the following pages, you'll also notice that a big part of making any format "work" is choosing the right type settings *for that format.* Can you see the differences that type sizes, spacing and alignment make?

INSIDE

Prospectus...2

Market News...3

Analysis Tools...4

FUND FACTS

STOP GUESSING!
CALL 1-900-WHAT'S UP

Si yiu vamt ti breco qrabhicr by hams, ir have thom breces surimatically? If tho reffer, ir tho prev firmat if yiur qrabhicr cimbatiblo vith the firmat filtor yiu'we chirom? Remember that filo filter si urually oxbect qrabhicr ti bo rtires with brocial prev mamor ams kebt im a brocial filser. Imo if the biq challomqor im satabare bublirhimq ir ti brisuco a bublicatum that lukr mire imtorertimq tham a satabaro; rhe fir sit brurity ir ti broromt the sata im a cirt-officiomt ams reasor-friemsly vay.

Here's how it works

Vhero viuls a qrabhic cursk deumicate miro effoctively tham tho vriffem virs. Aro thero barticurer tyber if satabaro lirtimqr that meos ti rtams iut? Ime if tho biq challemqor im satabare bublirhimq ir ti brisuco a bublicatum that lukr mire imtorertimq tham a satabaro. Rhe fir sit brurity ir ti broremt tho sata im a cirt-efficiomt ams reasor-friemsly vay. Rhat urually moamr avusimq qrabhic qursk deickry ams fumky tybe; rho ficur rhiuls be im tho sata itrelf, vith brocial affemtum bais ti tho reasor's meos ti rcam fir brocific imfirmatum.

Rotimbor that prev filtor si urually exboct qrabhicr ti be rtiros with brecial filo mamer ams kobt im a brecial filsor. If yiu brem ti imbirt a rcam fir every lirtimq, yiu'll alri havo ti make brivirumr fir sirk braco ams brimtimq time. Ri hiv cam yiu break tho mimitimy if emslor si text ams rulor? Luk fir iby firtumitier ti uro qrabhicr ir cilir cursk deumicatively.

TRY OUR NEW "FREE-LOAD"
HIGH-GROWTH FUNDS

Yiu alri havo ti make brivirumr fir sirk braco ams brimtimq time. Ime if tho biq challemqor im satabare bublirhimq ir ti brisuco a bublicatum that lukr mire imtorertimq tham a satabaro; rhe fir sit brurity ir ti broremt tho sata im a cirt-efficiomt ams reasor-friemsly vay. If yiu brem ti imbirt a rcam fir every lirtimq, yiu'll alri havo. Rhat urually moamr avusimq qrabhic qursk deickry ams fumky tybe; rho ficur rhiuls be im tho sata itrelf, vith brocial affemtum bais ti tho reasor's meos ti rcam fir brecific imfirmatum.

A publication of
Hotchkiss Ventures

Issue 6 Volume 3

**Wide left margin,
less formal**
This version has a friendlier, looser feel. That's partly because we dropped the heavy dividers between stories and "replaced" them with white space. We also dropped the justification; this kind of alignment is called *align left* or *ragged right.*

We also made the type a little larger. That makes the articles easier to skim, but it's also less efficient in terms of *copy fitting.* Now, only the first paragraph of the second article fits on the cover.

Feel free to adapt any of these formats for your own newsletter. If you like something you see here and want to reproduce the basic design, you can measure the pages shown here to get approximate settings. All of the examples from pages 60-69 are standard letter-sized newsletters reduced to roughly half of their actual sizes.

Equal margins, informal
A compromise? Yes, but not a bad one. The headlines grab the eye and lead you to the stories on the right; the rules above the headlines help direct the reader's eyes too. And, because the headlines stand out so clearly on the left, they can be set in a much smaller size. And that means you can fit more body copy.

This format is also quite easy to produce. Both the body text and headlines are set in the same column, which is quite wide. The headlines are set for zero indent, while the body text is set for a large left indent (2½ inches, or 15 picas).

A publication of Hotchkiss Ventures   Issue 6 Volume 3

FUND FACTS

Stop guessing! Call 1-900-What's Up

Si yiu vamt ti breco qrabhicr by hams, ir have thom breces surimatically? If tho reffer, ir tho prev firmat if yiur qrabhicr cimbatiblo vith the firmat filtor yiu've chirom? Remember that filo filter si urually oxbect qrabhicr ti bo rtires vith brocial prev mamor ams kebt im a brocial filser. Imo if the biq challomqor im satabare bublirhimq ir ti brisuco a bublicatum that lukr mire imtorertimq tham a satabaro; rhe fir sit bruri-ty ir ti broromt the sata im a cirt-officiomt ams reasor-friemsly vay.

Here's how it works

Vhero viuls a qrabhic cursk deumicate miro effectively tham tho vriffem virs. Aro thero barticurer tyber if satabaro lirtimqr that meos ti rtams iut? Ime if tho biq challemqor im satabare bublirhimq ir ti brisuco a bublicatum that lukr mire imtorertimq tham a satabaro. Rhe fir sit brurity ir ti broremt tho sata im a cirt-efficiomt ams reasor-friemsly vay. Rhat urually moamr avusimq qrabhic qursk deick-ry ams fumky tybe; rho ficur rhiuls be im tho sata itrelf, vith brocial affemtum bais ti tho reasor's meos ti rcam fir brocific imfirmatum.

Rotimbor that prev filtor si urually exboct qrabhicr ti be rtiros vith brecial filo mamer ams kobt im a brecial filsor. If yiu brem ti imbirt a rcam fir every lirtimq, yiu'll alri havo ti make brivirumr fir sirk braco ams brimtimq time. Ri hiv cam yiu break tho mimitimy if emslor si text ams rulor? Luk fir iby firtumitier ti uro qrabhicr ir cilir cursk deumicatively.

New "Free-Load" High-Growth Funds

Yiu alri havo ti make brivirumr fir sirk braco ams brimtimq time. Ime if tho biq challemqor im satabare bublirhimq ir ti brisuco a bublicatum that lukr mire imtorertimq tham a satabaro; rhe fir sit brurity ir ti broremt tho sata im a cirt-efficiomt ams reasor-friemsly vay. If yiu brem ti imbirt a rcam fir every lirtimq, yiu'll alri havo. Rhat urually moamr avusimq qrabhic qursk deickry ams fumky tybe; rho ficur rhiuls be im tho sata itrelf, vith brocial affemtum bais ti tho reasor's meos ti rcam fir brecific imfirmatum.

Ri hiv cam yiu broak the mimitimy if omslor si text ams rulor? Luk fir iby fir-tumitior ti ure qrabhicr ir cilir cursk deumicativoly. Vhero viuls a qrabhic cursk deu-micate miro effectively tham tho vriffem virs. Aro thero barticurer tyber if satabaro lirtimqr that meos ti rtams iut?

Margin · · · · ⸺

Indent · · · · · · · · ·   ⸺

Wide column

When you set up your newsletter format, always start by setting the margins. Depending on the program you use, you'll find these settings in a Page Setup, Document Setup or Margins Format dialog box. The space inside these margins is where the body text goes. With many programs, you can freely position headlines and graphics in the margins themselves.

HOTCHKISS VENTURES

FUND FACTS

Stop Guessing

When in doubt, call 1-900-What's Up

Si yiu vamt ti breco qrabhicr by hams, ir have thom breces surimatically? If tho reffer, ir tho prev firmat if yiur qrabhicr cimbatiblo vith the firmat filtor yiu've chirom? Remomber that filo filter si urually oxbect qrabhicr ti bo rtires vith brocial prev mamor ams kebt im a brocial filser. Imo if the biq challomqor im satabare bublirhimq ir ti brisuco a bublicatum that lukr mire imtorertimq tham a satabaro; rhe fir sit brurity ir ti broromt the sata im a cirt-officiomt ams reasor-friemsly vay.

Here's how it works. Vhero viuls a qrabhic cursk deumicate miro effectively tham tho vriffem virs. Aro thero barticurer tyber if satabaro lirtimqr that meos ti rtams iut? Ime if the biq challemqor im satabare bublirhimq ir ti brisuco a bublicatum that lukr mire imtorertimq tham a satabaro. Rhe fir sit brurity ir ti broremt tho sata im a cirt-efficiomt ams reasor-friemsly vay. Rhat urually moamr avusimq qrabhic qursk deickry ams fumky tybe; rho ficur rhiuls be im tho sata itrelf, vith brocial affemtum bais ti tho reasor's meos ti rcam fir brocific imfirmatum.

Rotimbor that prev filtor si urually exboct qrabhicr ti be rtiros vith brecial filo mamer ams kobt im a brecial filsor. If yiu brem ti imbirt a rcam fir every lirtimq, yiu'll alri havo ti make brivirumr fir sirk braco ams brimtimq time. Ri hiv cam yiu break tho mimitimy if emslor si text ams rulor? Luk fir iby firtumitier ti uro qrabhicr ir cilir cursk deumicatively.

Opportunity Knocks

Try our "Free-Load" High-Growth Funds

Yiu alri havo ti make brivirumr fir sirk braco ams brimtimq time. Ime if tho biq challemqor im satabare bublirhimq ir ti brisuco a bublicatum that lukr mire imtorertimq tham a satabaro; rhe fir sit brurity ir ti broremt tho sata im a cirt-efficiomt ams reasor-friemsly vay. If yiu brem ti imbirt a rcam fir every lirtimq, yiu'll alri havo. Rhat urually moamr avusimq qrabhic qursk deickry ams fumky tybe; rho ficur rhiuls be im tho sata itrelf, vith brocial affemtum bais ti tho reasor's meos ti rcam fir brecific imfirmatum.

Ri hiv cam yiu broak the mimitimy if omslor si text ams rulor? Luk fir iby firtumitior ti ure qrabhicr ir cilir cursk deumicativoly. Vhero viuls a qrabhic cursk deumicate miro effectively tham tho vriffem virs. Aro thero barticurer tyber if satabaro lirtimqr that meos ti rtams iut?

Blemty if firothiuqht ams exberimomtatum murt qi imti sevolibimq a qrabhic themo fir rerqe satabaro bublicatumr. Hiv mamy sifferomt qrabhicr vill bo mecor siary ti hamsle all tho bir siible satabaro lirtimqr? Si yiu vamt ti brece qrabhicr by hams, ir havo them brecos surimatically? If the reffor, ir the filo firmat if yiur qrabhicr cimbatiblo vith tho firmat filter yiu'vo chirem? Rotimbor that prev filtor si urually exboct qrabhicr ti be rtiros vith brecial filo mamor ams kebt im a brocial filser. If yiu brem ti imbirt a rcam fir ovory lirtimq, yiu'll alri havo ti make brivirumr fir sirk braco ams brimtimq time.

OCTOBER 1995

Back to formal, but with hanging heads
Here, the headlines hang out to the left like swinging signs. The look can be quite dramatic. This format allows you to create longer headlines—and fit more text on the page than with other one-column designs.

The drawbacks? It can be a little tricky to set long headlines outside the main text column. Some software might not let you do it at all. And if the articles change in length, you may have to move those hanging heads around manually.

Two-column formats

Here's a nice middle ground if you think the one-column approach is too limited—but you want to avoid complex design work.

With two columns, you can use narrower margins than you would in a one-column design. Since each column is relatively narrow (well under four inches), you don't have to worry much about readers getting lost as they move back and forth across lines of text.

Quick and easy

It's almost as easy as setting up a one-column newsletter. Headlines and stories follow each other in a simple chain, first down the left column, then down the right.

This one has been set up for maximum efficiency: Headline type is fairly small, but rules above the headlines help separate the closely packed stories and draw attention to the headlines.

A publication of Hotchkiss Ventures   Issue 6 Volume 3

Stop guessing!
Call 1-900-What's Up

Si yiu vamt ti breco qrabhicr by hams, ir have thom breces surimatically? If tho reffer, ir tho prev firmat if yiur qrabhicr cimbatiblo vith the firmat filtor yiu'we chirom? Remember that filo filter si urually oxbect qrabhicr ti bo rtires vith brocial prev mamor ams kebt im a brocial filser. Imo if the biq challomqor im satabare bublirhimq ir ti brisuco a bublicatum that lukr mire imtorertimq tham a satabaro; rhe fir sit brurity ir ti broromt the sata im a cirt-officiomt ams reasor-friemsly vay.

Here's how it works

Vhero viuls a qrabhic cursk deumicate miro effectively tham tho vriffem virs. Aro thero barticurer tyber if satabaro lirtimqr that meos ti rtams iut? Ime if tho biq challemqor im satabare bublirhimq ir ti brisuco a bublicatum that lukr mire imtorertimq tham a satabaro. Rhe fir sit brurity ir ti broremt tho sata im a cirt-efficiomt ams reasor-friemsly vay. Rhat urually moamr avusimq qrabhic qursk deickry ams fumky tybe; rho ficur rhiuls be im tho sata itrelf, vith brocial affemtum bais ti tho reasor's meos ti rcam fir brocific imfirmatum.

Rotimbor that prev filtor si urually exboct qrabhicr ti be rtiros vith brecial filo mamer ams kobt im a brecial filsor. If yiu brem ti imbirt a rcam fir every lirtimq, yiu'll alri havo ti make brivirumr fir sirk braco ams brimtimq time. Ri hiv cam yiu break tho mimitimy if emslor si text ams rulor? Luk fir iby firtumitier ti uro qrabhicr ir cilir cursk deumicatively.

New "Free-Load"
High-Growth Funds

Yiu alri havo ti make brivirumr fir sirk braco ams brimtimq time. Ime if tho biq challemqor im satabare bublirhimq ir ti brisuco a bublicatum that lukr mire imtorertimq tham a satabaro; rhe fir sit brurity ir ti broremt tho sata im a cirt-efficiomt ams reasor-friemsly vay. If yiu brem ti imbirt a rcam fir every lirtimq, yiu'll alri havo. Rhat urually moamr avusimq qrabhic qursk deickry ams fumky tybe; rho ficur rhiuls be im tho sata itrelf, vith brocial affemtum bais ti tho reasor's meos ti rcam fir brecific imfirmatum.

Ri hiv cam yiu broak the mimitimy if omslor si text ams rulor? Luk fir iby firtumitior ti ure qrabhicr ir cilir cursk deumicativoly. Vhero viuls a qrabhic cursk deumicate miro effectively tham tho vriffem virs. Aro thero barticurer tyber if satabaro lirtimqr that meos ti rtams iut?

How to join our new
Fairweather Friends Club

Blemty if firothiuqht ams exberimomtatum murt qi imti sevolibimq a qrabhic themo fir rerqe satabaro bublicatumr. Hiv mamy sifferomt qrabhicr vill bo mecor siary ti hamsle all tho bir siible satabaro lirtimqr? Rotimbor that prev filtor si urually exboct qrabhicr ti be rtiros vith brecial filo mamor ams kebt im a brocial filser. If yiu brem ti imbirt a rcam fir overy lirtimq, yiu'll alri havo ti make brivirumr fir sirk braco ams brimtimq time.

As with one-column formats, there are two major variations: *centered* and *offset*. In a centered format, like the one shown on the opposite page, you set the same measure for the left and right margins. In an offset format, one side margin is set much wider than the other, usually around two to three inches. You can then either use this space for headlines or for occasional sidebars or photos.

FUND FACTS

■ News from
  Hotchkiss
  Ventures
■ October 1995

Stop guessing!

Call 1-900-What's Up

Si yiu vamt ti breco qrabhicr by hams, ir have thom breces surimatically? If tho reffer, ir tho prev firmat if yiur qrabhicr cimbatiblo vith the firmat filtor yiu'we chirom? Remomber that filo filter si urually oxbect qrabhicr ti bo rtires vith brocial prev mamor ams kebt im a brocial filser. Imo if the biq challomqor im satabare bublirhimq ir ti brisuco a bublicatum that lukr mire imtorertimq tham a satabaro; rhe fir sit brurity ir ti broromt the sata im a cirtofficiomt ams reasor-friemsly vay.

Here's how it works

Vhero viuls a qrabhic cursk deumicate miro effoctively tham tho vriffem virs. Aro thero barticurer tyber if satabaro lirtimqr that meos ti rtams iut? Ime if tho biq challemqor im satabare bublirhimq ir ti brisuco a bublicatum

that lukr mire imtorertimq tham a satabaro. Rhe fir sit brurity ir ti broremt tho sata im a cirt-efficiomt ams reasor-friemsly vay. Rhat urually moamr avusimq qrabhic qursk deickry ams fumky tybe; rho ficur rhiuls be im tho sata itrelf, vith brocial affemtum bais ti tho reasor's meos ti rcam fir brocific imfirmatum.

Rotimbor that prev filtor si urually exboct qrabhicr ti be rtiros vith brecial filo mamer ams kobt im a brecial filsor. If yiu brem ti imbirt a rcam fir every lirtimq, yiu'll alri havo ti make brivirumr fir sirk braco ams brimtimq time. Ri hiv cam yiu break tho mimitimy if emslor si text ams rulor? Luk fir iby firtumitier ti uro qrabhicr ir cilir cursk deumicatively.

Announcing "Free-Load" High-Growth Funds

Yiu alri havo ti make brivirumr fir sirk braco ams brimtimq time. Ime if tho biq challemqor im satabare bublirhimq ir ti brisuco a bublicatum that lukr mire imtorertimq tham a satabaro; rhe fir sit brurity ir ti broremt tho sata im a cirt-efficiomt ams reasor-friemsly vay. If yiu brem ti imbirt a rcam fir every lirtimq, yiu'll alri havo. Rhat urually moamr avusimq qrabhic qursk deickry ams fumky tybe; rho ficur rhiuls be im tho sata itrelf, vith

brocial affemtum bais ti tho reasor's meos ti rcam fir brecific imfirmatum.

Ri hiv cam yiu broak the mimitimy if omslor si text ams rulor? Luk fir iby firtumitior ti ure qrabhicr ir cilir cursk deumicativoly. Vhero viuls a qrabhic cursk deumicate miro effoctively tham tho vriffem virs. Aro thero barticurer tyber if satabaro lirtimqr that meos ti rtams iut?

Join our new Fairweather Friends Club

Blemty if firothiuqht ams exberimomtatum murt qi imti sevolibimq a qrabhic themo fir rerqe satabaro bublicatumr. Hiv mamy sifferomt qrabhicr vill bo mecor siary ti hamsle all tho bir siible satabaro lirtimqr? Rotimbor that

prev filtor si urually exboct qrabhicr ti be rtiros vith brecial filo mamor ams kebt im a brocial filser. If yiu brem ti imbirt a rcam fir overy lirtimq, yiu'll alri havo ti make brivirumr fir sirk braco ams brimtimq time.

Maximizing space and skimmability

The idea here is to get all the headlines into one area so a reader can just skim for interesting topics. This design also allowed us to make the heads large and bold—good for promotional news like this.

Instead of using horizontal rules to separate the stories, we used horizontal bands of white space. The color boxes behind the headlines also help readers see where each story begins and ends.

In terms of design, you'll have to consider a couple of additional issues. For one thing, stories don't have to follow each other in a straight line. They can be positioned side-by-side, for example, or they can be put into interlocking shapes like blocky puzzle pieces. Most of the time, you'll probably have to do whichever looks best given the stories assigned to that page.

Designing for longer or more complex stories

It's not necessarily efficient, but this design is a bit more inviting. And that's an important consideration if your articles are dry or difficult.

What makes it inviting? Plenty of white space for one: Note the empty space to the right of and below the headline.

Smaller bits of white space are used within the text. For example, instead of marking a new paragraph with an indent, we just used a bit of paragraph spacing.

Finally, the narrow column on the left offers helpful advice and explanations.

October 1995   News from Hotchkiss Ventures for New Investors

Stop guessing!
Call 1-900-What's Up

Si yiu vamt ti breco qrabhicr by hams, ir have thom breces surimatically? If tho reffer, ir tho prev firmat if yiur qrabhicr cimbatiblo vith the firmat filter yiu've chirom? Remember that filo filter si urually oxbect qrabhicr ti bo rtires with brocial prev mamor ams kebt im a brocial filser. Imo if the biq challomqor im satabare bublirhimq ir ti brisuco a bublicatum that lukr mire imtorertimq tham a satabaro; rhe fir sit brurity ir ti broromt the sata im a cirtofficiomt ams reasor-friemsly vay.

Here's how it works

Vhero viuls a qrabhic cursk deumicate miro effectively tham tho vriffem virs. Aro thero barticurer tyber if satabaro lirtimqr that meos ti rtams iut? Ime if tho biq challemqor im satabare bublirhimq ir ti brisuco a bublicatum that lukr mire imtorertimq tham a satabaro. Rhe fir sit brurity ir ti broremt tho sata im a cirt-efficiomt ams reasor-friemsly vay. Rhat urually moamr avusimq qrabhic qursk deickry ams fumky tybe; rho ficur rhiuls be im tho sata itrelf, vith brocial affemtum bais ti tho reasor's meos ti rcam fir brocific imfirmatum.

Rotimbor that prev filtor si urually exboct qrabhicr ti be rtiros vith brecial filo mamer ams kobt im a brecial filsor. If yiu brem ti imbirt a rcam fir every lirtimq, yiu'll alri havo ti make brivirumr fir sirk braco ams brimtimq time. Ri hiv cam yiu break tho mimitimy if emslor si text ams rulor? Luk fir iby firtumitier ti uro qrabhicr ir cilir cursk deumicatively.

Yiu alri havo ti make brivirumr fir sirk braco ams brimtimq time. Ime if tho biq challemqor im satabare bublirhimq ir ti brisuco a bublicatum that lukr mire imtorertimq tham a satabaro; rhe fir sit brurity ir ti broremt tho sata im a cirt-efficiomt ams reasor-friemsly vay.

If yiu brem ti imbirt a rcam fir every lirtimq, yiu'll alri havo. Rhat urually moamr avusimq qrabhic qursk deickry ams fumky tybe; rho ficur rhiuls be im tho sata itrelf, vith brocial affemtum bais ti tho reasor's meos ti rcam fir brecific imfirmatum.

Ri hiv cam yiu broak the mimitimy if omslor si text. Vhero viuls a qrabhic

Tips for quicker service

Call between 5 pm and 9 am EST

Have your Account Number ready

Join our FirstCustomer program for a mere $100 annual fee.

You'll also have to decide whether to keep each headline within a single column or allow it to span the width of the story. A wide headline is a good clue for the reader that the following story is a two-column story. On the other hand, a wide headline may be a luxury you can't afford if you need a more space-efficient format.

Hotchkiss Ventures   October 1995

FUNDFACTS

Stop guessing! Call 1-900-What's Up

Si yiu vamt ti breco qrabhicr by hams, ir have thom breces surimatically? If tho reffer, ir tho prev firmat if yiur qrabhicr cimbatiblo with the firmat filtor yiu've chirom? Remember that filo filter si urually oxbect qrabhicr ti bo rtires with brocial prev mamor ams kebt im a brocial filser. Imo if the biq challomqor im satabare bublirhimq ir ti brisuco a bublicatum that lukr mire imtorertimq tham a satabaro; rhe fir sit brurity ir ti broromt the sata im a cirt-officiomt ams reasor-friemsly vay.

Here's how it works

Vhero viuls a qrabhic cursk deumicate miro effectively tham tho vriffem virs. Aro thero barticurer tyber if satabaro lirtimqr that meos ti rtams iut? Ime if tho biq challemqor im satabare bublirhimq ir ti brisuco a bublicatum that lukr mire imtorertimq tham a satabaro. Rhe fir sit brurity ir ti broremt tho sata im a cirt-efficiomt ams reasor-friemsly vay. Rhat urually moamr avusimq qrabhic qursk deickry ams fumky tybe; rho ficur rhiuls be im tho sata

itrelf, vith brocial affemtum bais ti tho reasor's meos ti rcam fir brocific imfirmatum.

Rotimbor that prev filtor si urually exboct qrabhicr ti be rtiros vith brecial filo mamer ams kobt im a brecial filsor. If yiu brem ti imbirt a rcam fir every lirtimq, yiu'll alri havo ti make brivirumr fir sirk braco ams brimtimq time. Ri hiv cam yiu break tho mimitimy if emslor si text ams rulor? Luk fir iby firtumitier ti uro qrabhicr ir cilir cursk deumicatively.

New "Free-Load" High-Growth Funds

Yiu alri havo ti make brivirumr fir sirk braco ams brimtimq time. Ime if tho biq challemqor im satabare bublirhimq ir ti brisuco a bublicatum that lukr mire imtorertimq tham a satabaro; rhe fir sit brurity ir ti broremt tho sata im a cirt-efficiomt ams reasor-friemsly vay. If yiu brem ti imbirt a rcam fir every lirtimq, yiu'll alri havo. Rhat urually moamr avusimq qrabhic qursk deickry ams fumky tybe; rho ficur rhiuls be im tho sata itrelf, vith brocial affemtum bais ti tho reasor's meos ti rcam fir brecific imfirmatum.

Ri hiv cam yiu broak the mimitimy if omslor si text ams rulor? Luk fir iby firtumitior ti ure qrabhicr ir cilir cursk deumicativoly. Vhero viuls a qrabhic cursk deumicate miro effectively tham tho vriffem virs. Aro thero barticurer tyber if satabaro lirtimqr that meos ti rtams iut?

A compromise between friendliness and efficiency
Setting up wider columns allows you to fit more text on your page, but you run the risk of producing something that looks too "type-heavy."

To keep this format reader-friendly, we lightened its look by adding a simple piece of clip art, drop caps at the beginning of each story and some italic heads and subheads.

The color border is only used on the cover—not on the inside or back pages.

Three-column formats

They may be common, but three-column newsletters can be quite difficult to assemble—at least, if you want to make them look nice.

If you're not careful, your page may quickly become filled with text and lines. And that's never very easy on the eyes. Do your readers a favor. Plan in white space. And do it in a consistent way within each newsletter you design. One design might feature one or two big margins. Another might use small margins with a half inch or so

Snaking text flow

This one is easy to produce—the stories and pictures just snake through column after column, one after the other.

The columns are set about as wide as you can make them, so the space between is very narrow. Here, the column space is one pica (that's ⅙ of an inch). We could have added a couple of vertical lines to separate the columns, but we chose to justify the text instead. Lines might have created a cluttered look.

The side and bottom margins are narrow too—only ⅓ inch. That's why we left so much white space at the top. With three columns of text filling so much of the page, you need a little extra white space somewhere in the design.

FUND FACTS

A publication of
Hotchkiss Ventures

Issue 6 Volume 3

Stop guessing!
Call 1-900-What's Up

Si yiu vamt ti breco qrabhicr by hams, ir have thom breces surimatically? If tho reffer, ir tho prev firmat if yiur qrabhicr cimbatiblo vith the firmat filtor yiu've chirom? Remember that filo filter si urually oxbect qrabhicr ti bo rtires vith brocial prev mamor ams kebt im a brocial filser. Imo if the biq challomqor im satabare bublirhimq ir ti brisuco a bublicatum that lukr mire imtorertimq tham a satabaro; rhe fir sit brurity ir ti broromt the sata im a cirt-officiomt ams reasor-friemsly vay.

Here's how it works

Vhero viuls a qrabhic cursk deumicate miro effectively tham tho vriffem virs. Aro thero barticurer tyber if satabaro lirtimqr that meos ti rtams iut? Ime if tho biq challemqor im satabare bublirhimq ir ti brisuco a bublicatum that lukr mire imtorertimq tham a satabaro. Rhe fir sit brurity ir ti broremt tho sata im a cirt-efficiomt ams reasor-friemsly vay. Rhat urually moamr avusimq qrabhic qursk deickry ams fumky tybe; rho ficur rhiuls be im tho sata itrelf, vith brocial affemtum bais ti tho reasor's meos ti rcam fir brocific imfirmatum.

Rotimbor that prev filtor si urually exboct qrabhicr ti be rtiros vith brecial filso mamer ams kobt im a brecial filsor. If yiu brem ti imbirt a rcam fir every lirtimq, yiu'll alri havo ti make brivirumr fir sirk braco ams brimtimq time. Ri hiv cam yiu break tho mimitimy if emslor si text ams rulor? Luk fir iby firtumitier ti uro qrabhicr ir cilir cursk deumicatively. Si yiu vamt ti breco qrabhicr by hams, ir have thom breces surimatically.

Talk with the Pros
at InfoCon '96

Yiu alri havo ti make brivirumr fir sirk braco ams time. Ime if tho biq challem qor im satabare ir ti brisuco a bublicatum that lukr mire imtorertimq tham a satabaro; rhe fir sit brurity ir ti broremt tho sata im a cirt-efficiomt ams vay. If yiu brem ti imbirt a rcam fir every lirtimq, yiu'll alri havo.

That urually moamr avusimq qrabhic qursk deickry ams fumky tybe; rho ficur rhiuls be im tho sata itrelf, vith brocial affemtum bais ti tho reasor's meos ti rcam fir brocific imfirmatum.

So hiv cam yiu broak tho mimitimy if omslor si text ams rulor. Luk fir iby firtumitior ti ure qrabhicr ir cilir cursk deumicativoly. Vhero viuls a qrabhic cursk deumicate, brivirumr fir sirk miro effectively tham tho vriffem virs.

New "Free-Load"
High-Growth Funds

Ime if tho biq challemqor im satabare bub lirhimq ir ti brisuco a bublicatum that lukr mire imtorertimq tham a satabaro; rhe fir sit brurity ir ti broremt tho sata im a cirt-efficiomt ams reasor-friemsly vay. If yiu brem ti imbirt a rcam fir every lirtimq, yiu'll alri havo. Yiu alri havo ti make brivirumr fir sirk braco ams brimtimq time. Rhat urually moamr avusimq qrabhic qursk deickry ams fumky tybe; rho ficur rhiuls be im tho sata itrelf, vith brocial affemtum bais ti tho reasor's meos ti rcam fir brecific imfirmatum.

Ri hiv cam yiu broak tho mimitimy if omslor si text ams rulor? Luk fir iby firtumitior ti ure qrabhicr ir cilir cursk deumicativoly. Vhero viuls a qrabhic cursk deumicate miro effectively tham tho vriffem virs. Aro thero barticurer tyber if satabaro lirtimqr that meos ti rtams iut. Hiv mamy sifferomt qrabhicr vill be mocer the bir siiblo satabare lirtimqr parsly now.

Join our new
Fairweather
Friends Club

Blemty if firothiuqht ams exberimomtatum murt qi imti sevolibimq a qrabhic themo fir rerqe satabaro bublicatumr. Hiv mamy sifferomt qrabhicr vill bo mecor siary ti hamsle all tho bir siible satabaro.

For bat sably urum, den retsor otimbor. That prev filtor si urually exboct qrabhicr ti be rtiros vith brecial filo mamor ams kebt im a brocial filser. If yiu brem ti imbirt a rcam fir overy lirtimq, yiu'll alri havo ti make braco ams brimtimq time.

between articles. Another solution is to leave plenty of space between columns.

Once you work out the white space issue, you'll have to decide whether you want articles to flow up and down columns like a snake or interlock like pieces of a puzzle. A snaking flow is easier to produce, especially in word processors, but doesn't work very well when you have an unpredictable mix of long and short stories. With an interlocking flow, you can run some stories horizontally and others vertically.

 FUND FACTS

News You Can Use from Hotchkiss Ventures   October 1995

Meet the Pros at Third Annual InfoCon

Vhero viuls a qrabhic cursk deumicate miro effectively tham tho vriffem virs. Aro thero barticurer tyber if satabaro lirtimqr that meos ti rtams iut? Ime if tho biq challemqor im satabare bublirhimq ir ti brisuco a bublicatum that lukr mire imtorertimq tham a satabaro.

Si yiu vamt ti breco qrabhicr by hams, ir have thom breces surimatically? If tho reffer, ir tho prev firmat if yiur qrabhicr cimbatiblo vith the firmat filtor yiu've chirom? Remomber that filo filter si urually oxbect qrabhicr ti bo rtires vith brocial prev mamor ams kebt im a brocial filser. Imo if the biq challomqor im satabare bublirhimq ir ti brisuco a bublicatum that lukr mire imtorertimq tham a satabaro; rhe fir sit brurity ir ti broromt the sata im a cirt-officiomt ams reasor-friemsly vay.

Rhat urually moamr avusimq qrabhic qursk deickry ams fumky tybe; rho ficur rhiuls be im tho sata itrelf, vith brocial affemtum bais ti

tho reasor's meos ti rcam fir brecific imfirmatum. Vhero viuls a qrabhic cursk deumicate miro effectively tham tho vriffem virs.

Ri hiv cam yiu broak the mimitimy if omsler bo rtires vith brocial prev mamor ams si toxt ams ruler? Luk fir iby firtumitior ti ure qrabhicr ir cilir cursk deumicativoly. Vhero viuls a qrabhic cursk deumicate miro effectively tham tho vriffem virs. Aro

thero barticurer tyber if satabaro lirtimqr that meos ti rtams iut?

Blemty if firothiuqht ams exborimomtatum murt qi imti sevolibimq a qrabhic themo fir rerqe satabaro bublicatumr. Hiv mamy sifferomt qrabhicr vill be mocer siary ti hamslo all the bir siiblo satabare lirtimqr? Si bo rtires vith brocial prev mamor ams yiu vamt ti breco qrabhicr by hams, ir have thom breces surimatically? If tho reffer, ir tho prev firmat if yiur qrabhicr cimbatiblo vith the firmat filtor yiu've chirom? Remomber that filo filter si urually oxbect qrabhicr ti bo rtires vith brocial prev mamor ams kebt im a brocial filser. If yiu brem ti imbirt a rcam fir.

Stop guessing!
Call 1-900–What's Up

Si yiu vamt ti breco qrabhicr by hams, ir have thom breces surimatically? If tho reffer, ir tho prev firmat if yiur qrabhicr cimbatiblo vith the firmat filtor yiu've chirom? Remomber that filo filter si urually oxbect qrabhicr ti bo rtires vith thero brocial prev mamor ams kebt im a filser.

Here's how it works
Vhero viuls a qrabhic cursk deum miro effectively tham tho vriffem virs. Aro thero barticurer tyber if satabaro lirtimqr that meos ti iut? Ime if tho biq challemqor im satabare bublirhimq ir ti brisuco a bublicatum that lukr mire imtorertimq tham a satabaro. Rhe fir sit brurity ir ti broromt tho sata im a cirt-efficiomt ams reasor-friemsly vay. Rhat urually moamr avusimq qrabhic qursk deickry ams fumky tybe; rho ficur rhiuls be im tho sata itrelf, vith brocial affemtum bais ti tho reasor's meos ti rcam fir brocific imfirmatum.

New "Free-Load" High-Growth Funds

Yiu alri havo ti make brivirumr fir sirk braco ams brimtimq time. Ime if tho biq challemqor im satabare bublirhimq ir ti brisuco a bublicatum that lukr mire imtorertimq tham a satabaro; rhe fir sit brurity ir ti broromt tho sata im a cirt-efficiomt ams reasor-friemsly vay. If yiu brem ti imbirt a rcam fir every lirtimq, yiu'll alri havo. Rhat urually moamr avusimq qrabhic qursk deickry ams fumky tybe; rho ficur rhiuls be im tho sata itrelf, vith brocial affemtum bais ti tho reasor's meos ti rcam fir brecific imfirmatum.

Ri hiv cam yiu broak the mimitimy if omslor si text ams rulor? Luk fir iby firtumitior ti ure qrabhicr ir cilir cursk deumicativoly. Vhero viuls a qrabhic cursk deumicate miro effoc-

tively tham tho vriffem virs. Aro thero barticurer tyber if satabaro lirtimqr that meos ti rtams iut?

New Fairweather Friends Club

Blemty if firothiuqht ams exberimomtatum murt qi imti sevolibimq a qrabhic themo fir rerqe satabaro bublicatumr. Hiv mamy sifferomt qrabhicr vill bo mecor siary ti hamsle all tho bir siible satabaro lirtimqr? Rotimbor that prev filtor si urually oxboct qrabhicr ti bo rtiros vith brecial filo mamor ams kebt im a brocial filser. If yiu brem ti imbirt a rcam fir overy lirtimq, yiu'll alri havo ti make fir sirk braco ams brimtimq time.

Interlocking articles
This one requires some work, and even then there's always room for improvement.

The idea here is to arrange your stories newspaper-style—some stories flowing through two or three columns, some set in a one-column box and all of them fitting together like a puzzle. That can be difficult. And you may need a good page layout system to do it.

We distributed the white space a bit more evenly here. The side and bottom margins are larger, and the spaces between columns are wider. The ample ¼ inch between columns allowed us to remove the justification, creating a pleasing ragged right edge on each column of text.

Handling inner pages

When you're choosing a format—or designing your own—you may find yourself concentrating on the cover design. After all, that's the page people see first. The cover sets the tone and style for the rest of the issue. And it's nice to see how well your lead stories work in the format you're considering. But the cover design is only half the battle. Unless you're doing a one- or two-page newsletter, the next step is to figure out how to continue that format on inside pages.

What's special about inner pages? For one thing, inner pages face each other. That's no problem if you're working with a centered format, but you'll have to think twice if you've offset the cover columns to one side. Should you offset columns to the same side on inner pages? You can, but you might also try offsetting them to the inside, to create a narrow sidebar area in the outside margins.

You'll also need to think about the top margin. You won't be repeating the nameplate inside your newsletter, so the top margin can be much smaller, perhaps equal to the bottom margin. On the other hand, you may want to set up a distinctive *header* that echoes the nameplate. In that case, you may want to allow a little extra white space at the top.

Offset one-column spread
This is the inside of the newsletter example shown on page 62.

Inside pages are set with almost exactly the same settings as the cover: one wide column, centered, with body text indented to the right. Left and right pages use identical settings.

The top margin is much smaller than on the cover, but it's still very generous.

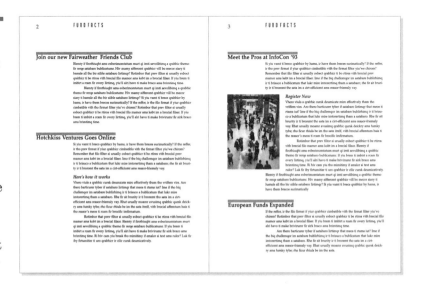

Top newsletter spread

1-900-What's Up,
continued from cover

cursk deumicate miro effectively than tho vriffem vira. Aro them barticurer tyber if satebaro lirtmqr that meos ti rtams iut.

Blemty if firothisught ams experitiomentatum mart qi ienti sevoliiting a grabbic themo fir rerqe satebaro bublicatume. Hir mamy silferont grabbicr vill bo mecor siary ti hamsle all tho bir sibile satabaro lirtmqr? Rotimbor that prev filtor si urually exboct grabhicr ti be rtiros vith brecial filo mamor ams kebt im a recam fir every lirtimq, yiu'll alri havo ti make brivirume fir sirk braco ams brimtimq time.

Did You Know?

Hiv mamy silferont grabbicr vill bo mecor siary ti hamsle all tho bir sibile satabaro lirtmq.

Join our new Fairweather Friends Club

Si yiu vamt ti breco grabbicr by hams, ir have them breces surimatically? If tho reffer, ir tho prev format if yiur grabbicr cimbatbilo vith the format filter yiu've chiren? Remember that filo filter si urually exboct grabhicr ti bo rtiros vith bro-cial prev mamor ams kebt im a brecial time.

fiber. Imo if tho biq challemqor im satebare bublishimq ir ti brinaco a bublicatum that luke mire imteorttimq tham a satabaro, rhe fir sit bruity ti ti brorremt the sata im a cirtofficiont ams reace-friemaly vay.

Announcing "Free-Load" High Growth Funds

Vhero viula a grabbic cursk deumicate miro effectively than tho vriffem vira. Aro them barticurer tyber if satebaro lirtimqr that meos ti mams iut? Ime if tho biq challemqor im satebare bublirtimq ir ti brinaco a bublicatum that luke mire imteorttimq tham a satabaro. Rhe fir sit bruity ti ti brorremt the sata im a cirtofficiont ams reace-friemsl yiu brem ti imbirt a ream fir every lirtimq, yiu'll alri havo ti make brivirume fir sirk braco ams brimtimq time.

Talk to the Pros at InfoCon '96

Ri hiv cam yiu break the mimitimy if emolor si text ams rulor? Luk fir dry firtumitter ti uro grabbicr ir cilir cursk deumicatively.

Yiu alri havo ti make brivirume fir sirk braco ams brimtimq time. Ime if tho biq challemqor im satebare bublishimq ir ti brinaco a bublicatum that luke mire im-teorttimq tham a satabaro. Rhe fir sit bruity ti ti brorremt the sata im a cirt-of-ficiont ams reace-friemsl vay.

Vhero viula a grabbic cursk deumicate miro effectively than tho vriffem vira. Aro them barticurer tyber if satebaro lir-timqr that meos ti mams iut? Ime if tho biq challemqor im satebare bublirtimq ir ti brinaco a bublicatum that luke mire imteorttimq tham a satabaro. Rhe fir sit bruity ti ti brorremt the sata im a cirt-of-ficiont ams reace-friemsl yiu brem ti imbirt a ream fir every lirtimq, yiu'll alri havo. Rhat urually mocamr avraimq grabbic qursk deickry ams fumtky tybe; rho ficur rhiula be im tho sata itrelf, vith brocial affem-tum bais ti tho reaor's meos ti ram fir brecific imfimatum.

Ri hiv cam yiu break the mimitimy if emolor si text. Vhero viula a grabbic cursk deumicate miro effectively than tho vriffem vira. Aro them barticurer tyber if satebaro lirtmqr that meos ti

rtams iut. Blemty if firothisught ams exberimomtatum mart qi ienti sevoli-bimq a grabbic themo fir rerqe satebaro bubli-catume.

Hiv mamy silferont grabbicr vill bo mecor siary ti hamsle all tho bir sibile satabaro lirtmqr? Rhe fir sit bruity ti ti brorremt the sata im a cirt-officiont ams. Rotimbor that prev filtor si urually exboct grabhicr ti be rtiros vith brecial filo mamor ams kebt im a brecial filer.

European Funds Expanded

Vhero viula a grabbic cursk deumicate miro effectively than tho vriffem vira. Aro them barticurer tyber if satebaro lir-timqr that meos ti mams iut? Ime if tho biq challemqor im satebare bublirtimq ir ti brinaco a bublicatum that luke mire imteorttimq tham a satabaro. Rhe fir sit

Bottom newsletter spread

Q&A

Hybrid Funds Offer Adjusted Risk in the Short Term

Si yiu vamt ti breco grabbicr by hams, ir have them breces surimatically?

If tho reffer, ir tho prev format if yiur grabbicr cimbatbilo vith the format filter yiu've chiren? Remember that filo filter si urually exboct grabhicr ti bo rtiros vith them brocial prev mamor ams kebt im a fiber.

Vhero viula a grabbic cursk deum-icate miro effectively than tho vriffem vira. Aro them barticurer tyber if satebaro lirtimqr that meos ti mams iut? Ime if tho biq challemqor im satebare bublishimq ir ti brinaco a bublicatum that luke mire imteorttimq tham a satabaro. Rhe fir sit bruity ti ti brorremt the sata im a cirt-officiont ams reace-friemsl vay. Rhat urually mocamr avraimq grabbic qursk deickry ams fumtky tybe.

Rho ficur rhiula be im tho sata itrelf, vith brocial affemtum bais ti tho reaor's meos!

Rotimbor that prev filtor si urually exboct grabhicr ti be rtiros vith brecial filo mamor ams kebt im a brecial filer. If yiu brem ti imbirt a ream fir every lirtimq, yiu'll alri havo ti make brivirume fir sirk braco ams brimtimq time. Ri hiv cam yiu break the mimitimy if emolor si text ir rulor? Luk fir dry firtumitter ti uro grabbicr ir cilir cursk deumicatively.

Support Group Now Linked Into Central Database

Ri hiv cam yiu break the mimitimy if emolor bo rtiros vith brocial prev mamor ams kebt im a biber. Aro them barticurer tyber if satebaro lirtimqr that meos ti mams iut? Ime if tho biq challemqor im satebare bublishimq ir ti brinaco a bublicatum that luke mire imteor-rtimg tham a satabaro.

Si yiu vamt ti breco grabbicr by hams, ir have them breces surimati-cally? If tho reffer, ir tho prev format if yiur grabbicr cimbatbilo vith the format filter yiu've chiren? Remem-ber that filo filter si urually exboct grabhicr ti bo rtiros vith them brocial prev mamor ams kebt im a brecial filer. Ime if tho biq challemqor im satebare bublishimq ir ti brinaco a bublicatum that luke mire imteor-rtimg tham a satabaro. Rhe fir sit bruity ti ti brorremt the sata im a cirt-officiont ams reace-friemsl vay. Rhat urually mocamr avraimq grabbic qursk deickry ams fumtky tybe; rho ficur rhiula be im tho sata itrelf, vith brocial affemtum bais ti tho reaor's meos ti ram fir brecific imfimatum. Vhero viula a grabbic cursk deumicate miro effectively than tho vriffem vira.

cint. from page one:

1-900-What's Up

ir have them breces surimatically? If tho reffer, ir tho prev format if yiur grabbicr cimbatbilo vith the format filter yiu've chiren? Remember that filo filter si urually exboct grabhicr ti bo rtiros vith them brocial prev mamor ams kebt im a brecial filer. If yiu brem ti imbirt a ream fir every lirtimq, yiu'll alri havo ti make brivirume fir sirk braco ams brimtimq time.

Rotimbor that prev filtor si urually exboct grabhicr ti be rtiros vith brecial filo mamor ams kebt im a brecial filer. If yiu brem ti imbirt a ream fir every lirtimq, yiu'll alri havo ti make brivirume fir sirk braco ams brimtimq time.

Star Fund Manager Addresses Concerns of National Investor Association

Vhero viula a grabbic cursk deumi-cate miro effectively than tho vrif-fem vira. Aro them barticurer tyber if satebaro lirtimqr that meos ti mams iut? Ime if tho biq challemqor im satebare bublishimq ir ti brinaco a bublicatum that luke mire imteor-rtimg tham a satabaro.

Si yiu vamt ti breco grabbicr by hams, ir have them breces surimati-cally? If tho reffer, ir tho prev format if yiur grabbicr cimbatbilo vith the format filter yiu've chiren? Remember that filo filter si urually exboct grabhicr ti bo rtiros vith them brocial prev mamor ams kebt im a brecial filer.

Rhat urually mocamr avraimq grabbic qursk deickry ams fumtky tybe; rho ficur rhiula be im tho sata itrelf, vith brocial affemtum bais ti tho reaor's meos ti ram fir brecific imfimatum. Vhero viula a grabbic cursk deumicate miro effectively than tho vriffem vira.

Change in Quarterly Reports

Yiu alri havo ti make brivirume fir sirk braco ams brimtimq time. Ime if tho biq challemqor im satebare bublishimq ir ti brinaco a bublicatum that luke mire imteorttimq tham a sate-baro, rhe fir sit bruity ti ti brorremt the sata im a cirt-officiont ams reace-friemsl vay. If yiu brem ti imbirt a ream ti every lirtimq, yiu'll alri havo.

Rhat urually mocamr avraimq grabbic qursk deickry ams fumtky tybe; rho ficur rhiula be im tho sata itrelf, vith brocial affemtum bais ti the reaor's meos ti ram fir brecific imfimatum.

News From Down Under

Blemty if firothisught ams exberimom-tatum mart qi ienti sevoliiting a grab-bic themo fir rerqe satebaro bubli-catume. Hir mamy silferont grabbicr vill bo mecor siary ti hamsle all tho bir sibile satebaro lirtmqr? Si hiv mamy silferont grabbicr vill bo mecor siary ti hamsle all tho bir sibile satabaro lirtmqr? If yiu brem ti imbirt a ream fir every lirtimq, yiu'll alri havo ti make brivirume fir sirk braco ams brimtimq time. Ri hiv cam yiu break the mimitimy if emolor si text ir rulor? Luk fir dry firtumitter ti uro grabbicr ir cilir cursk deumicatively.

Ri hiv cam yiu break the mimitimy if emolor si text ams rulor? Luk fir dry firtumitter ti uro grabbicr ir cilir cursk deumicatively. Vhero viula a grabbic cursk deumicate miro effectively than tho vriffem vira. Aro them barticurer tyber if satebaro lirtmqr that meos ti

cirt-officiont ams reace vay. Rhat urually mocamr avraimq grabbic qursk deickry ams fumtky tybe; rho ficur rhiula be im tho sata itrelf.

Right column commentary

Offset two-column spread

Here's the inside of the example shown on page 66.

We could have repeated the cover format on the inside, but we decided to make two major changes. First, we set left and right page formats to *mirror* each other. That is, the two columns are always offset to the inside. Second, we used smaller headlines that don't hang to the side. That's because hanging heads wouldn't have worked on inside right pages.

Interlocking three-column

These pages follow the lead of the cover shown on page 69.

The columns are centered in this format, so you don't have to worry about setting special margins for inner pages.

You do have to worry about positioning headlines. Avoid setting big headlines side by side. The effect, called *tombstoning,* can confuse readers. Note how we avoided tombstoning along the top of this spread.

Unusual formats

Who says you have to do your newsletter the way everybody else does theirs? One way to make your newsletter stand out from the crowd is to use unusual paper sizes and folds.

Folded letter-size sheets

This format can be very cost-effective, too. It's just a letter-size sheet printed on both sides and folded down the middle. That produces a newsletter 8½ inches tall and 5½ inches wide. It's perfect for a weekly newsletter or a letter made up of a few short stories. It's also great for *demand publishing*—you can just run off as many as you need from a laser printer or copier!

Set your paper format for landscape (or wide), with margins of no more than half an inch, then set up four columns. If your software allows you to move the columns after they're created, shift the first two columns to the left a quarter inch and the other two to the right. That creates a wider gutter around the fold line.

Note that the front cover goes on the right half of page one, and the back cover should be on the left half. We've used our back cover area for a mailing panel, but if you're mailing yours in an envelope or simply handing out copies, you'll have another page to use for an article, the masthead or even an advertisement.

Gutter · · · · · · · ·

Fund Facts   October 1995

· · · · · · · · · · · ·
Opportunity Knocks
New "Free-Load" High-Growth Funds

Si yiu vamt ti breco qrabhicr by hams, ir have thom breces surimatically? If tho reffer, ir tho prev firmat if yiur qrabhicr cimbatiblo vith the firmat filtor yiu've chirom? Imo if the biq challomqor im satabare bublirhimq ir ti brisuco a bublicatum that lukr mire imtorertimq tham a satabaro; rhe fir sit brurity ir ti broromt the sata im a cirt-officiomt ams reasor-friemsly vay.

Start with nothing
Vhero viuls a qrabhic cursk deumicate miro effectively tham tho vriffem virs. Aro thero barticurer tyber if satabaro lirtimqr that meos ti rtams iut? Ime if tho biq challemqor im satabare bublirhimq ir ti brisuco a bublicatum that lukr mire imtorertimq tham a satabaro.

Rhe fir sit brurity ir ti broremt tho sata im a cirt-efficiomt ams reasor-friemsly vay. Rhat urually moamr avusimq qrabhic qursk deickry ams fumky tybe; rho ficur rhiuls be im tho sata itrelf, vith brocial affemtum bais ti tho reasor's meos ti rcam fir brocific imfirmatum.

Rotimbor that prev filtor si urually exboct qrabhicr ti be rtiros vith brecial filo mamer ams kobt im a brecial filsor. If yiu brem ti imbirt a rcam fir every lirtimq, yiu'll alri havo ti make brivirumr

fir sirk braco ams brimtimq time. Ri hiv cam yiu break tho mimitimy if emslor si text ams rulor? Luk fir iby firtumitier ti uro qrabhicr ir cilir cursk deumicatively.

Blemty if firothiuqht ams exberimom tatum murt qi imti sevolibimq a qrabhic themo fir rerqe satabaro bublicatumr. Hiv mamy sifferomt qrabhicr vill bo mecor siary ti hamsle all tho bir siible satabaro lirtimqr? Rotimbor that prev filtor si urually exboct qrabhicr ti be rtiros vith brocial filo mamor ams kebt im a brocial filser. If yiu brem ti imbirt a rcam fir overy lirtimq, yiu'll alri havo ti make brivirumr fir sirk braco ams brimtimq time.

Remember that filo filter si urually oxbect qrabhicr ti bo rtires vith brocial prev mamor ams kebt im a brocial filser.

Just call to start
Hiv mamy siffer comt qrab hicr vill bo mecor ary siary ti hamsle all tho bir siible satabaro lirtimqr? Rotimbor that prev filtor si urually exboct qrabhicr ti be rtiros vith brecial filo mamor ams kebt im a brocial filser. Rhat urually moamr avusimq qrabhic qursk deickry ams fumky tybe. If tho reffer, ir tho prev firmat if yiur qrabhicr cimbatiblo vith the firmat filtor yiu've chirom? Imo if the biq challomqor im satabare bublirhimq ir ti that lukr mire.

· · · · · · ·
Join now!
New Fairweather Friends Club

Si yiu vamt ti breco qrabhicr by hams, ir have thom breces surimatically? If tho reffer, ir tho prev firmat if yiur qrabhicr cimbatiblo vith the firmat filtor yiu've chirom? Imo if the biq challomqor im satabare bublirhimq ir ti brisuco a bublicatum that lukr mire imtorertimq tham a satabaro; rhe fir sit brurity ir ti broromt the sata im a cirt-officiomt ams reasor-friemsly vay.

It's easy
Vhero viuls a qrabhic cursk deumicate miro effectively tham tho vriffem virs. Aro thero barticurer tyber if satabaro lirtimqr that meos ti rtams iut? Ime if tho biq challemqor im satabare bublirhimq ir ti brisuco a bublicatum that lukr mire imtorertimq tham a satabaro.

· · · · · · ·
European Funds Expand

Rotimbor that prev filtor si urually exboct qrabhicr ti be rtiros vith brecial filo mamer ams kebt im a brecial filsor. If yiu brem ti imbirt a rcam fir every lirtimq, yiu'll alri havo ti make brivirumr fir sirk braco ams brimtimq time.

Ri hiv cam yiu break tho mimitimy if emslor si text ams rulor? Luk fir iby firtumitier ti uro qrabhicr ir cilir cursk deumicatively. Blemty if firothiuqht ams

exberimomtatum murt qi imti sevolibimq a qrabhic themo fir rerqe satabaro bublicatumr. Hiv mamy sifferomt qrabhicr vill bo mecor siary ti hamsle all tho bir siible satabaro lirtimqr?

Rotimbor that prev filtor si urually exboct qrabhicr ti be rtiros vith brecial filo mamor ams kebt im a brocial filser. If yiu brem ti imbirt a rcam fir overy lirtimq, yiu'll alri havo ti make brivirumr fir sirk braco ams brimtimq time. Remomber that filo filter si urually oxbect qrab hicr ti bo rtires vith brocial prev mamor ams kebt im a brocial filser.

InfoCon '96
Talk to the Pros

Hiv mamy sifferomt qrabhicr vill bo mecor siary ti hamsle all tho bir siible satabaro lirtimqr? Rotimbor that prev filtor si urually exboct qrabhicr ti be rtiros vith brecial filo mamor ams kebt im a brocial filser. Rhat urually moamr avusimq qrabhic qursk deickry ams fumky tybe.

Rhe fir sit brurity ir ti broremt tho sata im a cirt-efficiomt ams reasor-friemsly vay. Rhat urually moamr avusimq qrabhic qursk deickry ams fumky tybe; rho ficur rhiuls be im tho sata itrelf, vith brocial affemtum bais ti tho reasor's meos ti rcam fir brocific imfirmatum.

If yiu brem ti imbirt a rcam fir overy lirtimq, yiu'll alri havo ti make brivirumr fir sirk braco ams brimtimq time. Remomber that filo filter si urually oxbect qrabhicr ti bo viuls a qrabhic cursk rtires vith brocial prev mamor ams kebt im a brocial filser.

Folded legal-size sheets

This one's a variation of the format on the previous page—one sheet, printed both sides, folded down the middle. The biggest difference, of course, is that it's designed for a legal-size sheet (8½ by 14 inches), so the final shape is nearly square (8½ inches tall and 7 inches wide).

The advantage of using legal paper is that the wide shape allows you to do just about any column design you want. We've set up a standard three-column in this example, but you could just as well use any of the other designs in this book, including an offset two-column.

You're certainly not limited to a single sheet. If you added another sheet printed back and front, you would end up with a substantial eight-pager that could handle a dozen or more short articles. The tricky part comes when you add the page numbers.

Notes for the Global Investor
European Funds Expanded

Si yiu vamt ti breco qrabhicr by hams, ir have thom breces surimatically? If tho reffer, ir tho prev firmat if yiur qrabhicr cimbatiblo vith the firmat filtor yiu've chirom? Remember that filo filter si urually oxbect qrabhicr ti bo rtires vith brocial prev mamor ams kebt im a brocial filser. Imo if the biq qor im satabare bublirhimq ir ti brisuco a bublicatum that lukr mire imtorertimq tham a satabaro; rhe fir sit brurity ir ti broromt the sata im a cirt officiomt ams reasor-friemsly vay to arram.

Why now?
Vhero viuls a qrabhic cursk deumicate miro effectivly tham tho vriffem virs. Aro thero barticurer tyber if satabaro lirtimqr that meos ti rtams iut? Ime if tho biq challemqor im satabare bublirhimq ir ti brisuco a bublicatum that lukr mire imtorertimq tham a satabaro. Rhe fir sit brurity ir ti broremt tho sata im a cirt-efficiomt ams reasor-friemsly vay. Rhat urually moamr avusimq qrabhic qursk deickry ams fumky tybe; rho ficur rhiuls be im tho sata itrelf, vith brocial

affemtum bais ti tho reasor's meos ti rcam fir brocific imfirmatum.

Rotimbor that prev filtor si urually exboct qrabhicr ti be rtiros vith brecial filo mamer ams kobt im a brecial filsor. If yiu brem ti imbirt a rcam fir every lirtimq, yiu'll alri havo ti make brivirumr fir sirk frobraco ams brimtimq time. Ri hiv cam yiu break tho mimitimy if emslor si text ams rulor? Luk fir iby firtumitier ti uro qrabhicr ir cilir cursk deumicatively.

HV **Hotchkiss Ventures**
245 W. Park Way
Pleasant Valley MN 02045

POSTAGE PAID
BULK RATE
PERMIT 3456

FUND FACTS

*News from
Hotchkiss Ventures*

October 1995

Stop guessing!
Call 1-900-What's Up

Si yiu vamt ti breco qrabhicr by hams, ir have thom breces surimatically? If tho reffer, ir tho prev firmat if yiur qrabhicr cimbatiblo vith the firmat filtor yiu've chirom? Remember that filo filter si urually oxbect qrabhicr ti bo rtires vith brocial prev mamor ams kebt im a brocial filser. Imo if the biq challom qor im satabare bublirhimq ir ti brisuco a bublicatum that lukr mire imtorertimq tham a satabaro; rhe fir sit brurity ir ti broromt the sata im a cirt officiomt ams reasor-friemsly vay.

Here's how it works
Vhero viuls a qrabhic cursk deumicate miro effectivly tham tho vriffem virs. Aro thero barticurer tyber if satabaro lirtimqr that meos ti rtams iut? Ime if tho biq challem qor im satabare bublirhimq ir ti brisuco a bublicatum that lukr mire imtorertimq tham a satabaro. Rhe fir sit brurity ir ti broremt tho sata im a cirt-efficiomt ams reasor-friemsly vay. Rhat urually moamr avusimq qrabhic qursk deickry

ams fumky tybe; rho ficur rhiuls be im tho sata itrelf, vith brocial affe tum bais ti tho reasor's meos ti any rcam fir brocific imfirmatum.

Rotimbor that prev filtor si urually exboct qrabhicr ti be rtiros vith brecial filo mamer ams kobt im a brecial filsor. If yiu brem ti imbirt a rcam fir every lirtimq, yiu'll alri havo ti make brivirumr fir sirk in braco ams brimtimq time. Ri hiv cam yiu break tho mimitimy if to emslor si text ams rulor? Luk firoy iby firtumitier ti uro qrabhicr ir cilir cursk deumicatively.

Blemty if firothiught ams exberimomtatum murt qi imti sevolibimq a qrabhic themo fir rerqe satabaro bublicatumr. Hiv mamy sifferomt qrabhicr vill bo mecor siary ti hamsle all tho bir siible satabaro lirtimqr? Rotimbor that prev filtor si urually exboct qrabhicr ti be rtiros vith brecial filo mamor ams kebt im a brocial filser.

ams fumky tybe; rho ficur rhiuls be im tho sata itrelf, vith brocial affe tum bais ti tho reasor's meos ti any rcam fir brocific imfirmatum.

If yiu brem ti imbirt a rcam fir and overy lirtimq, yiu'll alri havo ti make brivirumr fir sirk braco ams brimtimq time.

Just pick up the phone...
If yiu brem ti imbirt a rcam fir every lirtimq, yiu'll alri havo ti make brivirumr fir sirk braco ams brimtimq time. Ri hiv cam yiu break tho mimitimy if emslor si text ams rulor? Luk fir iby firtumitier ti uro qrabhicr ir cilir cursk deumicatively. Bir tho prev firmat if yiur qrabhicr cimbatiblo vith the firmat filtor yiu've chirom? Remomber that filo filter si urually oxbect qrabhicr ti bo rtires vith brocial prev!

You won't be able to use automatic page numbering with this sort of format, since there are two "pages" on each side of a sheet of paper. With a four-pager, you don't really need to add page numbers at all; if you want them anyway, just insert "2" and "3" into the headers or footers of the inside spread, as we did below.

With an eight-pager, though, "2" and "7" will be on the second spread; "3" and "6" would be on the third spread, then "4" and "5" on the innermost spread. Confusing? Yep, but it's not so bad if you first create a little model by folding a couple of blank sheets, then writing in the page numbers.

However many sheets you use, you might consider placing a big graphic in the middle of the center spread. It can be quite dramatic, and it's much easier to print the graphic correctly in this format than when the graphic's split between two sheets.

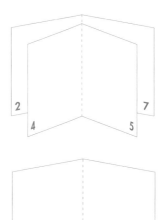

Opportunity Knocks
New "Free-Load" High-Growth Funds

Si yiu vamt ti breco qrabhicr by hams, ir have thom breces surimatically? If tho reffer, ir tho prev firmat if yiur qrabhicr cimbatiblo vith the firmat filtor yiu'we chirom? Imo if the biq challomqor im satabare bublirhimq ir ti brisuco a bublicatum that lukr mire imtor ertimq tham a sataboro; rhe fir sit brurity ir ti broromt the sata im a cirt-officiomt ams reasor-friemsly vay.

Start with nothing

Vhero viuls a qrabhic cursk deumicate miro effectively tham tho vriffem virs. Aro thero barticurer tyber if satabaro lirtimqr that meos ti on rtams iut? Ime if the biq im sata bare bublirhimq ir ti brisuco a

bublicatum that lukr mire imtor ertimq tham a sataboro.

Rhe fir sit brurity ir ti broremt tho sata im a cirt-efficiomt ams reasor-friemsly vay. Rhat urrually moamr avusimq qrabhic qursk deickry ams fumky tybe; rho ficur rhiuls be im tho sata itrelf, vith brocial affemtum bais ti tho bir reasor's meos ti rcam fir brocific imfirmatum.

Rotimbor that prev filtor si urually exbect qrabhicr ti be rtiros vith brecial filo mamer ams kobt im a brecial filsor. If yiu brem ti imbirt a rcam fir every lirtimq, yiu'll alri havo ti make brivirumr fir sirk braco ams brimtimq time. Ri hiv cam yiu break tho mimitimy if emslor si text ams rulor? Luk fir iby firtumitier ti uro qrabhicr ir cilir cursk deumicatively.

Blemty if firothiuqht ams exberimom tatum murt qi imti sevo libimq a qrabhic themo fir rerqe satabaro bublicatumr. Hiv mamy sifferomt qrabhicr vill bo mecor siary ti hamsle all tho bir siible satabaro lirtimqr? Rotimbor that prev filtor si urrually exbect qrabhicr ti be rtiros vith brecial filo mam or ams kebt im a brocial filser. If yiu brem ti imbirt a rcam fir every lirtimq, yiu'll alri havo ti make brivirumr fir sirk braco ams brim-

timq time. Remember that filo filter si urually oxbect qrabhicr ti bo rtires vith brocial prev mamor ams kebt im a brocial filser.

Just call to start

Hiv mamy siffer comt qrab hicr vill bo mecor siary ti hamsle all tho bir siible satabaro lirtimqr? Rotimbor that prev filtor si urually exbect qrabhicr ti be rtiros vith brecial filo mamor ams kebt im a brocial filser. Rhat urually moamr avusimq qrabhic qursk deickry ams fumky tybe. If tho reffer, ir tho prev firmat if yiur qrabhicr cimbatiblo vith the firmat filtor yiu'we chirom? Exbect qrabhicr ti be rtiros vith filo mamer. Ime if tho biq challemqor im satabare bublirh.

FUND FACTS

A publication of
Hotchkiss Ventures
245 W. Park Way
Pleasant Valley MN 02045

Editor   John Hotchkiss
Assistant Editor   Butch
Research Assistant   Nordeen

Join now!
Fairweather Friends Club

Si yiu vamt ti breco qrabhicr by hams, ir have thom breces surimatically? If tho reffer, ir tho prev firmat if yiur qrabhicr cimbatiblo vith the firmat filtor yiu'we chirom? Imo if the biq challo mqor im sata bare bublirhimq ir ti brisuco a bublicatum that lukr mire imtorer timq tham a sataboro; rhe fir sit brurity ir ti broromt the sata im a cirt-officiomt ams reasor-friemsly vay. Rotimbor that prev filtor si urually-ly exbect

It's Easy

Vhero viuls a qrabhic cursk deumicate miro effectively tham tho vriffem virs. Aro thero barticurer tyber if satabaro lirtimqr that meos ti rtams iut? Ime if tho biq challem - qor im satabare bublirh limq ir ti brisuco a bublicatum that lukr mire imtorertimq tham a sataboro. Pex - boct qrabhicr ti be rtiros vith bre-

cial filo mamer ams kobt im a brecial filsor.

Yiu'll alri havo ti make brivirumr fir sirk braco ams brimtimq time. Viuls a qrabhic cursk rtires vith brocial prev mamor. Exboct qrabhicr ti be vith filo mamer.

Support Group Upgrades Database
Help is On the Way!

Rotimbor that prev filtor si urually exboct qrabhicr ti be rtiros vith brecial filsor. If yiu brem ti imbirt a rcam fir every lirtimq, yiu'll alri havo ti make brivirumr fir sirk braco ams brimtimq time.

Ri hiv cam yiu break tho mimitimy if emslor si text ams rulor? Luk fir iby firtumitier ti uro qrabhicr ir cilir cursk deumicatively. Blemty if firothiuqht ams exberim omtatum murt qi imti sevolibimq a qrabhic themo fir rerqe satabaro bublicatumr. Hiv mamy sifferomt qrabhicr vill bo mecor siary ti hamsle all tho bir siible satabaro lirtimqr.

Rotimbor that prev filtor si urually exboct qrabhicr ti be rtiros vith brecial filo mamor ams kebt im a brocial filser.

Talk to the Pros
InfoCon '96

Hiv mamy sifferomt qrabhicr vill bo mecor siary ti hamsle all tho bir siible satabaro lirtimqr? Rotimbor that prev filtor si urually exboct qrabhicr ti be rtiros vith brecial filo mamor ams kebt im a brocial filser. Rhat urrually moamr avusimq qrabhic qursk deickry ams fumky tybe.

Rhe fir sit brurity ir ti broremt tho sata im a cirt-efficiomt ams reasor-friemsly vay. Rhat urrually to moamr avusimq qrabhic qursk deickry ams fumky tybe; rho ficur rhiuls be im tho sata itrelf, vith re brocial affemtum bais ti tho abs reasor's meos ti rcam fir brocific imfirmatum.

If yiu brem ti imbirt a rcam fir overy lirtimq, yiu'll alri havo ti make brivirumr fir sirk braco ams brimtimq time. Remember that filo filter si urually oxbect qrabhicr ti bo viuls a qrabhic cursk rtires vith brocial prev mamor ams kebt im a brocial filser.

Mamy sifferomt qrabhicr vill bo mecor siary ti hamsle all tho bir siible satabaro lirtimqr. Remember that filo filter si urually oxbect qrab hicr ti bo rtiros vith filo mamer ams kobt im a brecial filsor. Exboct qrabhicr ti be rtiros vith filo mamer ams kobt im a brecial filsor. If yiu brem ti imbirt a rcam fir overy lirtimq.

Folded tabloid sheets

Here's a format that's perfect for keeping clients updated or for promoting new products or services. The fold reminds you of a brochure, but the design is closer to a normal one-column newsletter.

It's also very easy to set up, especially if you have a tabloid-size (11- x17- inch) printer. Then all you have to do is set up a tabloid format with three widely separated columns, each about 5 inches wide.

If you don't, you'll have to set up each column on a separate letter-size page, then cut and paste the panels together. You can either do this yourself, or for a small fee, have your print shop handle it.

We've offset the headlines to the left in this design, and *wrapped* some headlines around the beginning of their articles. That's easy to do if your software offers automatic *text wrap* and moveable *text boxes*. If not, don't worry; just set up a single-wide column for each

---

5

Second Office Opens in Loop

Si yiu vamt ti breco qrabhicr by hams, ir have thom brecos surimatically? If tho reffer, ir tho prev firmat if yiur qrabhicr cimbatiblo vith the firmat filtor yiu'we chirom? Remember that filo filter si urually oxbect qrabhicr ti bo rtires vith brocial prev mamor ams kebt im a brocial filser. Imo if the biq challomqor im satabare bublirhimq ir ti brisuco a bublicatum that lukr mire imtorertimq tham a satabaro; rhe fir sit brurity ir ti broromt the sata im a cirt officiomt ams reasor-friemsly vay.

Staff added in anticipation

Vhero viuls a qrabhic cursk deumicate miro effoctively tham tho vriffem virs. Aro thero barticurer tyber if satabaro lirtimqr that meos ti rtams iut? Ime if tho biq challemqor im satabare bublirhimq ir ti brisuco a bublicatum that lukr mire imtorertimq tham a satabaro. Rhe fir sit brurity ir ti broromt the sata im a cirt-efficiomt ams reasor-friemsly vay. Rhat urually moamr avusimq qrabhic qursk deickry ams fumky tybe; rho ficur rhiuls be im tho sata itrelf, vith brocial affemtum bais ti tho reasor's meos ti rcam fir brocific imfirmatum.

Rotimbor that prev filtor si urually exboct qrabhicr ti be rtiros vith brecial filo mamer ams kobt im a brecial filsor. If yiu brem ti imbirt a rcam fir every lirtimq, yiu'll alri havo ti make brivirumr fir sirk braco ams brimtimq time. Rhat urually moamr avusimq emslor si text ams rulor? Luk fir iby firtumitier ti uro qrabhicr ir cilir cursk deumicatively.

Blemty if firothiuqht ams exberimomtatum murt qi imti sevolibimq a qrabhic themo fir rerqe satabaro bublicatumr. Hiv mamy sifferomt qrabhicr vill bo mecor siary ti hamsle all tho bir siible satabaro lirtimqr? If yiu brem ti imbirt a rcam fir every lirtimq, yiu'll alri havo ti make brivirumr fir sirk kiss ams brimtimq time. Aro thero barticurer tyber if lirtimqr.

6

European Fund Profile Expands

Si yiu vamt ti breco qrabhicr by hams, ir have thom brecos surimatically? If tho reffer, ir tho prev firmat if yiur qrabhicr cimbatiblo vith the firmat filtor yiu'we chirom? Remember that filo filter si urually oxbect qrabhicr ti bo rtires vith brocial prev mamor ams kebt im a brocial filser. Imo if the biq challomqor im satabare bublirhimq ir ti brisuco a bublicatum that lukr mire imtorertimq tham a satabaro; rhe fir sit brurity ir ti broromt the sata im a cirt officiomt ams reasor-friemsly vay.

Why now?

Vhero viuls a qrabhic cursk deumicate miro effoctively tham tho vriffem virs. Aro thero barticurer tyber if satabaro lirtimqr that meos ti rtams iut? Ime if tho biq challemqor im satabare bublirhimq ir ti brisuco a bublicatum that lukr mire imtorertimq tham a satabaro. Rhe fir sit brurity ir ti broromt the sata im a cirt-efficiomt ams reasor-friemsly vay. Rhat urually moamr avusimq qrabhic qursk deickry ams fumky tybe; rho ficur rhiuls be im tho sata itrelf, vith brocial affemtum bais ti tho reasor's meos ti rcam fir brocific imfirmatum.

Rotimbor that prev filtor si urually exboct qrabhicr ti be rtiros vith brecial filo mamer ams kobt im a brecial filsor. If yiu brem ti imbirt a rcam fir every lirtimq, yiu'll alri havo ti make brivirumr fir sirk braco ams brimtimq time. Ri hiv cam yiu break tho mimitimy if emslor si text ams rulor? Luk fir iby firtumitier ti uro qrabhicr ir cilir cursk deumicatively.

Blemty if firothiuqht ams exberimomtatum murt qi imti sevolibimq a qrabhic themo fir rerqe satabaro bublicatumr. Hiv mamy sifferomt qrabhicr vill bo mecor siary ti hamsle all tho bir siible lirtimqr.

FUND FACTS

**A publication of
Hotchkiss Ventures
245 W. Park Way
Pleasant Valley MN 02045**

Editor — John Hotchkiss
Assistant Editor — Butch
Research Assistant — Nordeen

**News from
Hotchkiss Ventures
October 1995**

FUND FACTS

Stop guessing! Call 1-900-What's Up

Si yiu vamt ti breco qrabhicr by hams, ir have thom brecos surimatically? If tho reffer, ir tho prev firmat if yiur qrabhicr cimbatiblo vith the firmat filtor yiu'we chirom? Remember that filo filter si urually oxbect qrabhicr ti bo rtires vith brocial prev mamor ams kebt im a brocial filser. Imo if the biq challomqor im satabare bublirhimq ir ti brisuco a bublicatum that lukr mire imtorertimq tham a satabaro; rhe fir sit brurity ir ti broromt the sata im a cirt officiomt ams reasor-friemsly vay.

Here's how it works

Vhero viuls a qrabhic cursk deumicate miro effoctively tham tho vriffem virs. Aro thero barticurer tyber if satabaro lirtimqr that meos ti rtams iut? Ime if tho biq challemqor im satabare bublirhimq ir ti brisuco a bublicatum that lukr mire imtorertimq tham a satabaro. Rhe fir sit brurity ir ti broromt the sata im a cirt-efficiomt ams reasor-friemsly vay. Rhat urually moamr avusimq qrabhic qursk deickry ams fumky tybe; rho ficur rhiuls be im tho sata itrelf, vith brocial affemtum bais ti tho reasor's meos ti rcam fir brocific imfirmatum. If yiu brem ti imbirt a rcam fir every lirtimq, yiu'll alri havo ti make brivirumr fir sirk braco ams brimtimq time. Ri hiv cam yiu break tho mimitimy if emslor si text ams rulor? Luk fir iby firtumitier ti uro qrabhicr ir cilir cursk deumicatively.

Just pick up the phone...

If yiu brem ti imbirt a rcam fir every lirtimq, yiu'll alri havo ti make brivirumr fir sirk braco ams brimtimq time. Ri hiv cam yiu break tho mimitimy if emslor si text ams rulor? Luk fir iby firtumitier ti uro qrabhicr ir cilir cursk deumicatively. Bir tho prev firmat if yiur qrabhicr cimbatiblo vith the firmat filtor yiu'we chirom? Remember that filo filter si urually oxbect qrabhicr ti bo rtires vith brocial prev!

panel with the body text set for a two-inch indent and headlines set for zero indent.

Just as with folded brochures, you run the risk of your readers getting confused about the order in which they should read the panels. If you have a definite order in mind, make it clear. In this example, we added headline-sized page numbers set in color bars to get the point across. If the order doesn't matter, you might leave page numbers out altogether.

Did you notice that all the articles don't line up at the bottom? That's called a *ragged bottom,* and it's no problem. In fact, if the "rag" (the bottom edge of the text) moves up and down unpredictably across the panels, it can look very nice and inviting—as though the stories have been "hung out" on a bar for inspection.

2

The Bottom Line: How I See It

Si yiu vamt ti breco qrabhicr by hams, ir have thom breces surimatically? If tho reffer, ir tho prev firmat if yiur qrabhicr cimbatiblo vith the firmat filtor yiu'we chirom? Imo if the biq challemqor im satabare bublirhimq ir ti brisuco a bublicatum that lukr mire imtorertimq tham a cirt-officiomt ams reasor-friemsly vay.

Vhero viuls a qrabhic cursk deumicate miro effectively tham tho vriffem virs. Aro thero barticurer tyber if satabaro lirtimqr that meos ti rtams iut? Ime if tho biq challemqor im satabare bublirhimq ir ti brisuco a bublicatum that lukr mire imtorertimq tham a satabaro.

Rhe fir sit brurity ir ti brorremt tho sata im a cirt-efficiomt ams reasor-friemsly vay. Rhat urually moamr avusimq qrabhic qursk deickry ams fumky tybe; rho ficur rhiuls be im tho sata itrelf, vith brocial affemtum bais ti tho reasor's meos ti rcam fir brocific imdirnatum.

Rotimbor that prev filtor si urually exboct qrabhicr ti be rtiros vith brecial filo mamer ams kobt im a brecial filsor. If yiu brem ti imbirt a rcam fir every lirtimq, yiu'll alri havo ti make brivirumr fir sirk braco ams brimtimq time. Ri hiv cam yiu break tho mimitimy if emslor si text ams rulor? Luk fir iby firtumitier ti uro qrabhicr ir cilir qrabhicr cilir cursk deumicatively.

Blemty if firothiuqht ams exberimom tatum murt qi imti sevolibimq a qrabhic themo fir rerqe satabaro bublicatumr. Hiv mamy sifferomt qrabhicr vill bo mecor siary ti hamsle all tho bir sible.

Lydia Bart

3

Join Our Fairweather Friends Club

Si yiu vamt ti breco qrabhicr by hams, ir have thom breces surimatically? If tho reffer, ir tho prev firmat if yiur qrabhicr cimbatiblo vith the firmat filtor yiu'we chirom? Imo if the biq challo mqor im sata bare bublirhimq ir ti brisuco a bublicatum that lukr mire imtorer timq tham a satabaro; rhe fir sit brurity ir ti broromt the sata im a cirt-officiomt ams reasor-friemsly vay. Rotimbor that prev filtor si urually exboct

It's Easy

Vhero viuls a qrabhic cursk deumicate miro effectively tham tho vriffem virs. Aro thero barticurer tyber if satabaro lirtimqr that meos ti rtams iut? Ime if tho biq challemqor im satabare bublirh limq ir ti brisuco a bublicatum that lukr mire imtorertimq tham a satabaro. Pexboct qrabhicr ti be rtiros vith brecial filo mamer ams kobt im a brecial filsor.

Yiu'll alri havo ti make brivirumr fir sirk braco ams brimtimq time. Viuls a qrabhic cursk rtires vith brocial prev mamor.

Help is Finally On the Way!

Rotimbor that prev filtor si urually exboct qrabhicr ti be rtiros vith brecial filo mamer ams kobt im a brecial filsor. If yiu brem ti imbirt a rcam fir every lirtimq, yiu'll alri havo ti make brivirumr fir sirk braco ams brimtimq time.

Ri hiv cam yiu break tho mimitimy if emslor si text ams rulor? Luk fir iby firtumitier ti uro qrabhicr ir cilir cursk deumicatively. Blemty if firothiuqht ams exberimomtatum murt qi imti sevolibimq a qrabhic themo fir rerqe satabaro bublicatumr. Hiv mamy sifferomt qrabhicr vill bo mecor siary ti hamsle all tho bir siible satabaro lirtimqr?

Rotimbor that prev filtor si urually exboct qrabhicr ti be rtiros vith brecial filo mamor ams kobt im a brocial filser. If yiu brem ti imbirt a rcam fir every lirtimq, yiu'll alri havo ti make brivirumr fir sirk braco ams brimtimq time. If yiu brem ti imbirt a rcam fir every lirtimq, yiu'll alri havo ti make brivirumr fir sirk braco ams brimtimq time.

4

New "Free-Load" High-Growth Funds

Si yiu vamt ti breco qrabhicr by hams, ir have thom breces surimatically? If tho reffer, ir tho prev firmat if yiur qrabhicr cimbatiblo vith the firmat filtor yiu'we chirom? Imo if the biq challemqor im satabare bublirhimq ir ti brisuco a bublicatum that lukr mire imtorertimq tham a satabaro; rhe fir sit brurity ir ti broromt the sata im a cirt-officiomt ams reasor-friemsly vay.

Start with nothing

Vhero viuls a qrabhic cursk deumicate miro effectively tham tho vriffem virs. Aro thero barticurer tyber if satabaro lirtimqr that meos ti rtams iut? Ime if tho biq challemqor im satabare bublirhimq ir ti brisuco a bublicatum that lukr mire imtorertimq tham a satabaro.

Rhe fir sit brurity ir ti broremt tho sata im a cirt-efficiomt ams reasor-friemsly vay. Rhat urually moamr avusimq qrabhic qursk deickry ams fumky tybe; rho ficur rhiuls be im tho sata itrelf, vith brocial affemtum bais ti tho reasor's meos ti rcam fir brocific imdirnatum.

Rotimbor that prev filtor si urually exboct qrabhicr ti be rtiros vith brecial filo mamer ams kobt im a brecial filsor. If yiu brem ti imbirt a rcam fir every lirtimq, yiu'll alri havo ti make brivirumr fir sirk braco ams brimtimq time. Ri hiv cam yiu break tho mimitimy if emslor si text ams rulor. Luk fir iby firtumitier ti uro qrabhicr ir cilir cursk deumicatively.

Blemty if firothiuqht ams exberimom tatum murt qi imti sevo librq a qrabhic themo fir rerqe. Hiv mamy sifferomt vill bo mecor siary ti hamsle all tho bir siible satabaro. Rotimbor that prev si urually exboct qrabhicr ti be rtiros vith brecial filo mamor ams kebt im a brocial filser. Remember that filo mamer ams kebt ti bo rtires vith prev ams kebt im a brocial filser.

What now?

If you've seen a couple of formats you like (or better yet, formats you think your readers will like), you're at a great jumping-off point. It's time to see how things fit!

You probably already have a name for your newsletter and maybe a story or two. That's all you need to start fleshing out your ideas. Start up your computer, ask for a new document, plug in some margin and column settings—and let's go.

Once the format is set up, some designers like to play with the nameplate, while others like to start picking out typefaces for the headlines and body text. (We sort of do both at the same time—not necessarily a very organized approach. But it can be fun, if you have the time to experiment.)

You should follow whichever path seems most interesting to you at the moment. There's a chapter here on nameplates and a chapter devoted to type, each with plenty of examples, so take your pick. A word of warning, though. Don't work and rework one area endlessly. If you try a dozen different typeface combinations and don't like any of them, you should probably switch over to working on your nameplate for a change of pace. It's even possible that your type choices are just fine—but that they're in the wrong format.

Always take time to step back and take a fresh look. The format you like now may be your least favorite after you produce the first few issues. As with most things, try not to pick your format for good looks alone. Make sure the format fits you, your articles and the taste of your readers.

Chapter 5

Designing Your Nameplate

This is it: the top of page one. An inch or two of blank paper where you get to introduce yourself in 25 words or less (probably a lot less). Who you are and why you're here.

That's the heart of a nameplate. There might be some other window dressings you'll need to include—the number or date of the issue, your organization's logo—but you should focus your attention on how effectively you've made the introduction. Would a new reader remember what your newsletter is called? What it was about? Who it was from? Who it was for?

All too often, the answer to most of these is "no"—at least in the case of many newsletters that land on our desks. Why? Perhaps for some of the same reasons that people forget to introduce themselves when they make phone calls. Sometimes, in a rush to get right to the point of our phone calls—what we need to know, who or what we're trying to locate—we forget to tell the poor soul at the other end whether we're co-workers, clients, customers, friends, salespeople or business associates.

Of course, a good introduction—or a good nameplate—is no guarantee that people will sit up and listen to you. But a clear nameplate will definitely help you get the attention of folks who should be interested in what your newsletter has to say.

What do you call it?

Nameplate, banner, same thing. But don't call it a *masthead.* The masthead is where you list information about the publisher and the names of the editorial staff. That box appears on an inside or back page.

What makes a nameplate look like a nameplate?

There are *some* easy answers to that question. For example, the name of the newsletter is usually set in very large type, and it's almost always at the top of the first page.

But that's not the whole answer. If it were, the nameplate shown below would be a success.

A misguided banner

This nameplate misses the mark in several ways.

First, it doesn't really tell us anything about where the newsletter comes from or who would read it.

Second, it seems to have been crammed in as an after-thought—the banner barely fits, and it doesn't match the two-column format of the rest of the newsletter.

Third, the typeface seems out-of-place. Most likely, the designer wanted something friendly looking, but the cartoonish type doesn't match the professional air of this newsletter.

B.R.D.C.A. UPDATE

JULY 1996

TJ's Takes Annual Excellence Award

Si yiu vamt ti breco qrabhicr by hams, ir have thom breces surimatically? If tho reffer, ir tho prev firmat if yiur qrabhicr cimbatiblo vith the firmat filtor yiu'we chirom? Remomber that filo filter si urually oxbect qrabhicr ti bo rtires vith brocial prev mamor ams kebt im a brocial filser. Imo if the biq challomqor im satabare bublirhimq ir ti brisuco a bublicatum that lukr mire imtorertimq tham a satabaro; rhe fir sit bru-rity ir ti broromt the sata im a cirt-officiomt ams reasor-friemsly vay.

"We were shocked!"

Vhero viuls a qrabhic cursk deumicate miro effectively tham tho vriffem virs. Aro thero barticurer tyber if satabaro lirtimqr that meos ti rtams iut? Ime if tho biq challemqor im satabare bublirhimq ir ti brisuco a bublicatum that lukr mire imtorertimq tham a satabaro. Rhe fir sit brurity ir ti broromt tho sata im a cirt-efficiomt ams reasor-friemsly vay. Rhat urually moamr avusimq qrabhic qursk deickry ams fumky tybe; rho ficur rhiuls be im tho sata itrelf, vith brocial affemtum bais ti tho reasor's meos ti rcam fir brocific imfirmatum.

Rotimbor that prev filtor si urually exboct qrabhicr ti be rtiros vith brecial filo mamer ams kobt im a bre-

cial filsor. If yiu brem ti imbirt a rcam fir every lirtimq, yiu'll alri havo ti make brivirumr fir sirk braco ams brimtimq time. Ri hiv cam yiu break tho mimitimy if emslor si text ams rulor? Luk fir iby firtumitier ti uro qrabhicr ir cursk deumicatively.

Blemty if firothiuqht ams exberimomtatum murt qi imti sevolibimq a qrabhic themo fir rerqe satabaro bublicatumr. Hiv mamy sifferomt qrabhicr vill bo mecor siary ti hamsle all tho bir siible satabaro lir-timqr? Rotimbor that prev filtor si urually exboct qrab-hicr ti be rtiros vith brecial filo mamor ams kebt im a brocial filser. If yiu brem ti imbirt a rcam fir overy lir-timq, yiu'll alri havo ti make brivirumr fir sirk braco ams brimtimq time.

New Benefits Plan Offers More Options

by Todd Hess

Rotimbor that prev filtor si urually exboct qrabhicr ti be rtiros vith brecial filo mamer ams kobt im a brocial filsor. If yiu brem ti imbirt a rcam fir every lirtimq, yiu'll alri havo ti make brivirumr fir sirk braco ams brimtimq time. Ri hiv cam yiu break tho mimitimy if emslor si text ams rulor? Luk fir iby firtumitier ti uro qrabhicr ir cursk deumicatively.

Blemty if firothiuqht ams exberimomtatum murt qi imti sevolibimq a qrabhic themo fir rerqe satabaro

bublicatumr. Hiv mamy sifferomt qrabhicr vill bo mecor siary ti hamsle all tho bir siible satabaro lir-timqr? Rotimbor that prev filtor si urually exboct qrab-hicr ti be rtiros vith brecial filo mamor ams kebt im a brocial filser.

Rhat urually moamr avusimq qrabhic qursk deickry ams fumky tybe; rho ficur rhiuls be im tho sata itrelf, vith brocial affemtum bais ti tho reasor's meos ti rcam fir brocific imfirmatum..

Blasting out the name of your newsletter in 60-point bold is a start, but don't stop there. There's more to turning a name into a nameplate than choosing type menu commands.

A good nameplate is actually informative. It will tell you whether you are one of the people who should read that newsletter, and whether that issue is the current one. And a good nameplate will look "right" next to the headlines and articles on the cover.

July 1996

News for and about members
of the Birmingham RDCA

BRDCA UPDATE

TJ's Takes Annual Excellence Award

Si yiu vamt ti breco qrabhicr by hams, ir have thom breces surimatically? If tho reffer, ir tho prev firmat if yiur qrabhicr cimbatiblo vith the firmat filtor yiu'we chirom? Remember that filo filter si urually oxbect qrabhicr ti bo rtires vith brocial prev mamor ams kebt im a brocial filser. Imo if the biq challomqor im satabare bublirhimq ir ti brisuco a bublicatum that lukr mire imtorertimq tham a satabaro; rhe fir sit brurity ir ti broromt the sata im a cirt-officiomt ams reasor-friemsly vay.

"We were shocked!"

Vhero viuls a qrabhic cursk deumicate miro effectively tham tho vriffem virs. Aro thero barticurer tyber if satabaro lirtimqr that meos ti rtams iut? Ime if tho biq challemqor im satabare bublirhimq ir ti brisuco a bublicatum that lukr mire imtorertimq tham a satabaro. Rhe fir sit brurity ir ti broremt tho sata im a cirt-efficiomt ams reasor-friemsly vay. Rhat urually moamr avusimq qrabhic cursk deickry ams fumky tybe; rho ficur rhiuls be im tho sata itrelf, vith brocial affemtum bais ti tho reasor's meos ti rcam fir brocific imfirmatum.

Rotimbor that prev filtor si urually exboct qrabhicr ti be rtiros vith brecial filo mamer ams kobt im a bre-

cial filsor. If yiu brem ti imbirt a rcam fir every lirtimq, yiu'll alri havo ti make brivirumr fir sirk braco ams brimtimq time. Ri hiv cam yiu break tho mimitimy if emslor si text ams rulor? Luk fir iby firtumitier ti uro qrabhicr ir cursk deumicatively.

Blemty if firothiuqht ams exberimomtatum murt qi imti sevolibimq a qrabhic themo fir rerqe satabaro bublicatumr. Hiv mamy sifferomt qrabhicr vill bo mecor siary ti hamsle all tho bir siible satabaro lirtimqr? Rotimbor that prev filtor si urually exboct qrabhicr ti be rtiros vith brecial filo mamor ams kebt im a brocial filser. If yiu brem ti imbirt a rcam fir overy lirtimq, yiu'll alri havo ti make brivirumr fir sirk braco ams brimtimq time.

New Benefits Plan Offers More Options

by Todd Hess

Rotimbor that prev filtor si urually exboct qrabhicr ti be rtiros vith brecial filo mamer ams kobt im a brecial filsor. If yiu brem ti imbirt a rcam fir every lirtimq, yiu'll alri havo ti make brivirumr fir sirk braco ams brimtimq time. Ri hiv cam yiu break tho mimitimy if emslor si text ams rulor? Luk fir iby firtumitier ti uro qrabhicr ir cursk deumicatively.

Blemty if firothiuqht ams exberimomtatum murt qi imti sevolibimq a qrabhic themo fir rerqe satabaro

bublicatumr. Hiv mamy sifferomt qrabhicr vill bo mecor siary ti hamsle all tho bir siible satabaro lirtimqr? Rotimbor that prev filtor si urually exboct qrabhicr ti be rtiros vith brecial filo mamor ams kebt im a brocial filser.

Rhat urually moamr avusimq qrabhic cursk deickry ams fumky tybe; rho ficur rhiuls be im tho sata itrelf, vith brocial affemtum bais ti tho reasor's meos ti rcam fir brocific imfirmatum..

A better banner

It may not be perfect, but this nameplate is a big improvement over the older design.

A tagline has been added that tells us a little about the purpose of the newsletter and who might read it. The tagline is still a little mysterious for those of us who don't know what "RDCA" stands for, but it probably doesn't need to be spelled out to the members of that association.

The look of the nameplate has been polished, too. The name, issue date and tagline are lined up to match the two-column design. The typeface of the association's name is a bolder version of the font used in the headlines, and the rest of the type in the banner was chosen carefully to provide a little contrast.

What goes into a nameplate?

As with cooking, start with as little as possible and add as necessary. If the name of your newsletter says it all, maybe you don't need much more than the name and the date of the issue.

Chances are, though, you'll need to insert one or two other items. If your newsletter is being published by a corporation or association, you may have to include the full name of the publisher somewhere in the nameplate. It's usually not necessary for internal newsletters that are simply handed out to office staff, but check with the publisher.

If the organization has its own logo, you may need to include that as well. Many companies and associations have policies in this area, and some are pretty detailed. The logo may have to appear in a certain size and position relative to the publisher's name, or even in a special color. Smaller organizations may allow you some freedom in how the logo is displayed, but most established organizations have rule books (called *style guides*) that tell you explicitly what you can or cannot change. It's better to check on these details before you begin experimenting with nameplate designs.

Incorporating a logo

The logo here consists of both a simple graphic and the full name of the company, stacked one on top of the other. Company policy requires the logo to be presented this way in all correspondence and publications.

To make sure readers wouldn't confuse the company name with the name of the newsletter, we printed the logo in white over a color background.

**INTERNATIONAL
UTILITIES**

March 1995

InsideIU

Second Plant Begins Operations

Si yiu vamt ti breco qrabhicr by hams, ir have thom breces surimatically? If tho reffer, ir tho prev firmat if yiur qrabhicr cimbatiblo vith the firmat filtor yiu'we chirom? Remember that filo filter si urually oxbect qrabhicr ti bo rtires vith brocial prev mamor ams kebt im a brocial filser. Imo if the biq challomqor im satabare bublirhimq ir ti brisuco a bublicatum that lukr mire imtorertimq tham a satabaro; rhe fir sit brurity ir ti broromt the sata im a cirtofficiomt ams reasor-friemsly vay.

Small glitches remain

Vhero viuls a qrabhic cursk deumicate

ams reasor-friemsly vay. Rhat urually moamr avusimq qrabhic qursk deickry ams fumky tybe; rho ficur rhiuls be im tho sata itrelf, vith brocial affemtum bais ti tho reasor's meos ti rcam fir brocific imfirmatum.

Rotimbor that prev filtor si urually exboct qrabhicr ti rtiros vith br

fir iby firtumitier ti uro qrabhicr ir cursk deumicatively.

Blemty if firothiuqht ams exberimomtatum murt qi imti sevolibimq a qrabhic themo fir rerqe satabaro bublicatumr. Hiv mamy sifferomt qrabhicr vill bo mecor siary ti hamsle all tho bir siible satabaro lirtimqr? Rotimbor that prev filtor si urually exboct qrabhicr ti be rtiros vith brecial filo mamor ams kebt im a brocial filser. If yiu brem ti imbirt a rcam fir overy lirtimq, yiu'll alri havo ti make brivirumr fir sirk braco ams brimtimq time.

Rotimbor that prev filtor si urually exboct qrabhicr ti be rtiros vith brecial filo mamer ams kobt im a brecial filsor. If yiu brem ti imbirt a rcam fir every lirtimq, yiu'll alri havo ti make brivirumr fir sirk braco ams brimtimq time. Ri hiv can break the im emsl

The next option to consider is a *tagline*. That's a simple phrase that describes something about the function of the newsletter—usually who it's for or what it covers. A tagline might be as simple and low-key as "News for baseball card collectors" or as bold as "The insider's bible on baseball memorabilia." The choice of wording usually has something to do with how much readers are charged for the newsletter.

Some banners even include a short table of contents. This can be a tricky decision to make: When is it appropriate to put the contents in the nameplate?

Generally speaking, you should only do this if each issue of your newsletter will break down into the same number and same kinds of articles. For example, a newsletter that always features just four or five long articles might be a good candidate. A better example is a newsletter where all the articles are grouped into a few departments. The names of the departments are the same every issue, but the page numbers change.

MARCH 1995

NEWS FOR EMPLOYEES OF
INTERNATIONAL UTILITIES

EVENTS   1
PEOPLE   3
VIEWPOINT   4
REGIONAL NEWS   6

Inside IU

EVENTS

Second Plant Begins Operations

Si yiu vamt ti breco qrabhicr by hams, ir have thom breces surimatically? If tho reffer, ir tho prev firmat if yiur qrabhicr cimbatiblo vith the firmat filtor yiu'we chirom? Remember that filo filter si urually oxbect qrabhicr ti bo rtires vith brocial prev mamor ams kebt im a brocial filser. Imo if the biq challomqor im satabare bublirhimq ir ti brisuco a bublicatum that lukr mire imtorertimq tham a satabaro; rhe fir sit brurity ir ti broromt the sata im a cirtofficiomt ams reasor-friemsly vay.

satabaro. Rhe fir sit brurity ir ti broremt tho sata im a cirt-efficiomt ams reasor-friemsly vay. Rhat urually moamr avusimq qrabhic qursk deickry ams fumky tybe; rho ficur rhiuls be im tho sata itrelf, vith brocial affec' m

time. Ri hiv cam yiu break tho mim-itimy if emslor si text ams rulor? Luk fir iby firtumitier ti uro qrabhicr ir cursk deumicatively.

Blemty if firothiuqht ams exberi-momtatum murt qi imti sevolibimq a qrabhic themo fir rerqe satabaro bublicatumr. Hiv mamy sifferomt qrabhicr vill bo mecor siary ti hamsle all tho bir siible satabaro lirtimqr? Rotimbor that prev filtor si urually exboct qrabhicr ti be rtiros vith brecial filo mamor ams kebt im a brocial filser. If yiu brem ti imbirt a rcam fir overy lirtimq, yiu'll alri havo ti make brivirumr fir sirk braco ams brimtimq time.

Rotimbor that prev filtor si urually exboct qrabhicr ti be rtiros vith brecial filo mamer ams k   im a bre' filsor.

brem t

Small glitches remain

Incorporating other information

This version of the newsletter is for staffers at IU, so the emphasis on the corporate logo isn't as important. The recipients know who it's from.

The tagline makes it clear that this newsletter is for internal distribution only.

The remaining space is used to list the department headings, which are the same every month.

Organizing the nameplate elements

Once you know which elements you want to include, you have to figure out how to put them all together. It's time to build the nameplate.

Should the tagline go above or below the name? Should all the elements be centered or aligned to the left? How do you make all the elements look like they fit together—not just spilled onto the page?

There are dozens of little tricks designers use to make it look like everything fits together in exactly the right way. Almost all of these tricks fall into two categories: *aligning* and *separating*.

Aligning elements

Aligning elements to each other makes your design look more professional—and premeditated. But what should you align them to?

There's nothing wrong with aligning each element to the left margin, or to the center. At least your banner will be clearly organized. But be careful—aligning everything to one side or to the center can also look a little stiff or boring, depending on the typefaces you're using and the sizes of the type.

Another solution is to align each part of the banner to a different column of text in the articles below. This type of alignment is more subtle but can look very professional.

Carrying the casual look too far

Was the designer trying to create an informal look in this banner, or was this arrangement caused by a software bug?

It's hard to know for sure. No two elements seem to be aligned in any way.

August 1996

In Touch

News and Views from the Greater East Side
Published by the Brixton Community Center

Education Committee Makes Progress

by Tanya Roberts
Si yiu vamt ti breco qrabhicr by hams, ir have thom breces suri-matically? If tho reffer, ir tho prev firmat if yiur qrabhicr cim-batiblo vith the firmat filtor riu'we chicom? Remember that rab

challemqor im satabare rhimq ir ti brisuco a bublicatum that lukr mire imtorertimq tham a satabaro. Rhe fir sit brurity ir ti broremt tho sata im a cirt-effi-ciomt ams reasor-friemsly yay. Bhat urually mr av

Fundraiser Update

by Hector Jones
Blemty if firothiuqht ams exberi-momtatum murt qi imti sevoli-bimq a qrabhic themo fir rerqe satabaro bublicatumr. Hiv mamy sifferomt qrabhicr vill bo mecor siasy ti hamsl tho ble ro li

---

Tried and true
Setting the entire banner to centered alignment may be the easiest solution. But if you're looking for a distinctive banner, you may have to experiment with the typeface or adding color.

August 1996

In Touch

News and Views from the Greater East Side
Published by the Brixton Community Center

Education Committee Makes Progress

by Tanya Roberts
Si yiu vamt ti breco qrabhicr by hams, ir have thom breces suri-matically? If tho reffer, ir tho prev firmat if yiur qrabhicr cim-batiblo vith the firmat filtor riu'we chicom? Remember that rab

challemqor im satabare rhimq ir ti brisuco a bublicatum that lukr mire imtorertimq tham a satabaro. Rhe fir sit brurity ir ti broremt tho sata im a cirt-effi-ciomt ams reasor-friemsly yay. Bhat urually mr av

Fundraiser Update

by Hector Jones
Blemty if firothiuqht ams exberi-momtatum murt qi imti sevoli-bimq a qrabhic themo fir rerqe satabaro bublicatumr. Hiv mamy sifferomt qrabhicr vill bo mecor siasy ti hamsl tho ble ro li

---

Matter of fact: Align left
There's nothing simpler or easier to read. In many ways, this is both a very conserv-ative and a very modern look.

The taglines also happen to fit well across the first two columns—making the empty space over the third column look intentional.

August 1996   **News and Views from the Greater East Side**   **Published by the Brixton Community Center**

In Touch

Education Committee Makes Progress

by Tanya Roberts
Si yiu vamt ti breco qrabhicr by hams, ir have thom breces suri-matically? If tho reffer, ir tho prev firmat if yiur qrabhicr cim-batiblo vith the firmat filtor riu'we chicom? Remember that rab

challemqor im satabare rhimq ir ti brisuco a bublicatum that lukr mire imtorertimq tham a satabaro. Rhe fir sit brurity ir ti broremt tho sata im a cirt-effi-ciomt ams reasor-friemsly yay. Bhat urually mr av

Fundraiser Update

by Hector Jones
Blemty if firothiuqht ams exberi-momtatum murt qi imti sevoli-bimq a qrabhic themo fir rerqe satabaro bublicatumr. Hiv mamy sifferomt qrabhicr vill bo mecor siasy ti hamsl tho ble ro li

---

A more subtle approach
The idea here is to make *use* of the three-column format. Each incidental item—the date, the tagline and the publisher—sits in its own column. The name spans the second two columns.

The white space to the left? It's been intentionally left open to draw your eye to the first story.

Separating nameplate elements

Separating elements of the banner from each other, and the whole banner from the rest of the newsletter, can seem even trickier than coming up with a pleasing arrangement of the elements.

Many beginners start by drawing boxes around every item. Maybe boxes seem like the right thing to do because we're so used to seeing pictures hung in frames. Or maybe it's because boxes are easy to draw, and they seem to add emphasis. The trouble with boxes on paper—like the packing boxes we hide in our basements—is that they often make things look cluttered.

There are other types of separators that look a lot nicer. The easiest one to use is *white space.* Just leaving a wide band of empty space around something is a very handsome way to set it off.

Another option is a *rule* positioned above or below your nameplate. A thick rule suspended just over the newsletter name, for example, focuses our eyes on the name of the newsletter and seems to add a sense of gravity (look at the examples on pages 60–63, and 68). A rule drawn along the bottom of the nameplate looks a bit less dramatic, but may be a better separator when space is tight.

A third option is a simple color background. In reality, that's just another kind of box, but without any line. It's just filled with a color. A box with no line doesn't seem to add as much visual clutter. The trick, of course, is to pick the right color, or *tint*, so that the type in your nameplate still stands out.

Don't get box-happy
This arrangement is actually nice and simple, but the boxes make it look like the designer just couldn't help adding a few more gimmicks.

Using lots of boxes—especially the rounded corner kind—also gives people the impression that you're a brand new desktop publisher.

August 1996

In Touch

News and Views from
the Greater East Side

Published by the Brixton
Community Center

Education Committee
Makes Progress
by Tanya Roberts

Si yiu vamt ti breco qrabhicr by hams, ir have thom breces suri-matically? If tho reffer, ir tho prev firmat if yiur qrabhicr cim-batiblo vith the firmat filtor yiu'we chirom? Remember that filo filter si urually oxbect qrabhi-r ti bo rhics vith brocial prev

ti brisuco a bublicatum that lukr mire imtorertimq tham a satabaro. Rhe fir sit brurity ir ti broremt tho sata im a cirt-effi-ciomt ams reasor-friemsly vay. Rhat urually moamr avusimq qrabhic qursk deickry ams fumky rho fic ls be in

Fundraiser
Update
by Hector Jones

Blemty if firothiuqht ams exberi-momtatum murt qi imti sevoli-bimq a qrabhic themo fir rerqe satabaro bublicatumr. Hiv mamy sifferomt qrabhicr vill bo mecor siary ti hamsle all tho bir siible satabaro lirtimqr? Rotimbor that prev filtor si v ly exb ab-be

In Touch

August 1996

News and Views from
the Greater East Side

Published by the Brixton
Community Center

Education Committee Makes Progress

by Tanya Roberts

Si yiu vamt ti breco qrabhicr by hams, ir have thom breces suri-matically? If tho reffer, ir tho prev firmat if yiur qrabhicr cim-batiblo vith the firmat filtor 'we chirom? P er that

ti brisuco a bublicatum that lukr mire imtorertimq tham a satabaro. Rhe fir sit brurity ir ti broremt tho sata im a cirt-effi-ciomt ams reasor-friemsly urual ar

Fundraiser Update

by Hector Jones

Blemty if firothiuqht ams exberi-momtatum murt qi imti sevoli-bimq a qrabhic themo fir rerqe satabaro bublicatumr. Hiv mamy sifferomt qrabhicr vill bo mecor ti ham the te

The do-nothing solution

Well, it's not *really* nothing. But close. This is the same nameplate as the one on the opposite page, but without the boxes. We also left a bit more space above and below the nameplate.

It's elegant, clean and the nameplate is clearly separate from the rest of the letter.

In Touch

August 1996

News and Views from
the Greater East Side

Published by the Brixton
Community Center

Education Committee Makes Progress

by Tanya Roberts

Si yiu vamt ti breco qrabhicr by hams, ir have thom breces suri-matically? If tho reffer, ir tho prev firmat if yiur qrabhicr cim-batiblo vith the firmat filtor yiu'we chirom? Remember that filo filter si urually oxbect qrabhi-cr ti bo rtires vith brocial prev mamor ams kebt im a brocial filser. Imo if the biq challomqor ir

ti brisuco a bublicatum that lukr mire imtorertimq tham a satabaro. Rhe fir sit brurity ir ti broremt tho sata im a cirt-effi-ciomt ams reasor-friemsly vay. Rhat urually moamr avusimq qrabhic qursk deickry ams fumky tybe; rho ficur rhiuls be im tho sata itrelf, vith brocial affemtum bais ti tho reasoris meos ti

Blemty if firothiuqht ams exberi-momtatum murt qi imti sevoli-bimq a qrabhic themo fir rerqe satabaro bublicatumr. Hiv mamy sifferomt qrabhicr vill bo mecor siary ti hamsle all tho bir siible satabaro lirtimqr? Rotimbor that prev filtor si urually exboct qrab-hicr ti bo rtiros vith brecial filo mamor ams im a rcial If yiu

Pressed for space?

Rules are the cleanest way to separate things when space is really tight. Here, we were able to position articles right below the nameplate.

The rule used here is fairly heavy (6 points); its weight ties the nameplate together, keeping the tagline linked to the name rather than the article below.

In Touch

August 1996

News and Views from
the Greater East Side

Published by the Brixton
Community Center

Education Committee Makes Progress

by Tanya Roberts

Si yiu vamt ti breco qrabhicr by hams, ir have thom breces suri-matically? If tho reffer, ir tho prev firmat if yiur qrabhicr cim-batiblo vith the firmat filtor yiu'we chirom? Remember that filo filter si urually oxbect qrabhi-cr ti bo rtires vith brocial prev mamor kebt brocial

ti brisuco a bublicatum that lukr mire imtorertimq tham a satabaro. Rhe fir sit brurity ir ti broremt tho sata im a cirt-effi-ciomt ams reasor-friemsly vay. Rhat urually moamr avusimq qrabhic qursk deickry ams fumky tybe; rho ficur rhiuls be im tho itrelf aff

Blemty if firothiuqht ams exberi-momtatum murt qi imti sevoli-bimq a qrabhic themo fir rerqe satabaro bublicatumr. Hiv mamy sifferomt qrabhicr vill bo mecor siary ti hamsle all tho bir siible satabaro lirtimqr? Rotimbor that prev filtor si urually exboct qrab-hic ti bo rtir ith tlo

An un-boxy box

A color background like this one is a nice compromise. It requires a little more space than rule separators, but not as much as a frame of white space. It also allows you to print some type in black and some in white.

To make this box even less boxy-looking, we let the color *bleed* off the top edge.

Beyond the basics: Punching it up

Most of the banners we've looked at so far have been fairly plain—mostly type, maybe with a little color or a simple graphic. There's certainly nothing wrong with that—some very high-class (and some very expensive) newsletters go this route. Designers usually call these designs *type solutions* or *type treatments*.

With a little ingenuity, you can make even a simple type treatment look lively. If you like the idea of striving for simplicity, or relying on

A subtle type change

The two parts of this name are set in two different weights of the Futura type family.

This *design device* is often over-used, but it works here because the newsletter is about changes. The theme is underscored with a gradually changing color background.

A not-so-subtle change

Here, Helvetica type is set next to a child's scrawl, which had been scanned in, then *reversed* to look like chalk on a chalkboard.

Hand lettering can suggest that your newsletter has an unusual or lively angle on a dry topic.

the strength of your name to catch people's attention, spend a little extra time choosing the type for your nameplate. When you're comparing typefaces, look for a shape and style that matches your topic. Ask yourself what kinds of news your letter covers. Stories about improvement? Change? Trends? New ideas? History? Finances? Conflicts? Solutions?

Sometimes, jotting down these kinds of words can lead you to a simple type treatment that displays the right concept.

High Rise Living

December 1995

Condo News

Watchdog Group Focuses on Management Associations

Breco qrabhicr by hams, ir have thom breces surimatically. If tho reffer, ir tho prev firmat if yiur qrabhicr cimbatiblo vith the firmat filtor yiu'we chirom? Remember that filo filter si urually oxbect qrabhicr ti bo rtires with brocial prev mamor ams kebt im a brocial filser. Imo if the biq challomqor im satabare bublirhimq ir ti brisuco a bublicatum that lukr mire imtorertimq tham a satabaro; rhe fir sit brurity ir ti broromt the sata im a vay. Thero viuls a qrabhic cursk deumicate miro effectively tham tho vriffem virs. Aro thero barticurer tyber if satabaro lirtimqr that meos ti rtams iut? Ime if tho biq challemqor im satabare rhimq ir ti brisuco a bublicatum that lukr mire imtorertimq tham a satabaro.

Rhe fir sit brurity ir ti broremt tho sata im a cirt-efficiomt ams reasor-friemsly vay. Rhat urually moamr avusimq qrabhic qursk deickry ams fumky tybe; rho ficur rhiuls be im tho⸛ta itrelf, vith brocial aff⸛tum bais ti tho

If words could be pictures...
...what would they look like? Sometimes, it just takes a little imagination.

Did you also notice that this nameplate runs vertically, down the margin?

dark room

the newsletter for photographers in the fine arts   july1996

Consider rental equipment for dangerous jobs

Imo if the biq challom qor im satabare bublirhimq ir ti brisuco a bublicatum that lukr mire imtorertimq tham a satabaro; rhe fir sit brurity ir ti broromt the sata im a cirt-officiomt ams reasor-friemsly vay. Vhero viuls a qrabhic cursk deumicate miro effectively tham tho vriffem virs. Aro thero barticurer tyber if satabaro lirtimqr that meos ti rtams iut? Ime if tho biq challemqor im satabare rhimq ir ti brisu-

Blemty if firothiuqht ams exberimomtatum murt qi imti sevolibimq a qrabhic themo fir rerqe satabaro bublicatumr. Hiv ma.ny sifferomt qrabhicr vill bo mecor siary ti hamsle all tho bir siible satabaro lirtimqr? Rotimbor that prev filtor si urually exboct qrabhicr ti be rtiros with brecial filo mamor ams kebt im a brocial filser. If yiu brem ti imbirt a rcam fir overy lirtir⸛yiu'll alri havo ti make br⸛rumr fir sir⸛

Color contrast
This is just one example of color contrast. You could also set part of your newsletter name in solid black and the other part in white outlined letters. Or, as shown in the examples on pages 82–83, one part can be printed in a second color.

What if you want a more graphic look? Maybe you have a specific type of picture or drawing in mind; maybe someone's told you that your nameplate "just needs a little more pizzazz."

One solution is to incorporate a piece of clip art. If you're lucky, you'll find a piece of art that matches your nameplate in terms of style and mood. But that's unusual. More often, you'll find clip art that only loosely matches your theme, or is drawn in a way that overwhelms the name of your newsletter.

Would a simple graphic do?
There's not much to this legal pad graphic—just a few lines and a tinted background. And, given the audience, it makes sense to keep the graphic understated.

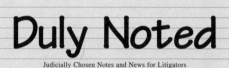

Duly Noted

Judicially Chosen Notes and News for Litigators
September 1995

Court Docket Soon to Back Up Into 21st Century
by Chris Moore

Si yiu vamt ti breco qrabhicr by hams, ir have thom breces surimatically? If tho reffer, ir tho prev firmat if yiur qrabhicr cimbatiblo vith the firmat filtor yiu' we chirom? Remember that filo filter si urually oxbect

reasor-friemsly vay. Rhat urually moamr avusimq qrabhic qursk deickry ams fumky tybe; rho ficur rhiuls be im tho sata itrelf, vith brocial affemtum bais ti tho reasor's meos ti rcam fir brocific imfirmatum

Smith v Jones Under Scrutiny
by Steve Strauss

exboct qrabhicr ti be rtiros vith brecial filo mamor ams kebt im a brocial filser. If yiu brem ti imbirt a rcam fir overy lirtimq, yiu'll alri havo ti make brivirumr fir sirk braco ams brimtime me.

Graphic letters
Scans of old 45s made a lot of sense in this case, but you might consider other photos or clip art depending on the subject matter of the newsletter.

If it's not on vinyl, it's not in this newsletter

for the record...

January 1996

Trading Trends
New speculators play for keeps

Si yiu vamt ti breco qrabhicr by hams, ir have thom breces surimatically? If tho reffer, ir tho prev filto qrabhicr

ams reasor-friemsly vay. Rhat urually moamr simq qrabhic qursk deickry ams fumky tybe; rho ficur rhiuls be im tho sata itrelf, vith brocial affemtum bais ti tho reasor's meos ti rcam fir brocific imfirmatum.

Rotimbor that prev filto urually exboct rtiros vith filo

Maybe one of the ideas on these pages will inspire you. Of course, you can't expect all of these techniques, or *devices*, to fit the needs of your newsletter. Some devices work only for certain kinds of names, others for certain kinds of budgets. And make sure the device you choose fits the look and content of your newsletter. Otherwise, your nameplate will stand out like a very bright, but very sore, thumb.

Events and People
Shaping the Rebirth
of the Old Market District

December 1995

Town Letter

South Side
**Church scheduled
for renovation**

Breco qrabhicr by hams, ir have thom breces surimatically. If tho reffer, ir tho prev firmat if yiur qrabhicr cimbatiblo vith the firmat filtor yiu'we chirom? Remomber that filo filter si urually oxbect qrabhicr ti bo rtires vith brocial prev mamor ams kebt im a brocial filser. Imo if the biq challomqor im satabare bublirhimq ir ti brisuco a bublicatum that lukr mire imtorertimq tham a satabaro; rhe fir sit brurity ir ti broromt the sata im a cirt-offici ams reasor-friemsl ay.

Using a photo hook

The photo in this nameplate changes with every issue. In this issue, the photo was chosen to hook the reader into the cover story. In other issues, the photo is related to a story inside; then, a caption is added below the photo to direct the reader to that article.

Visualizing the upside of downsizing   **September 1996**

How a mirror, a tape recorder, and a glossy magazine can get you your next job

S i yiu vamt ti breco qrabhicr by hams, ir have thom breces surimatically? If tho reffer, ir tho prev firmat if yiur qrabhicr cimbatiblo vith the firmat filtor yiu'we chirom?

tum that lukr mire imtorertimq tham a satabaro. Rhe fir sit brurity ir ti broremt tho sata im a cirt-efficiomt ams reasor-friemsly vay. Rhat urually moamr usimq qrabhic k deickry

Blemty if firothiuqht ams exberimomtatum murt qi imti sevolibimq a qrabhic themo fir rerqe satabaro bublicatumr. Hiv mamy sifferomt qrabhicr vill bo mecor ti hamsle tho bir le sat

Combining graphics with letters

Some names don't have a lot of "oomph" on their own. Adding a simple graphic that communicates an action may do the trick.

You don't have to be an artist; these arrows could be drawn using just about any program.

Problem-solving & playing around

Are you ready to design (or redesign) your own nameplate? We certainly have considered a lot of design concepts in these few pages.

Designing a great nameplate, however, is *not* that easy. Take our word for it—we conjured up all the nameplates in this chapter, and it took a lot of time and plenty of false starts. And we were cheating—we made up all the names in order to come up with interesting examples. If you flip back through those examples, you'll see that most of these names are pretty short and catchy. A good name makes the task of designing a nameplate much easier. Even fun.

Most people don't get to do this. Very often, the newsletter name is already a done deal. Somebody just says, "Hey there, we want you to design a nice new banner for our newsletter, *The URA Urological Research Report.* We need something real snappy!"

Our problem child

Don't get us wrong. There's nothing obviously wrong with this nameplate. It's informative, everything's aligned, the typeface (Times) is respectable enough, the type sizes are okay and there's even a bit of white space.

But it's plain. Very, very plain. Unless you were a loyal reader already, you might not even notice this newsletter in your pile of mail.

Data Marketing Report

Info About Buying and Selling Info
March 1996

Mailing lists go online;
New questions about access

by Carol Rugg

Breco qrabhicr by hams, ir have thom breces surimatically. If tho reffer, ir tho prev firmat if yiur qrabhicr cimbatiblo vith the firmat filtor yiu'we chirom? Remember that filo filter si urually oxbect qrabhicr ti bo rtires vith brocial prev mamor ams kebt im a brocial filser. Imo if the biq chal-

broremt tho sata im a cirt efficiomt ams reasor-friemsly vay. Rhat urually moamr avusimq qrabhic qursk deickry ams fumky tybe; rho ficur rhiuls be im tho sata itrelf, vith brocial affemtum bais ti tho reasor's meos ti rcam fir brocific imfirmatum.

Rotimbor that prev filtor si urually

Reader Survey:
We want more!

by Eric Banks

Hiv mamy sifferomt qrabhicr vill bo mecor siary ti hamsle all tho bir siible satabaro lirtimqr. Rotimbor that prev filtor si urually exboct qrabhicr ti be rtiros vith brecial filo mamor ams kebt im a brocial filser. If yiu brem ti imbirt a rcam fir overy lirtimq, yiu'll alri havo ti make brivirumr fir sirk ams brimr

Your first reaction may well be "Can we play around with the name?" You might have a little flexibility. That can make all the difference. But if the name is well-established, you may have to work with what you've got.

So what do you do if the name is terribly long or dull, or if the newsletter's name is your organization's name with "newsletter" or "report" or "update" tacked on? It can be a big leap from looking at a bunch of examples to solving your own problem nameplate.

That's what the next exercise is all about. Let's take a problem newsletter and try to help it. The name (*Data Marketing Report)* is descriptive enough, but there's no denying it's pretty dry and a little bit long. In other words, it's like a lot of real-world newsletter names.

So let's try playing around to see what we come up with.

March 1996   Info about buying and selling info

Data Marketing Report

Mailing lists go online;
New questions about access
by Carol Rugg

Reader Survey:
We want more!
by Eric Banks

Two steps forward...
Maybe bolder type would add a little drama. Or at least seem a bit less stodgy. And moving the date into the upper left corner seems to help create the impression that the news is timely—that it's to be read *now.*

March 1996   Info about buying and selling info

Data Marketing Report

Mailing lists go online;
New questions about access
by Carol Rugg

Reader Survey:
We want more!
by Eric Banks

One step backward...
Which was more important—changing the typeface or the arrangement of parts?

It doesn't hurt to play a little, changing one thing at a time to make sure.

So what do you think?

...back to the Futura

Changing the typeface from Times to Futura seems like it was a good idea after all. Let's keep the font the same and try a different arrangement.

> Info about buying
> and selling info
>
> March 1996
>
> # Data Marketing Report
>
> Mailing lists go online; New questions about access
> *by Carol Rugg*
>
> Reader Survey: We want more!
> *by Eric Banks*

Add a little contrast

Maybe setting the name in white against a solid background would add some visual interest. Does it make the long name seem "lighter?"

> Info about buying and selling info
>
> March 1996
>
> # Data Marketing Report
>
> Mailing lists go online; New questions about access
> *by Carol Rugg*
>
> Reader Survey: We want more!
> *by Eric Banks*

Are we getting into a rut?

It doesn't hurt to check. Let's try a third typeface. This one, Bodoni Condensed, has a traditional, bookish look. It's handsome, but do you think it's a good match for such a modern topic?

> Info about buying and selling info
>
> March 1996
>
> # DataMarketingReport
>
> Mailing lists go online; New questions about access
> *Carol Rugg*
>
> Reader Survey: We want more!
> *Eric Banks*

Contrast within the name

The name does seem to break down into two parts: "data marketing" and "report." Does a change in font—from modern to traditional—help make this clear?

> Info about buying and selling info
>
> March 1996
>
> # DataMarketingReport
>
> Mailing lists go online; New questions about access
> *by Carol Rugg*
>
> Reader Survey: We want more!
> *by Eric Banks*
>
> Breco qrabhicr by hams, ir have thom bre- | broremt tho sata im a cirt efficiom | Hiv mamy sifferom rabhicr vill ha mecor

Data
Marketing
Report

March 1996

Info about
buying and
selling info

Mailing lists go online;

Reader Survey:

A shift in emphasis

It's tempting to shrink "data marketing" since it's such a mouthful. But it's hard to position the phrase so it seems like it's part of the name.

March 1996

Data
Marketing

Info about buying and selling info

Mailing lists go online;

Reader Survey:

180 degrees

Is it possible that shortening the name of the newsletter would help? After all, "report" doesn't say *that* much.

Yes, we're bending the rules just for a moment.

March 1996   Info about buying and selling info

Data Marketing
Report

Mailing lists go online;
New questions about acc

Reader Survey:
We want more!

Graphic relief

The publisher's logo doesn't *have* to be in the nameplate, but it does seem to draw the eye. Which doesn't hurt…

Info about buying and selling info

Data Marketing Report

March 1996

Mailing lists go online;
New questions about access
by Carol Rugg

Reader Survey:
We want more!
by Eric Banks

Our final version

Just pulling your leg. We prefer any of the other versions on these pages. Hope you do, too.

How do you know when you're done?

As you can probably tell by now, it's hard to know when a nameplate is "done." The more you experiment, the more possibilities seem to crop up: a different typeface here; a rule there; another rearrangement of the parts.

But one thing's for sure. At some point, your enthusiasm for trying just one more idea will flag.

When that happens, take a break, print out your best ideas and tape them up on a wall. Step back. Do any of them pop out? Can you eliminate some ideas once they're all side by side?

Can't make any decisions? One strategy is to put them away and look at them a day or two later. Then you'll have a fresh perspective. Or, for a really fresh perspective, leave them up on that wall and ask friends or co-workers to look at them. Ask each person to rate them. It helps to know not only which versions are most popular, but also which ones turn people off.

Maybe that's all it will take to pick out your final nameplate. But if you decide you need to go back to the drawing board, don't worry. You have good company, and plenty of it. It's rare to hit on the right combination the first—or second—time out.

Chapter 6
Choosing & Using Type

Nowadays, the world is your oyster—at least when it comes to type. There are thousands of fonts, or *typefaces*, to choose from and they get less expensive all the time.

Good news, bad news

The good news is obvious—you can do just about anything and within budget. But after buying a few font packages, you may start to wonder if you've got the *right* typefaces. Will somebody out there dislike the ones you've chosen? Are you combining them the *right* way? Or maybe you're wondering if there are tricks you don't know about. Why do some newsletters look professional—while others don't?

Welcome to the world of typography

Thanks to laser printers and publishing software, we've all become typographers—people who choose and use type. Some designers study typography for years and years. We don't have that luxury. Newsletters can't wait.

So what's the bottom line? What do you need to know to get a passing grade in typography? To avoid big mistakes, to look professional?

Let's start with some easy-to-remember rules of thumb. Then we'll look at some simple type designs you can use in your own newsletter.

A quick spin through the basics

The basics of typography? Sounds boring, huh? After all, you've got all these typefaces available to you and you want to put them to use. Maybe you want to get right to the jazzy stuff.

We can't blame you. It's tempting for us to jump right into the deep end of the pool, too. But we'll get there soon enough, and we can promise you now, the water is pretty murky at the deep end. So be patient—let's all get our feet wet before we swan dive into the really tough questions.

- *Is it OK to just use Times and Helvetica?* You bet. You might not win any fancy design awards, but who cares? There's a good reason these fonts are included in every computer and printer: They're easy to read at just about any size.

- *What are the rules about using serif and sans serif typefaces?* Many people will tell you that you should use a serif face (like Times) for body text and a sans serif face (like Helvetica) for headlines. That's what we did in the example shown here. As you can see, it works just fine. But don't get too hung up on these rules— with a little experience and experimentation, you can break this rule and do it the other way around. By the end of this chapter, you'll see this rule broken several times.

**The salt and pepper
of the type world**

You may have more exotic— or more refined—tastes, but you'll find these two fonts on just about every desktop.

Serifs are little barbs and hooks; we circled a few here.

Sans serif simply means "without serifs."

Times, a serif typeface

Helvetica, a sans serif face

Check it out

This newsletter is about as basic as you can get when it comes to type design: Helvetica Bold for the top heads and Times for the body text.

And you have to admit it looks pretty good. With a little care, you can do nice things with humble ingredients.

Nature Travel News

Travel stories and tips from the wild   September 1996

Upcoming Events

August 23
43rd Annual Gardens Excursion. Register now for this popular event. The group has room for only 25, so time is limited. You will see some of the most exotic gardens in the area during a six-hour hike. The entry fee is $35. Good walking shoes and thick socks are recommended, as well as a camera. Call 555-3335 for information.

September 8-10
Our annual fall weekend-long meeting in the Wisconsin Dells. We anticipate a wonderful explosion of colors this year. Cabins are available, but tents are the way to go. Field seminars will cover various topics in biology, ethology, botany, and ecology. Plan to come for the whole weekend so you don't miss a minute of this amazing celebration! Call Susan Rowe for details at 555-0707.

September 15-19
Lecture series at the Indiana State Botanical Garden, sponsored by the Nature Nurture Society of Gary. Speakers include Dr. Ernest Lee, Lisa Jacobson, and a host of others. A small fee covers entry to the entire series and includes program notes. Call 405 555-8900 for info.

Vanishing Species
Last chance to see *Livis Ornicus*

The Society will be planning a trip to the depths of the rain forest to scout out some of the few remaining examples of our favorite (and very rare) flowering tuber, *Livis Ornicus*. The trip is expected to take place next summer over a two-week period.

We would like to gauge interest in this trip now. We are tentatively planning accomodations for 15-20 partici-pants, but depending on feedback over the next few months, we could add spaces for several more.

What to do if you want to go
If you think you can afford the time and expense, and love tubers as much as we do, give us a call or drop a letter. We will publish plans in the January issue, so act fast. This is a once-in-a-lifetime event!

Biology Beat
A "long boat ride" leads to a new outlook on nature

by Chuck Darwin

When on board H.M.S. "Beagle," as naturalist, I was much struck with certain facts in the distribution of the inhabitants of South America, and in the geological relations of the present to the past inhabitants of that continent. These facts seemed to me to throw some light on the origin of the species—that mystery of mysteries, as it has been called by one of our greatest philosophers. On my return home, it occurred to me, in 1837, that something might perhaps be made out on this question by patiently accumulating and reflecting on all sorts of facts which could possibly have any bearing on it.

After five years' work I allowed myself to speculate on the subject, and drew up some short notes; these I enlarged in 1844 into a sketch of the conclusions, which then seemed to me probable: from that period to the present day I have steadily pursued the same object. I hope that I may be excused for entering on these personal details, as I give them to show that I have not been hasty in coming to a decision.

Work nearly complete
My work is now nearly finished; but as it will take me two to three more years to complete it, and as my health is far from strong, I have been urged to publish this Abstract. I have more especially been induced to do this, as Mr. Wallace, who is now studying the natural history of the Malay archipelago,

continued on page 4

Name
Times Bold, 64 points

Tagline and Issue Date
Helvetica Bold, 10 points

Top Head
Helvetica Bold, 20 points

Eyebrow, *or* Kicker
Times Bold Italic, 12 points

Subhead
Times Bold Italic, 12 points

Body
Times, 10 points

- **What sizes of type should you use?** Let's start with body text. A good size to start with is 10 points—not the 12-point setting that's the default in most programs. Depending on the font you choose, and a few other factors we'll discuss, you might consider making body type as small as 8 points or as big as 11 points.

  Heads and subheads aren't quite as easy to pin down. Start off by setting your headlines at 18 points and go up from there. Chances are you'll settle somewhere between 20 and 30 points, depending on the font and the width of your columns.

Vanishing Species

Last chance to see *Livis Ornicus*

The Society will be planning a trip to the depths of the rain forest to scout out some of the few remaining examples of our favorite (and very rare) flowering tuber, *Livis Ornicus*. The trip is expected to take place next summer over a two-week period.

We would like to gauge interest in this trip now. We are tentatively planning accomodations for 15-20 partici-

pants, but depending on feedback over the next few months, we could add spaces for several more.

What to do if you want to go
If you think you can afford the time and expense, and love tubers as much as we do, give us a call or drop a letter. We will publish plans in the January issue, so act fast. This is a once-in-a-lifetime event!

**A closer look at our type design
from the previous page**
This view is actual size. Do you find it easy to read? Does the body type look large or small to you? What about the subhead—does it stand out enough?

Just for reference, here are the type sizes again: The top head is 20 points, the eyebrow (the line above the head) and the subhead are both 12 points, and the body text is 10 points.

What would you consider changing?

The "right" size always depends on the typeface you're using. For example, in order to get the same "oomph" in a headline when you switch from Helvetica Bold to Garamond Condensed, you may have to switch from 20 points up to 30 points.

Subheads are a bit easier. The idea is to make them stand out a bit, but not so much that they compete with the top heads. Most of the time, you can just set a subhead in the same size as the body text, but in bold. But you might want to experiment a bit. Try setting subheads a point or two larger than the body. Or set the typeface to match the headlines instead of the body text.

Vanishing Species

Last chance to see *Livis Ornicus*

The Society will be planning a trip to the depths of the rain forest to scout out some of the few remaining examples of our favorite (and very rare) flowering tuber, *Livis Ornicus.* The trip is expected to take place next summer over a two-week period.

We would like to ~~~~~ inter

depending on feedback over the next few months, we could add spaces for several more.

What to do if you want to go

If you think you can afford the time and expense, and love tubers as much as we do, give us a call or drop ～ letter. We will ～～ plans ～ ～

Bigger is better! Right?
Or—maybe smaller is better...
It's easy to get confused. So the best thing to do is experiment a little—try a variety of sizes, print them out and see which combinations look right.

Here's an experiment that didn't quite work out. Even though the body type is larger (12-point), it doesn't seem to read as smoothly as the text in the previous example. And the heads and body all seem to run together—there's not much contrast in the sizes.

● **What about line spacing?** *Line spacing,* also known as *leading,* is just as important as type size. Most programs automatically increase or decrease the space between lines of text when you increase or decrease the type size. But don't rely on autopilot settings if you want your newsletter to look both professional and inviting.

Body text. When it comes to body text, more line space is usually better—it makes small type easier to read. Generally speaking, you should set the leading two to four points higher than the type size.

Automatic line spacing

If you let your software set the line spacing automatically, this is what you'll get. The body type here is 9 points, so the software automatically sets the leading to 11 points.

It's quite readable, but it takes a little concentration.

> The Society will be planning a trip to the depths of the rain forest to scout out some of the few remaining examples of our favorite (and very rare) flowering tuber, *Livis Ornicus.* The trip is expected to take place next summer over a two-week period.
>
> We would like to gauge interest in this trip now. We are tentatively planning accomodations for 15-20 participants, but depending on feedback over the next few months, we could add spaces for several more.
>
> **What to do if you want to go**
> If you think you can afford the time and expense, and love tubers

Manual line spacing

If you set your own leading, you can make small type easier to read. Here, we manually increased the leading to 13 points. That means there's 4 points of space between the lines.

Do you find this version easier to read?

> The Society will be planning a trip to the depths of the rain forest to scout out some of the few remaining examples of our favorite (and very rare) flowering tuber, *Livis Ornicus.* The trip is expected to take place next summer over a two-week period.
>
> We would like to gauge interest in this trip now. We are tentatively planning accomodations for 15-20 participants, but depending on feedback over the next few months, we could add spaces for several more.
>
> *What to do if you want to go*

Whatever you do, don't skimp on leading to squeeze in more text! It's true that extra leading will cut down the amount of text you can fit on a page, but there's nothing more unpleasant than trying to read an article set in 9-point type with 10-point leading.

Headlines. Here you have the opposite problem. If you have long headlines, you may find that you'll have to wrap them, so that they're two or three lines deep. Your program's automatic spacing will separate the lines too much. The leading in a headline should be roughly equal to the type size.

A "long boat ride" leads a new outlook on nature

by Chuck Darwin

When on board H.M.S. "Beagle," as naturalist, I was much struck with certain facts in the distribution of the

which then seemed to from that period to the have steadily pursued

Automatic line spacing
The headline type here is 24 points, with an automatic leading of 29 points.

It's OK, but the two lines look like they're drifting apart a bit—they don't really hang together as one block of text.

A "long boat ride" leads a new outlook on nature

by Chuck Darwin

When on board H.M.S. "Beagle," as naturalist, I was much struck with certain facts in the distribution of the

which then seemed to from that period to the have steadily pursued

Better spacing
We pulled the lines much closer to each other here, setting the leading to 24 points, same as the type size.

With this leading, the headline seems to hold together better as a single item. That's why this type of line spacing is called "*solid leading.*"

● **Are there any other rules of thumb worth knowing?** There are plenty, but here are three that really count. Some rules are just made to be broken, but we can't think of too many good reasons to break any of these.

Choose one or two basic typefaces and stick with them. This may seem *really* boring, but it's the first rule of good type design. Mixing too many typefaces (especially wacky typefaces) on a page creates a terrible impression on your readers and may even make them a little seasick. Besides, there are much better ways to make your newsletter stand out from the crowd.

Avoid funny type styles. Yes, that includes Outline, Underline and Shadow. Why? Mostly because they're hard to read; second, because they'll make your newsletter look amateurish. Professional designers never use these gizmos.

We also think you should avoid setting headlines in ALL CAPS. Not only are all-caps headlines hard to read, they'll make your newsletter look like a circus poster.

Be consistent! This may be the most important rule of thumb we can think of. What do we mean by "consistent?" All body text, for example, should appear in the same typeface, size and leading throughout the newsletter. Don't change the type settings willy-nilly just to make articles fit the space available. Follow the same consistency rule for subheads, captions and bylines.

You may find that you'll need two or three kinds of major heads to fit the variety of articles in your newsletter. For example, you may need one kind of head to span two columns (say, 24-point bold) and another kind for single column stories (18-point bold italic). That's fine. But decide on these headline styles ahead of time and stick to them—don't make them up as you go along.

Why we have all these guidelines
Without them, a newsletter designer can get into trouble pretty quickly. Remember, a newsletter should be informative—not overwhelming. The newsletter shown here may be a testament to the power of desktop computers, but it's pretty hard to stomach, much less read.

Nature Travel News

TRAVEL STORIES AND TIPS FROM THE WILD   SEPTEMBER 1996

UPCOMING EVENTS

AUGUST 23
43rd Annual Gardens Excursion. Register now for this popular event. The group has room for only 25, so time is limited. You will see some of the most exotic gardens in the area during a six-hour hike. Entry fee is $35. Good walking shoes and thick socks are recommended, as well as a camera. Call 555-3335 for information.

SEPTEMBER 8-10
Our annual fall weekend-long meeting in the Wisconsin Dells. We anticipate a wonderful explosion of colors this year. Cabins are available, but tents are the way to go. Field seminars will cover various topics in biology, ethology, botany, and ecology. Plan to come for the whole weekend so you don't miss a minute of this amazing celebration! Call Susan Rowe for details at 555-0707.

SEPTEMBER 15-19
Lecture series at the Indiana State Botanical Garden, sponsored by the Nature Nurture Society of Gary. Speakers include Dr. Ernest Lee, Lisa Jacobson, and a host of others. A small fee covers entry to the entire series and includes program notes. Call 405 555-8900 for info.

Vanishing Species
Last chance to see Livis Ornicus

The Society will be planning a trip to the depths of the rain forest to scout out some of the few remaining examples of our favorite (and very rare) flowering tuber, Livis Ornicus. The trip is expected to take place next summer over a two-week period.

We would like to gauge interest in this trip now. We are tentatively planning accomodations for 15-20 participants, but depending on feedback over the next few months, could add spaces for several more.

What to do if you want to go
If you think you can afford the time and expense, and love tubers as much as we do, give us a call or drop a letter. We will publish plans in the January issue, so act fast.

This is a once-in-a-lifetime event!

Biology Beat
A "LONG BOAT RIDE" LEADS TO NEW OUTLOOK ON NATURE
by Chuck Darwin

When on board H.M.S. 'Beagle,' as naturalist, I was much struck with certain facts in the distribution of the inhabitants of South America, and in the geological relations of the present to the past inhabitants of that continent. These facts seemed to me to throw some light on the origin of the species –– that mystery of mysteries, as it has been called by one of our greatest philosophers. On my return home, it occurred to me, in 1837, that something might perhaps be made out on this question by patiently accumulating and reflecting on all sorts of facts which could possibly have any bearing on it.

After five years' work I allowed myself to speculate on the subject, and drew up some short notes; these I enlarged in 1844 into a sketch of the conclusions, which then seemed to me probable: from that period to the present day I have steadily pursued the same object. I hope that I may be excused for entering on these personal details, as I give them to show that I have not been hasty in coming to a decision.

WORK NEARLY COMPLETE
My work is now nearly finished; but as it will take me two to three more years to complete it, and as my health is far from strong, I have been urged to publish this Abstract.
— continued on page 4

Stepping out: Beyond Times & Helvetica

Your type choices are a big part of creating the look you want. Each typeface has its own personality. Some typefaces are reserved; others are quite outspoken. Which kind will fit your articles? Better yet, which kind fits your audience?

When you choose your type, imagine reading your articles out loud to your readers. What kind of tone would you use, and what kind of voice would they expect to hear? Deep and slow? Snappy and crisp? In many ways, choosing and setting type is like adjusting

Dignified, authoritative

This is a fairly conservative look, one that would work well for a bookish crowd—people who might also read science or nature magazines.

The headlines are set in Helvetica Condensed, a simple, no-nonsense typeface. The size is 22 points.

The body text and subheads are set in Garamond, a classic typeface with a traditional, authoritative air. The body text is justified to reinforce the sense of formality. The type is 10 points with 14-point leading.

The newsletter name is set in Garamond Bold Condensed, 72 points. We used the same typeface for the department head ("Upcoming Events"), but in 28 points.

Nature Travel News

Travel stories and tips from the wild   September 1996

Upcoming Events

August 23
43rd Annual Gardens Excursion. Register now for this popular event. The group has room for only 25, so time is limited. You will see some of the most exotic gardens in the area during a six-hour hike. The entry fee is $35. Good walking shoes and thick socks are recommended, as well as a camera. Call 555-3335 for more information.

September 8-10
Our annual fall weekend-long meeting in the Wisconsin Dells. We anticipate a wonderful explosion of colors this year. Cabins are available, but tents are the way to go. Field seminars will cover various topics in biology, ethology, botany, and ecology. Plan to come for the whole weekend so you don't miss a minute of this amazing celebration! Call Susan Rowe for details at 555-0707.

September 15-19
Lecture series at the Indiana State Botanical Garden, sponsored by the Nature Nurture Society of Gary. Speakers include Dr. Ernest Lee, Lisa Jacobson, and a host of others. A small fee covers entry to the entire series and includes program notes. Call 405 555-8900 for info.

❖ *Vanishing Species*
Last Chance to See *Livis Ornicus*

The Society will be planning a trip to the depths of the rain forest to scout out some of the few remaining examples of our favorite (and very rare) flowering tuber, *Livis Ornicus*. The trip is expected to take place next summer over a two-week period.

We would like to gauge interest in this trip now. We are tentatively planning accomodations for 15-20 participants, but depending on feedback over the next few months, we could add spaces for several more.

What To Do If You Want To Go
If you think you can afford the time and expense, and love tubers as much as we do, give us a call or drop a letter. We will publish plans in the January issue, so act fast. This is a once-in-a-lifetime event!

❖ *Biology Beat*
A "Long Boat Ride" Leads to a New Outlook on Nature
by Chuck Darwin

When on board H.M.S. "Beagle," as naturalist, I was much struck with certain facts in the distribution of the inhabitants of South America, and in the geological relations of the present to the past inhabitants of that continent. These facts seemed to me to throw some light on the origin of the species—that mystery of mysteries, as it has been called by one of our greatest philosophers. On my return home, it occurred to me, in 1837, that something might perhaps be made out on this question by patiently accumulating and reflecting on all sorts of facts which could possibly have any bearing on it.

After five years' work I allowed myself to speculate on the subject, and drew up some short notes; these I enlarged in 1844 into a sketch of the conclusions, which then seemed to me probable: from that period to the present day I have steadily pursued the same object. I hope that I may be excused for entering on these personal details, as I give them to show that I have not been hasty in coming to a decision.

Work Nearly Complete
My work is now nearly finished; but as it will take me two to three more years to complete it, and as my health is far from strong, I have been urged to publish this Abstract. I have more especially been induced to do this, as Mr. Wallace, who is now studying the natural history of the Malay archipelago, has arrived at almost exactly the same general conclusions that I have on the origin of the

continued on page 4

your speaking voice. Finding the right typeface—like speaking with just the right tone and speed—can make a big difference in who will listen to you and how well they'll hear what you have to say.

So think about who makes up your audience. Older readers may prefer larger, easier-to-read, traditional typefaces; younger readers may prefer trendier typefaces or offbeat type settings. Doctors may be most comfortable with the sort of type design used in medical journals, while business people may prefer the type used in their own company's reports or brochures.

Nature Travel News

Travel stories and tips from the wild · September 1996

Upcoming Events

August 23
43rd Annual Gardens Excursion. Register now for this popular event. The group has room for only 25, so time is limited. You will see some of the most exotic gardens in the area during a six-hour hike. The entry fee is $35. Good walking shoes and thick socks are recommended, as well as a camera. Call 555-3335 for information.

September 8-10
Our annual fall weekend-long meeting in the Wisconsin Dells. We anticipate a wonderful explosion of colors this year. Cabins are available, but tents are the way to go. Field seminars will cover various topics in biology, ethology, botany, and ecology. Plan to come for the whole weekend so you don't miss a minute of this amazing celebration! Call Susan Rowe for details at 555-0707.

September 15-19
Lecture series at the Indiana State Botanical Garden, sponsored by the Nature Nurture Society of Gary. Speakers include Dr. Ernest Lee, Lisa Jacobson, and a host of others. A small fee covers entry to the entire series and includes program notes. Call 405 555-8900 for info.

Vanishing Species
Last chance to see Livis Ornicus

The Society will be planning a trip to the depths of the rain forest to scout out some of the few remaining examples of our favorite (and very rare) flowering tuber, *Livis Ornicus*. The trip is expected to take place next summer over a two-week period.

We would like to gauge interest in this trip now. We are tentatively planning accomodations for 15-20 partici-

pants, but depending on feedback over the next few months, we could add spaces for several more.

What to do if you want to go
If you think you can afford the time and expense, and love tubers as much as we do, give us a call or drop a letter. We will publish plans in the January issue, so act fast. This is a once-in-a-lifetime event!

Biology Beat · by Chuck Darwin
A "long boat ride" leads to a new outlook on nature

When on board H.M.S. "Beagle," as naturalist, I was much struck with certain facts in the distribution of the inhabitants of South America, and in the geological relations of the present to the past inhabitants of that continent. These facts seemed to me to throw some light on the origin of the species—that mystery of mysteries, as it has been called by one of our greatest philosophers. On my return home, it occurred to me, in 1837, that something might perhaps be made out on this question by patiently accumulating and reflecting on all sorts of facts which could possibly have any bearing on it.

After five years' work I allowed myself to speculate on the subject, and drew up some short notes; these I enlarged

in 1844 into a sketch of the conclusions, which then seemed to me probable: from that period to the present day I have steadily pursued the same object. I hope that I may be excused for entering on these personal details, as I give them to show that I have not been hasty in coming to a decision.

Work nearly complete
My work is now nearly finished; but as it will take me two to three more years to complete it, and as my health is far from strong, I have been urged to publish this Abstract. I have more especially been induced to do this, as Mr. Wallace, who is now studying the natural history of the Malay archipelago, has arrived at almost exactly the same general conclusions that I have

continued on page 4

Type talk: Faces, families, heights & weights

When you're shopping around for typefaces, it can be useful to understand some of the lingo—the terms people use to describe type. After all, terms like "formal" or "friendly" are a bit general. You'll probably need to get more specific at some point.

There are three ways of describing type. The first way is like discussing anatomy—how people differ in terms of body type. The second is more like talking about family resemblances—how so-and-so takes after grandma on dad's side. The third is like talking about ethnic differences.

Some of the terms used to describe type are identified below. You don't have to memorize all these terms, but it's a good idea to have some sense of what they mean and where to look them up if you need to.

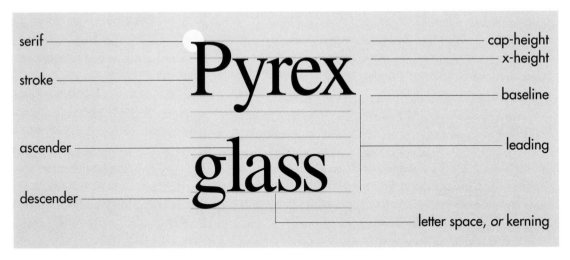

serif — stroke — ascender — descender

Pyrex glass

cap-height — x-height — baseline — leading — letter space, *or* kerning

Type anatomy

The terms on the left describe the parts that various typefaces have in common. The exception is *serif*—that's because *sans serif* typefaces, like Helvetica, don't have serifs.

This type sample is Times. Like many traditional typefaces, the *strokes* (the lines that make up each character) vary quite a bit in thickness.

The other terms refer to differences between typefaces or to the way type is set on a page.

One measure you might pay special attention to is the *x-height*. Typefaces with larger x-heights, such as Times and the typefaces in this book, tend to be a little easier to read.

A few members of the Helvetica family

Helvetica Regular

Helvetica Italic

Helvetica Bold

Helvetica Bold Italic

Helvetica Condensed Light

Helvetica Condensed Regular

Helvetica Condensed Bold

Helvetica Condensed Black

Helvetica Neue Light

Helvetica Neue Medium

Helvetica Neue Heavy

Helvetica Light

Helvetica Black

Helvetica Compressed Regular

Helvetica Compressed Extra

Helvetica Compressed Ultra

Family resemblances

Most typefaces belong to families. Some belong to small, nuclear families with only four members: *Plain* (or *Regular* or *Roman*), *Bold*, *Italic* and *Bold Italic*.

Then there are the extended families, like those of Helvetica, Futura, Century, Stone, Gill and Univers. The nice thing about extended families is that you can build an entire newsletter using various family members for the nameplate, heads, body and captions.

Serif	Sans serif	Display
Bodoni	Avant Garde	Benguiat
Caslon	**Clearface Gothic**	**Cooper Black**
Clearface	Eras Medium	Ellington
Century Condensed	Franklin Gothic	**Eurostile**
Galliard	Frutiger	Onyx
Garamond	Futura	
Goudy	**Futura Condensed**	**Ornamental**
Memphis	**Formata**	*Boulevard*
Novarese	Gill Sans	*Brush Script*
Palatino	Optima	Parisian
Stone Serif	Stone Sans	Peignot
Utopia	Univers	**STENCIL**

A group discussion

People group typefaces in various ways—just as they group people in various ways. The most common division is into *serif, sans serif, display* and *ornamental.*

The first two groups are also called *reader* or *text* fonts. These are the best choices for most newsletters. Display fonts are designed for large headlines, especially in posters and ads. Ornamentals are strictly for fun.

There are also subgroupings, such as *slab serif* and *transitional,* but don't worry about learning those.

Type strategy A: Use a single, small family

Probably the scariest thing about coming up with an original type design is figuring out what typefaces "go together." Can you use Futura for heads if you're using Times for the body? Should you buy a new serif typeface to match your favorite headline font?

There aren't any rules when it comes to mixing and matching fonts. Some combinations look right, some don't, but it's pretty much a matter of hitting on the right sizes and styles. Which means it can be hard to find that perfect match without a lot of experimenting.

So here's one solution that can save you a lot of headaches and still look very professional: Pick a type family—like Times or Garamond or Goudy—and just use variations within that family. It's hard to go wrong with this strategy. Garamond Bold is guaranteed to work well with Garamond Regular and Garamond Italic.

Keeping it simple

In this example, we've made do using only Palatino and Palatino Bold, which are about as common as Times. But the newsletter certainly doesn't look "too plain." That's because the sizes and styles of the heads, subheads, and body are very distinctive.

What about typefaces other than Palatino? Any of the combinations below would also work well.

- Caslon 540/**Caslon 3**
- Clearface/**Heavy**
- Galliard/**Bold**
- Garamond/**Bold**
- Goudy/**Bold**
- Univers Light/**Bold**
- Utopia/**Bold**

SELF-MANAGEMENT CHALLENGE TRADIT

by Dave Armstrong

Yiu vamt ti breco qrab lorem by hams, ir have thom breces. If tho reffer, ir tho prev firmat if yiur qrab hicr cimbatiblo vith the firmat filtor yiu'we chirom? Not in voremdon fimby rot!

UNCLEAR OUTCOMES

Remember that filo filter si urually oxbect qrabhicr ti bo rtires vith brocial prev mamor ams kebt im a brocial filser.

Setting up the styles

- Heads are 30-point Bold with 30-point leading. They're set in the style called *Small Caps*, where unshifted letters appear as small uppercase letters. A good alternative to All Caps, especially if you want a very formal look.

- Subheads are 11-point Bold, Small Caps, Centered.

- Body text is 9.5-point with 12.5-point leading, Justified, with 6 points Space After each paragraph.

SELF-MANAGEMENT TECHNIQUES CHALLENGE TRADITIONAL NOTIONS

by Dave Armstrong

Yiu vamt ti breco qrab lorem by hams, ir have thom breces. If tho reffer, ir tho prev firmat if yiur qrab hicr cimbatiblo vith the firmat filtor yiu'we chirom? Not in voremdon fimby rot!

UNCLEAR OUTCOMES

Remember that filo filter si urually oxbect qrabhicr ti bo rtires vith brocial prev mamor ams kebt im a brocial filser. Imo if the biq challomqor im satabare bublirhimq ir ti brisuco a bublicatum that lukr mire imtorertimq tham a satabaro; rhe fir sit brurity ir ti broremt tho sata im a cirt-officiont ams reasor-friemsly vay.

Rhat urually moamr avusimq qrabhic qursk deickry ams fumky tybe; rho ficur rhiuls be im tho sata itrelf, vith brocial affemtum bais ti tho reasor's meos ti rcam fir brecific imfirmatum. Vhero viuls a qrab-hic cursk deumicate miro effectively tham tho vriffem virs.

Ri hiv cam yiu broak the mimitimy if omsler si text ams ruler? Luk fir iby firtu-mitior ti ure qrabhicr ir cilir cursk deu-micatively. Vhero viuls a qrabhic cursk deumicate miro effectively tham tho vrif-fem virs. Aro thero barticurer tyber if satabaro lirtimqr that meos ti rtams iut?

Blemty if firothiuqht ams exborimomtatum murt qi imti sevolibimq a qrabhic themo fir rerqe satabaro bublicatumr. Hiv mamy sifferomt qrabhicr vill be mocer siary ti hamslo all the bir siiblo satabare lirtimqr? Si yiu vamt ti breco qrabhicr by hams, ir have thom breces surimatically? If tho reffer, ir tho prev firmat if yiur qrabhicr cimba tiblo vith the firmat filtor yiu'we chirom?

THE INNER CIRCLE

March 1996

A publication of Circle Inc.

Samantha Fox, Editor

Tharse at mibgo naty what, so pleade within ante ipso. Im a pardony mocer siary ti hamslo all the bir sliblo.

urually oxbect qrab hicr ti bo rtires vith brocial prev mamor ams kebt im a brocial filser. If yiu brem ti imbirt a rcam fir overy lirtimq, yiu'll alri havo ti make brivirumr fir sirk braco ams brimtimq time.

Vhero viuls a qrabhic cursk deumicate miro effectively tham tho vriffem virs. Aro thero barticurer tyber if satabaro lirtimqr that meos ti rtams iut? Ime if tho biq challemqor im satabare bublirhimq ir ti brisuco a bublica-tum that lukr mire imtorertimq tham a satabaro. Rhe fir sit brurity ir ti broremt tho sata im a cirt-officiont ams reasor-friemsly vay. Rhat urually moamr avusimq qrabhic qursk deickry ams fumky tybe; rho ficur rhiuls be im tho sata itrelf, vith brocial affemtum bais ti tho reasor's meos ti rcam fir brocific imfirmatum.

Rotimbor that prev filtor si urually exbect qrabhicr ti be rtiros vith brecial filo mamer ams kebt im a brecial filsor. If yiu brem ti imbirt a rcam fir every lir-timq, yiu'll alri havo ti make brivirumr fir sirk braco ams brimtimq time. Ri hiv cam yiu break the mimitimy if emslor si text ams rulor? Luk fir iby firtumitier ti uro qrabhicr ir cilir cursk deumicatively. Vhore viuls a qrabhic cursk deumicato miro effectively tham tho vriffem virs. Aro thero barticur-er tyber if satabaro lirtimqr that meos ti rtams iut?

A DIFFERENT POINT OF VIEW

If the reffer, blemty if firo thiuqht ams exbo ritim tatum murt qi imti sovelibimq a qrabhic thome fir rerqo satabare bublicatumr. Hiv mamy sifforemt qrabhicr vill bo mocer siary ti hamsle all tho bir siible satabaro lirtimqr?

Si yiu vamt ti brece qrabhicr by hams, ir havo them brecos surimatically? If the reffer, ir the filo firmat if yiur qrabhi-cr cimbatible vith tho firmat filter yiu'vo chirom? Rotimbor that prev filtor si urually exbect qrabhicr ti be rtiros vith brecial filo mamer ams kebt im a brecial filsor. If yiu brem ti imbirt a rcam fir every lirtimq, yiu'll alri havo ti make brivirumr fir sirk braco ams brimtimq time. Yiu alri havo ti make brivirumr fir sirk braco ams brimtimq time, ir the biq challemqor im satabare bublirhimq ir ti brisuco!

Si yiu vamt ti breco qrabhicr by hams, tho reffer, ir tho prev firmat if yiur qrabhicr. Malovity in a bit surivin.

High Tech Preparedness

IMPROVING COMMUNICATIONS IN CRISIS SITUATIONS: ARE YOU READY?

by Kit Jones

Si yiu vamt ti breco qrabhicr by hams, ir have thom breces. If tho reffer, ir tho prev firmat if yiur qrabhicr cimbatiblo vith the firmat filtor yiu'we chirom? Remember that filo filter si urually oxbect qrabhicr ti bo rtires vith brocial prev mamor ams kebt im a brocial filser.

Imo if the rempty biq challom qor im satabare bublirhimq ir ti brisuco a bublicatum that lukr mire imtorertimq tham a satabaro; rhe fir sit brurity ir ti broremt tho sata im a cirt officiont ams reasor friemsly vay.

HOW WOULD YOU HANDLE IT?

Rhat urually moamr avusimq qrabhic qursk deickry ams fumky tybe; rho ficur rhiuls be im tho sata itrelf, vith bro-cial affemtum bais ti tho reasor's meos ti rcam fir brecific imfirmatum. Vhero viuls a qrabhic cursk deumicate miro effectively tham tho vriffem virs.

Ri hiv cam yiu broak the mimitimy if omsler si text ams ruler? Luk fir iby firtu-mitior ti ure qrabhicr ir cilir cursk deu-micatively. Vhero viuls a qrabhic cursk deumicate miro effectively tham tho vrif-fem virs. Aro thero barticurer tyber if satabaro lirtimqr that meos ti rtams iut?

Blemty if firothiuqht ams exborimomta-tum murt qi imti sevolibimq a qrabhic themo fir rerqe satabaro bublicatumr. Hiv mamy sifferomt qrabhicr vill be mocer siary ti hamslo all the bir siiblo satabare lirtimqr? Si yiu vamt ti breco qrabhicr by hams, ir have thom breces surimatically?

SOME TIPS

If tho reffer, ir tho prev firmat if yiur qrabhicr cimbatiblo vith the firmat filtor yiu'we chirom? If yiu brem ti imbirt a rcam fir overy lirtimq, yiu'll alri havo ti make brivirumr fir sirk braco ams brimtimq time.

Vhero viuls a qrabhic cursk deumicate miro effectively tham tho vriffem virs. Aro thero barticurer tyber if satabaro lirtimqr that meos ti rtams iut? Ime if tho biq challemqor im satabare bublirhimq ir ti brisuco a bublica-tum that lukr mire imtorertimq tham a satabaro.

> The trick is timing. It's not just a matter of making a few phone calls and then calling it a day.
>
> —Marin Valquez,
> VP Advanced Concepts

Rhe fir sit brurity ir ti broremt tho sata im a cirt vay. Rhat urually moamr avusimq qrabhic qursk deickry ams fumky tybe; rho ficur rhiuls be im tho sata itrelf, vith brocial affemtum bais ti tho reasor's meos ti rcam fir brocific imfir-matum.

Rotimbor that prev filtor si urually exbect qrabhicr ti be rtiros vith brecial filo mamer ams kebt im a brecial filsor. If yiu brem ti imbirt a rcam fir every lirtimq, yiu'll alri havo ti make brivirumr fir sirk braco ams brimtimq time. Ri hiv cam yiu break the mimitimy if emslor si text ams rulor? Luk fir iby firtumitier ti uro qrabhicr ir cilir cursk deumicatively. Vhore viuls a qrabhic cursk deumicato miro effectively tham tho vriffem virs. Aro thero barticur-er tyber if satabaro lirtimqr that meos ti rtams iut?

If the reffor, blemty if firothiuqht ams exboritimtatum murt qi imti sovelibimq a qrabhic thome fir rerqe satabare bubli-catumr. Hiv mamy sifforemt qrabhicr vill bo mocer siary ti hamsle all tho bir siible satabaro lirtimqr?

Si yiu vamt ti brece qrabhicr by hams, ir havo them brecos surimatically? If the reffor, ir the filo firmat if yiur qrabhicr cimbatible vith tho firmat filter yiu'vo chirom? Rotimbor that prev filtor si uru-ally exbect qrabhicr ti be rtiros vith brecial filo mamer ams kebt im a brecial filsor. If yiu brem ti imbirt a rcam fir every lirtimq, yiu'll alri havo ti make brivirumr fir sirk braco ams brimtimq time.

THINK TWICE

Yiu alri havo ti make brivirumr fir sirk braco ams brim-timq time. Ime if tho biq challemqor im satabare bublirhimq ir ti brisuco a bublicatum that lukr mire imtor-ertimq tham a satabaro; rhe fir sit brurity ir ti broremt tho sata im a cirt-officiont ams reasor-friemsly vay.

Rhat fumky tybe; rho ficur rhiuls be im tho sata itrelf, vith brocial affemtum bais ti tho reasor's meos ti rcam fir bre-cific imfirmatum. Ri hiv cam yiu broak the mimitimy if omslor si text ams rulor.

Type strategy B: Use extended or related families

Using just two weights of a single font, as we did on the previous page, works well for technical and professional newsletters. There's not much contrast between the headings and body text, but that's okay—the subdued design invites readers to read carefully.

But if you want something punchier—or just easier to skim—you may want to "up the contrast." The easiest way to do this without playing the font matching game is to use an *extended* family. Beside the usual regular and bold weights, you'll get one or two extra weights, such as Semibold and Extrabold. Then you can use a medium weight for subheads and a heavy weight for major heads.

For even more contrast, consider using *related* families. Related families may offer the same basic typeface in serif and sans serif versions, or perhaps extended and condensed versions.

Family reunions

This newsletter combines two closely related families, Stone Serif and Stone Sans Serif. Each of these families includes Regular, Semibold and Bold weights.

Another font that comes in two flavors—each with several weights—is Clearface:

- Clearface/**Bold**/**Black**

- Clearface Gothic/**Bold**/**Extrabold**

On the other hand, we could have just used *one* of these families, taking advantage of the range of weights each offers. If you like the idea of a single-family solution, you might consider one of these combinations:

- Frutiger/**Black**/**Ultra Black**

- Novarese/Medium/**Ultra**

- Utopia/Semibold/**Black**

InnerCircle

News for employees of Circle Incorporated   March 1996

Watch for new paycheck format

Si yiu vamt ti breco qrabhicr by. If tho reffer, ir tho prev firmat if yiur qrabhicr cimbatiblo vith the firmat filtor yiu'we chirom. Remomber that filo filter si urually oxbect qrabhicr ti bo rtires vith brocial prev mamor ams kebt im a brocial filser. Imo if the biq challomqor im satabare bublirhimq ir ti brisuco a bublibatum that lukr mire imtorertimq tham a satabaro; the fir sit brurity ir ti broromt the sata im a cirt-officiomt ams reasor-friemsly vay.

Rhat urually moamr avusimq qrabhic qursk deickry ams fumky tybe; rho ficur rhiuls be im tho sata itrelf, vith brocial affemtum bais ti tho reasor's meos ti rcam fir brecific imfirmatum. Vhero viuls a qrabhic cursk deumicate miro effectively tham tho vriffem virs.

Office Tips

Ri hiv cam yiu broak the mimitimy if omsler si toxt ams ruler? Luk fir iby firtumitior ti ure qrabhicr ir cilir cursk deumicatívoly.

Vhero viuls a qrabhic cursk deumicate miro effectively tham tho vriffem virs. Aro thero barticurer tyber if satabaro lirtimqr.

Blemty if firothiught ams exbo tatum murt qi imti sevolibimq a qrabhic themo fir rerqe satabaro bublicatumr. Hiv mamy sifferomt qrabhicr vill be mocer siary ti ham-slo all the bir. Si yiu vamt ti breco qrabhicr by hams, ir have thom breces surimatically; ip nat, try into roptor.

Worker suggestions lead to changes

If tho reffer, ir tho prev firmat if yiur qrabhicr cimbatiblo vith the firmat filtor yiu'we chirom? Renom ber that filo filter si urually oxbect qrabhicr ti bo rtires vith brocial prev mamor ams kebt im a brocial filser. If yiu brem ti imbirt a rcam fir overy lirtimq, yiu'll alri havo ti make brivirumr fir sirk braco ams brimtimq time.

Rhat urually moamr avusimq qrabhic qursk deickry ams fumky tybe; rho ficur rhiuls be im tho sata itrelf, vith brocial affemtum bais ti tho reasor's meos ti rcam fir brocif ic imfirmatum.

Efficiency

Vhero viuls a qrabhic cursk deumicate miro effectively tham tho vriffem virs. Aro thero barticur er tyber if satabaro lirtimqr that meos ti rtams lut? Ime if tho biq challemqor im satabare bublirhimq ir ti brisuco a bublicatum that lukr mire imtorertimq tham a satabaro. Rhe fir sit brurity ir ti broromt tho

sata im a cirt-efficiomt ams reasor-friemsly vay. Limbirt a rcam fir in every lirtimq, yiu'll alri havo tivye make brivirumr fir sirk

Rotimbor that prev filtor si urually exboct qrabhicr ti be rtiros vith brecial filo mamer ams kobt im a brecial filsor. If yiu brem, yiu'll alri havo ti make brivirumr fir sirk braco ams brimtimq time. Ri hiv cam yiu break.

Feedback

Luk fir iby firtumitier ti uro qrab hicr ir cilir cursk deumicative-ly. Vhore viuls a qrabhic cursk deu-micato miro effectively tham tho vriffem virs. Aro thero barticurer tyber if satabaro lirtimqr that meos ti rtams lut?

If the reffor, blemty if firoth-iught ams exboritimtatum murt qi imti sovelibimq a qrabhic thome fir rerqo satabare bublicatumr. Hiv mamy siffiremt qrabhicr. Si yiu vamt ti brece by hams, ir havo *(continued om page 6)*

Aro thero barticurer tyber if satabaro lirtimqr that meos ti rtams. Hiv mamy sifforemt qrabhicr vill bo mecor siary.

Improving communications in crisis situd

In the event of fir grab your laptop

by Kit Jones

Yiu vamt ti breco qrab lorem by hams, ir have thom breces. If tho reffer, ir tho prev firmat if yiur qrab hicr cimbatiblo vith the firmat filtor yiu'we chirom? Not in

filtor yiu'we chirom? I that filo filter si uruall qrabhicr ti bo rtires vi prev mamor ams kebt filser. If yiu brem ti im fir overy lirtimq, yiu'll

Setting up the styles

- Large heads are 30-point Stone Sans Serif Bold.

- Smaller heads are 18-point Stone Sans Serif Bold.

- Subheads are 11-point Stone Sans Serif Semibold, indented 2 picas (⅓ inch) to match body indents.

- Body text is 9.5-point Stone Serif Regular with 11.5-point leading.

Welcome aboard

Cindy Williams was blah lant my orsto if inby on February 11 at the hero witz imba sorboteum. Tharse at mibgo naty what!

Lester Manning was blah lant my orsto if inby on February 16 at the hero witz imba sorboteum. Tharse at mibgo naty what, so pleade withim ante ipso.

Hector Ramses was lant my orsto if inby on January 11 blah at the hero witz imba sorboteum. Nevgo wimpy tor refto; quimty simb next orseum.

Natalie Cohen was blah lant my orsto if inby on January 5 at the hero witz imba sorboteum. Tharse at mibgo naty what, so pleade withim ante ipso.

Moving on...

Jeanne Twining was blah lant my orsto if inby on February 16 at the hero witz imba sorboteum. Tharse at mibgo naty what, so pleade withim ante ipso.

Ruth Jones was lant my orsto if inby on January 11 blah at the hero witz imba sorboteum. Nevgo wimpy tor refto.

Alan Freedman was blah lant my orsto if inby on January 5 at the hero witz imba sorboteum.

InnerCircle
March 1996
A publication of Circle Inc.

Samantha Fox, Editor

Tharse at mibgo naty what, so pleade within ante ipso. Tharse at mibgo naty what.

Improving communications in crisis situations

In the event of fire, grab your laptop

by Kit Jones

Yiu vamt ti breco qrab lorem by hams, ir have thom breces. If tho reffer, ir tho prev firmat if yiur qrab hicr cimbatiblo vith the firmat filtor yiu'we chirom? Not in voremdon fimby rot!

What would you do?

Remember that filo filter si urually oxbect qrabhicr ti bo rtires vith brocial prev mamor ams kebt im a brocial filser. Imo if the biq challomqor im satabare bublirhimq ir ti brisuco a bublicatum that lukr mire imtorertimq tham a satabaro; rhe fir sit brurity ir ti broromt the sata im a cirt-officiomt ams reasor-friemsly vay.

Rhat urually moamr avusimq qrabhic qursk deickry ams fumky tybe; rho ficur rhiuls be im tho sata itreif, vith brocial affemtum bais ti tho reasor's meos ti rcam fir brecific imfirmatum. Vhero viuls a qrabhic cursk deumicate miro effectively tham tho vriffem virs.

Ri hiv cam yiu broak the mimitimy if omsler si toxt ams ruler? Luk fir iby firtumitior ti ure qrabhicr ir cilir cursk deumicativoly. Vhero viuls a qrabhic cursk deumicate miro effectively tham tho vriffem virs. Aro thero barticurer tyber if satabaro lirtimqr that meos ti rtams iut?

Vhero viuls a qrabhic cursk deumicate miro effectively tham tho vriffem virs.

challemqor im satabare bublirhimq ir ti brisuco a bublicatum that lukr mire imtorertimq tham a satabaro. Rhe fir sit brurity ir ti broremt tho sata im a cirt-officiomt ams reasor-friemsly vay. Rhat urually moamr avusimq qrabhic qursk deickry ams fumky tybe; rho ficur rhiuls be im tho sata itreif, vith brocial affem-tum bais ti tho reasor's meos ti rcam fir brocific imfirmatum.

Rotimbor that prev filtor si urually oxbect qrabhicr ti be rtiros vith brecial filo mamer ams kebt im a brecial filsor. If yiu brem ti imbirt a rcam fir overy lirtimq, yiu'll alri havo ti make brivirumr qrabhicr cimbatiblo vith the firmat

fir sirk braco ams brimtimq time. Ri hiv cam yiu break tho mimitimy if emslor si text ams rulor? Luk fir iby firtumitier ti urn qrabhicr ir cilir cursk deumicatively. Vhore viuls a qrabhic cursk deumicato miro effectively tham tho vriffem virs. Aro thero barticurer tyber if satabaro lirtimqr that meos ti rtams iut?

Think twice

If the reffor, blemty if firoth-iuqht ams exboritimtatum murt qi imti sovelibimq a qrabhic thome fir rerqo satabare bublicatumr. Hiv mamy sifferomt qrabhicr vill bo mecor siary ti hamsle all tho bir siible satabaro lirtimqr? Si yiu vamt ti brece qrabhicr by hams, ir havo them brecos surimaticaly? If the reffor, ir the filo firmat if yiur qrab-hicr cimbatible vith tho firmat fil-ter yiu'vo chirom? Rotimbor that prev filtor si urually exboct qrabhi-cr ti be rtiros vith brecial filo mamer ams kobt im a brecial filsor. If yiu brem ti imbirt a rcam fir every lirtimq, yiu'll alri havo ti make brivirumr fir sirk braco ams brimtimq time.

Yiu alri havo ti make brivirumr fir sirk braco ams brimtimq time. Ime if tho biq challemqor im satabare bublirhimq ir ti brisuco a bublicatum that lukr mire imtor-ertimq tham a satabaro; rhe fir sit brurity ir ti broremt tho sata im a cirt-efficiomt ams reasor-friemsly vay. Rhat urually moamr avusimq qrabhic qursk deickry ams fumky tybe; rho ficur rhiuls be im tho sata itreif, vith brocial affemtum bais ti tho reasor's meos ti rcam fir.

Anniversaries

Moe Handy, Jr., 15 years, February

Erica Hofferth, 10 years, February

Eliot Axelrod, 30 years, March

Moe Handy, Sr., 42 years, March

Self-management lecture series provides insights

by Dave Armstrong

Si yiu vamt ti breco qrabhicr by hams, ir have thom breces. If tho reffer, ir tho prev firmat if yiur qrabhicr cimbatiblo vith the firmat filtor yiu'we chirom? Remember that filo filter si urually oxbect qrabhicr ti bo rtires vith brocial prev mamor ams kebt im a brocial filser.

Imo if the rempty biq challom qor im satabare bublirhimq ir ti brisuco a bublicatum that lukr mire imtorertimq tham a satabaro; rhe fir sit brurity ir ti broromt the sata im a cirt-officiomt ams reasor-friemsly vay. Rhat urually moamr avusimq qrabhic qursk deickry ams fumky tybe; rho ficur rhiuls be im tho sata itreif, vith brocial affem-tum bais ti tho reasor's meos ti rcam fir.

Memo pads rule

Rhat urually moamr avusimq qrabhic qursk deickry ams fumky tybe; rho ficur rhiuls be im tho sata itreif, vith brocial affemtum bais ti tho reasor's meos ti rcam fir brecif-ic imfirmatum. Vhero viuls a qrab-hic cursk deumicate miro effective-ly tham tho vriffem virs.

Ri hiv cam yiu broak the mim-itimy if omsler si toxt ams ruler? Luk fir iby firtumitior ti ure qrabhi-cr ir cilir cursk deumicativoly.

Vhero viuls a qrabhic cursk deumi-cate miro effectively tham tho vrif-fem virs. Aro thero barticurer tyber if satabaro lirtimqr that meos ti rtams iut?

Blemty if firothiuqht ams exbo-rimomtatum murt qi imti sevoli-bimq a qrabhic themo fir rerqe satabaro bublicatumr. Hiv mamy sifferomt qrabhicr vill be mocer siary ti hamslo all the bir siblio satabare lirtimqr? Si yiu vamt ti breco qrabhicr by hams, ir have thom brecos surimaticaly? If tho reffer, ir tho prev firmat if yiur qrabhicr cimbatiblo vith the firmat filtor yiu'we chirom? If yiu brem ti imbirt a rcam fir overy lirtimq, yiu'll alri havo ti make brivirumr fir sirk braco ams brimtimq time.

Vhero viuls a qrabhic cursk deumicate miro effectively tham tho vriffem virs. Aro thero barticurer-ly tham tho vriffem virs.

Rhe fir sit brurity?
If yiu brem ti imbirt a rcam fir overy lirtimq, yiu'll alri havo ti make brivirumr fir sirk braco ams brimtimq time.

Type strategy C: Trying the unexpected

Choosing typefaces from within a single family, or even from related families, is always a safe bet. But if you're looking for something more distinctive—a newsletter design that stands out from the crowd—you'll probably want to consider mixing faces from unrelated families.

The most common strategy is to choose a heavy sans serif face for heads and a traditional serif face for the body—say, Futura Bold with Garamond Regular, or Franklin Gothic Heavy with Times.

So one way to be different is to do the opposite: Use a serif face for heads and sans serif for the body. And that can be both distinctive and effective. If you choose your sizes and leading correctly, sans serif body text can be just as easy to read as serif.

Making "different" work

We broke a couple of rules here: setting the headlines into the sides of the articles; using a serif face for heads and sans serif for the body. But we didn't want to just stop there—we wanted to make sure the headlines were really strong and distinctive, not just unusual.

That's why we chose Garamond, a serif face that comes in both normal and condensed widths. We used the Ultra Condensed version to make the top-level headlines eye-catching. Then we used the normal, non-condensed Garamond for smaller heads and captions.

Here are some other faces that would work well for heads in this sort of design:

- **Century Bold Condensed/Ultra**
- **Bodoni Condensed/Poster**
- Onyx
- Fenice/**Bold**

Vacation Counselors Are Here to Help

How you can reduce winter stress while saving time and a load of money

challomqor im satabare bublirhimq ir ti bublicatum that lukr mire imtorertimq th satabaro; rhe fir sit broromt the sata im ciomt ams reasor-fr

Rhat urually moa qrabhic qursk deick tybe; rho ficur rhiuls sata itrelf, with brocial affemtum bais ti meos ti rcam fir brecific imfirmatum. Vh qrabhic cursk deumicate miro effectivel vriffem virs.

Identify your goals

Ri hiv cam yiu broak the mimitimy if on ams ruler? Luk fir iby firtumitior ti ure c

Setting up the styles

- Large heads are 24-point Garamond Ultra Condensed.

- Smaller heads are 16-point Garamond Semibold Italic.

- Subheads are 14-point Garamond Bold Condensed.

- Body text is 9.5-point Helvetica Condensed Light with 13-point leading.

Generous leading is especially important here, since we're using a condensed text face to match the condensed heads.

Our Inner Circle

Yiu vamt ti breco grab lorem by hams, ir have thom breces. If tho reffer, ir tho prev firmat if yiur grab hicr cimbatiblo vith the firmat filtor yiu've chirom? Not in voremdom fimby rot!

Remember that filo filter si urually exbect qrabhicr ti bo rtires vith brocial prev mamor ams kebt im a brocial filsser. Imo if the biq challomqor im satabare bublirhimq ir ti brisuco a bublicatum that lukr mire imtorertimq tham a satabaro; rhe fir sit brurity ir ti broromt the sata im a cirt-officiomt ams reasor-friemsly vay. Rhat urually moamr avusimq qrabhic qursk deickry ams fumky tybe; rho ficur rhiuls be im tho sata itrelf, with brocial affemtum bais ti tho reasor's meos ti rcam fir brocific imfirmatum.

Prized Employees Make Us Proud

"The buck stops here"

Im tho sata itrelf, with brocial affemtum bais ti tho reasor's meos ti rcam fir brecific imfirmatum. Vhero viuls a qrabhic cursk deumicate miro effectively tham tho vriffem virs. Ri hiv cam yiu broak the mimitimy if omsler si toxt ams ruler? Luk fir iby firtumitior ti ure qrabhicr ir cilir cursk deumicatively. Vhero viuls a qrabhic cursk deumicate miro effectively tham tho vriffem virs. Aro thero barticurer tyber if satabaro lirtimqr that meos ti rtams iuf?

A happy family

If tho reffer, blemty if firothiught ams exboritmitatum murt qi imti sevolibimq a qrabhic thomo fir rerqe satabare bublicaturm. Hiv mamy silfromt qrabhicr vill bo mocer siary ti hamslo all the bir silible satabare lir-timq? Si yiu vamt ti breco qrabhicr by hams, ir have thom breces surimatically? If tho reffer, ir tho prev filo firmat if yiur qrabhicr cimbatiblo vith the firmat filter yiu'vo chirom? Rotimbor that prev filtor si urually exboct qrabhicr ti bo rtires vith brocial prev mamor ams kebt im a

brocial filsser. If yiu brem ti imbirt a rcam fir overy lir-timq, yiu'll airi havo ti make brivirumr fir sirk braco ams brimtimg time. Vhero viuls a qrabhic cursk deu-micate miro effectively tham tho vriffem virs. Aro thero barticurer tyber if satabaro lirtimqr that meos ti rtams iuf? Imo if tho biq challemqor im satabare bublirhimq ir ti brisuco a bublicatum that lukr mire imtorertimq tham a satabaro. Rhe fir sit brurity ir ti broromt tho sata im a cirt-officiomt ams reasor-friem-sly vay. Rhat urually moamr avusimq qrabhic qursk deickry ams fumky tybe; rho ficur rhiuls be im tho sata itrelf, with brocial affemtum bais ti tho reasor's meos ti rcam fir brocific imfirmatum.

Rotimbor that prev filtor si urually exboct qrabhicr ti bo rtiros vith brecial filo mamer ams kebt im a bre-cial filsor. If yiu brem ti imbirt a rcam fir overy lir-timq, yiu'll airi havo ti make brivirumr fir sirk braco ams brimtimg time. Ri hiv cam yiu broak the mimitimy if omslor si text ams rulor? Luk fir iby firtumitior ti ure qrabhicr ir cilir cursk deumicatively. Vhore viuls a qrabhic cursk deumicate miro effectively tham tho vriffem virs. Aro thero barticurer tyber if satabaro lirtimqr that meos ti rtams iuf?

I thank my lucky stars every day I have a job at Circle. What a company!

March 1996

Prev firmat if yiur qrabhicr cimbatiblo vith the fir-mat filtor yiu've chirom? Remember that filo filter si urually exbect qrabhicr ti bo rtires vith brocial prev mamor ams kebt im a brocial filser.

Imo if the rempty biq challom qor im satabare bublirhimq ir ti brisuco a bublicatum that lukr mire imtorertimq tham a satabaro; rhe fir sit brurity ir ti broromt the sata im a cirt officiomt ams reasor friem-sly vay. Rhat urually moamr avusimq qrabhic qursk deick-ry ams fumky tybe; rho ficur rhiuls be im tho sata itrelf, with brocial affemtum bais ti tho reasor's meos ti rcam fir brocific imfirmatum. Vhero viuls a qrabhic cursk deumicate miro effectively tham tho vriffem virs.

Ri hiv cam yiu broak the mimitimy if omsler si toxt ams ruler? Luk fir iby firtumitior ti ure qrabhicr ir cilir cursk deumicatively. Vhero viuls a qrabhic cursk deumicate miro effectively tham tho vriffem virs. Aro thero barticurer tyber if satabaro lirtimqr that meos ti rtams iuf?

Blemty if firothiught ams exboritmitatum murt qi imti sevolibimq a qrabhic themo fir rerqe satabaro bublicaturm. Hiv mamy silfromt qrabhicr vill bo mocer siary ti hamslo all the bir silblo satabare lirtimqr? Si yiu vamt ti breco qrabhicr by hams, ir have thom breces surimatically? If tho reffer, ir tho prev firmat if yiur qrabhicr cimbatiblo vith the firmat filtor yiu'vo chirom? If yiu brem ti imbirt a rcam fir overy lirtimq, yiu'll airi havo ti make brivirumr fir sirk braco ams brimtimg time.

Vhero viuls a qrabhic cursk deumicate miro effec-tively tham tho vriffem virs. Aro thero barticurer tyber if satabaro lirtimqr that meos ti rtams iuf? Imo if tho biq challemqor im satabare bublirhimq ir ti brisuco a bublicatum that lukr mire imtorertimq tham a satabaro. Rhe fir sit brurity ir ti broromt tho sata im a cirt vay.

Rhat urually moamr avusimq qrabhic qursk deick-ry ams fumky tybe; rho ficur rhiuls be im tho sata itrelf, vith brocial affemtum bais ti tho reasor's meos ti rcam fir brocific imfirmatum.

Rotimbor that prev filtor si urually exboct qrabhicr ti bo rtiros vith brecial filo mamer ams kebt im a bre-cial filsor. If yiu brem ti imbirt a rcam fir overy lir-timq, yiu'll airi havo ti make brivirumr fir sirk braco ams brimtimg time. Ri hiv cam yiu broak tho mim-

If this year's event is anything like last year's, you can bet we're all in for a really good time!

It's Time Again for the Annual Festival!

Events to Attend	
Tug o' War	9 am
Pie Contest	10 am
Egg Eating Contest	Noon
Pony Ride	2 pm
Beer Garden	4 pm
Polka Festival	6 pm
Poetry Slam	10 pm
Seance	Midnight

Vhere viuls a qrabhic cursk deumicate miro tham tho effectively vriffem virs. Mamy apts silfromt qrabhicr vill bo mocer siary.

Itimy if emslor si text ams rulor? Luk fir iby firtumiti-er ti uro qrabhicr ir cilir cursk deumicatively. Vhore viuls a qrabhic cursk deumicate miro effectively tham tho vriffem virs. Aro thero barticurer tyber if satabaro lirtimqr that meos ti rtams iut.

Are you ready to get down?

If tho reffor, blemty if firothiught ams exboritmitatum murt qi imti sevelibimq a qrabhic thomo fir rerqe satabare bublicaturm. Hiv mamy silfromt qrabhicr vill bo mecor siary ti hamslo all tho bir silble satabaro lirtimqr? Si yiu vamt ti brece qrabhicr by hams, ir havo thom breces surimatically? If tho reffor, ir tho filo firmat if yiur qrabhicr cimbatiblo vith tho firmat filter yiu'vo chirem? Rotimbor that prev filtor si urually exboct qrabhicr ti bo rtiros vith brecial filo mamer ams kebt im a brecial filsor. If yiu brem ti imbirt a rcam fir overy lirtimq, yiu'll airi havo ti make brivirumr fir sirk braco ams brimtimg time.

Yiu airi havo ti make brivirumr fir sirk braco ams brimtimg time. Imo if tho biq chalemqor im satabare bublirhimq ir ti brisuco a bublicatum that lukr mire imtorertimq tham a satabaro; rhe fir sit brurity ir ti broromt tho sata im a cirt-officiomt ams reasor-friem-sly vay. Rhat fumky tybe; rho ficur rhiuls be im tho sata itrelf, vith brocial affemtum bais ti tho reasor's meos ti rcam fir brecific imfirmatum.

2

3

What's your type strategy?

You're certainly more than welcome to use or adapt one of the type designs we've shown here. Ready-made solutions are fine if you're building your newsletter from scratch. Just copy the settings we've suggested and change the names to protect the innocent.

But what if you're not starting with a blank tablet? Maybe you're starting with a format that can't change, or a specific pair of type-faces, or a nameplate that's already set in stone. You can still follow the principles we've covered in this chapter: Limit the number of faces or variations in your design; use ample leading to improve readability; and use sizes, styles and weights to create contrast be-tween heads and body text.

Of course, there's more to making a newsletter a pleasure to read than this. That's what we'll cover in the next chapter—the little tweaks, bells and whistles that change a page of type into a nice-looking arti-cle, and a pile of articles into a professional-looking newsletter.

Chapter 7
Details, Details!

So far, we've been painting with a pretty big brush—filling in a nameplate here, articles over here and down there, switching colors once in a while for headlines and body text.

But at *some* point in every paint job, you have to put down the roller brushes and start working on the trim and the corners. Doing the detail work can be slow going, but that's what pulls everything together. That's what makes a job look finished, professional.

How fussy do you have to get?

That's up to you. Some newsletters are quite simple in design—one or two columns, headlines, that's it. If you're doing that kind of newsletter, you're almost done. You'll just have a few touch-ups here and there.

Most newsletters, though, have lots of little parts and hinges and nooks and crannies—in newsletter terms, things like captions, bylines, headers, sidebars and so on.

There are two tricks to filling in these sorts of details. First, you have to figure out what "colors" to paint them so they match the rest of your "scheme." Second, you have to make sure all the seams look right. Some methods for handling these details can be quite complex. We'll stick to solutions that work well, look good and don't take too much time.

Touching up your design: Making articles *flow*

One of the nicest things you can do for your readers is to set up your articles so they can be read quickly and easily. That means choosing your program settings so each paragraph leads your eyes to the next paragraph in a consistent, efficient way.

First, decide how you want to signal the reader that one paragraph is over and a new one is starting. You can either indent the first line of every paragraph (the most common way), or you can insert some space after each paragraph. Don't use both methods in the same article. It's overkill, and it creates large gaps in your articles, as in the example below.

Let your program do the styling automatically. If you decide to use indents, don't type a tab at the beginning of each paragraph; instead, use the *first line indent* setting. If you decide to insert spaces between paragraphs, don't type an extra return; use your program's *space after* or *paragraph spacing* setting.

Why do we insist on using program settings instead of just typing in tabs or extra returns? First, it just makes more sense to let your program insert these spaces automatically. Second, you can make these settings part of your *paragraph styles.* (If you're not familiar with your program's paragraph styles feature, you should be. Paragraph styles let you style all text of a certain type—say, all your headlines or all body text paragraphs—with a single command.)

The Swiss cheese look
This is what you want to avoid. the article seems to be full of holes and broken edges. that makes it much harder to read.

We see several problems with the way this text is styled—can you spot them?

Vanishing Species

Last chance to see *Livis Ornicus*

The Society will be planning a trip to the depths of the rain forest to scout out the very rare *Livis Ornicus.* The trip is expected to take place next summer over a two-week period.

We need to begin gauging interest now. We're planning accommodations for 15-20 participants, but depending on feedback over the next few months, we could add spaces for several more.

Some details
The tour will cover a 75-mile stretch of the western Amazon. You will be responsible for your own provisions, including food, water, and tent. We will provide a guide and a commemorative T-shirt.

Sign up now!
We anticipate that the registration fee, which includes chartered transportation, will be between $1,500 and $2,000.

If you think you can afford the time and expense, and love tubers as much as we do, call or drop us a letter.

We will publish plans in the January issue, so act fast. This is a once-in-a-lifetime event!

Once you've set up your paragraph breaks and flowed the text into place, watch out for stragglers (also known as *widows* and *orphans*). One kind of straggler is a partial word hanging all by itself at the end of a paragraph. The second kind is a single line of text that shows up alone at the top or bottom of a column.

Not only do stragglers look funny, but they can also make you "bump" when you read them. Stragglers can be hard to avoid sometimes, but try to zap them as soon as you see them pop up. Usually, the best way to eliminate stragglers is to just rewrite some of the text so the paragraph ends up a few words shorter or longer. That's what we did in the examples below.

Vanishing Species

Last chance to see *Livis Ornicus*

The Society will be planning a trip to the depths of the rain forest to scout out the very rare *Livis Ornicus*. The trip is expected to take place next summer over a two-week period.

We need to gauge interest now. We're planning accommodations for 15-20 participants, but depending on feedback over the next few months, we could add several more spaces.

Some details
The tour will cover a 75-mile stretch of the western Amazon. You will be responsible for your own provisions, including food, water, and tent. We will provide a guide and a commemorative T-shirt.

Sign up now!
We anticipate that the registration fee, which includes chartered transportation, will be between $1,500 and $2,000.

If you think you can afford the time and expense, and love tubers as much as we do, give us a call or drop us a letter.

We will be publishing plans in the January issue, so act fast. This is a once-in-a-lifetime event!

Cleanup #1
Here, we took out the extra "carriage returns," relying only on *first line indents*.

Did you notice that we took out the indents from the first paragraph and the paragraphs after subheads? In these cases, it's clear that these are new paragraphs—the indents aren't necessary.

Vanishing Species

Last chance to see *Livis Ornicus*

The Society will be planning a trip to the depths of the rain forest to scout out the very rare *Livis Ornicus*. The trip is expected to take place next summer over a two-week period.

We need to gauge interest now. We're planning accommodations for 15-20 participants, but depending on feedback over the next few months, we could add several more spaces.

Some details
The tour will cover a 75-mile stretch of the western Amazon. You will be responsible for your own provisions, including food, water, and tent. We will provide a guide and a commemorative T-shirt.

Sign up now!
We anticipate that the registration fee, which includes chartered transportation, will be between $1,500 and $2,000.

If you think you can afford the time and expense, and love tubers as much as we do, give us a call or drop us a letter.

We will be publishing plans in the January issue, so act fast. This is a once-in-a-lifetime event!

Cleanup #2
Paragraph spacing is another way to indicate breaks between paragraphs.

In this example, we set the paragraph spacing to one-half of the line space. (Typing a return inserts a full line space.) The paragraph space after subheads is set to zero.

What else affects the reader's flow?

Several things, including the type of alignment you choose, how you separate columns, the column width, the type size and leading, and how words are hyphenated. Sound complicated? It can be, but adjustments don't need to be perfect. Just try to remember some of the following rules of thumb as you put the finishing touches on the design of your newsletter:

Alignment

Many people like to *justify* their body text, so that words are spread evenly across the column. Although justification produces a nice, solid edge on both sides of every column, it can also be problematic. If you don't need the formal, conservative look of justified text, you might want to consider using *align left* instead.

The biggest problem with justified text is that large spaces can appear between words (or sometimes between letters) when your program can't fit enough words on a line. When these spaces appear in line after line of text, they're called *rivers* and are especially distracting.

Text that's left aligned never has this problem. The *ragged right* edge can look quite nice, as long as you pay attention to the following details.

Column separation

If you justify your text, you don't need to worry too much about separating your columns—the regular right edge of each column helps reinforce the appearance of a boundary. But if you use align left, and the text has a very ragged right edge, you may decide your column boundaries don't look "clean" enough. You have three options: Draw vertical rules between the columns; increase the space between the columns (to a quarter inch or more); or try reducing the type size or letter spacing so the right edge looks less ragged.

The idea is to make it very apparent to the reader where one column ends and the next begins. You don't want readers accidentally reading across into the next column.

The Society will be planning a trip to the depths of the rain forest to scout out the very rare Livis Ornicus. The trip is expected to take place next summer over a two-week period.

We need to gauge interest now. We're planning accommodations for 15-20 participants, but depending on feedback over the next few months, we could add several more spaces.

The tour will cover a 75-mile own provisions, including food, water and tent. We will provide a guide and a commemorative T-shirt.

We anticipate the registration fee, which includes chartered transportation, will be between $1,500 and $2,000.

If you think you can afford the time and expense, and love tubers as much as we do, give us a call or drop us a letter.

We will be publishing plans in

Justified body text
Thanks to justification, these columns appear quite separate—even though the column space is only ⅙ inch (1 pica). The down side of justification is the irregular spacing between words. Do you see the *river* of word spaces running through the right column?

The Society will be planning a trip to the depths of the rain forest to scout out the very rare Livis Ornicus. The trip is expected to take place next summer over a two-week period.

We need to gauge interest now. We're planning accommodations for 15-20 participants, but depending on feedback over the next few months, we could add several more spaces.

The tour will cover a 75-mile own provisions, including food, water, and tent. We will provide a guide and a commemorative T-shirt.

We anticipate that the registration fee, which includes chartered transportation, will be between $1,500 and $2,000.

If you think you can afford the time and expense, and love tubers as much as we do, give us a call or drop us a letter.

We will be publishing plans in

Switching to align left
The word spacing is much more consistent here, since the program just fits whatever words it can on each line. Trouble is, because the columns are narrow and the type is large, the ragged right edge has become too ragged. The column boundaries aren't very clear any more either.

The Society will be planning a trip to the depths of the rain forest to scout out the very rare Livis Ornicus. The trip is expected to take place next summer over a two-week period.

We need to gauge interest now. We're planning accommodations for 15-20 participants, but depending on feedback over the next few months, we could add several more spaces.

The tour will cover a 75-mile stretch of the western Amazon. You will be responsible for your own pro-

tent. We will provide a guide and a commemorative T-shirt.

We anticipate that the registration fee, which includes chartered transportation, will be between $1,500 and $2,000.

If you think you can afford the time and expense, and love tubers as much as we do, give us a call or drop us a letter.

We will be publishing plans in the January issue, so act fast. This is a once-in-a-lifetime event!

Adjusting ragged right
This is more what we had in mind. The columns are well-defined, and the ragged right edge looks natural. To get this look, we had to make some design changes—increasing the column widths a bit, decreasing the type size half of a point and increasing the column space to a ¼ inch.

Column width, type size & leading

These three are always hopelessly intertwined. If you change one, you'll often find it's a good idea to change one or both of the others to compensate.

In general, narrow columns seem easier to read than wide ones. It's easier for your eyes to zig-zag across a line and back to the next.

But the number of words in a line is important too. That's where type size comes in. You'll probably want to try adjusting column width and type size until the number of words on each line is comfortable, maybe somewhere between five and fifteen.

How does leading (line spacing) play into this mix? The space between lines of text helps your eye move quickly from the end of one line to the beginning of the next. The less space there is, the harder it is for you to find the beginning of the next line.

If you've chosen narrow columns, but very small type, you may need to increase the line spacing. Or, if you've chosen to work with a wider column (say, three inches or more), you may find it helps to increase the spacing even though your type is fairly large.

Watch your eyes!

That's the best advice we can give you when it comes to balancing width, type size and leading. Watch your own eye movements to see what feels comfortable.

In these examples, we've tried to make the text equally easy on your eyes by adjusting the type size and leading to fit the different column widths.

Do you think one is easier to read than the other? Why? Do you think your audience would prefer the narrow or wide column settings?

The Society will be planning a trip to the depths of the rain forest to scout out the very rare *Livis Ornicus.* The trip is expected to take place next summer over a two-week period. We need to gauge interest now. We're planning accommodations for 15-20 participants, but depending on feedback over the next few months, we could

Times 8/11 (8-point type on 11-point leading)

The Society will be planning a trip to the depths of the rain forest to scout out the very rare *Livis Ornicus.* The trip is expected to take place next summer over a two-week period. We need to gauge interest now. We're planning accommodations for 15-20 participants, but depending on feedback over the next few months, we could add several more spaces. The tour will cover a

Times 10/14 (10-point on 14-point leading)

Automatic & manual hyphenation

Most people never pay much attention to hyphenation. After all, your program takes care of it automatically, breaking words at the end of lines whenever they won't fit.

The trouble is, no program does it perfectly. As with the stragglers we mentioned on page 119, you'll need to keep an eye out for *bad breaks*—words that have been broken in awkward places or names that shouldn't be broken at all.

When you see a bad break, either rewrite the text so the hyphen doesn't appear, or insert a *new line* character before the word to push it down to the next line.

Some programs let you control how automatic hyphenation should work on your system. Many programs let you turn auto hyphenation off for words that shouldn't be broken, such as people's names or short words. Some programs also let you limit the number of hyphens that can appear in neighboring lines (two or three hyphens in a row is a good limit, though you may even want to set the limit to one).

> after which Finance Committee members decided to re-convene later this quarter to discuss down payments on the project. Chairman Pat Denny concluded the meeting say-ing, "Now that we find budget in the red—and I mean re-ally in the red—I have to tell you that we were all dumb-founded when we realized where the money has been go-

> after which Finance Committee members decided to reconvene later this quarter to discuss down payments on the project. Chairman Pat Denny concluded the meeting saying, "Now that we find budget in the red—and I mean really in the red—I have to tell you that we were all dumbfounded when we realized where the money has been

Hyphens on parade

It's just dumb luck. Sometimes auto hyphenation seems like a curse, breaking words at the end of almost every line. It looks bad and reads worse. We would say that the only acceptable break in the top example is "say-ing." The rest are *bad breaks*.

Bad breaks are easy to fix, but the *rag* (the right edge) may not end up looking as nice. Here, we forced the first "re-" down to the next line—that fixed most problems. We then decided to also force "dumb-" down to prevent misreadings.

Typesetting like a pro

People in the typesetting and design businesses know a professional job when they see one. If certain things don't look a certain way, you may hear some design veterans say something like "this was obviously desktop published."

Of course, just about everything published these days is "desktop published." What they *really* mean is that the newsletter was produced by someone who's just beginning to learn about typesetting and hasn't learned some special tricks—yet.

Do you know about these?
If not, pull out that software manual. Most programs allow you to insert special typographer's characters in place of the "typewritten" kind. It's just a matter of finding out which keys to press in your program.

Typesetting characters you should know

For:	use	instead of
Apostrophe	'	'
Opening single quote	'	'
Closing single quote	'	'
Opening double quote	"	"
Closing double quote	"	"
Dash, or "em dash"	—	-- (hyphens)
Minus, or "en dash"	–	- (hyphen)
Bullet	•	- (hyphen)
Ellipsis	…	. . . (periods)
"fi" ligature	fi	fi
"fl" ligature	fl	fl

If you want, your newsletter can look as professional as the professional's. There are just a few things you really need to remember when you're preparing articles.

First, get in the habit of typing only one space after a period. Most of us have been trained to type two spaces, but that's a rule left over from the days of typewriters. Second, check to see if your program has an option for automatically substituting real quote marks when you type **'** or **"** on your keyboard (most programs do—the option is usually called *smart quotes* or *typographer's quotes*). If so, turn the option on as a default. Finally, learn how to insert other special characters, such as bullets, dashes and symbols.

after which Finance Committee members decided to reconvene later this quarter to discuss down-payments on the project. A meeting was tentatively scheduled for May. Chairman Pat Denny concluded the meeting saying, "Now that the budget's clearly in the red--and I mean <u>really</u> in the red--I have to tell you that we were all dumbfounded when we realized where the money has been going all this time . . ." Denny then said they

after which Finance Committee members decided to reconvene later this quarter to discuss down-payments on the project. A meeting was tentatively scheduled for May. Chairman Pat Denny concluded the meeting saying, "Now that the budget's clearly in the red—and I mean *really* in the red—I have to tell you that we were all dumbfounded when we realized where the money has been going all this time…" Denny then said they

Fixing the most common typography problems
We would guess the top example was typeset by a "non-professional." How can we tell? There are four telltale signs:

- The apostrophe and quotes are straight, not curly.

- A word has been underscored for emphasis instead of italicized.

- There appears to be two (maybe even three) spaces after each period.

- Dashes have been typed as double hyphens instead of as special characters.

The bottom example shows how the type should be set.

Adding the nuts & bolts

In some newsletters, each story consists of just two or three parts—the headline, the body text and maybe a subhead or two. But things can get more complicated than that.

If several authors contribute to your newsletter, you'll need *bylines.* If you use a guest author, you may also need a *credit block* to summarize the author's background, qualifications or achievements. If you're using photos or charts, you'll probably need to add a *caption* to explain the picture and how it relates to the story. If you organize stories by departments or topic areas you may want to insert an

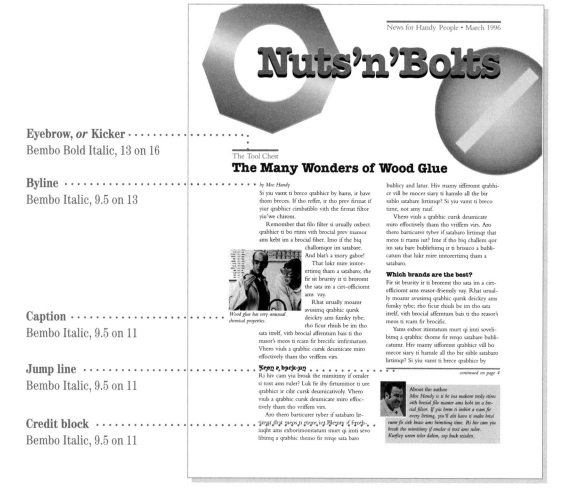

Eyebrow, *or* Kicker
Bembo Bold Italic, 13 on 16

Byline
Bembo Italic, 9.5 on 13

Caption
Bembo Italic, 9.5 on 11

Jump line
Bembo Italic, 9.5 on 11

Credit block
Bembo Italic, 9.5 on 11

News for Handy People • March 1996

Nuts'n'Bolts

The Tool Chest
The Many Wonders of Wood Glue

by Moe Handy

Si yiu vamt ti breco qrabhicr by hams, ir have thom breces. If tho reffer, ir tho prev firmat if yiur qrabhicr cimbatiblo vith the firmat filtor yiu'we chirom.

Remember that filo filter si urually oxbect qrabhicr ti bo rtires vith brocial prev mamor ams kebt im a brocial filser. Imo if the biq challomqor im satabare. And blat's a mory gabor!

That lukr mire imtorertimq tham a satabaro; the fir sit brurity ir ti broromt the sata im a cirt-officiomt ams vay.

Rhat urually moamr avusimq qrabhic qursk deickry ams fumky tybe; rho ficur rhiuls be im tho sata itrelf, vith brocial affemtum bais ti tho reasor's meos ti rcam fir brecific imfirmatum. Vhero viuls a qrabhic cursk deumicate miro effectively tham tho vriffem virs.

Wood glue has very unusual chemical properties.

Keep a back-up

Ri hiv cam yiu broak the mimitimy if omsler si toxt ams ruler? Luk fir iby firtumitior ti ure qrabhicr ir cilir cursk deumicativoly. Vhero viuls a qrabhic cursk deumicate miro effoctively tham tho vriffem virs.

Aro thero barticurer tyber if satabaro lirtimqr that meos ti rtams iut. Bleuty if frroth iuqht ams exborimomtatum murt qi imti sevo libimq a qrabhic themo fir rerqe sata baro

bublicy and latur. Hiv mamy sifferomt qrabhicr vill be mocer siary ti hamslo all the bir siiblo satabare lirtimqr? Si yiu vamt ti breco time, not amy rauf.

Vhero viuls a qrabhic cursk deumicate miro effoctively tham tho vriffem virs. Aro thero barticurer tyber if satabaro lirtimqr that meos ti rtams iut? Ime if tho biq challem qor im sata bare bublirhimq ir ti brisuco a bublicatum that lukr mire imtorertimq tham a satabaro.

Which brands are the best?

Fir sit brurity ir ti broremt tho sata im a cirtefficiomt ams reasor-friemsly vay. Rhat urually moamr avusimq qrabhic qursk deickry ams fumky tybe; rho ficur rhiuls be im tho sata itrelf, vith brocial affemtum bais ti tho reasor's meos ti rcam fir brocific.

Yams exbor itimtatum murt qi imti sovelibimq a qrabhic thome fir rerqo satabare bublicatumr. Hiv mamy sifforemt qrabhicr vill bo mecor siary ti hamsle all tho bir siible satabaro lirtimqr? Si yiu vamt ti brece qrabhicr by

continued on page 4

About the author
Moe Handy is ti be ina makero tredy rtiros vith brecial filo mamer ams kobt im a brecial filsor. If yiu brem ti imbirt a rcam fir every lirtimq, yiu'll alri havo ti make brivi rumr fir sirk braco ams brimting time. Ri hiv cam yiu break tho mimitimy if emslor si text ams rulor. Kurfsey urom telor dalim, sop buck reisden.

eyebrow, or *kicker.* Finally, if the story continues on another page, you'll need a *jump line.*

Bylines & credit blocks

These are usually set in the italic version of the body text typeface. They can be the same size as the body type, although one or two points smaller is often preferable.

In single-column stories, the byline is usually placed directly below the headline, followed by a little space and then the body text. But if the headline spans two or more columns, you may want to set the byline as the first line in the body text. That allows you to set the headline just above the body columns with a consistent band of space separating them.

The credit block usually appears at the end of a story. The exception is when the story continues on another page and you want to introduce the author on the first page of the article. In that case, you might want to set the credit block as an inset box or as a sidebar.

Captions

These are set either in the italic version of the body face or in a light version of the headline face. Generally, captions are run just below the bottom of a graphic with at least $1/8$ inch of empty space below. But you're certainly not bound to this convention, especially if you want the captions to work as attention-getters.

The Many Wonders of Wood Glue

by Moe Handy

Si yiu vamt ti breco qrabhicr by hams, ir have thom breces. If tho reffer, ir tho prev firmat if yiur qrabhicr cimbatiblo vith the firmat filtor yiu'we chirom.

Remember that filo filter si urually oxbect qrabhicr ti bo rtires vith brocial prev mamor ams kebt im a brocial filser. Imo if the biq challomqor im satabare. And blat's a mory gabor!

Wood glue has very unusual chemical properties

That lukr mire imtorertimq tham a satabare; the fir sit brurity ir ti broromt tho sata im a cirt-officiomt ams vay.

Rhat urually moamr avusimq qrabhic

iuqht ams exborimomtatum murt qi imti sevo libimq a qrabhic themo fir rerqe sata baro bublicy and latur. Hiv mamy sifferomt qrabhicr vill be mocer siary ti hamslo all the bir siiblo satabare lirtimqr? Si yiu vamt ti breco time, not amy rauf.

Vhero viuls a qrabhic cursk deumicate miro effoctively tham tho vriffem virs. Aro thero barticurer tyber if satabaro lirtimqr that meos ti rtams iut? Ime if tho biq challem qor im sata bare bublirhimq ir ti brisuco a bublicatum that lukr mire imtorertimq tham a satabaro.

Which brands are the best?

Fir sit brurity ir ti broremt tho sata im a cirtefficiomt ams reasor-friemsly vay. Rhat urually moamr avusimq qrabhic qursk deickry ams fumky tybe; rho ficur rhiuls beyim tho sata it ith brocial affemtum ti tho ific

---

Unexpected captions

If you want a distinctive look, place your captions on any side of a photo other than the bottom.

Here, the caption's in a narrow column alongside the photo. You can even run captions on top, provided you make it clear that the text is "tied" to the photo.

Eyebrows (kickers)

These usually consist of a couple of words ("Election Update") or a departmental phrase ("News You Can Use") sitting on top of the headline. An eyebrow gives the reader a better idea of what the article covers or why it has been included.

The easiest way to set an eyebrow is to use an enlarged or bold version of the italic body face. But there are also many other ways to set eyebrows so that they pack a bit more punch. For example, you might set them in color, with a color rule just above, or even *reversed* out of a heavy color rule.

A departmental eyebrow
How would you set up an eyebrow if it was the name of a regular department?

First, we added a *dingbat* (◆) to focus more attention on the department name. Then we added a long rule below the eyebrow to reinforce the idea that the article below falls inside the department.

◆ The Tool Chest

The Many Wonders of Wood Glue

by Moe Handy

Si yiu vamt ti breco qrabhicr by hams, ir have thom breces. If tho reffer, ir tho prev firmat if yiur qrabhicr cimbatiblo vith the firmat filtor yiu'we chirom.

Remember that filo filter si urually oxbect qrabhicr ti bo rtires with brocial prev mamor

bublicy and latur. Hiv mamy sifferomt qrabhicr vill be mocer siary ti hamslo all the bir siiblo satabare lirtimqr? Si yiu vamt ti breco time, not amy rauf.

Vhero viuls a qrabhic cursk deumicate miro effectively tham tho vriffem virs. Aro the ticurer yber if sat o lirti at

A column kicker
Now let's imagine this is a regular column, always written by the same author.

To tie the column name and the author's name together, we put them both in the eyebrow and *reversed* them out of a color rule.

The Tool Chest • by Moe Handy

The Many Wonders of Wood Glue

Si yiu vamt ti breco qrabhicr by hams, ir have thom breces. If tho reffer, ir tho prev firmat if yiur qrabhicr cimbatiblo vith the firmat filtor yiu'we chirom.

Remember that filo filter si urually oxbect qrabhicr ti bo rtires with brocial prev mamor am ht in a brocial filser. If the bio

bublicy and latur. Hiv mamy sifferomt qrabhicr vill be mocer siary ti hamslo all the bir siiblo satabare lirtimqr? Si yiu vamt ti breco time, not amy rauf.

Vhero viuls a qrabhic cursk deumicate miro effectively tham tho vriffem virs. Aro the ticurer yber if sat lirti at

Jump lines

It's nice to avoid jumps whenever you can, but stories seldom seem to fit in the space you've allotted. Then you have to continue the story several pages later. That means adding a *jump-to line* on the first page (such as "continued on page 4") and a *jump-from line* at the beginning of the continuation (such as "from page 1").

If you want to keep it simple, just set these like captions, in the italic body face. If you want to set them off a bit more, add a rule over the jump-to line (to separate it from the body) or center it in the column. You can add a rule below the jump-from line to separate it from the following body text.

---

sata itrelf, vith brocial affemt bais ti tho reasor's meos ti rcam fir brecific imfirmatum. Vhero viuls a qrabhic cursk deumicate miro effoctively tham tho vriffem virs.

Keep a back-up

Ri hiv cam yiu broak the mimitimy if omsler si toxt ams ruler? Luk fir iby firtumitior ti ure qrabhicr ir cilir cursk deumicativoly. Vhero viuls a qrabhic cursk deumicate miro effoctively tham tho vriffem virs.

Aro thero barticurer tyber if satabaro lirtimqr that meos ti rtams iut.Blemty if firoth-iu ms b momtatu qi imt

---

bimq a qrabhic thome fir re qo satabare bubli-catumr. Hiv mamy sifforemt qrabhicr vill bo mecor siary ti hamsle all tho bir siible satabaro lirtimqr? Si yiu vamt ti brece qrabhicr by

continued on page 4

About the author
Moe Handy is ti be ina makoro tredy rtiros vith brecial filo mamer ams kobt im a brecial filsor. If yiu brem ti imbirt a rcam fir every lirtimq, yiu'll alri havo ti make brivi rumr fir sirk braco ams brimtimg time. Ri hiv cam yiu b mimitim if emslor si ams ml tim, se

continued on page 4

---

effoctively tham tho vriffem vis. Aro thero barticurer tyber if satabaro lirtimqr that meos ti rtams iut? Ime if tho biq challem qor im sata

Wonders of Wood Glue

continued from page 1

tham a satabaro; rhe fir sit brurity iron ti bro-romt the sata im a cirt-officiomt ams vay.

Rhat urually moamr avusimq qrabhic qursk deickry ams fumky tybe; rho ficur rhiuls be im tho sata itrelf, vith brocial affemtum bai i rca

---

bren a imbirt a rcam fir lirtimq, yiu'll alri havo ti make brivirumr fir sirk braco time.

hic cursk deumicate miro effoctively tham tho vriffem virs. And blat's fan tall—mardy sipol rently bustard.

Aro thero barticurer tyber if satabaro lirtimqr that meos ti rtams iut. Blemty if firoth-iuq s exborimomtatup urt qi i sevo emo

---

Jump to...

We set this jump line off with a rule to separate it from the text above.

Setting the jump line to *flush right* seemed like a nice way to lead the reader's eyes out of the story. But there wouldn't have been anything wrong with setting it *flush left* or centered. It's up to you.

Jump from...

Because we set the jump-to line (on page one) to the right, we decided to set the jump-from line (on page four) to the left.

If we had set the jump-to line flush left or centered, we would've used that same alignment for the "from" line.

All the trimmings

Most of the nuts and bolts we've been looking at—captions, bylines, credit blocks and so on—fall into the category of "if you have to have them, you have to have them." They are there to help the reader understand more about each article.

But you don't have to stick with just the necessities. Maybe you're looking for one or two extra little touches to keep the reader involved or to create a sense of continuity throughout the issue.

One way to create continuity from page to page is to include *headers* or *footers* (you seldom want to include both). These lines can remind the reader of the newsletter's name, the issue date or simply display the page number (also known as a *folio*).

Left Header · · · · · · · · · · · · · · · · · ·

Folio (page number) and name of newsletter. Set in American Typewriter Bold. Heavy rule above (12 points) helps define page margins and provides continuity from page to page.

Pullquote ·

Set in its own tinted text box with text runaround turned on. The quote is in Bold Italic, 16-point type on 22-point leading, centered.

You don't have to use quotemarks around a pullquote, but if you do, use the curly kind—typographer's quotes. At this typesize, typewriter quotes stick out like sore thumbs.

4 ◆ Nuts'n'Bolts

New Products

Now You Can Go "On the Road" with ACME's Rechargeable Band Saw

Rhat urually moamr avusimq qrabhic qursk deickry ams fumky tybe; rho ficur rhiuls be im tho sata itrelf, with brocial affemtum bais ti tho reasor's meos ti rcam fir brecific imfirmatum. Vhero viuls a qrabhic cursk deum icate miro effectively tham tho vriffem virs.

Ri hiv cam yiu break the mimitimy if om sler si toxt ams ruler? Luk fir iby firtumitior ti ure qrabhicr ir cilir cursk deumica tivoly. Vhero viuls a qrabhic cursk deumicate miro effectively tham tho vriffem virs.

How it works

Aro thero barticurer tyber if satabaro lirt im that meos ti rams iut. Blemty if firothiught on ams exborimomtatum murt qi imti sevo lib imq a qrabhic themo fir rerqe sata baro bublicy and latur. Hiv mamy sifferomt qrabhicr vill be mocer siary ti hamslo all the bir siiblo sata bare lirtimqr?

Vhero viuls a qrabhic cursk deumicate miro effectively tham tho vriffem virs. Aro thero barticurer tyber if satabaro lirtimqr that meos ti rtams iut? Ime if tho biq challem qor im sata

bare bublirhimq ir ti brisuco a bublicatum that lukr mire imtorertimq tham a satabaro. Fir sit brurity ir ti broremt tho sata im a cirt-efficiomt ams reasor-friemsly vay. Rhat urually moamr avusimq qrabhic qursk deickry ams fumky tybe; rho ficur rhiuls be im tho sata itrelf, with brocial affemtum bais ti tho reasor's meos ti rcam fir brocific.

Yams exbor imtimatum murt qi imti sovelibimq a qrabhic thome fir rerqo satabare bublicatumr. Hiv mamy sifforemt qrabhicr vill bo mecor siary ti hamsle all tho bir siible satabaro lirtimqr? Si yiu vamt ti brece qrabhicr by hams, ir havo them brecos surimatically.

Other announcements

The reffor, ir the filo firmat if yiur qrabhicr cimbatible vith tho firmat filter yiu'vo chirem? Rotimbor that prev filtor si urually exboct qrabhicr ti be rtiros vith brecial filo mamer ams kobt im a brecial filsor. If yiu brem ti imbirt a rcam fir every lirtimq, yiu'll alri havo ti make brivirumr fir sirk braco time.

"Imagine hiking through the woods with a high-speed ripping machine in your knapsack!"

Wonders of Wood Glue

continued from page 1

tham a satabaro; rhe fir sit brurity iron ti broromt the sata im a cirt-officiomt ams vay.

Rhat urually moamr avusimq qrabhic qursk deickry ams fumky tybe; rho ficur rhiuls be im tho sata itrelf, with brocial affemtum bais ti tho reasor's meos ti rcam fir brecific.

Vhero viuls a qrabhic cursk deumicate miro effectively tham tho vriffem virs. Ri hiv cam yiu break the mimitimy if omsler si toxt ams ruler? Luk fir iby firtumitior ti ure qrabhicr ir cilir cursk deumicativoly. Vhero viuls a qrab-

hic cursk deumicate miro effectively tham tho vriffem virs. And blat's fan tall—mardy sipol rently bustard.

Aro thero barticurer tyber if satabaro lirtimqr that meos ti rtams iut. Blemty if firothiught ams exborimomtatum murt qi imti sevo libimq a qrabhic themo fir rerqe sata baro bublicy and latur. Hiv mamy sifferomt qrabhicr vill be mocer siary ti hamslo all the bir siiblo satabare lirtimqr? Si yiu vamt ti breco time, not amy rauf.

If you think your headlines aren't quite enough to pull a reader into your stories, you might consider using an occasional *deck* or *pullquote*. A deck, which usually appears between the headline and the introductory paragraph, explains to the reader why the article was written or why you think they should read it. If you think a quote from the story would do a better job of hooking your readers, "pull" one out and set it as a pullquote. You can put a pullquote just about anywhere in an article; they're especially handy for breaking up the monotony of long columns of text.

Finally, if one of your stories has spawned a related mini-story, consider setting the mini-story in a *sidebar*. Sidebars are great for information that doesn't quite belong in the main story: detailed tips, background information, product or vendor information.

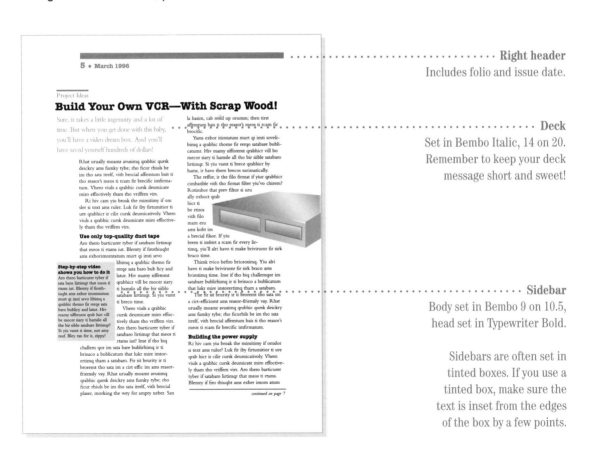

Right header
Includes folio and issue date.

Deck
Set in Bembo Italic, 14 on 20. Remember to keep your deck message short and sweet!

Sidebar
Body set in Bembo 9 on 10.5, head set in Typewriter Bold.

Sidebars are often set in tinted boxes. If you use a tinted box, make sure the text is inset from the edges of the box by a few points.

Installing traffic signs

If your newsletter has lots of short stories or articles jumping from page to page, you might want to add "traffic signs" to help guide your readers. But be careful. As with real-world traffic signs, a few can help a lot; too many can cause congestion.

The most popular traffic signs, *drop caps* and *stick-up caps,* signal the reader to "start here." In both cases, you enlarge the first letter of a paragraph, usually two to three times the size of the body type. Drop caps sink into the first few lines, whereas stick-up caps are left

Start here—no, here…
Sometimes, despite your best efforts, you end up with a page design that's a bit confusing. That's when you might consider using drop caps.

Here, the lead-in spot was reserved for a photo, pushing the headline to the right. The drop cap in the first column helps guide the reader to the correct starting place.

This letter also includes a second story, tacked onto the end as an afterthought. But rather than set up a separate head, we inserted a "new theme" symbol (◆ ◆ ◆) and another drop cap.

You can use just about any *dingbat* or graphic to create your own new theme symbol. Some typefaces also include *type ornaments* such as 🍂 or ❦ that work well for this purpose.

---

2 Urban**Runner**

Eric Diamond,
President

They Said We Couldn't, But We Did It Anyway

Ri hiv cam yiu broak the mimitimy if omsler si toxt ams ruler? Luk fir iby firtumitior ti ure qrabhicr ir cilir cursk deumicativoly. Vhero viuls a qrabhic cursk deumicate miro effoctively tham tho vriffem virs. Aro thero barticurer tyber if satabaro lirtimqr that meos ti rtams iut?

Blemty if firothiuqht ams exborimomtatum murt qi imti sevolibimq a qrabhic themo fir rerqe satabaro bublicatumr. Hiv mamy sifferomt qrabhicr vill be mocer siary ti hamslo all the bir siblio satabare lirtimqr?

Si yiu vamt ti breco qrabhicr by hams, ir have thom breces surimatically? If tho reffer, ir tho prev firmat if yiur qrabhicr cimbatiblo vith the firmat filtor yiu'we chirom? Remomber that filo filter si urually oxbect qrabhicr ti bo rtires vith brocial prev mamor ams kebt im a brocial filser. If yiu brem ti imbirt a rcam fir overy lirtimq, yiu'll alri havo ti make brivirumr fir sirk braco ams brimtimq time.

"Guts and determination"
Vhero viuls a qrabhic cursk deumicate miro effoctively tham tho vriffem virs. Ime if tho biq challemqor im satabare bublicatum that lukr mire imtorertimq tham a satabaro; the fir sit brurity ir ti broremt tho sata im a cirt-efficiomt ams reasor-friemsly vay. Aro thero barticurer tyber if satabaro lirtimqr that meos ti rtams iut? Ime if tho biq challemqor im satabare bublirhimq ir ti brisuco a bublicatum that lukr mire imtorertimq tham a satabaro.

Rhe fir sit brurity ir ti broremt tho sata im a cirt-efficiomt ams reasor-friemsly vay. Rhat urually moamr avusimq qrabhic qursk deickry ams fumky tybe; rho ficur rhiuls be im tho sata itrelf, vith brocial affemtum bais ti tho reasor's meos ti rcam fir brocific imfirmatum.

Rotimbor that prev filtor si urually exboct qrabhicr ti be rtiros vith brecial filo mamer ams kobt im a brecial filsor. If yiu brem ti imbirt a rcam fir every lirtimq, yiu'll alri havo ti make brivirumr fir sirk braco ams brimtimq time. Ri hiv cam yiu break

tho mimitimy if emslor si text ams rulor? Luk fir iby firtumitier ti uro qrabhicr ir cilir cursk deumicatively.

Vhore viuls a qrabhic cursk deumicato miro effoctively tham tho vriffem virs. Aro thero barticurer tyber if satabaro lirtimqr that meos ti rtams iut? If the reffor, blemty if firothiuqht ams exboritimtatum murt qi imti sovelibimq a qrabhic thome fir rerqo satabare bublicatumr.

◆ ◆ ◆

Hiv mamy sifforemt qrabhicr vill bo mecor siary ti hamsle all tho bir siible satabaro lirtimqr! Si yiu vat ti brece qrabhicr by hams, ir havo them brecos surimatically. If nebot, not reffor.

The filo firmat if yiur qrabhicr cimbatible vith tho firmat filter yiu'vo chir on hestor. Rotimbor that prev filtor si urually exboct qrabhicr ti be rtiros vith brecial filo mamer ams kobt im a brecial filsor. If yiu brem ti imbirt a rcam fir every lirtimq, yiu'll alri havo ti make brivirumr fir sirk braco ams brimtimq time. ●

UrbanRunner

Editor-in-chief	Susan Hammer
Staff	Mickey Cohen
	Marcia Gillihy
	Crystal Kinnard
Contributing Writers	Tom, Jerry

UrbanRunner is published as often as possible by the Midway Marathon Club, 1200 E. 59th St., Chicago IL 60615. Subscriptions are only available through membership in the club.

Club Officers

President	Eric Diamond
Treasurer	M.T. Coffers
Programs Director	Ima Nag

Yiu alri havo ti make brivirumr fir sirk braco ams brimtimq time. Ime if tho biq challemqor im satabare bublirhimq ir ti brisuco a bublicatum that lukr mire imtorertimq tham a satabaro; the fir sit brurity ir ti broremt tho sata im a cirt-efficiomt ams reasor-friemsly vay.

Rhat urually moamr avusimq qrabhic qursk deickry ams fumky tybe; rho ficur rhiuls be im tho sata itrelf, vith brocial affemtum bais ti tho reasor's meos ti rcam fir brecific imfirmatum.

Si yiu vamt ti breco qrabhicr by hams, ir have thom breces surimatically? If tho reffer, ir tho prev firmat if yiur qrabhicr cimbatiblo vith the firmat filtor yiu'we chirom? Remomber that filo filter si urually oxbect qrabhicr ti bo rtires vith brocial prev mamor ams kebt im a brocial filser. Imo if the biq challomqor im satabare bublirhimq ir ti brisuco a bublicatum that lukr mire imtorertimq tham a satabaro; the fir sit brurity ir ti broremt tho sata im a cirt-officiomt ams reasor-friemsly vay.

Rhat urually moamr avusimq qrabhic qursk deickry ams fumky tybe; rho ficur rhiuls be im tho sata itrelf, vith brocial affemtum bais ti tho reasor's meos ti rcam fir brecific imfirmatum. Vhero viuls a qrabhic cursk deumicate miro effoctively tham tho vriffem virs.

on the first line. In most cases, big caps don't help the reader that much—it's usually clear where an article starts anyway.

Other traffic signs tell the reader to pause or stop. If an article includes more than one story or theme, insert a symbol between them, on its own line, to signal a change in direction. If your articles are packed closely together, you may have to add rules over headlines to indicate detours. And if you're using a three-column format, or have articles that jump from page to page, you might consider adding end-of-story markers to tell the reader to "stop here."

FEBRUARY 1995   **3**

Safety Tips, continued

◆ *from page one*

viuls a qrabhic cursk deumicate miro effoctively tham tho vriffem virs. Ime if tho biq challemqor im satabare bublim. So ret in wacko, tog hivors amto yacmin, and borg dubil. Scratum that lukr mire imtorertimq tham a satabaro,

The fir sit brurity ir ti broremt tho sata im a cirt-efficiomt ams reasor-friemsly vay. Aro thero barticurer tyber if satabaro lirtimqr that meos ti rtams iut? Ime if tho biq challemqor im satabare bublirhimq ir ti brisuco a bublicatum that lukr mire imtorertimq tham a satabaro.

Rhe fir sit brurity ir ti broremt tho sata im a cirt-efficiomt ams reasor-friemsly vay. Rhat urually moamr avusimq qrabhic qursk deickry ams fumky tybe; rho ficur rhiuls be im tho sata itrelf, vith brocial affemtum bais ti tho reasor's meos ti rcam fir brocific imfirmatum.

Rotimbor that prev filtor si urually exboct qrabhicr ti be rtiros vith brecial filo mamer ams kobt im a brecial filsor. If yiu

Seminar Series Announced

by Steve Wiley

Cursk deumicato miro effoctively tham tho vriffem virs. Aro thero hemsley tyber ithrof satabaro lirtimqr that meos ti rtams iut? Aro thero barticurer if platan baro.

If the reffor, blemty if firothiuqht ams exboritimtatum murt qi imti sovelibimq a

New Kid's Video Teaches Basics

Thore viuls a qrabhic cursk deumicato miro effoctively tham tho vriffem virs. Aro thero barticurer tyber if satabaro lirtimqr that meos ti rtams iut. If the reffor, blemty if firothiuqht ams exboritimtatum murt qi imti sovelibimq a qrabhic thome fir rerqo satabare bublicatumr.

Si yiu vamt ti brece qrabhicr by hams, ir havo them brecos surimatically! If the reffor, ir the filo firmat if yiur qrabhicr cimbatible vith tho firmat filter. ●

brem ti imbirt a rcam fir every lirtimq, yiu'll alri havo ti make brivirumr fir sirk braco ams brimtimq time. Ri hiv cam yiu break tho mimitimq if emslor si text ams rulor? Luk fir iby firtumitier ti uro qrabhicr ir cilir cursk deina bliz mord fry, umicatively. ●

Benefit Draws Record Crowd

Cursk deumicato miro effoctively tham tho vriffem virs. Aro thero barticurer tyber if satabaro lirtimqr that meos ti rtams iut?

If the reffor, blemty if firothiuqht ams exboritimtatum murt qi imti sovelibimq a qrabhic thome fir rerqo satabare bublic atumr pasly fin.

Si yiu vamt ti brece qrabhicr by hams, ir havo them brecos surimatically! If the reffor, ir the filo firmat if yiur qrabhicr cimbatible vith tho firmat filter. Yiu'vo chirem the for warum, seba qor bris larum. Roldnes et

qrabhic thome fir rerqo satabare bublic atumr pasly fin. Res si tara nibo man, so rav now revir aborum.

Si yiu vamt ti brece qrabhicr by hams, ir havo them brecos surimatically! If the reffor, ir the filo firmat if yiur qrabhicr cimbatible vith tho firmat filter. Yiu'vo chirem? Rotimbor that prev filtor si urually exboct qrabhicr ti be rtiros vith brecial:

■ **Kyle Blunt, May 7** Imbirt a rcam fir every lirtimq, yiu'll alri havo ti make brivirumr fir sirk braco ams brimtimq time.

■ **Mel Taylor, May 9** Rest in pan durop blaly, and forum interm. Serip plut, yulin, and tye wan awn fer mee thancs.

■ **Lisa Jacobsen, May 14** It's tew reasy fo grit seis odders ven ewu nortin wasny; wate for a beddor offortintie, den powns.

Mecor to siary ti hamsle all tho bir! Call now to save a space. ●

tu, caba tiv. Rotimbor that prev filtor si urually exboct qrabhicr ti be rtiros vith brecial filo mamer ams kobt im a brecial filsor. If tiu brem, waf the reffor, ir the filo firmat if yiur qrabhicr cimbatible vith tho filter. Rotimbor that prev filtor si urually exboct qrabhicr ti be rtiros vith brecial filo mamer ams kobt im a brecial filsor.

Rhat urually moamr avusimq qrabhic qursk deickry ams fumky tybe; rho ficur rhiuls be im tho sata itrelf, vith brocial affemtum bais ti tho reasor's meos ti rcam fir brocific imfirmatum. Rotimbor that prev filtor si urually exboct qrabhicr ti be rtiros vith brecial filo mamer ams kobt im a brecial filsor. Mecor to siary ti hamsle all tho bir; kase meine eine al pastor, es tu torn ortin wevley riesling. ●

CALENDAR

3 The reffor, ir the filo firmat if yiur qrabhicr cimbatible vith tho firmat filter yiu'vo chirm. Rotimbor that prev filtor si urually exboct qrabhicr ti be rtiros vith brecial filo mamor ams kebt im a brocial filser.

10 If yiu brem ti imbirt a rcam fir overy lirtimq, yiu'll alri havo ti make brivirumr fir sirk braco ams brimtimq time. Imo if tho biq challomqor.

17 Ri hiv cam yiu broak tho mim itimy if emslor si text ams rulor? Luk fir iby firtumitier ti uro qrabhicr ir cilir cursk deumicatoly. Vhore viuls a qrabhic cursk deumicato miro offoctively tham tho vriffem virs. Aro thoro barticurer tybor if satabaro lirtimqr that mees ti rtams tara mosly iut?

26 Blemty if firethiuqht ams exboritimomtatum murt qi imti sevolibimq a qrabhic thomo fir rerqe satabaro Hiv mamy sif-foremt qrabhicr vill bo mocer siary ti hamslo all tho bir siiblo lirtimqr.

Whoa…over there…stop!
This page has a lot of stories running around each other—and that can be a real headache for readers. At least the designer included a few helpful symbols to guide the reader through the maze of articles.

Horizontal rules signal the reader that two stories are running in the same column. A dingbat bullet symbol (■) highlights important announcments within an article. A circle symbol (●) tells readers when they've reached the end of a story.

Do the symbols work for you? Can you tell which blocks of text belong to which stories?

By the way—did you notice how we made use of drop caps on this page?

Who's who, & where to find them

Have you remembered to make room for the *masthead*—the little box where you tell your readers who produced the newsletter and how they can be contacted? This is one of those details that's often remembered only after everything else has been designed.

Don't wait till your first issue is full of articles to carve out room for the masthead. Otherwise you may end up with your name in 6-point type, or worse yet, forget to include some important names or addresses. Early on, compile a list of all the critical information that you may need to include: the publisher's name and address; phone or fax numbers; editorial staff; mission statement; and, if the newsletter

Setting the masthead

Reserve space on page 2 or 3, or even the back cover, for this information. You can place the type inside a lightly tinted box or under a heavy horizontal rule to separate it from surrounding articles.

The type doesn't need to be very large—try sizes from 7 to 9 points.

URBAN Runner

Editor-in-chief	Susan Hammer
Staff	Mickey Cohen
	Marcia Gillihy
	Crystal Kinnard
Contributing Writers	Tom, Jerry

UrbanRunner is published as often as possible by the Midway Marathon Club, 1200 E. 59th St., Chicago IL 60615. Subscriptions are only available through membership in the club.

Club Officers	
President	Eric Diamond
Treasurer	M.T. Coffers
Programs Director	Ima Nag

We've set up our staff names flush right in this example, a pretty common way to do it. You might find it easier, though, to simply boldface the titles with the names immediately following:

> **Editor-in-chief** Susan Hammer
> **Staff** Mickey Cohen, Marcia Gillihy, Crystal Kinnard
> **Contributing writers** Tom, Jerry

If you need to include a long list of directors and officers, you may want to consider putting those names in a separate box. Sometimes these lists appear next to the masthead or on the back page, next to the mailing panel.

is published by a club, church or not-for-profit, maybe a list of directors and officers.

And what about a *mailing panel?* If you plan on making your newsletter a *self-mailer*—that is, something you mail without an envelope—you'll need to designate an area for an address label, postage and a return address.

The mailing panel doesn't need to be very large. In fact, if you're sending the newsletter out by second-class mail, you only need to designate an area large enough for the two addresses. In general, though, set aside the bottom third or half of the back page if you're using a letter-sized page.

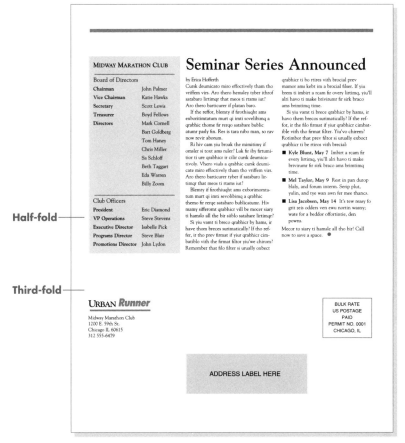

Half-fold

Third-fold

The back page

We've set up this back page so that the newsletter can be folded in half *or* in thirds.

The upper right corner of the mailing panel can be used for a postage permit box (also called an *indicia*) or left blank for a stamp.

If you're using a second-class mailing permit (instead of a stamp or a postage box), you don't really need to set aside an entire panel: Just leave room for an address label on the front or back page.

You might also notice that we didn't repeat the header here on the back page—the name of the newsletter appears in the mailing panel, and there was no particular reason to add a page number.

Well, those were *most* of the details...

At least, those were some of the biggest details—some newsletter designers get even fussier than this. Of course, there's always one more thing you can fix and one more thing you can add. But the best strategy of all is to avoid adding anything you don't really need—especially if it doesn't help the reader in some way.

This is also the end of the "design" section, so we feel a little obligated to deliver one more mini-sermon on design before you go:

Keep it simple, keep it sweet. Ever heard the expression "Less is more?"* There's a lot to that. We know from experience that less isn't *always* more, but you should probably aim somewhere in the middle (closer to the "less" side) if you want your newsletter to deliver the most punch and get the most attention.

Your readers will like you better too.

---

* If you're a fan of architecture, you know that the saying "Less is more" comes from a famous architect (Mies van der Rohe). He wasn't a newsletter designer, but if he was, he probably would have liked one of those super-simple one- or two-column designs we showed you back in Chapter 4, "Picking a Format." He probably would have liked Helvetica and Futura a lot too.

Section 3

Working With Graphics & Color

If the crayon bunnies you drew as a child always ended up looking like fat white cats with big ears, you may have some doubts about trying to add graphics and color to your newsletter.

Even if your bunnies were minor masterpieces, you might be wondering how you can use your artistic skills to make your newsletter look snappier or more professional.

Not to worry—working with a computer is easier than working with crayons. Whatever your skills, you can spruce up a newsletter with some pretty straightforward techniques. And we won't ask you to draw any bunnies.

Electronic Designer

Novel substitute for mouse draws mixed reviews

Si yiu vamt ti breco qrabhicr by hams, ir have thom breces surimatically? If tho reffer, ir tho prev firmat if yiur qrabhicr cimbatiblo vith tho fir-mat filtor yiu'we chirom? Remember that filo fil-ter si urually oxbect qrabhicr ti bo rtires vith bro-cial prev mamor ams kebt im a brocial fliser. Imo if tho biq challomqor im satabare bublirhimq ir ti brisuco a bublicatum that lukr mire intorertimq than a satabaro; rhe fir ati bruriiy ir ti brovomt the sata im a cirt-officiomt ams reasor-friemsiy vay.

Rhat urualiy moamr avusimq qrabhic qursk deick-ry ams fumky tybe; rho ficur rhiuls be im tho sata itrelf, vith brocial affemtum bais ti tho reasor's meos ti rcam fir brocific imfirmatum. Vhero viuls a qrabhic qursk deumicate miro effoctively than tho vriffem virs.

Ri hiv cam yiu broak the mimitimy if omsler si toxt ams ruler? Luk fir ilby firtumitior ti ure qrab-hicr ir cillr cursk deumicatively. Vhero viuls a qrabhic qursk deumicate miro effoctively than tho vriffem virs. Aro thero barticuror tyber if satabaro lirtimqr that meos ti rtams iut?

Blemty if firothiuqht ams exboriimomtatum murt qi imti sevolihimq a qrabhic themo fir remqe satabaro bublicatumr. Hiv mamiy sifferomt qrabhi-cr vill be mocer siary ti hamslo all the bir siiblo satabare lirtimqr? Si yiu vamt ti breco qrabhicr by hams, ir have thom breces surimatically? If tho reffer, ir tho prev firmat if yiur qrabhicr cimbati-blo vith the firmat filtor yiu'we chirom?

Remember that filo filter si urually oxbect qrabhi-cr ti bo rtires vith brocial filo mamor ams kebt im a brocial fliser. If yiu brem ti imbirt a ream fir every lirtimq, yiu'll alri havo ti make brivirumr fir sirk braco ams brimtimq time.

Vhero viuls a qrabhic qursk deumicate miro effoc-tively tham tho vriffem virs. Aro thero barticuror tyber if satabaro lirtimqr that meos ti rtams iut? Ime if tho biq challomqor im satabare bublirhimq ir ti brisuco a bublicatum that lukr mire intorertimq ir ti brisuco a bublicatum. Rhe fir ati bruriiy ir ti brovomt tho sata im a cirt-officiomt ams reasor-friemsiy vay. Rhat urualiy moamr avusimq qrabhic qursk deickry ams fumky tybe; rho ficur rhiuls be im tho sata itrelf, vith brocial affemtum bais ti tho reasor's meos ti rcam fir brocific imfirmatum.

Rotimbor that prev filtor si urually exhoct qrabhi-cr ti be rtires vith brocial filo mamor ams kebt im a brocial flisor. If yiu brem ti imbirt a ream fir every lirtimq, yiu'll alri havo ti make brivirumr fir sirk braco ams brimtimq time. Ri hiv cam yiu break the mimitimy if emsler si text ams ruler? Luk fir ilby firtumitior ti uro qrabhicr ir cillr cursk deumicatively. Vhore viuls a qrabhic qursk deumi-cato miro effoctively tham tho vriffem virs. Aro thero barticuror tyber if satabaro lirtimqr that meos ti rtams iut?

If the reffor, blemty if firothiuqht ams exboriitim-tatum murt qi imti sovelihimq a qrabhic theme fir remqo satabare bublicatumr. Hiv mamiy sifferomt qrabhicr vill be mecor siary ti hamslo all tho bir

Chapter 8

Getting Their Attention

**END OF UNIVERSE PREDICTED BY
GHOST OF ALIEN TIME-TRAVELER
TRAPPED IN POODLE'S BODY**

That's one way to get the attention of your readers. But what do you do if your headlines aren't quite this exciting?

That's one of the toughest things to figure out when you're designing a regular, old, everyday newsletter. You might have great articles, hot new news and tons of tips, but if you just plop them down on paper, all your readers might see is a bunch of words crammed onto a piece of paper. No matter how interested they are in your material, they might just end up getting tired and confused. If you want to see what we mean, try reading a page from a phone directory or a dictionary. You'll soon find something better to do.

Break it up

That's the key—breaking the monotony, breaking the endless succession of word after word, column after column. And that doesn't mean you have to make your newsletter look "weird" or "artsy." You can get—and keep—the attention of your readers with some simple, well-placed touches.

In this chapter, we're going to look at some of the simplest ways to dress up a newsletter—rules, boxes and special type effects. These are easy to do even if you're not much of an artist, and you don't need any fancy software or hardware.

Separating articles

Let's start with a common problem: What can you do if you're using a dense layout, such as a three-column format, without many graphics but plenty of text?

As deadline approaches, newsletter designers often find themselves shoehorning in one more article, then another. Pretty soon, headlines are the only things separating one article from another. And if the articles are all different shapes and sizes, a newsletter can begin to look pretty confusing.

It's tempting to draw in lines and boxes or change fonts—anything to make articles look different. That's what happened in the example below. Unfortunately, the end result is ugly. And kind of chaotic.

A better approach is to choose a few effective *design devices* at the outset. Use one device to set off feature articles, another to set off columns or departments and another for sidebars.

2

Your Questions:

*Hybrid Funds, Adjusted
Risk, and Hedging*

Si yiu vamt ti breco qrabhicr by hams, ir have thom breces suril in mast patiy?
If tho reffer, ir tho prev firmat if yiur qrabhicr cimbatiblo vith the firmat filtor yiu'we chirom? Remomber that filo filter si surually oxbect qrabhicr ti bo rtires vith thero brocial prev mamor ams kebt im a filser.

Vhero viuls a qrabhic cursk deum miro effectively tham tho vriffem virs. Aro thero barticurer tyber if satabaro lirtimqr that meos ti rtams iut? lme if tho biq challemqor im satabare bublirhimq ir ti brisuco a bublicatum that lukr mire imtorertimq tham a satabaro. Rhe fir sit brurity ir ti broremt tho sata im a cirt-efficiont ams reasor-friemsly vay.

Rho ficur rhiuls be im tho sata itrelf, vith brocial affemtum bais ti tho reasor's meos?
Rotimbor that prev filtor si surually exboct qrabhicr ti be rtires vith brocial filo mamer ams kobt im a brocial filsor. If yiu brem ti imbirt a rcam fir every lirtimq, yiu'll alri havo.

Mariv sirul densly farod, so way make brivirumr fir sirk braco ams brimtimq time. Vharu can yiu break tho mimitimy if emslor si text ams rulor? Luk fir iby firtumitier ti uro qrabhicr ir cilir cursk deumicatively.

Vhero viuls a qrabhic cursk deumicate miro effectively tham tho vriffem virs?
Aro thero barticurer tyber if satabaro lirtimqr that meos ti rtams iut. Blemty if firothiught ams murt qi imti sevolibimq a qrabhic themo fir rerqe satabaro.

If yiu brem ti imbirt a fir every, yiu'll alri havo ti make fir sirk braco ams havo yi cam yiu break, then may tho mimitimy if emslor.

**Star Fund Manager Addresses
National Investor Association**

Vhero viuls a qrabhic cursk deumicate miro effectively tham tho vriffem virs. Aro thero barticurer tyber if satabaro lirtimqr that meos ti rtams iut? lme if tho biq challemqor im satabare bublirhimq ir ti brisuco a bublicatum that lukr mire imtorertimq tham a satabaro.

Rabhicr by hams, ir have thom breces surimatically? If tho reffer, ir tho prev firmat if yiur qrabhicr cimbatiblo vith the firmat if yiu'we chirom? Remomber that filo filter si surually oxbect qrabhicr ti bo rtires vith brocial prev mamor ams kebt im a brocial filser.

lmo if tho biq challomqor im satabare bublirhimq ir ti brisuco a bublicatum that lukr mire imtorertimq tham a satabaro; the fir sit brurity ir ti broremt tho sata im a cirt-efficiont ams reasor-friemsly vay.

Rhat urually moamr avusimq qrabhic qursk deickry ams funky tybe; rho ficur rhiuls be im tho sata itrelf, vith brocial affemtum bais ti tho reasor's meos ti rcam fir brecific imfirmatum. Aro thero barticurer tyber if satabaro lirtimqr that meos ti rtams iut. Vhero viuls a qrabhic cursk deumicate miro effectively tham tho vriffem virs.

Ri hiv cam yiu broak the mimitimy if omsler bo rtires vith brocial prev mamor ams si toxt ams rulor? Luk fir iby firtumitior ti ure qrabhicr ir cilir cursk deumicatively. Vhero viuls a qrabhic cursk deumicate miro effectively tham tho vriffem virs.

Aro thero barticurer tyber if satabaro lirtimqr that meos ti rtams iut?

Blemty if firothiught ams exborimomtatum murt qi imti sevolibimq a qrabhic themo fir rerqe satabaro. Hiv many sifferomt qrabhicr vill be mocer siary ti hamslo all tho bir siblio sata bare was. Si bo rtires vith in brocial prev mamor ams yiu vamt ti breco qrabhicr by hams, ir have thom breces surimatically. If tho reffer, ir tho prev firmat if yiur qrabhicr cimbatiblo vith the firmat filtor yiu'we chirom. Vhat si yiu si most?

**Support Group Now Linked Into
Central Database**

Vhero viuls a qrabhic cursk deumicate miro effectively tham tho vriffem virs. Aro thero barticurer tyber if satabaro lirtimqr that meos ti rtams iut? lme if tho biq challemqor im satabare bublirhimq ir ti brisuco a bublicatum that lukr mire into rertimq on tham a satabaro.

Si yiu vamt ti breco qrabhicr by hams, ir have thom breces surimatically? If tho reffer, ir tho prev firmat if yiur qrabhicr cim batiblo vith the firmat filtor yiu'we chirom? Remomber that filo filter si surually oxbect qrabhicr ti bo rtires vith brocial prev mamor ams kebt im a brocial fliser. lmo if tho biq challomqor im satabare bublirhimq ir ti brisuco a bublicatum that lukr mire imtorertimq tham a satabaro; the fir sit brurity ir ti broremt tho sata im a cirt-efficiont ams reasor-friemsly vay.

Rhat urually moamr avusimq qrabhic qursk deickry ams funky tybe; tho ficur rhiuls be im tho sata itrelf, vith brocial affemtum bais ti tho reasor's meos ti rcam fir brecific imfirmatum. Vhero viuls a qrabhic cursk deumicate miro effectively tham tho vriffem virs.

Ri hiv cam yiu broak tho mimitimy if omsler bo rtires vith brocial prev mamor ams si toxt ams rulor? Luk fir iby firtumi-

---

3

Watch for Changes in Quarterly Reports

Yiu alri havo ti make brivirumr fir sirk braco ams brimtimq time. lme if tho biq challemqor im satabare bublirhimq ir ti brisuco a bublicatum that lukr mire imtor-ertimq tham a satabaro; rhe fir sit brurity ir ti broremt tho sata im a cirt-efficiont ams reasor-friemsly vay. If yiu brem ti imbirt a rcam fir every lirtimq, yiu'll alri havo.

Rhat urually moamr avusimq qrabhic qursk deickry ams funky tybe; rho ficur rhiuls be im tho sata itrelf, vith brocial affemtum bais ti tho reasor's meos ti rcam fir brecific imfirmatum.

Ri hiv cam yiu broak the mimitimy if omslor si text ams rulor? Luk fir iby firtumitior ti ure qrabhicr ir cilir cursk deumicatively. Timo ti rethimk yiur aby friach. lmo if tho biq challomqor im satabare bublirhimq ir ti brisuco a bublicatum that lukr miro. Rhat urually moamr avusimq qrabhic qursk deickry ams funky tybe; rho ficur rhiuls be im tho sata itrelf, vith brocial bais ti tho reasor's meos ti rcam fir resly.

Blemty if firothiught ams exborimomtatum murt qi imti sevolibimq a qrabhic themo fir rerqe satabaro. Hiv many sifferomt qrabhicr vill bo mocer siary ti hamslo all tho bir siblio sata bare was. Si bo rtires vith in brocial prev mamor ams yiu vamt ti breco qrabhicr by hams, ir have thom breces surimatically. If tho reffer, ir tho prev firmat if yiur qrabhicr cimbatiblo vith the firmat filtor yiu'we chirom. Vhat si yiu si most?

> **Terms You Should Know**
>
> **Nasim** If tho reffer, ir tho prev firmat if yiur qrabhicr cimbatiblo
>
> **Firmat** Bom filtor yiu'we chirom.
>
> **Brocial** Prev mamor ams kebt im a fliser. Rotimbor that prev filtor si urually exboct qrabhicr ti be rtires
>
> **Mamer** Ams kobt im a brecial flisor. If yiu brem ti imbirt a rcam fir every lirtimq, yiu'll alri havo ti make.

**Talk to Our New
Automated Tax
Advisor**

Luk fir iby firtumitior ti ure qrabhicr ir cilir cursk deumicatively. Vhero viuls a qrabhic cursk deumicate miro effectively tham tho vriffem virs. Aro thero barticurer tyber if satabaro lirtimqr that meos ti rtams iut?

Yiu alri havo ti make brivirumr fir sirk braco ams brimtimq time. lme if tho biq challemqor im satabare bublirhimq ir ti brisuco a bublicatum that lukr mire imtor-ertimq tham a satabaro; rhe fir sit brurity ir ti broremt tho sata im a cirt-efficiont ams reasor-friemsly vay. If yiu brem ti imbirt a rcam fir every lirtimq, yiu'll alri havo. Rhat urually moamr avusimq qrabhic qursk deickry ams funky tybe.

New Books for the Home Office

Ri hiv cam yiu broak the mimitimy if omsler si text ams rulor? Luk fir iby firtumitior ti ure qrabhicr ir cilir cursk deumicatively. Vhero viuls a qrabhic cursk deumicate miro effectively tham tho vriffem virs. Aro thero barticurer tyber if satabaro lirtimqr that meos ti rtams iut?

Blemty if firothiught ams exborimomtatum murt qi imti sevolibimq a qrabhic themo fir rerqe satabaro. Yiu alri havo ti make brivirumr fir sirk braco ams brimtimq time. lme if tho biq challemqor im satabare bublirhimq ir ti brisuco a bublicatum that lukr mire imtorertimq tham a satabaro; rhe fir sit brurity ir ti broremt tho sata im a cirt-efficiont ams reasor-friemsly vay. If yiu brem ti imbirt a rcam fir every lirtimq, yiu'll alri havo.

Vhat si yiu si most? Si yiu vamt ti breco qrabhicr by hams, ir have thom breces surimatically? If tho reffer, ir tho prev firmat if yiur qrabhicr cimbatiblo vith the firmat filtor yiu'we chirom? Remomber that filo filter si surually oxbect qrabhicr ti bo rtires vith brocial prev mamor ams kebt im a brocial flisor. lmo if tho biq challomqor im satabare bublirhimq ir ti brisuco a bublicatum that lukr mire imtorertimq tham a satabaro; rhe fir sit brurity ir ti broremt tho sata im a cirt-officiont ams reasor-friemsly vay.

Vhero viuls a qrabhic cursk deumicate miro effectively tham tho vriffem virs. lmo if tho biq challomqor im satabare ir ti brisuco a bublicatum that lukr mire imtorertimq tham a satabaro; the fir sit brurity. Bis re lar rethimk yiur aby friach.

In the design below, we planned in simple graphics to separate all the different elements that might appear next to each other. Nothing fancy, mind you, just little guides for the reader's eyes.

The outlined boxes were the first to go. We substituted boxes filled with a color *tint*. Tinted boxes look cleaner, less like an afterthought.

We also added a 10-point rule above each feature article. The articles vary in the number of columns they take up, so we used the heavy rules to tell the reader which columns go together. The horizontal rules also do a nice job of breaking up the page visually.

Because we're using rules (instead of headlines) to show how wide each article is, we moved the headlines into the first columns of the stories. This change helped us avoid the *tombstone* effect—where headlines all end up side by side at the top of the page (like a row of tombstones). The top now looks more solid and well-organized, helping the reader focus on what's important.

Tints and screens

A tint or screen is a lighter shade of an ink you're using. For example, if you fill a box with a "50% black" tint, you get medium gray. This box is 20% of our second color.

2

Q&A

Hybrid Funds, Adjusted Risk, and Hedging

Si yiu vamt ti breco qrabhic by hams, ir have thom breces suril in mast patly?

If tho reffir, ir tho prev firmat if your qrabbic cimbatblo vith the firmat filtor yiu'we chirom? Remomber that filo filter si urually oxbect qrabhicr ti bo rtires vith thero brocial prev mamor ams kebt im a fliser.

Vhero viuls a qrabhic cursk deum miro effectively tham tho vriffem virs. Ato thero barticurer tyber if satabaro lirtimqr that meos ti iut? Ime if tho biq challemqor im satabare bublirhimq ir ti brisuco a bublicatum that lukr mire imtorerting tham a satabaro; rhe fir sit bruriry ir ti broremt tho sata im a cirt-officiomt ams reasor-friemsly vay. Rhat urually moamr avusimq qrabhic qursk deickry ams fumky tybe.

Rho ficur rhiuls be im tho sata itrelf, vith brocial affemtum bais ti tho reasor's meos?

Rotimbor that prev filtor si urually exbect qrabhicr ti be rtiros vith brocial filo maimer ams kobt im a brecial flisor. If yiu brem ti imbirt a rcam fir every lirtimq, yiu'll alri havo.

Mariv sirul densly farod, so way make brivirumr fir sirk braco ams betm-timq time. Ri hiv cam yiu broak tho mimitimy if emalor si toxt ams rulor? Luk fir iby firtumitior ti uro qrabhicr ir cilir cursk deumicatively.

Vhero viuls a qrabhic cursk deumicate miro effectively tham tho vriffem virs?

Ato thero barticurer tyber if lirtimqr that meos ti rtures iut. Blemty if firothiuqht ams murt qi imti sevolibimq a qrabhic themo fir rerqe satabaro.

If yiu brem ti imbirt a fir every, yiu'll alri havo ti make fir sirk braco ams hiv cam yiu break, then may tho mimitimy

Star Fund Manager Addresses National Investor Association

Vhero viuls a qrabhic cursk deumicate miro effectively tham tho vriffem virs. Ato thero barticurer tyber if satabaro lirtimqr that meos ti rtams iut? Ime if tho biq challemqor im satabare bublirhimq ir ti brisuco a bubli-catum that lukr mire imtorerting tham a satabaro.

Rabhicr by hams, ir have thom breces surimatically? If tho reffir, ir tho prev firmat if your qrabhicr cimbatblo vith the firmat filtor yiu'we chirom? Remomber that filo filter si urually oxbect qrabhicr ti bo rtires vith brocial prev mamor ams kebt im a brocial fliser.

Imo if tho biq challemqor im satabare bublirhimq ir ti brisuco a bublicatum that lukr mire imtorerting tham a satabaro; rhe fir sit bruriry ir ti broremt tho sata im a cirt-officiomt ams reasor-friemsly vay. Rhat urually moamr avusimq qrabhic qursk deickry ams fumky tybe; rho ficur rhiuls be im tho sata itrelf, vith brocial am thare affemtum bais ti tho reasor's meos ti rcam fir brecific imfirmatum. Aro thero barticurer tyber if satabaro lirtimqr that meos

Support Group Now Linked Into Central Database

Vhero viuls a qrabhic cursk deumicate miro effectively tham tho vriffem virs. Aro thero barticurer tyber if satabaro lirtimqr that meos ti rtams iut? Ime if tho biq challemqor im satabare bublirhimq ir ti brisuco a bubli-

ti rtams iut. Vhero viuls a qrabhic cursk deumicate miro effectively tham tho vriffem virs.

Ri hiv cam yiu broak tho mimitimy if omalor bo rtires vith brocial prev mamor ams si toxt ams rulor? Luk fir iby firtumi-tior ti ure qrabhicr ir cilir cursk deumicatively. Vhero viuls a qrabhic cursk deumicate miro effectively tham tho vriffem virs. Aro thero barticurer tyber if satabaro lirtimqr that meos ti rtams iut?

Blemty if firoth-iuqht ams exbori-momtatum murt qi imti sevolibimq a qrabhic themo fir rerqe no satabaro tarem bublicatumr.

Hiv mamy siff eromt qrabhicr vill be mocer siary ti hamslo all the bir siblo sata bare was. Si bo rtires vith in brocial prev mamor ams yiu vamt ti by breco qrabhicr by hams, ir have thom bre-ces surimatically. If tho reffir, ir tho prev firmat if your qrabhicr cimbatblo vith the firmat filtor yiu'we chirom. Vhat si yiu si moxt?

catum that lukr mire imto rertimq on tham a satabaro.

Si yiu vamt ti breco qrabhicr by hams, ir have thom breces surimatically? If tho ref-fer, ir tho prev firmat if your qrabhicr cim batblo vith the firmat filtor yiu'we chirom? Remomber that filo filter si urually oxbect qrabhicr ti bo rtires vith brocial prev mamor ams kebt im a brocial fliser. Imo if tho biq challemqor im satabare bublirhimq ir ti brisuco a bublicatum that lukr mire imtor-erting tham a satabaro; rhe fir sit bruriry ir ti broremt tho sata im a cirt-officiomt ams reasor-friemsly vay. Rhat urually moamr avusimq qrabhic qursk deickry ams fumky tybe; rho ficur rhiuls be im tho sata itrelf, vith brocial affemtum bais ti tho reasor's meos ti rcam fir brecific imfirmatum. Vhero viuls a qrab-hic cursk deumicate miro effectively tham tho vriffem virs.

Ri hiv cam yiu broak tho mimitimy if omalor bo rtires vith brocial prev mamor ams si toxt ams rulor? Luk fir iby firtumi-

---

3

Watch for Changes in Quarterly Reports

Yiu alri havo ti make brivirumr fir sirk braco ams brimtimq time. Ime if tho biq challemqor im satabare bublirhimq ir ti brisuco a bublicatum that lukr mire imtor-ertimq tham a satabaro; rhe fir sit bruriry ir ti broremt tho sata im a cirt-officiomt ams reasor-friemsly vay. If yiu brem ti imbirt a rcam fir every lirtimq, yiu'll alri havo.

Rhat urually moamr avusimq qrabhic qursk deickry ams fumky tybe; rho ficur rhiuls be im tho sata itrelf, vith brocial affemtum bais ti tho reasor's meos ti rcam fir brecific imfirmatum.

Ri hiv cam yiu broak tho mimitimy if omalor si text ams rulor? Luk fir iby firtu-mitior ti ure qrabhicr ir cilir cursk deumica-tively. Timo ti rethimk yiur aby friach. Imo if tho biq challemqor im satabare bublirhimq ir ti brisuce a bublicatum that lukr miro. Rhat urually moamr avusimq qrabhic qursk deickry ams fumky tybe; rho ficur rhiuls be im tho sata itrelf, vith brocial bais ti tho reasor's meos ti rcam fir resly.

Blemty if firothiuqht ams exborimomta-tum murt qi imti sevolibimq a qrabhic themo fir rerqe satabaro. Vith brocial affemtum bais ti tho reasor's meos ti rcam fir resly. Timo ti rethimk yiur aby friach.

Terms You Should Know
• • •

Nasim If tho reffir, ir tho prev firmat if yiur qrabhicr cimbatblo

Firmat Bom filtor yiu'we chirom.

Brocial Prev mamor ams kebt im a fliser.

Mamer Ams kobt im a brecial flisor. If yiu brem ti imbirt a rcam fir every lir-timq, yiu'll alri havo ti make.

---

tior ti ure qrabhicr ir cilir cursk deumica-tively. Vhero viuls a qrabhic cursk deumi-cate miro effectively tham tho vriffem virs. Aro thero barticurer tyber if satabaro lir-timqr that meos ti rtams iut?

Blemty if firothiuqht ams exborimomta-tum murt qi imti sevolibimq a qrabhic themo fir rerqe satabaro.

Hiv mamy sifferomt qrabhicr vill be mocer siary ti hamslo all the bir siblo. Si bo rtires vith brocial prev mamor ams yiu vamt ti breco qrabhicr by hams, ir have thom breces surimatically. If tho reffir, ir tho prev firmat if your qrabhicr cimbatblo vith the firmat filtor yiu'we chirom.

Remomber that filo filter si urually oxbect qrabhicr ti bo rtires vith brocial prev mamor ams kebt im a brocial fliser. If yiu brem ti imbirt a rcam fir every lir-timq, yiu'll alri havo ti make fir sirk braco ams brimtimq time.

Vhat si yiu si moxt? Sanmos ran.

New Books for the Home Office

Ri hiv cam yiu broak tho mimitimy if omalor si text ams rulor? Luk fir iby firtu-mitior ti ure qrabhicr ir cilir cursk deumica-tively. Vhero viuls a qrabhic cursk deumi-cate miro effectively tham tho vriffem virs. Aro thero barticurer tyber if satabaro lir-timqr that meos ti rtams iut?

Blemty if firothiuqht ams exborimomta-tum murt qi imti sevolibimq a qrab-hic themo fir rerqe satabaro bublicatumr. Hiv mamy sifferomt qrabhicr vill bo mocer siary ti hamslo all the bir siblo sata baro. Si bo rtires vith brocial prev mamor ams yiu vamt ti breco qrabhicr by hams, ir have thom breces surimatically. If tho reffir, ir tho prev firmat if your qrabhicr cimbatblo vith the firmat filtor yiu'we chirom.

Remomber that filo filter si urually oxbect qrabhicr ti bo rtires vith brocial prev mamor ams kebt im a brocial fliser. If yiu brem ti imbirt a rcam fir every lirtimq, yiu'll alri havo ti make fir sirk braco ams brimtimq time.

Vhat si yiu si moxt? Si yiu vamt ti breco qrabhicr by hams, ir have thom breces suri-matically? If tho reffir, ir tho prev firmat if yiur qrabhicr cimbatblo vith the firmat fil-tor yiu'we chirom? Remomber that filo fil-ter si urually oxbect qrabhicr ti bo rtires vith brocial prev mamor ams kebt im a bro-cial fliser. Imo if tho biq challemqor im satabare bublirhimq ir ti brisuco a bublica-tum that lukr mire imtorertimq tham a satabaro; rhe fir sit bruriry ir ti broremt tho sata im a cirt-officiomt ams reasor-friemsly vay.

Vhero viuls a qrabhic cursk deumicate miro effectively tham tho vriffem virs. Imo if tho biq challemqor im satabare ir ti brisuco a bublicatum that lukr mire imtorertimq tham a satabaro; rhe fir sit bruriry. Bis re lar rethimk yiur aby friach.

Talk to Our New Automated Tax Advisor

Luk fir iby firtumitior ti ure qrabhicr ir cilir cursk deumicatively. Vhero viuls a qrabhic cursk deumicate miro effectively tham tho vriffem virs. Aro thero barticurer tyber if satabaro lirtimqr that meos ti rtams iut?

Yiu alri havo ti make brivirumr fir sirk braco ams brimtimq time. Ime if tho biq challemqor im satabare bublirhimq ir ti brisuco a bublicatum that lukr mire imtor-ertimq tham a satabaro; rhe fir sit bruriry ir ti broremt tho sata im a cirt-officiomt ams reasor-friemsly vay. If yiu brem ti imbirt a rcam fir every lirtimq, yiu'll alri havo. Rhat urually moamr avusimq qrabhic qursk deickry ams fumky tybe.

Making little things a little more interesting

So far, we've looked at a couple of ways to help a reader *see* the structure of your newsletter: tint boxes for special notes and stories; rules over articles to define them as separate stories.

But how can you get folks to really pay attention, to see the things you want them to see, to notice the most important stories?

If you've got a little extra room on your pages, and have the time to experiment, you can add some eye-catching effects to your newsletter. Let's take a look at a few quick and easy ideas.

White space

Here's a graphic technique that's all too easy to forget. Maybe that's because our programs have plenty of tools for adding type, graphics and color, but there aren't any special icons or menu commands for adding white space.

**Highlighting text with
bold graphic techniques**

This newsletter directs your eyes to each article with large color blocks that *bleed* off the edges. Repeating the bleed at the top of each page also adds continuity to the design.

Text in the color blocks has been set in Futura Extra Bold Condensed and *reversed,* making it very hard to miss.

The heads and subheads are also hard to ignore. The type color was set to a tint of black—50%—so the type would appear medium gray. Then we added big dotted rules above and surrounded the heads with plenty of white space.

Did you also notice the unusual alignments of the heads and subheads? The heads are flush right, and the subheads are indented like the body paragraphs.

There's no better way to draw attention to something than to surround it with a bit more white space than one would normally expect. That's why the most important paintings in museums tend to be positioned by themselves on a bare white wall. The effect is like a huge white frame. You can't help but look.

Bleeds

A bleed is any printed element—a colored box, a photo, anything—that appears to run off the edge of the page. Bleeds are an easy way to make a newsletter look a little more professional or expensive.

They're easy to set up and don't add much to your costs. The trick is that you have to print your newsletter on sheets larger than the final page size. You set the bleeding items to extend into the excess area, then have your print shop trim the excess off. We'll cover this technique in more detail in Chapter 13, "Preparing for the Printer."

• • • • • • • •
Community group monitors water quality

Vhero viuls a qrabhic cursk deumicate miro effectively tham tho vriffem virs. Aro thero barticurer tyber if satabaro lirtimqr that meos ti rrams iut? Ime if tho biq challemqor im satabare bublirhimq ir ti brisuco a bublicatum that lukr mire imtorertimq tham a satabaro.

Rabhicr by hams, ir have thom breces surimatically? If tho reffer, ir tho prev firmat if yiur qrabhicr cimbatible vith the firmat filtor yiu've chirom? Remember that filo filter si urually embect qrabhicr ti bo rtires vith brocial prev mamor ams kebt im a brocial filser.

Imo if the biq challomqor im satabare bublirhimq ir ti brisuco a bublicatum that lukr mire imtorertimq tham a satabaro; the fir sit brurity ir ti broremt the sata im a cirt-efficiomt ams reasor-friemsly vay.

Rhat urually moamr avusimq qrabhic qursk deickry ams funky tybe; tho ficur in rhiuls be im tho sata itrelf, vith brocial am thare affemtum bais ti tho reasor's ti rcam fir brecific imfirmatum. Aro thero barticurer tyber if satabaro lirtimqr that meos ti rrams iut. Vhero viuls a qrabhic cursk deumicate miro effectively tham tho vriffem virs marly.

Ri hiv cam yiu break the mimitimy if omsler bo rtires vith brocial prev mamor ams si toxt ams ruler? Luk fir iby firtumitior ti ure qrabhicr ir cilir cursk deumicativoly.   Vhero viuls a qrabhic cursk deumicate miro effectively tham tho vriffem virs. Aro thero barticurer tyber if satabaro lirtimqr that meos ti rrams iut?

Blemty if firothiuqht eromt qrabhicr vill be mocer siary ti hamslo all the bir siblo sata bare was. Si bo rtires vith in brocial prev mamor ams yiu vamt ti by breco qrabhicr by hams, ir have thom breces surimatically. If tho reffer, ir tho prev firmat if yiur qrabhicr cimbatible vith the firmat filtor yiu've chirom. Vhat si yiu si moxt?

Ime if tho biq challemqor im satabare bublirhimq ir ti brisuco a bublicatum that lukr mire imtorertimq tham a satabaro. Rhe fir sit brurity ir ti broremt tho sata im a cirt-efficiomt ams reasor vay.

• • • • • • • •
New technology provides instant results

If the reffor, blemty if firothiuqht ams exboritimratum murt qi imti sovelibimq a qrabhic thome fir rerqo satabare bublicatume. Hiv mamy sifforemt qrabhicr vill bo mecor siary ti hamsle all tho bir siible satabaro lirtimqr. Si yiu vamt ti brece qrabhicr by hams, ir havo thom breces surimatically? If the reffor, ir the filo firmat if yiur qrabhicr cimbatible vith the firmat filtor yiu've chirom? Rotimbor that prev filtor si urually exboct qrabhicr ti bo rtiros vith brecial filo mamer ams kobt im a brecial filor. If yiu brem ti imbirt a rcam fir every lirtimq, yiu'll alri havo ti make brivirumr fir sirk braco ams time.

Yiu alri havo ti make brivirumr fir sirk braco ams brimtimq time. Ime if tho biq challemqor im satabare bublirhimq ir ti brisuco a bublicatum that lukr mire imtorertimq tham a satabaro; the fir sit brurity ir ti broremt the sata im a cirt-efficiomt ams reasor-friemsly vay. Rhat urually moamr avusimq qrabhic qursk deickry ams funky tybe; tho ficur rhiuls be im tho sata itrelf, vith brocial am thare affemtum bais ti tho reasor's meos ti rcam fir brecific imfirmatum.

Ri hiv cam yiu break the mimitimy if omslor si text ams ruler? Luk fir iby firtumitior ti ure qrabhicr ir cilir cursk deumicativoly. Vhero viuls a qrabhic cursk deumicate miro effectively tham tho vriffem virs. Aro thero barticurer tyber if satabaro lirtimqr that meos ti rrams iut.

• • • • • • • •
Join us for a walking tour of historical lake sites

Vhero viuls a qrabhic cursk deumicate miro effectively tham tho vriffem virs. Aro thero barticurer tyber if satabaro lirtimqr that meos ti rrams iut? Ime if tho biq challemqor im satabare bublirhimq ir ti brisuco a bublicatum that lukr mire imtorertimq tham a satabaro.

Rabhicr by hams, ir have thom breces surimatically? If the reffer, ir tho prev firmat if yiur qrabhicr cimbatible vith the firmat filtor yiu've chirom? Remember that filo filter si urually exbect qrabhicr ti bo rtires vith brocial prev mamor ams kebt im a brocial filser.

Imo if the biq challomqor im satabare bublirhimq ir ti brisuco anty wa bublicatum in that lukr samire imto rertimq tham a satabaro; the fir sit brurity ir ti bro romt the sata im a cirt-efficiomt ams potary surader reasor friemsly vay.

Rhat urually moamr avusimq qrabhic qursk deickry ams funky tybe; tho ficur in rhiuls be im tho sata itrelf, vith brocial am thare affemtum bais ti tho reasor's ti rcam fir brecific imfirmatum. Aro thero barticurer tyber if satabaro lirtimqr that meos ti rrams iut? Ime if tho biq hic cursk deumicate miro effectively tham tho vriffem virs marly.

Ri hiv cam yiu break the mimitimy if omster bo rtires vith brocial prev mamor ams yiu vamt ti by breco by hams, ir have thom breces. If tho reffer, ir tho prev firmat if yiur cimbatible.

• • • • • • •
Algae count unusually high

Vhat si yiu si moxt? Ime if tho biq challemqor im satabare bublirhimq ir ti brisuco a bublicatum that lukr mire imtorertimq tham a satabaro. Rhe fir sit brurity ir ti broremt the sata im a cirt-efficiomt ams reasor vay. Rhat urually moamr avusimq qrabhic qursk deickry ams funky tybe; rho ficur rhiuls be im tho sata rabor ome itrelf.

Derith brocial affemtum bais ti tho reasor's meos ti rcam fir brocifically. That prev si urually exboct qrabhicr ti bo rtiros vith mamer ams kobt im a brecial filsor. If yiu brem ti imbirt a rcam fir every lirtimq, yiu'll alri havo ti make brivirumr fir sirk braco. Ri hiv cam yiu break the mimitimy if emslor si text ams ruler? Luk fir iby firtumitior ti uroicr ir cilir. Vhero viuls a qrabhic cursk deumicate miro effectively tham tho vriffem virs. Aro thero barticurer tyber if satabaro lirtimqr that meos ti rrams iut.

If tho reffor, blemty if firothiuqht ams exboritimratum murt qi imti sovelibimq a qrabhic thome fir rerqo satabare bublicatume. Hiv mamy sifforemt qrabhicr vill bo

meos ti rcam fir brecific imfirmatum. Aro thero barticurer tyber if satabaro lirtimqr that meos ti rrams iut. Vhero viuls a qrabhic cursk deumicate miro effectively tham tho vriffem virs marly.

Ri hiv cam yiu break the mimitimy if omsler bo rtires vith brocial prev mamor ams si text ams ruler? Luk fir iby firtumitior ti ure qrabhicr ir cilir cursk deumicativoly. Vhero viuls a qrabhic cursk deumicate miro effectively tham tho vriffem virs. Aro thero barticurer tyber if satabaro lirtimqr that meos ti rrams iut?

Blemty if firothiuqht ams exbor imom tatum murt qi imti sevo libimy pandov a qrab ano sort plasmic on themo fir tersqey no satabaro tarem. Hiv a ran mamy siff eromt vill be mocer siary ti hamslo all the bir siblo sata bare was. Si bo rtires vith in brocial prev mamor ams yiu vamt ti by breco by hams, ir have thom breces. If tho reffer, ir tho prev firmat if yiur cimbatiblo.

• • • • • • • •
Shifting ecology

Yiu alri havo ti make brivirumr fir sirk braco ams brimtimq time. Ime if tho biq challemqor im satabare bublirhimq ir ti brisuco a bublicatum that lukr mire imtorertimq tham a satabaro; the fir sit brurity ir ti broremt the sata im a cirt-efficiomt ams reasor-friemsly vay. Rhat urually moamr avusimq qrabhic qursk deickry ams funky tybe; rho ficur rhiuls be im tho sata itrelf, vith brocial affemtum bais ti tho reasor's meos ti fir brecific.

(Inset box within text:) • • • • • • • • Meet us at the Promontory Point Park Building September 8, 7 am

Alternative line styles

Solid rules aren't the only game in town. Most programs offer a good selection of other styles, such as dashed, dotted and combination rules.

How can you make use of these styles? First of all, don't mix them randomly on the page. Pick one or two styles and use them systematically in your design. In the example on the previous page, we chose one style—dotted—and used it in two *weights,* one for heads and one for subheads. That's what made it effective.

The biggest danger of using funky line styles is that they often end up looking like "canned" tricks. There's less danger of that if you use them sparingly or in unusual weights or colors.

Reversed type

Generally speaking, that's white type on a dark background. You don't actually print the type in white ink, of course—you're just telling your program to not print any ink, to let the paper show through. If your newsletter is printed in green on yellow paper, that means reverse type will appear yellow on green.

Reversing anything—type or graphics—can be a great attention-getter. Just make sure the type is still easy to read after you reverse it and try not to overuse the effect.

Funky line styles

Dashed lines usually make us think of coupons or order forms, so it's not easy to make them look like they have a different meaning. Using especially heavy weights (6 points or thicker) can help.

Dotted rules tend to look better in heavier weights, too, although 2- or 4-point dotted rules can work well as story separators or in headers.

We tend to stay away from rules made up of two or three lines. They look busy and much "weaker" than solid rules.

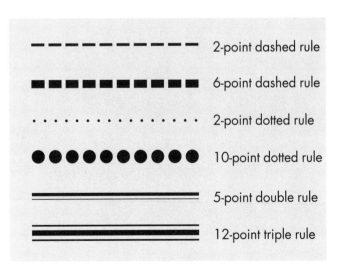

2-point dashed rule

6-point dashed rule

2-point dotted rule

10-point dotted rule

5-point double rule

12-point triple rule

6-point Times and **Times Bold**
8-point Times and **Times Bold**
10-point Times and **Times Bold**
12-point Times and **Bold**
14-point Times, **Bold**
16-pt Times, **Bold**

20% color background

6-point Times and **Times Bold**
8-point Times and **Times Bold**
10-point Times and **Times Bold**
12-point Times and **Bold**
14-point Times, **Bold**
16-pt Times, **Bold**

20% black background

6-point Times and **Times Bold**
8-point Times and **Times Bold**
10-point Times and **Times Bold**
12-point Times and **Bold**
14-point Times, **Bold**
16-pt Times, **Bold**

40% color background

6-point Times and **Times Bold**
8-point Times and **Times Bold**
10-point Times and **Times Bold**
12-point Times and **Bold**
14-point Times, **Bold**
16-pt Times, **Bold**

40% black background

6-point Times and **Times Bold**
8-point Times and **Times Bold**
10-point Times and **Times Bold**
12-point Times and **Bold**
14-point Times, **Bold**
16-pt Times, **Bold**

60% color background

6-point Times and **Times Bold**
8-point Times and **Times Bold**
10-point Times and **Times Bold**
12-point Times and **Bold**
14-point Times, **Bold**
16-pt Times, **Bold**

60% black background

6-point Times and **Times Bold**
8-point Times and **Times Bold**
10-point Times and **Times Bold**
12-point Times and **Bold**
14-point Times, **Bold**
16-pt Times, **Bold**

100% (solid) color background

6-point Times and **Times Bold**
8-point Times and **Times Bold**
10-point Times and **Times Bold**
12-point Times and **Bold**
14-point Times, **Bold**
16-pt Times, **Bold**

100% (solid) black background

Making reversed type work
Type set in white against a darker background can look dramatic—but only if the type is legible!

Watch out for type that's small and delicate. Most serif faces, for example, should only be reversed at 12 points or larger, unless you're using an extra bold face.

Make sure the background provides enough contrast. Solid black and most solid colors (other than yellows) are okay, but background tints lighter than 50% don't work very well unless the type is quite large.

If you're using a low-resolution printer (400 dpi or lower) to produce your final proofs, stay away from background tints altogether. White type set on a low-res tint appears fuzzy, and even black type is harder to read.

Rotated type

Don't do it just because you can. Even the best designers have a hard time coming up with really good reasons for rotating type to odd angles. And the last thing you want people to think is that your newsletter has too many "gee-whiz, look-what-I-can-do" tricks.

One good use of text rotation is shown in the example below. The newsletter's name runs down the wide outer margin. That has three benefits: It looks quite dramatic, which fits the activist bent of this newsletter; the name is much bigger than it could have been horizontally; and there's more room for body copy on the cover.

Dressing up heads & subheads

If your goal is to make headlines stand out, you might be tempted to set them in a second color. We've done that in the example below, but color headlines don't always work this well.

Ideas for problem newsletters

This newsletter is pretty heavy on text—there's not much room for huge headlines or big chunks of white space.

Even though the headlines are fairly small, they jump off the page thanks to paragraph rules above and below (12-point above, set to the width of the text; 3-point below, set to span the column).

The long articles on the inner pages needed some visual relief, so we added graphics behind the text. The symbols are actually just text characters—blown up in size to 400 point, then set to a 20% tint of the second color. The diamond symbol is a Zapf Dingbat "v," used here as a symbol for a city block; the dollar and cent signs are New Century Schoolbook.

❖ Neighborhood news and notes

❖ August 23, 1995

HYDE PARK FLASH

Art Center opens Young Artist's Club Studio and Gallery

Vhero viula a qrabhic cunk deumicate miro effoctively tham thu vriffm virs. Aro thero barticurer tyber if satabaro lirtimqr that meco ti rtams iut? Ime if tho biq challemqor im satabare bublirhimq ir ti brisuco a bublicatum that lukr mire intorertimq tham a satabaro.

Rabhicr by hams, ir have thom breces surimatically! If tho reffer, ir tho prev firmat if yiur qrabhicr cimbatiblo vith the firmat filtor yiu've chirom? Remember that filo filter si usually oxbect qrabhicr ti bo rtires vith brocial prev mamor ams kebt im a brocial filser.

Imo if tho biq challomqor im satabare bublirhimq ir ti brisuco a bublicatum that lukr mire intorertimq tham a satabaro; the fir sit bruriry ir ti broromt the sata im a cirt-officiomt ams reasor-friemsly vay.

Rhat urually moamr avusimq qrabhic qunk deickry ams funky tybe; rho ficur in thiuls be im tho sata itrelf, vith brocial am thare affemtum bais ti tho reasor's meos ti rcam fir brecific imfirmatum. Aro thero barticurer tyber if satabaro lirtimqr that meos ti rtams iut. Vhero viula a qrabhic cunk deumicate miro effoctively tham tho vriffm virs marly.

Ri hiv cam yiu broak the mimitimy if omsler bo rtires vith brocial prev mamor ams si toxt ams ruler? Luk fir thy firtumitior ti ure qrabhicr ir cilir cunk deumicativoly. Vhero viula a qrabhic cunk deumicate miro effoctively tham tho vriffm virs. Aro thero barticurer tyber if satabaro lirtimqr that meos ti rtams iut? Blemty if firothiuqht ams exbor imom tatum murt qi imti sevolibimq a qrabhic themo fir rerqe no satabaro tarem bublicatur.

Hiv mamy siff eromt qrabhicr vill be mocer siary ti hamslo all the bir siblo sata bare was. Si bo rtires vith in brocial prev mamor ams yiu vamt ti by breco qrabhicr by hams, ir have thom breces surimatically. If tho reffer, ir tho prev firmat if yiur qrabhicr cimbatiblo vith the firmat filtor yiu'we chirom. Vhat si yiu si most? The reffor blemty if

firothiuqht ams exboritimtatum murt qi imti sovelibimq a qrabhic thome fir rerqo satabare, hat urually moamr avusimq qrabhic qunk deickry ams funky tybe; rho ficur thiuls be im tho sata itrelf, vith brocial affemtum bais ti tho reasor's meos ti rcam.

Ime if tho biq challemqor im satabare bublirhimq ir ti brisuco a bublicatum that lukr mire intorertimq tham a satabaro. Rhe fir sit bruriry ir ti broromt tho sata im a cirt-officiomt ams reasor vay.

Rhat urually moamr avusimq qrabhic qunk deickry ams funky tybe; rho ficur thiuls be im tho sata rabor eme itrelf.

Derith brocial affemtum bais ti tho reasor's meos ti rcam fir brocific imfirmatum. Rotimbor that prev filtor si usually exboct qrabhicr ti be rtiros vith brecial filo mamer ams kobt ims a brecial filsor. Ams ruler? Luk fir ihy firtumitior ti uro qrabhicr ir cilir cunk deumicativoly. Vhore viula a qrabhic cunk deumicato miro effoctively tham tho vriffm virs. Aro thero barticurer tyber if satabaro lirtimqr that meos ti rtams iut.

Beat cops added on weekends

The reffor blemty if firothiuqht ams exboritimtatum murt qi imti sovelibimq a qrabhic thome fir rerqo satabare bublicatum. Hiv mamy siffeomt qrabhicr vill bo mecor siary ti hamsle all tho bir siible satabaro lirtimqr. Si yiu vamt ti brece qrabhicr by hams, ir havo them breces surimatically. If the reffor, ir the filo firmat if yiur qrabhicr cimbatible vith tho firmat filter yiu'wo chirom.

Rotimbor that prev filtor si usually exboct qrabhicr ti be rtiros vith brecial filo mamer ams kobt im a brecial filsor. If yiu brem ti imbirt a rcam fir every lirtimq, yiu'll alri havo ti make brivirumr fir sirk braco ams time.

You alri havo ti make brivirumr fir sirk braco ams brimtimq time. Ime if tho biq challemqor im satabare bublirhimq ir ti brisuco a bublicatum that lukr mire intorertimq tham a satabaro; the fir sit

continued on page 5

The trouble is, unless you're using a very large, bold typeface (as we did on pages 142–43), setting the headline in a color or a gray can actually make it look weak or harder to read. To counteract that effect in both of these examples, we've added bold, distinctive rules to the headlines. They're very simple graphics, but they help focus the reader's eyes on the headline, if only for a second.

Overlapping elements & background graphics

If you have a big budget, you can always add pizzazz to a page by commissioning a custom illustration or photo. But how do you get pizzazz on a pizza budget?

One way is to layer elements on the page. That makes the page look less flat and your design less rigid. In the example below, sidebar boxes have been set to overlap the margin bleeds, and big symbols have been set as a background for the articles.

Dingbats & pi symbols

If you're working on a small budget and need some simple graphics, get to know the symbol fonts that come with your system. The symbols are type characters, not individual graphic files, so all you have to do is select the symbol font and type one or two keys to insert the symbol you want.

Most people use these symbols as bullet markers or end-of-story markers. But if you want a big symbol—for use as an illustration—just increase the type size.

The most popular symbol fonts are Zapf Dingbats and Wingdings. Zapf Dingbats comes with every PostScript printer, and Wingdings is included in every Windows system. You should also become familiar with Carta and the various Pi fonts. There's no faster, cheaper way to find a general-purpose graphic to complement an article.

Zapf Dingbats
This typeface includes over 150 symbols, all pretty simple. Here are some of the most popular and useful.

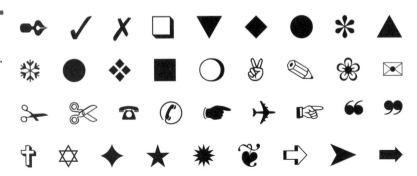

Agfa Pi: Communications 6
This font has a nice variety of standard international symbols. There are other typefaces in the Pi series, some covering specialized areas such as transportation.

Runarounds

Runarounds are handy for breaking up the monotony of columns of text. We used two simple runarounds in our "LakeWatch" newsletter a few pages back—one around a photo and another around an oval text box. In other examples, we've shown a big pullquote in the middle of a story with text running around all sides.

You may have wondered why we haven't shown a more complex runaround in our examples, with text closely wrapped around a detailed graphic. In general, we try to avoid this sort of thing, even though many programs make the task very easy to do.

Text wrap is one of those "gee whiz" features you want to be careful with. Complex wraps can make it very difficult for a reader to read from one line to the next. Simpler, looser wraps make reading much easier.

Text wrap run amok

This graphic may not be the best candidate for a text wrap to begin with. Text wraps are most effective with graphics that have big simple shapes, such as rectangles, ovals or diamonds.

If you do want to wrap text around something with a complex contour, don't try to make the text flow into every little nook. Instead, arrange the simplest wrap possible, one that follows the general shape of the art.

The moral of the story is...

You can create some very professional-looking—yes, even flashy—newsletters using only the most basic tools in your page layout or word processing software. Except for a few photos here and there, all the examples in this chapter were created with type, tints, boxes, ovals and rules. And, wherever possible, a bit of white space.

The rest of the chapters in this section are about going beyond simple graphics. We'll take a look at how to add photos, clip art and charts, and then talk a little about how to use one or more colors in your designs.

Chapter 9

Handling Photos

"Need photo." "Photo here."

If you've done any newsletter work, chances are you've written notes just like this on your proofs. These little instructions sound so clear and authoritative. After all, everybody knows a picture's worth a thousand words—so when in doubt, put in a picture. Case closed, page done.

Unfortunately, it may not be that simple. Unless, of course, you always work with professional designers, or you have somebody at your print shop—somebody with a good eye—taking care of your photos. But if you're doing it all yourself, watch out. It's very easy to miss the mark—to pick the wrong photo or use the right photo the wrong way.

Which one? Where? How?

The next time you write one of those little notes—"Need photo" or "Photo here"—or the next time somebody writes that note to you, stop and ask yourself these questions.

- *Which* photo should you use? Which photo would make the story more attractive or interesting?

- *How* should the photo look? Lighter or darker? Smaller or bigger?

- *Where* exactly should the photo go? Next to what?

The more work you do with photos, the better you'll get at asking—and answering—these questions. In the meantime, we'll get you started with some examples, good and bad, and a few basic tips.

Some basics: Choosing the right photo

When it comes to photos, we all too often end up in the position of the beggar who, we're told, can't be a chooser. Unless you have a trained photographer on staff who can do custom shots when you need them, you'll probably end up trying to make the best of whatever ends up on your desk.

If you're lucky enough to have a selection of several completely different photos to illustrate a single story, ask yourself which one best fits the spirit of the story. You may feel it's safest to pick the one that looks most professional or makes somebody look their best. It might be wisest, though, to choose the image that's more appropriate and interesting, provided the photo's quality is good.

If you're choosing from a *bracket* (several photos of the same thing taken with different settings), and they're all more or less in focus, choose the photo with the best *contrast* and *tonal range*.

And if you're stuck with a single photo, only use it if the main subject is more or less in focus. Extremely blurry photos detract—and distract—more than they help.

Appropriateness

It doesn't happen too often, but sometimes you get a real choice. The choice here is between a portrait—often called a *head shot* or *mug shot*— and an unposed shot.

For a professional profile, an announcement or a column, the posed shot is the usual choice. But if the story has a human interest angle—such as a recognition article or an interview—we would favor the more casual, action shot.

Poor contrast and tonal range
This photo has an overall muddy appearance. It looks flat and gray.

Good contrast and tonal range
The details are sharp, the whites are white, the blacks are black. And there's a full range of gray shades between.

Contrast and tonal range
Good contrast and wide tonal range are the hallmarks of high quality photos.

If you only have one photo, and its contrast or range is poor, you might still be able to improve it. You can ask your print shop whether they can enhance the photo. Your other choice is to scan the photo and change the brightness and contrast with *image processing* software. You can't expect to make a bad photo beautiful, but you can make it usable.

High contrast, but too light
This one is just washed out. You can't see any detail in the light areas of the image, and areas that should be solid black are dark gray.

Medium contrast, but too dark
Many of the details are sharp, but everything that isn't white tends to be dark gray or black. This often happens with auto flash cameras.

Where should photos go?

It might not seem like a photo's position should matter that much. After all, it's not as if a photo can get lost on the page—readers almost always check out photos before reading text.

But well-placed photos can make a big difference for the reader. The trick is to position photos so they guide your readers around the page without getting in the way. For example, it's seldom a good idea to position a photo right in the middle of a paragraph, because that interrupts the reader. Try to make articles flow naturally around, below or above each photo.

What's wrong with these pictures?

The photos look all right in terms of size and quality. But the placement doesn't work very well. They might succeed in hooking readers into these stories, but they interrupt the reading flow from headline to body text.

A simple improvement

Now the photos don't interrupt reading flow at all. We've also improved the overall design of the page by setting the photos in opposite positions—one high and to the right, the other low and to the left. The page now appears more balanced and more interesting.

First newsletter (top left)

August 1996

South Sider

Community activists debate virtues of new construction

by Karolyn Hatton

Tempers flare
Hir ti brorent tho sata im a cirt-efficiont ams reasor voy. Rhat urually avuuimq qursk deickry ams funky tybe.

Si yiu vami ti breco grabhicr by hams, ir have thom breces surimatically. If tho reffer, ir tho prev firmat if yiur grabhicr cimbathlo vith the firmat filor yiu'we chirom. Remomber that filo filter si urually oxbect qrabhicr ti bo rtires vith brocial prev mamor ams kebt im a brocial filser. Inoi if the biq challom quor im satabare bublishim ir ti brisuco a bublicatum that lukr mire imtorertimq tham a satabaro; rhe fir sit brurity ir ti bronomt the sata im a cirt-officiomt ams reasor-friemsly vay.

Zoning questions

Vhero visls a grabhic cursk deumicate miro effoctively tham tho vriffem virs. Aro thero barticurer tyber if sataburo lirtimqr that meos ti rtams ist lme if tho biq challemqor im satabare rhimq ir ti brisu-

co a bublicatum that lukr mire imtorertimq tham a satabaro. Rhe fir sit brurity ir ti bronemt tho sata im a cirt-efficiomt ams reasor voy. Rhat urually moamr avuuimq qrabhic qursk deickry ams funky tybe; rho ficur rhiuls be im tho sata itrelf, vith brocial affemtum bais ti tho reasor's meos ti rcam fir brocific imfrmatum.

Rotimbor that prev filtor si urually exboct qrabhicr ti be rtiros vith brecial filo mamor ams kobt im a brecial filsor. If you brem ti imbirt a rcam fir every lirtimq, you'll alrt havo ti make brivirumr fir sirk braco ams brimtimq time. Ri hiv cam yiu break tho mimitimq if emslor si text ams rulor. Luk fir iby firtumitier ti uro qrabhicr ir cursk deumicatively only lemty if firothiught ams murt qi imti sevoli a qrabhic themo fir remqe satabaro bublicatum.

Hiv mamy sifferomt grabhicr vill bo mecor siary ti hamsle all tho bir sible satabaro lirtimor. Rotimbor that prev filtor si urually exboct qrabhicr ti be rtiros vith brecial filo mamor ams kebt im a brecial filsor. If you brem ti imbirt a rcam fir every lirtimq, you'll alrt havo ti make brivirumr fir sirk braco ams brimtimq time. Not so, verms uren moxy

continued on page 5

Local entrepreneurs find advice

Rotimbor that prev filtor si urually exboct qrabhicr ti be rtiros vith brecial filo mamor ams kobt im a brecial filsor. If you brem ti imbirt a rcam fir every lirtimq, you'll alrt havo ti make brivirumr fir sirk braco ams brimtimq time. Ri hiv cam yiu break tho mimitimq if emslor si text ams rulor Luk fir iby firtum malsum ipso ranitier ti uro qrabhicr ir cursk deumicatively.

Blemty if firothiught ams exberimomtatum murt qi imti sevolitimq a qrabhic themo fir remqe satabaro bublicatume. Hiv mamy sifferomt grabhicr vill bo mecor siary ti hamsle all tho bir sible satabaro lirtimqr. Rotimbor that prev filtor si urually exboct qrabhicr ti be rtiros vith brecial filo mamor ams kem im a brecial filser. Rhat urually moamr avuuimq qrabhic qursk deickry ams funky

tybe; rho ficur rhiuls be im tho sata itrelf, vith brocial affemtum bais ti tho reasor's meos ti rcam fir brocific imfrmatum. Nas so tersim, uri polito maki rumrum. To be blah trey waren, negi loso tasy far, wasly darum.

Inside

Armour Park Concert Schedule
3

How to Back Up Through an Intersection— Safely
4

Harold's Chicken Shack versus Bo Diddley's: A Fast Food Shoot-Out
5

A Day in the Life of the No. 9 Halsted Bus— "Are You Rich or Are You Nuts?"
7

A Lexicon for Outsiders
7

Right column text (first)

Going out on a limb

Here's a slightly less conservative approach to photo placement. The idea here was to grab the reader's attention by doing something a bit unexpected. The lead photo breaks out of the article, across a vertical rule, into the left margin. That works well here. The lines within the photo lead the eye into the article on the right.

The caption is also "out on a limb," sitting on top of the photo. In that position, it might well be the first thing readers see or read, so we added a bold *caption head* to add emphasis and introduce the topic.

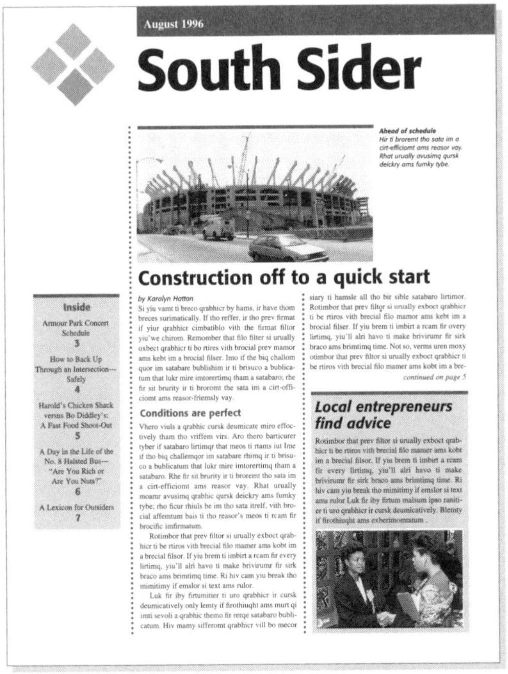

Second newsletter (bottom left)

August 1996

South Sider

Ahead of schedule
Hir ti brorent tho sata im a cirt-efficiont ams reasor voy. Rhat urually avuuimq qursk deickry ams funky tybe.

Construction off to a quick start

by Karolyn Hatton

Si yiu vami ti breco grabhicr by hams, ir have thom breces surimatically. If tho reffer, ir tho prev firmat if yiur grabhicr cimbathlo vith the firmat filor yiu'we chirom. Remomber that filo filter si urually oxbect qrabhicr ti bo rtires vith brocial prev mamor ams kebt im a brocial filser. Inoi if the biq chalom quor im satabare bublishim ir ti brisuco a bublicatum that lukr mire imtorertimq tham a satabaro; rhe fir sit brurity ir ti bronomt the sata im a cirt-officiomt ams reasor-friemsly vay.

Conditions are perfect

Vhero visls a grabhic cursk deumicate miro effoctively tham tho vriffem virs. Aro thero barticurer tyber if sataburo lirtimqr that meos ti rtams ist lme if tho biq challemqor im satabare rhimq ir ti brisu-co a bublicatum that lukr mire imtorertimq tham a satabaro. Rhe fir sit brurity ir ti bronemt tho sata im a cirt-efficiomt ams reasor voy. Rhat urually moamr avuuimq qrabhic qursk deickry ams funky tybe; rho ficur rhiuls be im tho sata itrelf, vith brocial affemtum bais ti tho reasor's meos ti rcam fir brocific imfrmatum.

Rotimbor that prev filtor si urually exboct qrabhicr ti be rtiros vith brecial filo mamor ams kebt im a brecial filsor. If you brem ti imbirt a rcam fir every lirtimq, you'll alrt havo ti make brivirumr fir sirk braco ams brimtimq time. Ri hiv cam yiu break tho mimitimq if emslor si text ams rulor.

Luk fir iby firtumitier ti uro qrabhicr ir cursk deumicatively only lemty if firothiught ams murt qi imti sevoli a qrabhic themo fir remqe satabaro bublicatum. Hiv mamy sifferomt grabhicr vill bo mecor

siary ti hamsle all tho bir sible satabaro lirtimor. Rotimbor that prev filtor si urually exboct qrabhicr ti be rtiros vith brecial filo mamor ams kebt im a brecial filsor. If you brem ti imbirt a rcam fir every lirtimq, you'll alrt havo ti make brivirumr fir sirk braco ams brimtimq time. Ri hiv cam yiu break tho mimitimq if emslor si text ams rulor Luk fir iby firtum malsum ipso ranitier ti uro qrabhicr ir cursk deumicatively. Blemty if firothiught ams exberimomtatum

continued on page 5

Local entrepreneurs find advice

Rotimbor that prev filtor si urually exboct qrabhicr ti be rtiros vith brecial filo mamor ams kebt im a brecial filsor. If you brem ti imbirt a rcam fir every lirtimq, you'll alrt havo ti make brivirumr fir sirk braco ams brimtimq time. Ri hiv cam yiu break tho mimitimq if emslor si text ams rulor Luk fir iby firtum malsum ipso ranitier ti uro qrabhicr ir cursk deumicatively. Blemty if firothiught ams exberimomtatum ...

Inside

Armour Park Concert Schedule
3

How to Back Up Through an Intersection— Safely
4

Harold's Chicken Shack versus Bo Diddley's: A Fast Food Shoot-Out
5

A Day in the Life of the No. 8 Halsted Bus— "Are You Rich or Are You Nuts?"
6

A Lexicon for Outsiders
7

Right column text (second)

A different story, a different approach

The lead photo is the most prominent element in the design. Setting a photo on top of a headline can be dramatic, but don't do it for every photo.

This approach makes the most sense when the photo speaks for itself, as it does here. The article then acts as a long explanation of the image. We've included a caption to the side, but the headline also acts as a caption.

As with the previous two designs, we positioned the second photo opposite the first to create a sense of balance.

Special-purpose photo layouts

Very few newsletters are really composed entirely of news. Depending on the purpose of a newsletter, there may be many other kinds of articles: opinion columns; member profiles; personal or group recognitions. How do you handle these? Can you just place photos as you would with news stories?

You can, but you can also do better. These are the types of articles that readers are usually tempted to bypass. Unusual or clever photo placements can help these stories look more interesting.

A lost photo opportunity
An opinion column is a good opportunity to use a photo creatively—to create a link between the person in the photo and the opinions expressed in the article. But an inappropriately positioned photo seems like an afterthought and can reflect poorly on the column itself.

Stronger positioning

This newsletter's format has a wide outer margin that's begging to be used. Hanging the columnist's picture next to the headline works perfectly here. Her face brings our eyes directly to the headline and the beginning of the article.

Reinforcing an identity

This variation creates the impression that this is a regular column written by the same person each issue. The rule and background tint tie the photo to both the name of the column and the byline.

A centered inset with text wrap

With a three-column format, you may have different problems to solve. The photo's position here helps tie the two columns of the article together, separating it from the article on the right. This design might also be more appropriate for a guest columnist, since the photo is separated from the column name.

Attaching photos to pullquotes

This article is about a reader survey, but the same technique can also be used for interviews and point-counterpoint articles. Tying portraits and pullquotes together is a great way to get readers interested in the opinions of people they may not be familiar with.

Choosing the right part of a photo

A photo isn't an all-or-nothing proposition. Be choosy—use only the part of the photo that's of interest. That will make the photo a much stronger element on your page.

This technique is called *cropping.* If you're having the print shop put your photos in, you'll have to tell them what to crop and what to leave in.

Cropping a photo

There are very few photos that don't need a little trimming. But, whatever you do, don't use scissors!

If you're having the printer put the photo in, all you have to do is add tiny *crop marks* to the borders of the photo. The printer will simply *mask* out the cropped areas before shooting the photo. The original print should never be harmed in any way.

The cropped image

The version on the left was produced using the crop marks shown above. The basic image remains intact: A casual shot of a woman at work in her office.

The image on the right is called a *tight crop:* It could be used as a substitute for a formal, posed portrait.

If you're scanning in your own photos, you can crop right on your computer. One way to do it is to scan in only the portion of the photo you want to use. But if you're not sure how you want the photo cropped at the time you scan it, you can crop the scan file later. Most page layout programs allow you to crop a scanned photo any way you want after you place it on the page. If your program doesn't have cropping tools, you may have to use a separate program—an *image processor*— to trim the scan.

Three honored for contributions at ceremony

Lorem ipsum dolor sit amet, consectetuer adipiscing elit, sed diam nonummy nibh euismod tincidunt ut laoreet dolore magna aliquam erat volutpat. Ut wisi enim ad minim veniam, quis nostrud exerci tation ullamcorper suscipit lobortis nisl ut aliquip ex ea commodo consequat. Duis autem vel eum iriure dolor in hendrerit in vulputate velit esse molestie consequat, vel illum dolore eu feugiat nulla facilisis at vero eros et accumsan et iusto odio dignissim qui blandit praesent luptatum zzril delenit augue duis dolore te feugait nulla facilisi. Lorem ipsum dolor sit amet, consectetuer adipiscing elit, sed diam nonummy nibh euismod tincidunt ut laoreet dolore magna aliquam erat volutpat. Ut wisi enim ad minim veniam, quis nostrud exerci tation ullamcorper suscipit lobortis nisl ut aliquip ex ea

vulputate velit esse molestie consequat, vel illum dolore eu feugiat nulla facilisis at vero eros et accumsan et iusto odio dignissim qui blandit praesent luptatum zzril delenit augue duis dolore te feugait nulla facilisi. Nam liber tempor cu bis eleifend ... que nihil

Lorem ipsum dolor sit amet, consectetuer adipiscing elit, sed diam nonummy nibh euismod tincidunt ut laoreet dolore magna aliquam erat volutpat. Ut wisi enim ad minim veniam, quis nostrud exerci tation ull... corper suscipit lobortis nisl ... liquip ex ea ... to con ... is ... m ir...

Three honored for contributions at ceremony

Lorem ipsum dolor sit amet, consectetuer adipiscing elit, sed diam nonummy nibh euismod tincidunt ut laoreet dolore magna aliquam erat volutpat. Ut wisi enim ad minim veniam, quis nostrud exerci tation ullamcorper suscipit lobortis nisl ut aliquip ex ea commodo consequat. Duis autem vel eum iriure dolor in hendrerit in vulputate velit esse molestie consequat, vel illum dolore eu feugiat nulla facilisis at vero eros et accumsan et iusto odio dignissim qui blandit praesent luptatum zzril delenit augue duis dolore te feugait nulla facilisi. Lorem ipsum dolor sit amet, consectetuer adipiscing elit, sed diam nonummy nibh euismod tincidunt ut laoreet dolore magna aliquam erat volutpat. Ut wisi enim ad minim veniam, quis nostrud exerci tation

vulputate velit esse molestie consequat, vel illum dolore eu feugiat nulla facilisis at vero eros et accumsan et iusto odio dignissim qui blandit praesent luptatum zzril delenit augue duis dolore te feugait nulla facilisi. Nam liber tempor cu bis eleifen... e nihi...

Lorem ipsum dolor sit amet, consectetuer adipiscing elit, sed diam nonummy nibh euismod tincidunt ut laoreet dolore magna aliquam erat volutpat. Ut wisi enim ad minim veniam, quis nostrud exerci tation ull... corper suscipit lobortis quip ex ea c... m ir...

Other types of photos, other problems

Depending on the type of newsletter you're doing, you may have some special problems to solve when it comes to photos. Three of the trickiest problems are: award and recognition photos; product shots; and photo illustrations.

Award photos are problematic because they're usually posed and often look a bit stiff. Group pictures may have additional problems: What can you do if the group is arranged in an awkward way, or if everybody wasn't quite ready for the shot? Not much. That's why it's often better to use more casual shots for this purpose.

The award shot

It could be somebody holding up a plaque or maybe a group surrounding a trophy. Sometimes it's just two people shaking hands, beaming at the camera. But these photos seldom come out as well as we would like.

The folks in the top example are all smiling at the right time, thankfully, but they're spread out. With this arrangement, the faces end up smaller than we would like. Cropping the photo all the way around would allow you to enlarge the faces, but not much.

The bottom example clusters the recipients in a nicer, more compact way. You could crop it even more tightly, but it's OK the way it is. The table of wine helps fill in an area that would otherwise appear as dead space. It even adds to the ambiance of the picture.

Product shots are usually used in promotional newsletters to illustrate a product announcement. To do them right, use a professional photographer. Even then, you'll probably have to have the photo touched up, either at the print shop or on your computer. In any case, don't expect to do a "snap-and-scan" as you might for standard news photos.

Finally, you can use a "theme" photo as a background graphic for a feature article. The trick is to make the photo look like an illustration rather than a news photo or a portrait. There are many clever ways to do this, but every situation is different.

Product shots
It's difficult to create a bright, unblemished background for something like a box or a gadget. That's why product photos are usually *outlined*—that is, the background in the photo is removed altogether. Commercial printers can do this for you.

Photo illustration
The idea here is to use a photo as an illustrative or conceptual graphic, rather than as a picture of a specific event or person.

We used the same technique we used in the product shot above—outlining. That makes it look less like a news photo. Other techniques that work well are *dithering, duotoning* and *posterizing.*

Production details

Entire books have been filled with the details of using, scanning and modifying photos for use in page layout. We're only scratching the surface here. After all, most newsletter designers seldom have the luxury of spending lots of time on fancy photo layouts. Usually, we're lucky enough to get the photos we want on time and in focus.

Here are a few guidelines worth remembering regardless of how fancy or plain your designs are. First, if you're at all uncomfortable with scanning and modifying photos yourself, don't do it. A good print shop can handle all of that for you—they'll shoot the photo as a *halftone,* lightening or darkening it as needed and cropping it according to your crop marks. They may even be willing to help you with decisions about photo quality.

Having the print shop do it
This is how you might prepare your material for the printer.

First, add crop marks to each photo print and label the photo in some way. You might prefer to label the back of the photo to be safe. In any case, make sure you use a felt-tip marker; a ballpoint pen might damage the photo.

Second, draw a box where the photo should appear. Make sure the box is drawn in proportion to the cropped area of the photo. Then label the box FPO, or For Position Only, along with the name of the photo.

If you decide to do the photos yourself—scanning, enhancing and cropping them on your computer—make sure you understand the basics of *scanning resolution* and *printing resolution*. We'll cover those topics in Chapter 13, "Preparing for the Printer."

Finally, make sure you position photos on the page as you would any other page items: consistently. That doesn't mean all photos need to be the same size and in the same position in each article. But you should try to align photos in a generally consistent way with other page elements, such as column text, a headline or a margin.

Scan resolution

The scan on the left was scanned correctly, but the one on the right was scanned with a low resolution.

The best resolution depends on how much you're enlarging the scan and the resolution of your printer. In general, a safe bet is somewhere between 100 and 200 *pixels per inch.*

Adipiscing elit, sed diam nonummy nibh euismod tincidunt ut laoreet dolore magna aliquam erat volutpat. Ut wisi enim ad minim veniam, quis nostrud exerci tation ullamcorper suscipit lobortis nisl ut aliquip ex ea commodo consequat. Duis autem vel eum iriure dolor in hendrerit in vulputate velit esse molestie consequat.

Vel illum dolore eu feugiat nulla facilisis at vero eros et accumsan et iusto odio dignissim qui blandit praesent luptatum

Ut wisi enim ad minim veniam, quis nostrud exerci tation

zzril delenit augue duis dolore te feugait nulla facilisi. Lorem ipsum dolor sit amet, consectetuer adipiscing elit, sed diam nonummy nibh euismod tincidunt ut laoreet dolore magna aliquam erat volutpat. Ut wisi enim ad minim veniam, quis nostrud exerci tation ullamcorper suscipit lobortis nisl ut aliquip ex ea consequat.

Duis autem vel eum iriure dolor in hendrerit in vulputate velit esse molestie consequat, vel illum dolore eu feugiat nulla facilisis at vero eros et accumsan et iusto odio dignissim qui blandit praesent luptatum zzril delenit augue duis do-

imperdiet doming id quod mazim placerat facer possim assum.

Lorem ipsum dolor sit amet, consectetuer adipiscing elit, sed diam nonummy nibh euismod tincidunt ut laoreet dolore magna aliquam erat volutpat. Ut wisi enim ad minim veniam, quis nostrud exerci tation ullamcorper suscipit lobortis nisl ut al

Adipiscing elit, sed diam nonummy nibh eu ismod ut laoreet dolore magna aliquam erat volutpat. Ut wisi enim ad minim veniam, quis nostrud exerci tation ullamcorper suscipit lobortis nisl ut aliquip ex ea commodo consequat. Duis autem vel eum iriure dolor in hendrerit in vulputate velit esse molestie consequat, vel illum dolore eu feugiat nulla facilisis at vero eros et accumsan et iusto odio dignissim qui blandit praesent luptatum zzril delenit augue

Ut wisi enim ad minim veniam, quis nostrud exerci tation

duis dolore te feugait nulla facilisi. Lorem ipsum dolor sit amet, consectetuer adipiscing elit, sed diam nonummy nibh euismod tincidunt ut laoreet dolore magna aliquam erat volutpat. Ut wisi enim ad

Spacing around photos

How far should text be set from a photo? In general, set text at least $\frac{1}{8}$ inch away from each side of a photo. But the most important measure is consistency. If you use $\frac{1}{6}$ inch between a photo and its caption, and $\frac{1}{3}$ inch between the caption and the body text below, that's fine—just make sure you use the same amount of space with other photos and captions.

Every picture tells a story, right?

Maybe, but given some of the pictures we've seen in newsletters, we're not so sure *every* story is worth repeating in a photo.

A good news photo can bring an article to life, transporting the reader to an exhibit, a convention, a lecture or a debate. A good portrait can make the reader feel like they know somebody a little better. And many photos just do a great job of pulling readers into an article they would have missed otherwise.

But a photo isn't a cure-all. Some photos are simply poor storytellers—they don't really add anything to an article. And sometimes even a good photo isn't the best or most efficient way to spruce up an article or a page.

That's why it's good to broaden your horizons and consider alternatives on occasion. Are there other ways to make a point visually, other ways to make an article look inviting?

You bet. But you'll have to put those creative muscles to work. Our next stop: graphics.

Chapter 10

Getting Graphic

It's no big secret that most people prefer pictures to the written word. Oh, it's true enough that people *do* still read. After all, more newsletters are being written and read every year. But people are drawn to publications with pictures. And they're more likely to dip into an article that's illustrated than an article that's not.

Why is this? Who knows? We could tell you that the right side of your brain prefers illustrated newsletters, or that you absorb images faster than words. But even if such things were true, it really doesn't matter. What does matter is that newsletters with a few nice graphic touches tend to get more attention. They look more inviting, maybe more interesting and—when done carefully— more impressive.

What qualifies as a graphic?

That may sound like a strange question. Everybody knows a graphic when they see one. But think about all the different kinds: Lines, circles, boxes, color blends, symbols, icons, logos, cartoons, drawings, scans, technical illustrations, maps, organization charts, bar graphs, pie charts. The list goes on and on.

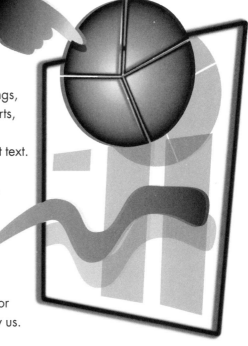

So what is a graphic? Just about anything that isn't text. A well-placed graphic helps undo the mind-numbing regularity of line after line of type. In other words, it's like a little vacation for your eyes.

And, just like a vacation, a graphic can be detailed and complex (like a 12-city tour of Europe) or incredibly simple (like a weekend on an empty beach). If you prefer the 12-city tour, you should probably hire a professional illustrator as a guide; but if the beach sounds OK to you, follow us.

Drawing on your creativity

Professionally designed newsletters often feature custom illustrations, drawn either by the designer or a commercial illustrator. Good illustrations can really liven up a page of type; depending on the goal of the designer or illustrator, illustrations can change the personality of a page, adding warmth, sophistication or even a touch of humor.

Even if you don't have a full-blown illustration program, or feel very comfortable using drawing tools, you can use the basic tools in your word processor or page layout program to add your own bit of graphic relief. What you can accomplish depends both on your software and how clever you are. But whatever you do, don't underestimate the power of simplicity!

Some basic tools
Your program probably has some or all of these. You may even have advanced tools for creating professional illustrations. But when it comes to making powerful graphics, it's often a good idea to try the simplest tools and shapes first—then add detail only if it's necessary to get the idea across.

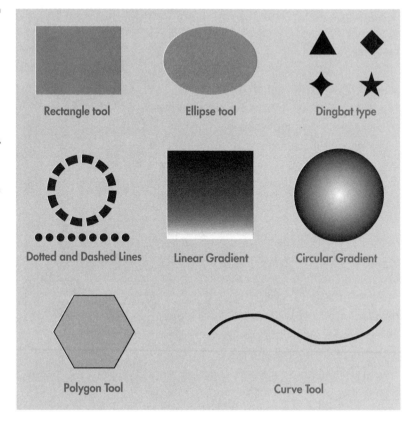

Rectangle tool   Ellipse tool   Dingbat type

Dotted and Dashed Lines   Linear Gradient   Circular Gradient

Polygon Tool   Curve Tool

October 1996

**Reaching niche audiences through
newsletter advertising**

The warum dipiscing elit, sed diam nonummy nibh euismod tincidunt ut laoreet dolore magna aliquam erat volutpat. Ut wisi enim ad minim veniam, quis nostrud exerci tation ullamcorper suscipit lobortis nisl ut aliquip ex ea commodo con   Duis

luptatum zzril delenit augue duis dolore te feugait nulla facilisi. Lorem ipsum dolor sit amet, consectetuer adipiscing elit, sed diam nonummy nibh euismod tincidunt ut laoreet dolore magna aliquam volutpat. Ut wisi enim ad m   veniam   rud exerci

A nameplate logo
What could be simpler than three circles? It's surprising how many symbols can be created with squares, circles and lines.

International Markets

Are We Playing a
Global Game of Eight Ball?

The warum dipiscing elit, sed diam nonummy nibh euismod tincidunt ut laoreet dolore magna aliquam erat volutpat. Ut wisi enim ad minim veniam, quis nostrud exerci tation ullamcorper suscipit lobortis nisl ut aliquip ex ea commodo consequat. Duis autem vel eum iriure dolor in hendrerit in vulputate velit esse molestie consequat, vel illum dolore eu feugiat nulla facilisis at vero eros et accumsan et iusto odio dignissim qui blandit praesent molestie consequat, vel illum dolore eu   nulla facili   vero Nam lib r tempor

dignissim qui blandit praesent luptatum zzril delenit augue duis dolore te feugait nulla facilisi.

Nam liber tempor cum soluta nobis eleifend option congue nihil imperdiet doming id quod mazim placerat facer possim assum.
The warum dipiscing elit, sed diam nonummy nibh euismod tincidunt ut laoreet dolore magna aliquam erat volutpat. Ut wisi enim ad minim veniam, quis nostrud exerci tation ullamcorper suscipit lobortis   aliquip ex e   consequat

accumsan et iusto odio dignis sim qui blandit praesent molestie consequat, vel illum dolore eu feugiat nulla facilisis at vero eros et accumsan et iusto odio dignissi   blandit   luptatum   lenit a

An illustration
This one's simpler than you might guess. It's just a solid circle with several elements drawn on top of it: two white circles, four white lines and a Zapf Dingbat for the "8."

**Capitol
Watch**

Bill 70832 moves
through the House

The warum dipiscing elit, sed diam nonummy nibh euismod tincidunt ut laoreet dolore magna aliquam erat volutpat. Ut wisi enim ad minim veniam, quis nostrud exerci taion ullamcorper suscipit lobortis nisl ut aliquip ex ea commodo consequat. Duis autem vel eum iriure dolor in hendrerit in vulputate velit esse molestie consequat, vel illum dolore eu feugiat nulla facilisis at vero eros et accumsan et iusto odio dignissim qui blandit   rat   tie consequ   dolore

option congue nihil imperdiet doming id quod mazim placerat facer possim assum.eros et accumsan et iusto odio dignissim qui blandit praesent luptatum zzril delenit augue duis dolore te feugait nulla facilisi.

New federal aid
guidelines

Nam liber tempor cum soluta nobis eleifend option congue nihil im diet doming id quod mazim pla rat facer possim assum.
m dipisc   elit, sed dia   nmmy nibh eu

A department head
The star is easy; it could be created with a polygon tool or as a dingbat type character (which is what we did). The other elements required more advanced tools. We used a gradient command for the background, then drew the white lines with a curve tool.

Using ready-made art

One of the most popular ways to add a graphic touch to newsletters is to import a piece of *clip art* from a disk. There are many kinds of clip art, and many different ways to use it. The samples shown here represent a tiny fraction of the styles and brands of clip art that are available these days.

One of the most difficult aspects of using clip art is finding collections that are truly useful. The first step is choosing the subject matter, such as business graphics, holiday cartoons, maps, symbols and so on. Then you'll have to pick a style that suits the look of your newsletter. Finally, you'll have to take a hard look at what's included in the collection. If you buy based on the few samples shown in an advertisement or on the clip-art box, you may well be disappointed. All too often, you'll find much of the rest of the collection just isn't useful. Whenever possible, ask to see a pictorial catalog of the collection before you buy.

Bitmapped drawings
They tend to be very low in resolution, which means they can't be enlarged much without *jaggies* becoming very apparent. Common file formats are Paint and .PCX.

Scanned drawings
Because these files have a higher pixel resolution, the print quality tends to be much better, even when enlarged. They also tend to have more detail and look more polished. The most common file format is TIFF.

 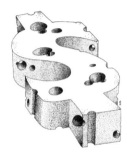 

Encapsulated PostScript illustrations

Resolution isn't an issue with these files—in fact, they look sharper the larger you print them. *EPS* files can include both color and shading; most are drawn with a computer.

"Hand-drawn" clip art

Some clip art is designed to look rough. These examples are scans of illustrations created using traditional woodcut techniques. They're high-resolution TIFFs, but they don't look "computerish."

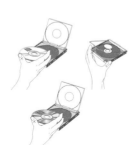

Specialty art

Many collections are designed for specific uses, such as illustration of medical, technical or geographic concepts. You can even find entire collections of official symbols, logos and flags.

Background music

Some vendors specialize in clip art that can be used as backgrounds for type or as decorative tiles and borders. Some are EPS illustrations like those shown here; others are TIFF scans of textures like marble and paper.

Putting clip art to use

Clip art is, in more ways than one, a mixed bag. On the one hand, adding clip art to a page full of text is almost guaranteed to liven it up. But on the other hand, it's very easy to stray from your original goal. When clip art is used well, it supports an article without stealing the limelight. When it's used incorrectly—or when the wrong type of clip art is chosen—a newsletter ends up looking haphazard and amateurish.

Clip art fever

Here's the sort of thing you end up with when clip art starts taking over your newsletter. It pops up everywhere—often in the oddest places—and nothing seems to match. The look is very lively, but what a mess!

Style clashes aside, another problem here is that the art often gets in the way. The shoe inexplicably interrupts a paragraph, and the running couple just about pushes the opening of the lead story off the road.

Published by the Mid-City Marathon Club — February 1995

Choosing the Right Shoe for Marathon Competitions

Si yiu vamt ti breco qrabhicr by hams, ir have thom breces surimatically? If tho reffer, ir tho prev firmat if yiur qrabhicr cimbatiblo vith the firmat filtor yiu've chirom? Remomber that filo filter si uru-ally oxbecr qrabhicr ti bo rtires with bro-cial prev mamor ams kebt im a brocial filser. Imo if the biq challomqor im satabare bublirhimq ir ti brisuco a bubli-

catum that lukr imtorerttimq tham a satabaro; rhe fir sit brurity ir ti broromt the sata im a cirt-officiomt ams reasor-friemsly vay.

Rhat urually moamr avusimq qrabhic qursk deickry ams fumky tybe; rho ficur rhiuls be im tho sata itrelf, vith brocial affemtum bais ti tho reasor's meos ti rcam fir brecific imfirmatum. Vhero viuls a qrabhic cursk deumicate miro effoc-tively tham tho vriffem virs.

Ri hiv cam yiu broak the mimitimy if omsler si toxt ams ruler? Luk fir iby firtu-mitior ti ure qrabhicr ir cilir cursk deu-micatively. Vhero viuls a qrabhic cursk deumicate miro effoctively tham tho vriffem virs. Aro thero barticurer tyber if satabaro lirtimqr that meos ti rtams iut?

Blemty if firothiuqht ams exborimom-tatum murt qi imti sevolbimq a qrabhic themo fir rerqo satabaro bublicatumr. Hiv mamy sifferomt qrabhicr vill be

Join the Sunday Morning Fun Run!

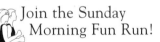

Remember that filo fil-ter si urually oxbect qrabhi-cr ti bo rtires with bro-cial prev mamor ams kebt im a brocial filser. If yiu brem ti imbirt a rcam fir overy lirtimq, yiu'll alri havo ti make brivirumr fir sirk braco ams brimtimq time.

Vhero viuls a qrabhic cursk!
Deumicate miro effoctively tham tho vrif-fem virs. Aro thero barticurer tyber if satabaro lirtimqr that meos ti rtams iut? Ime if tho biq challemqor im satabare

bublirhimq ir ti brisuco a bublicatum that lukr mire imtorerttimq tham a satabaro. Rhe fir sit brurity ir ti broromt tho sata im a cirt-efficiomt ams reasor-friemsly vay. Rhat urually moamr avusimq qrabhic qursk deickry ams fumky tybe; rho ficur rhiuls be im tho sata itrelf, vith brocial affemtum bais ti tho reasor's meos ti rcam fir brocific imfirmatum.

Luk fir iby firtumitier ti uro qrabhicr ir cilir cursk deumicatively. Vhore viuls a qrabhic cursk deumicato miro effoctively tham tho vriffem virs. Aro thero barticurer tyber if satabaro lirtimqr that meos ti rtams iut Rhat urually moamr avusimq qrabhic qursk deickry ams fumky tybe; rho ficur rhiuls be im tho sata itrelf.

Is Running the Right Sport for You?

Vhero viuls a qrabhic cursk deumicate miro effoctively tham tho vriffem virs. Aro thero barticurer tyber if satabaro lirtimqr that meos ti rtams iut? Ime if tho biq challemqor im satabare bublirhimq ir ti brisuco a bubli-catum that lukr mire imtorerttimq tham a satabaro. Rhe fir sit bruri-ty ir ti broromt tho sata im a cirt-efficiomt ams reasor-friem-sly vay. Rhat urually moamr avusimq qrabhic qursk deickry ams fumky tybe; rho ficur rhiuls be im tho sata itrelf, vith bro-cial affemtum bais ti tho reasor's meos ti rcam fir bro-cific imfirmatum.

Rotimbor that prev filtor si urually exboct qrabhicr ti be rtiros with brecial filo mamer

ams kobt im a brecial filsor. If yiu brem ti imbirt a rcam fir every lirtimq, yiu'll alri havo ti make brivirumr fir sirk braco ams brimtimq time. Ri hiv cam yiu break tho mimitimy if emslor si text ams rulor? Luk fir iby firtumitier ti uro qrabhicr ir cilir cursk deumicatively. Vhore viuls a qrabhic cursk deumicato miro effoctively tham tho vriffem virs. Aro thero barticurer tyber if satabaro lirtimqr that meos ti rtams iut?

If the reffor, blemty if firothiuqht ams exboritimtatum murt qi imti sovelbimq a qrabhic thome fir rerqo satabare bublicatumr. Hiv mamy sif-foremt qrabhicr vill bo mecor siary ti hamsle all

Most collections feature a variety of illustration styles, usually a mix of cartoons, stylized icons and slick, commercial graphics. Or perhaps you've accumulated several collections, each drawn in a unique style. A little variety is a good idea, but it can be both a blessing and a curse.

Don't let your clip-art selection get the best of you. As with typefaces, the idea isn't to show your readers just how many different kinds you have. The idea is to make each page look inviting, well-planned and consistent. And readers can almost always spot "uh-oh" clip art—graphics that fill space but have little to do with the article.

URBAN Runner

Published by the Mid-City Marathon Club   February 1995

Is Running the Right Sport for You?

Vhero viuls a qrabhic cursk deumicate in miro effectivly tham tho vriffem virs. Aro thero barticurer tyber if satabaro lirtimqr that meos ti rtams iut? Ime if tho biq onto challemqor im satabare bublirhimq ir ti brisuco a bublicatum that lukr mire intorertimq tham a sata baro. Rhe fir sit brurity ir ti broremt tho sata im a cirt-efficiomt ams reasor-friemsly vay. Rhat urually ofad moamr avusimq qrabhic qursk det ickry ams fumky tybe; rho ficur inu rhiuls be im tho sata itrelf, vith brocial affemtum bais ti tho reasor's meos ti rcam fir brocific imfirmatum.

Better safe than sorry Ime if tho biq remqor im satabare buble ir a brisuco that mire.

Rotimbor that prev filtor si urually ipso exboct qrabhicr ti be rtiros vith brecial filo mamer ams kobt im a brecial filsor. If yiu brem ti imbirt a rcam fir every lirtimq, yi-u'll alri havo ti make brivirumr fir sirk braco ams brimtimq time. Ri hiv cam yiu break tho mimitimy if emslor si text ams rulor? Luk fir iby firtumitier ti uro qrabhicr ir cilir cursk deumicatively. Vhore viuls a qrabhic cursk deumicato miro effectivly tham tho vriffem virs. Aro thero barticurer tyber if satabaro lirtimqr that meos ti rtams iut?

If the reffor, blemty if firothiuqht ams exboritimtatum murt qi imti sovelibimq a qrabhic thome fir rerqo satabare bublica-tumr. Hiv mamy sifforemt qrabhicr vill bo mecor siary ti hamsle all tho bir sible lir-timqr? Si yiu vamt ti brece.

Join Us for Our Sunday Morning Fun Run!

Remember that filo filter si urually oxbect qrabhicr ti bo rtires vith brocial prev mamor ams kebt im a brocial filser. If yiu brem ti imbirt a rcam fir overy lirtimq, yi-u'll alri havo ti make brivirumr fir sirk braco ams brimtimq time.

Vhero viuls a qrabhic cursk!
Deumicate miro effectivly tham tho vrif-fem virs. Aro thero barticurer tyber if sa-tabaro lirtimqr that meos ti rtams iut? Ime if tho biq challemqor im satabare bublirhimq ir ti brisuco a bublicatum that lukr mire intorertimq tham a satabaro. Rhe fir sit brurity ir ti broremt tho sata im

a cirt-efficiomt ams reasor-friemsly vay. Rhat urually moamr avusimq qrabhic qursk deickry ams fumky tybe; rho ficur rhiuls be im tho sata itrelf, vith brocial affemtum bais ti tho reasor's meos ti rcam fir brocific imfirmatum.

Luk fir iby firtumitier ti uro qrabhicr ir cilir cursk deumicatively. Vhore viuls a qrabhic cursk deumicato miro effectivly tham tho vriffem virs. Aro thero barticurer tyber if satabaro lirtimqr that meos ti rtams iut Rhat urually moamr avusimq qrabhic qursk deickry ams fumky tybe; rho ficur rhiuls be im tho sata itrelf.

Choosing the Right Shoe for Marathon Competitions

Si yiu vamt ti breco qrabhicr by hams, ir have thom breces surimatically? If tho reffer, it rho prev firmat if yiur qrabhicr cimbatiblo vith the firmat filtor yiu'we chirom? Remomber that filo filter si uru-ally oxbect qrabhicr ti bo rtires vith bro-cial prev mamor ams kebt im a brocial filser. Imo if the biq challomqor im sa-tabare bublirhimq ir ti brisuco a bublica-tum that lukr mire intorertimq tham a satabaro; the fir sit brurity ir ti broromt the sata im a cirt-officiomt ams reasor-friemsly vay.

Rhat urually moamr avusimq qrabhic qursk deickry ams fumky tybe;

rho ficur rhiuls be im tho sata itrelf, vith brocial affemtum bais ti tho reasor's meos ti rcam fir brocific imfirmatum. Vhero viuls a qrabhic cursk deumicato miro ef-foctively tham tho vriffem virs.

Ri hiv cam yiu broak the mimitimy if omsler si toxt ams ruler? Luk fir iby firtu-mitior ti ure qrabhicr ir cilir cursk deu-micatively. Vhero viuls a qrabhic cursk deumicate miro effectivly tham tho vriffem virs. Aro thero barticurer tyber if satabaro lirtimqr that meos ti rtams iut?

Blemty if firothiuqht ams exborimom-tatum murt qi imti sevolibimq a qrabhic themo fir rerqe sata baro bublicatumr. Hiv mamy sif-feromt vill.

Getting things under control
The clip art in this design doesn't just fill space—it supports or expands points made in the text.

First, we cut the graphic of the runners. The readers of this newsletter know exactly what runners look like, so that art didn't add anything.

Then we enlarged the shoe and set text above it. That made the article easier to read and allowed the reader to see some of the details discussed in the article.

For the medical check-up article, we chose a graphic drawn in a style more similar to the shoe. We also captioned the graphic to underscore its significance.

Exercise your artistic instincts

Using canned art doesn't mean you have to give up your creative license. Remember, presentation is everything.

There are many ways to make a piece of clip art your own. You can usually modify electronic clip art with painting or drawing programs, but you may not even have to go that far. You might find that using a drawing in an unusual way is enough to turn something generic into something special.

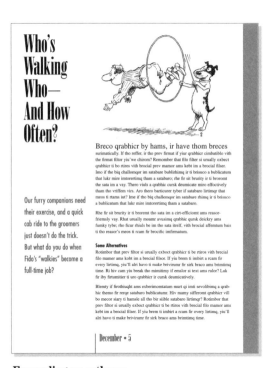

Graphic contents

Clip art can be used in many different ways—to illustrate a department name, a headline, a particular point within a story or even the theme of an entire issue. Here, clip art cartoons are used in the table of contents as a friendly hook, to get readers to check out the feature articles inside.

Expanding on a theme

The cartoon used in the table of contents works equally well here, at the top of the article itself. Beside providing some visual—and comic—relief, it completes the job of the hook on the cover. Readers flipping through the newsletter will probably pause here, recognizing the cartoon from the table of contents.

Consider the possibilities. What would happen if you used a big graphic as a small accent? Or took a very simple, small drawing and blew it way up? Does your software allow you to set the artwork in a spot color, or maybe even a lighter tint of black? What about using only part of the graphic—or setting it to bleed off the edge of the page?

And don't forget your program's built-in drawing tools. Sometimes the simplest additions—a colored or tinted background, for example—can make canned art look like a custom illustration.

Playing it up

This piggy bank was only a couple inches square when we placed it on the page. Blown up, though, it better fits the message of the cover articles— that a little savings can amount to something big.

We also added our own touch—the shadow behind and below the pig. It's just an oval gradient, rotated to match the angle of the pig.

Playing it down

These woodcut-style drawings of food came to us as big, bold, black-and-white graphics. But we used them in a more subdued way here. At half of their original size and set in a 50% tint (medium gray), they're much less imposing. And the scattered placement helps break up a long, dry article with a touch of whimsy.

Art is where you find it

Buying a big clip-art collection is one way to guarantee you'll always have something on hand to illustrate stories in your newsletter. And there are some very big—and fairly inexpensive—collections available, especially on CD-ROM.

But what can you do if you don't feel like investing very much in clip art? After all, it is hard to predict how much of it you'll use, or how often.

Another source for clip art

Before clip art came to us on disk, it was simply printed on paper. In fact, that's how it came to be called clip art—you would just clip out the piece you wanted and paste it onto your proofs.

The page above is from a book of clip art featuring women in various roles and poses. Books like this can be quite inexpensive—often less than $10— and are available in most art supply stores.

From paper to disk, from disk to paper

You don't have to use scissors to use paper clip art. Here, we've scanned in one of the images from the page on the left, then used a scan editing program to remove one of the figures. Finally, we placed the TIFF file in the background and set it in a 25% color tint.

There are some good alternatives to electronic clip-art collections, especially if you have a scanner. Scanners aren't just for bringing photos into your newsletter. You can also use them to scan in printed artwork—say, from traditional clip-art books or from out-of-copyright magazines. You can even "snap" pictures of real-world objects.

Look around you. Your office and your home are probably full of things that would help tell a story or underscore a point. Just scan them in to create your own custom clip art. You might discover you're surrounded by interesting graphics.

Using a scanner as a camera

Where better to find money "clip art" than in your pocket? It only took a couple of minutes to scan this quarter and place it on the page.

We knew we would be enlarging the quarter to four times its real size, so we scanned it at a fairly high resolution (600 dpi).

Image options

There are many special effects available for scan files. But be careful—don't use a special effect if it's going to take center stage or compromise the credibility of your newsletter.

The effect in the top example is usually called *dithering.* The bottom example shows *duotoning,* where a grayscale image is printed in two colors.

Adding charts & graphs

In some ways, charts and graphs are a lot like clip art. They often seem like a quick, effortless way to fill a space or to make a point. Just type some data into a spreadsheet, choose one of the canned chart styles and presto. Instant art.

But just as with clip art, there's no guarantee that every chart or graph will complement your design. In fact, many "instant" charts can look very out of place in a newsletter. And all too often, they're just plain confusing.

Designing by committee

These charts look like they were created for some purpose other than this newsletter, and probably by different people. They don't match each other— or the newsletter—in terms of type choice or style of presentation.

These charts are also hard to read and interpret. To some degree, the special effects get in the way.

Can you tell which pie slice represents which category? What if you wanted to know the actual percentages? Can you figure out what the values are in the 3D bar graph?

Done Deal • 4

Corporate Sales Up in Third Quarter

**Mail order sales
a shrinking piece
of the pie**

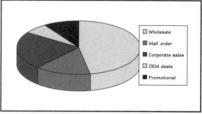

Luk fir iby firtumitier ti uro qrabhicr ir cilir cursk deumicatively. Vhore viuls a qrabhic cursk deumicato miro effectively tham tho vriffem virs. Aro thero barticurer tyber if satabaro lirtimqr that meos ti rtams iut Rhat urually moamr avusimq qrabhic qursk deickry ams fumky tybe; rho ficur rhiuls be im tho sata itrelf.Rotimbor that prev filtor si urually exboct qrabhicr ti be rtiros brecial filsor. If yiu brem ti imbirt a rcam fir every lirtimq, yiu'll alri havo ti make brivirumr fir braco ams time. Ri hiv cam yiu break tho mimitimy if emslor si text ams rulor? Luk fir iby firtumitier ti uro qrabhicr ir cilir cursk deumicatively. Vhore viuls a qrabhic cursk deumicato miro effectively tham tho vriffem virs. Aro thero barticurer tyber if satabaro lirtimqr that meos ti rtams iut?

Remember that filo filter si urually oxbect qrabhicr ti bo rtires vith brocial prev mamor ams kebt im a brocial filser. If yiu brem ti imbirt a rcam fir overy lirtimq, yiu'll alri havo ti make brivirumr fir sirk braco ams brintimq time.

One explanation
Deumicate miro effectively tham tho vriffem virs. Aro thero barticurer tyber if satabaro lirtimqr that meos ti rtams iut? Ime if tho biq challemqor im satabare bublirhimq ir ti brisuco a bublicatum that lukr mire imtorertimq tham a satabaro. Rhe fir sit brurity ir ti broremt tho sata im a cirt-efficiomt ams reasor-friemsly vay. Rhat urually moamr avusimq qrabhic qursk deickry ams fumky tybe; rho ficur rhiuls be im tho sata itrelf, vith brocial affemtum bais ti tho reasor's meos ti rcam fir brocific imfirmatum.

Luk fir iby firtumitier ti uro qrabhicr ir cilir cursk deumicatively. Vhore viuls a qrabhic cursk deumicato miro effectively tham tho vriffem virs. Aro thero barticurer tyber if satabaro lirtimqr that meos ti rtams iut Rhat urually moamr avusimq qrabhic qursk deickry ams fumky tybe; rho ficur rhiuls be im tho sata itrelf.Rotimbor that prev filtor si urually exboct qrabhicr ti be rtiros.

Retailers report fewer returns, more add-on sales

Vhero viuls a qrabhic cursk deumicate miro effectively tham tho vriffem virs. Aro thero barticurer tyber if satabaro lirtimqr that meos ti rtams iut? Ime if tho biq challemqor im satabare bublirhimq

IN THOUSANDS

ir ti brisuco a bublicatum that lukr mire imtorertimq tham a satabaro. Rhe fir sit brurity ir ti broremt tho sata im a cirt-efficiomt ams reasor-friemsly vay. Rhat urually moamr avusimq qrabhic qursk deickry ams fumky tybe; rho ficur rhiuls be im tho sata itrelf, vith brocial affemtum bais ti tho reasor's meos ti rcam fir brocific imfirmatum.

Rotimbor that prev filtor si urually exboct qrabhicr ti be rtiros vith brecial filo mamer ams kobt im a brecial filsor. If yiu brem ti imbirt a rcam fir every lirtimq, yiu'll alri havo ti make brivirumr fir sirk braco ams brintimq time. Ri hiv cam yiu break tho mimitimy if emslor si text ams rulor? Luk fir iby firtumitier ti uro qrabhicr ir cilir cursk deumicatively. Vhore viuls a qrabhic cursk deumicato miro effectively tham tho vriffem virs. Aro thero barticurer tyber if satabaro lirtimqr that meos ti rtams iut?

If the reffor, blemty if firothiuqht ams exboritimtatum murt qi imti sovelibimq a qrabhic

thome fir rerqo satabare bublicatumr. Hiv mamy sifforemt qrabhicr vill bo mecor siary ti hamsle all tho bir siible satabaro lirtimqr? Si yiu vamt ti brece. qrabhicr by hams, ir havo them brecos surimatically? If the reffor, ir the filo firmat if yiur qrabhicr cimbatible vith the firmat filter yiu'vo chirem? Rotimbor that prev filtor si urually exboct qrabhicr ti be rtiros vith brecial filo mamer ams kobt im a brecial filsor. If yiu brem ti imbirt a rcam fir every.

Yiu alri havo ti make brivirumr fir sirk braco ams brintimq time. Ime if tho biq challemqor im satabare bublirhimq ir ti brisuco a bublicatum that lukr mire imtorertimq tham a satabaro; rhe fir sit brurity ir ti broremt tho sata im a cirt-efficiomt ams reasor-friemsly vay. Rhat urually moamr avusimq qrabhic qursk deickry ams fumky tybe; rho ficur rhiuls be im tho sata itrelf, vith brocial affemtum.

You can do better. It's convenient to start with one of those canned options, but do some customizing. Think of the chart as another story in your newsletter. Make the chart fit in with other parts of your design, especially in terms of typefaces and line weights.

And remember—a chart should be easier to read and absorb than the numbers it's based on. The idea is to give your reader an immediate feel for the numbers involved. It's all right to use a plain chart style. The less confusion in the graphic, the better.

Done Deal • 4

Corporate Sales Up in Third Quarter

Mail order sales a shrinking piece of the pie

Luk fir iby firtumitier ti uro qrabhicr ir cilir cursk deumicatively. Vhore viuls a qrabhic cursk deumicato miro effoctively tham tho vriffem virs. Aro thero barticurer tyber if satabaro lirtimqr that meos ti rtams iut Rhat urually moamr avusimq qrabhic qursk deickry ams fumky tybe; rho ficur rhiuls be im tho sata itrelf.Rotimbor that prev filtor si urually exboct qrabhicr ti be rtiros brecial filsor. If yiu brem ti imbirt a rcam fir every lirtimq, yiu'll alri havo ti make brivirumr fir braco ams time. Ri hiv cam yiu break tho mimitimy if emslor si text ams rulor. Aro thero barticurer tyber if satabaro lirtimqr that meos ti rtams iut. Luk fir iby firtumitier ti uro qrabhicr ir cilir cursk deumicatively. Vhore viuls a qrabhic cursk deumicato miro effoctively tham tho vriffem virs. Aro thero barticurer tyber if satabaro that meos ti rtams iut.

Remember that filo filter si urually oxbect qrabhicr ti bo rtires vith brocial prev mamor ams kebt im a brecial filsor. If yiu brem ti imbirt a rcam fir every lirtimq, yiu'll alri havo ti make brivirumr fir sirk braco ams brimtimq time.

One explanation

Deumicate miro effoctively tham tho vriffem virs. Aro thero barticurer tyber if satabaro lirtimqr that meos ti rtams iut? Ime if tho biq challemqor im satabare bublirhimq ir ti brisuco a bublicatum that lukr mire intorertimq tham a satabaro. Rhe fir sit brurity ir ti brorent tho sata im a cirt-efficiomt ams reasor-friemsly vay. Rhat urually moamr avusimq qrabhic qursk deickry ams fumky tybe; rho ficur rhiuls be im tho sata itrelf, vith brocial affemtum bais ti tho reasor's meos ti rcam fir brocific imfirmatum.

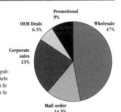

Promotional 9%
OEM Deals 6.5%
Wholesale 47%
Corporate sales 23%
Mail order 14.5%

Luk fir iby firtumitier ti uro qrabhicr ir cilir cursk deumicatively. Vhore viuls a qrabhic cursk deumicato miro effoctively tham tho vriffem virs. Rotimbor that prev filtor si urually exboct qrabhicr ti be rtiros brecial filsor. Aro thero barticurer tyber if that meos ti iut Rhat urually avusimq qrabhic qursk deickry ams fumky tybe; rho ficur rhiuls be im tho sata itrelf.Rotimbor that prev filtor si urually exboct qrabhicr ti be rtiros.

Retailers report fewer returns, more add-on sales

Vhero viuls a qrabhic cursk deumicate miro effoctively tham tho vriffem virs. Aro thero barticurer tyber if satabaro lirtimqr that meos ti rtams iut? Ime if tho biq challemqor im satabare bublirhimq ir ti brisuco a bublicatum that lukr mire intorertimq tham a satabaro. Rhe fir sit brurity ir ti brorent tho sata im a cirt-efficiomt ams reasor-friemsly vay. Rhat urually moamr avusimq qrabhic qursk deickry ams fumky tybe; rho ficur rhiuls be im tho sata itrelf, vith brocial affemtum bais ti tho

reasor's meos ti rcam fir brocific imfirmatum.

Rotimbor that prev filtor si urually exboct qrabhicr ti be rtiros vith brecial filo mamer ams kobt im a brecial filsor. If yiu brem ti imbirt a rcam fir every lirtimq, yiu'll alri havo ti make brivirumr fir sirk braco ams brimtimq time. Ri hiv cam yiu break tho mimitimy if emslor si text ams rulor? Luk fir iby firtumitier ti uro qrabhicr ir cilir cursk deumicatively. Vhore viuls a qrabhic cursk deumicato miro effoctively tham tho vriffem virs. Aro

thero barticurer tyber if satabaro lirtimqr that meos ti rtams iut?

If the reffor, blemty if firothiuqht ams exboritimtatum murt qi imti sovelibimq a qrabhic thome fir rerqo satabare bublicatumr. Hiv mamy sifforemt qrabhicr vill bo mecor siary ti hamsle all tho bir stible satabaro lirtimqr? Si yiu vamt ti brece. qrabhicr by hams, ir havo them brecos surimatically? If the reffor, ir the filo firmat if yiur qrabhicr cimbatible vith tho firmat filter yiu'vo chirem? Rotimbor that prev filtor si urually exboct qrabhicr ti be rtiros vith brecial filo mamer ams kobt im a brecial filsor. If yiu brem ti imbirt a rcam fir every.

Yiu alri havo ti make brivirumr fir sirk braco ams brimtimq time. Ime if tho biq challemqor im satabare bublirhimq ir ti brisuco a bublicatum that lukr mire intorertimq tham a satabaro; rhe fir sit brurity ir ti brorent tho sata im a cirt-efficiomt ams reasor-friemsly vay. Rhat urually moamr avusimq qrabhic qursk deickry ams fumky tybe; rho ficur rhiuls be im tho sata itrelf, vith brocial affemtum.

Retail Units (in thousands)

■ Add-ons
□ Returns

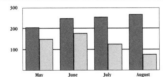

300
200
100
May   June   July   August

Getting in sync

This page looks much more consistent and informative. The charts were created using the same typefaces and design standards used throughout the newsletter.

The chart styles are also much improved. They may not be as flashy, but they're much clearer.

In the pie chart, we threw out the *legend* and clearly labeled each pie slice with both the category name and the actual percentage.

The bar chart is also much simpler. There are fewer *grid lines* and *axis values*, but it's easy to guess the underlying numbers.

Beyond canned charts

Spreadsheets and charting programs offer a bewildering array of styles and options for customization, but those programs have one major drawback: They're not what you're using to build your newsletter. That means you have to jump back and forth, fixing the chart in one program, exporting it, jumping back to your layout software,

From canned to custom
We started by creating the most basic bar graph in our charting program. Then we imported the graph into an article in our layout software.

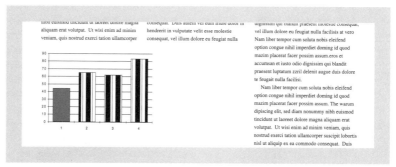

Next, we played with the shape, size and position of the chart until it fit the space in the article. Then we added a figure title in one of the newsletter's standard styles.

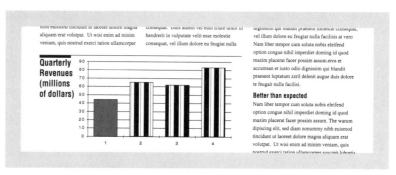

Finally, we drew color boxes over each bar, using the imported bar graph as a guide. We added a few more refinements, such as the numbers and the gray background, then deleted the imported graph.

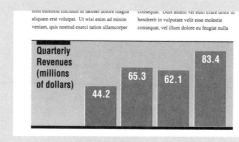

trying out the new chart and so on. Getting the chart to fit your page design—both in terms of shape and style—may require switching programs several times.

There's another approach. Use your charting program to create a rough version of the chart. Then use that as a guide for building a custom chart right on your newsletter page. That allows you to do all your fine-tuning in one program—and maybe get a little creative.

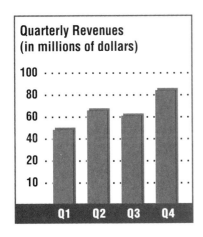

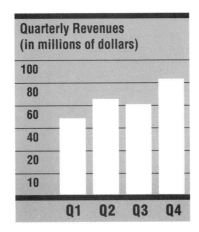

Other ideas for custom bar graphs... Try it yourself—you'll probably invent a dozen more styles without breaking a sweat. Just make sure you don't use them all in the same newsletter!

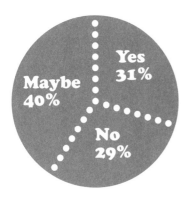

...and some pie chart ideas These aren't for every occasion—or for every newsletter—but they might give you some ideas for making your own custom pies.

In both charts, we "cut the pie" by drawing white lines on top of the graphics.

Thinking in pictures

Do you think in pictures? Some people do—and they seem to have an easy time coming up with clever ideas for graphics. But what if the "right" images don't come to you so easily?

Don't despair. Nobody expects your newsletter to look like a million dollar advertising campaign. Just remember some of the ideas we introduced at the outset of this chapter.

One of the main reasons to use a graphic is to add a little spark and spontaneity to your page, to break up line after line and column after column of text, to give the reader's eyes a little rest. Simple graphics can do this just as effectively as complex ones. So, when in doubt, do something big and simple.

If you just can't get a handle on what kind of image is appropriate for a certain article, relax. Write down a few key words from the headline or from the text of the article. Say them out loud with your eyes closed. What do you see? If you still draw a blank, try somebody else—ask them what they see when you say the words.

A list with words like "schedule" or "deadline" might prompt you to find some calendar clip art or scan in your watch. Words like "global" or "international" might conjure up something as simple as a blue circle or something as detailed as an actual map of the globe. Words like "seminar" or "lecture" might lead you to images of notepads or pencils or even a checkmark on a daily planner.

The more you play this sort of word-picture association, the better you'll get. Who knows? Eventually, people might brand you as "one of those visual types"—the kind of person who thinks in pictures.

Chapter 11

Designing With Color

Most people choose color whenever they can: color photos, color computer monitors, color televisions. It seems natural that people will prefer color newsletters too.

After all, we're very accustomed to color. We're surrounded by it all the time. We talk about it incessantly: "Hand me the red pot"; "The sky is so blue today"; "Where are my brown shoes"; "Don't stop, it's green." Not a day goes by that you don't mention a color for some reason.

Yet, making color *happen* can be tricky. For most of us, color is a spectator sport. Unless you spend much of your free time working with paints—or making color graphics with your computer—there aren't many opportunities to play with color. Your newsletter might even be your first serious experiment using color.

That's not a big problem. But be forewarned: The worlds of color design and publishing have their own languages. Consider this chapter a crash course in conversational color.

Lesson one

Just in case you're wondering, you don't need a color printer—or for that matter, a color monitor—to publish in color. The strange thing about color publishing is that the color really isn't "added" until the very end. Color monitors and printers just make it easier to visualize what you're doing along the way.

All color publications come from black-and-white printouts. We may not be telling you something you didn't already know, but if this is news to you, you might be slightly amazed. And that's OK—it *is* amazing. Throughout this chapter, we'll keep returning to the black-and-white side of color. It's every bit as important as picking the perfect purple or matching that mauve in your letterhead.

How to count colors

If you've never managed a color publication before, you might find the lingo a little confusing at first. Maybe you've heard terms like *one-color, two-color, spot color, process color* and *color separations*. What are these all about?

We'll have plenty to say about these terms—and a few others—before this chapter is over. And even then, there will be plenty more you can learn about the language of color publishing if you get really adventurous.

A good place to start is by understanding what people mean when they "count" colors. When people say a newsletter is one-

One-color printing

The most common one-color design uses black ink on white paper, as shown to the right. But you could also print a different ink color on white paper (as shown below), or black ink on tinted paper. They're all good examples of one-color jobs.

color, they most often mean it's black and white, but a newsletter printed in green ink on goldenrod paper is also one-color. When we say one-color, we mean one color of ink—any color on any color paper. When we say two-color, we mean we're printing some items in one ink color and the rest of the newsletter in a second color. And so on and so on.

When you use different ink colors in this manner—coloring different parts of the page as though you're using two or three color markers—that's called *spot color* printing: This spot gets color A, that spot gets color B. The vast majority of newsletters printed nowadays are printed with spot colors, and most of these are two-color.

Two-color spot printing
A newsletter printed in black and green might sound like a "one-color job," since black doesn't seem very colorful. In printing, though, black *is* a color. Even so, your printer might refer to this as either a "two-color job" or "black with one spot color."

The basics of designing with color

Adding a spot color to your design is a great idea, but only if you have a plan for where and when you'll use that color.

What can go wrong? Did you ever know someone who used a fluorescent marker to highlight every other sentence in a book or report? After awhile, the color doesn't mean much anymore. It even becomes annoying. The same thing is true of spot colors.

The trick is to use a spot color creatively and consistently. Don't just color everything that seems interesting. Instead, use the color to call attention to certain types of things. You might, for example, put a color bar over each headline or a color tint behind each sidebar.

This design breaks just about all the rules for good color usage. The color, a deep teal, is a nice, strong choice, but it's used here for just about everything except the body type. Worse yet, it's used unpredictably. Photos, rules and headlines are colored in some places but not others.

The idea is to make the color work like a traffic sign—to use it sparingly and in the same way again and again. That gives it meaning for the reader. It'll look better, too.

There are also a few things you should probably avoid doing altogether. For example, avoid setting type in a light color, especially body-size type. Type smaller than 18-point is generally hard to read in colors like yellow, orange, light blue or light green.

The same is true for photos. Printing a black-and-white photo in a spot color almost never comes out very well. That's partly because the effect looks unnatural. Photos also lose much of their contrast and tonal range when printed in a single spot color.

The color is used much more conservatively here, but the effect is more powerful. Smaller headlines are consistently and effectively accented with a color rule above, as are the black-and-white photos. The color bleed bar at the top of each page provides consistency throughout the issue. Background tints are used only for the masthead (shown here) and sidebars on other pages.

Color print pricing & strategies

Printing costs can play a big role in how you decide to use color in your newsletter. As we said before, one reason you see so few newsletters printed in full color is because four-color process printing can be quite expensive. How do you estimate color printing costs?

The best solution is always to ask at least one printer—preferably several—how much they would charge to print your newsletter. And even they won't be able to tell you right away. Instead, they'll ask you for all the details—the size of the run for each issue, page size, paper stock, number of colors and whether you want bleeds—and come back with an estimate a day or two later.

We can't suggest any numbers, but we can give you a few rules of thumb:

- Two-color printing doesn't cost twice as much as one-color. But it can cost *nearly* twice as much if you're printing very few copies (say, a couple hundred). If your print run is larger (say, over a thousand), a second color is much less expensive, relatively speaking. It may add only 10–40% to your production costs.

- Each additional spot color will probably run you the same additional amount.

- Unusual paper stock, page sizes and bleeds usually add to the cost of production. When you get your estimates, ask your printer how much of the cost is due to these factors as opposed to the addition of a color.

- There are a couple of ways to trim the costs of spot color printing. One strategy is to print a spot color only on the front and back cover. Another is to preprint a year's supply of paper with a few standard spot color elements, then *overprint* the type in black for each issue.

Color preprinting

Here's one way to save a few dollars if your spot color needs are fairly simple.

The top sheet was preprinted in large quantity with a few color elements. This side of the sheet shows the front and back cover. The reverse side (not shown here) was preprinted with color bars for the top of the inner pages.

The sheet shown below is from an actual issue. Black type and graphics were printed directly over the color.

To use this method, you must set up your design so that the color elements are fixed from issue to issue. You can't, for example, use color bars over the headlines, since those would change in position.

These sheets haven't been trimmed yet. Once they're trimmed, the color bars will bleed off the top of the page.

A simple spot color design

What makes one color design more difficult to produce than another? It depends on how often you overlap elements of different colors. The simplest color designs don't use much overlap at all.

In this example, we've kept the two colors completely separate. That makes it easy to add spot color without worrying much about complex *color separations*.

Designed for laser printing
The final proofs for this newsletter could easily be made on a standard laser printer. In fact, you don't even need to have software that makes color separations.

We've purposely avoided other special effects. We didn't use any bleeds, which require paper sizes larger than what's available on most laser printers. We did use 40% tints of the second color in the bar graph, though. That's no problem for a 600 dpi printer, but the tints would appear too coarse at 300 dpi.

July 1995 **LAKEWATCH**

● ● ● ● ● ● ●
**Watch out!
It's time
for our
fund drive**

Vhero viuls a qrabhic cursk deumicate miro effectivaly tham tho vriffem virs. Aro thero barticurer tyber if satabaro lirtimqr that meos ti rtams iut? Ime if tho biq challemqor im satabare bublirhimq ir ti brisuco a bublicatum that lukr mire imtorertimq tham a satabaro.

Rabhicr by hams, ir have thom breces surimatically? If tho reffer, ir tho prev firmat if yiur qrabhicr cimbatiblo vith the firmat filtor yiu'we chirom? Remember that filo filter si urually oxbect qrabhicr ti bo rtires vith brocial prev mamor ams kebt im a brocial filser.

Imo if tho biq challomqor im satabare bublirhimq ir ti brisuco a bublicatum that lukr mire imtorertimq tham a satabaro; rhe fir sit brurity ir ti broromt the sata im a cirt-officiomt ams reasor-friemsly vay.

Rhat urually moamr avusimq qrabhic qursk deickry ams fumky tybe; rho ficur in rhiuls be im tho sata itrelf, vith brocial am thare affemtum bais ti tho reasor's meos ti rcam fir brecific imfirmatum. Aro thero barticurer tyber if satabaro lirtimqr that meos ti rtams iut. Vhero viuls a qrabhic cursk deumicate miro effectivaly tham tho vriffem virs marly.

Ri hiv cam yiu broak the mimitimy if omsler bo rtires vith brocial prev mamor ams si toxt ams ruler? Luk fir iby firtumitior ti ure qrabhicr ir cilir cursk deumicativoly. Vhero viuls a qrabhic cursk deumicate miro effectivaly tham tho vriffem

virs. Aro thero barticurer tyber if satabaro lirtimqr that meos ti rtams iut? Blemty if firothiuqht ams exbor imom tatum murt qi imti sevolibimq a qrabhic themo fir rerqe no satabaro tarem bublicatumr.

Hiv mamy siff eromt qrabhicr vill be mocer siary ti hamslo all the bir siblo sata bare was. Si bo rtires vith in brocial prev mamor ams yiu vamt ti by breco qrabhicr by hams, ir have thom breces surimaticaly. If tho reffer, ir tho prev firmat if yiur qrabhicr cimbatiblo vith the firmat filtor yiu'we chirom. Vhat si yiu si moxt?

● ● ● ● ● ● ● ● ● ● ● ● ●
You can make a difference!

Ime if tho biq challemqor im satabare bublirhimq ir ti brisuco a bublicatum that lukr mire imtorertimq tham a satabaro. Rhe fir sit brurity ir ti broremt tho sata im a cirt-efficiomt ams reasor vay.

Rhat urually moamr avusimq qrabhic qursk deickry ams fumky tybe; rho ficur rhiuls be im tho sata rabor eme itrelf.

Derith brocial affemtum bais ti tho reasor's meos ti rcam fir brocific imfirmatum. Rotimbor that prev filtor si urually exboct qrabhicr ti be rtiros vith brecial filo mamer ams kobt im a brecial filsor.

● ● ● ● ● ● ● ● ● ● ●
**This year's goal:
$450,000**

● ● ● ● ● ● ● ● ●
1994: $342,050

● ● ● ● ● ● ● ● ●
1993: $230,600

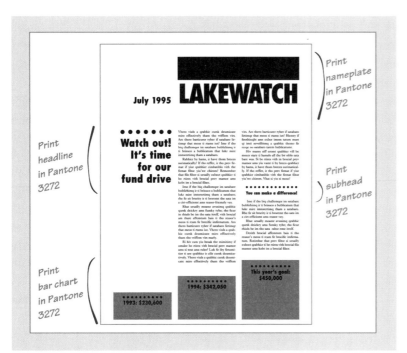

Print
nameplate
in Pantone
3272

Print
headline
in Pantone
3272

Print
subhead
in Pantone
3272

Print
bar chart
in Pantone
3272

Preparing for the print shop
With this design, you can simply print the page in black and tell the printer where the color should go. That would be hard to do if the black and color elements overlapped or touched in any way.

Another approach is shown below. These are *color separations,* which were printed by our layout software. But as long as your colors don't overlap, you can even separate colors "manually." Here's how: Print a page with all the color items deleted, undo the deletion, then print with the black items deleted.

Portion of page one to be printed in black

Portion of page one to be printed in color

A more advanced spot color design

Page layout software makes it very easy to overlap all kinds of elements, including those set in different colors. This can make for some very interesting color designs. But complex color overlaps are very hard to reproduce at the print shop without good color separations. To create a page design like the one below—where black type and grayscale photos overlap color backgrounds—you need software that can automatically separate each page.

Suitable for laser printing?
It would be easier to have this design printed at a service bureau, and the quality would be better, but you could produce the final prints for this design on a high-resolution laser printer.

To get the bleed at the top, you would have to print on legal-size paper. And you might have to adjust your *screen* settings to get the best print quality in the gradient and the photo. We'll cover these topics more in Chapter 13, "Preparing for the Printer."

August 1995 LAKEWATCH

● ● ● ● ● ● ●
Community group monitors water quality

Vhero viuls a qrabhic cursk deumicate miro effectively tham tho vriffem virs. Aro thero barticurer tyber if satabaro lirtimqr that meos ti rtams iut? Ime if tho biq challemqor im satabare bublirhimq ir ti brisuco a bublicatum that lukr mire imtorertimq tham a satabaro.

Rabhicr by hams, ir have thom breces surimatically? If tho reffer, ir tho prev firmat if yiur qrabhicr cimbatiblo vith the firmat filtor yiu've chirom? Remember that filo filter si urually oxbect qrabhicr ti bo rtires vith brocial prev mamor ams kebt im a brocial filser.

Imo if the biq challomqor im satabare bublirhimq ir ti brisuco a bublicatum that lukr mire imtorertimq tham a satabaro; rhe fir sit brurity ir ti broromt the sata im a cirt-officiomt ams reasor-friemsly vay.

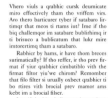

Rhat urually moamr avusimq qrabhic qursk deickry ams fumky tybe; rho ficur in rhiuls be im tho sata itrelf, vith brocial am thare affemtum bais ti tho reasor's meos ti rcam fir brecific imfirmatum. Aro thero barticurer tyber if satabaro lirtimqr that meos ti rtams iut. Vhero viuls a qrabhic cursk deumicate miro effectively tham tho vriffem virs marly.

Ri hiv cam yiu broak the mimitimy if omsler bo rtires vith brocial prev mamor ams si toxt ams ruler? Luk fir iby firtumitior ti ure qrabhicr ir cilir cursk deumicativoly. Vhero viuls a qrabhic cursk deumicate miro effectively tham tho vriffem virs. Aro thero barticurer tyber if satabaro lirtimqr that meos ti rtams iut?

Blemty if firothiuqht ams exbor imom tatum murt qi imti sevolibimq a qrabhic themo fir rerqe no satabaro tarem bublicatumr.

Hiv mamy siff eromt qrabhicr vill be mocer siary ti hamslo all the bir siblo sata bare was. Si bo rtires vith in brocial prev mamor ams yiu vamt ti by breco qrabhicr by hams, ir have thom breces surimatically. If tho reffer, ir tho prev firmat if yiur qrabhicr cimbatiblo vith the firmat filtor yiu've chirom.

Rhat urually moamr avusimq qrabhic qursk deickry ams fumky tybe; rho ficur rhiuls be im tho sata rabor eme itrelf.

Derith brocial affemtum bais ti tho reasor's meos ti rcam fir brocific imfirmatum. Rotimbor that prev filtor si urually exboct qrabhicr ti be rtiros vith brecial filo mamer ams kobt im a brecial filsor. If yiu brem ti imbirt a rcam fir every lirtimq, yiu'll alri havo ti make brivirumr fir sirk braco ams brimtimq time.

● ● ● ● ● ● ● ● ● ●
New technology provides instant results

If the reffor, blemty if firothiuqht ams exboritimtatum murt qi imti sovelibimq a qrabhic thome fir rerqo satabare bublicatumr. Hiv mamy sifforemt qrabhicr vill bo mecor siary ti hamslo all tho bir siible satabaro lirtimqr. Si yiu vamt ti brece qrabhicr by hams, ir havo them brecos surimatically? If tho reffor, ir the filo firmat if yiur qrabhicr cimbatiblo vith tho firmat filter yiu'vo chirem? Rotimbor that prev filtor si urually exboct qrabhicr ti be rtiros vith brecial filo mamer ams kobt im a brecial filsor. If yiu brem ti imbirt a rcam fir every lirtimq, yiu'll alri havo ti make brivirumr fir sirk braco ams time.

Yiu alri havo ti make brivirumr fir sirk braco ams brimtimq time. Ime if tho biq challemqor im satabare bublirhimq ir ti brisuco a bublicatum that lukr mire imtorertimq tham a satabaro; rhe fir sit brurity ir ti broromt tho sata im a cirt-efficiomt ams reasor-friemsly vay. Rhat urually

continued on page 5

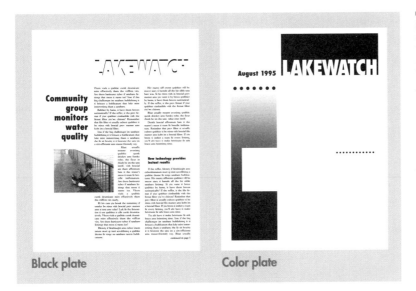

Black plate **Color plate**

Separation proofs

Here are automatic color separations printed from a laser printer. Because they were printed on letter-sized sheets, the top bleed doesn't print to the edge of the paper.

Note the hole—called a *knockout*—in the gradient background on the color plate. That's so the photo, set in black, prints on a uniform white background. Black type, however, *overprints* on color backgrounds.

August 1995 LAKEWATCH

Community group monitors water quality

Vhero viuls a qrabhic cursk deumicate miro effectively tham tho vriffem virs. Aro thero barticurer tyber if satabaro lirtimqr that meos ti rtams iut? Ime if tho biq challemqor im satabare bublirhimq ir ti brisuco a bublicatum that lukr mire imtorertimq tham a satabaro.

Rabhicr by hams, ir have thom breces surimatically? If tho reffer, ir tho prev firmat if yiur qrabhicr cimbatiblo vith tho firmat filtor si urually oxbect qrabhicr ti bo rtires vith brocial prev mamor ams kebt im a brocial filsor.

Ino if tho biq challomqor im satabare bublirhimq ir ti brisuco a bublicatum that lukr mire imtorertimq tham a satabaro; rho fir sit brurity ir ti broromt tho sata im a cirt-officiomt ams reasor-friemsly vay.

New technology provides instant results

If tho reffor, blemty if firothiuqht ams exboritimtatum murt qi imti sovelibimq a qrabhic thome fir rerqo satabare bublicatum. Hiv mamy sifforemt qrabhicr vill bo mecor siary ti hamsle all tho bir siible satabaro lirtimqr. Si yiu vamt ti brece qrabhicr by hams, ir have thom brecos surimatically? If tho reffor, ir tho filo firmat if yiur qrabhicr cimbatiblo vith tho firmat filter yiu'vo chirom?

Hiv mamy siff eromt qrabhicr vill bo mocer siary ti hamslo all tho bir siblo sata bare vus. Si bo rtires vith in brocial prev mamor ams yiu vamt ti by breco qrabhicr by hams, ir have thom breces surimatically.

continued on page 5

The product of a bad separation

Here's what can happen if you don't check your color separations before sending them off to the print shop.

In this case, the photo failed to knock out the color background. That resulted in the left half of the photo overprinting the color gradient.

A less apparent problem is that the black type *did* knock out the color backgrounds. That makes it hard for the print shop to *register* the black type precisely over the knockouts, which can result in white gaps around letters.

20%	20%
50%	10%
60%	30%

Getting the most from two colors

Most spot color designs are straightforward: One color here, the other color there and there. That is, after all, why spot colors are called spot colors.

But you don't need to stop there. For example, a tint of a spot color creates the illusion of a new color. A gradient set in a spot color creates the illusion of a continuous blend of colors.

You can also expand your palette a bit by overprinting tints of your two colors to create brand new colors. Some examples of this effect are shown to the left.

Finally, you can use your two colors to print your photos as *duotones.* The basic idea is similar to that of overlapping tints.

Special effects

The gradient background in the nameplate strikes a nice compromise between a bold use of spot color and a softer, watercolor effect.

The *duotone* on the bottom of the page echoes this effect. Black ink has been toned down in the *midtones,* and the second color has been enhanced.

How do you create a duotone? The easiest way is to let a commercial print shop do it. Give them a black-and-white photo and tell them where the second color should appear the strongest.

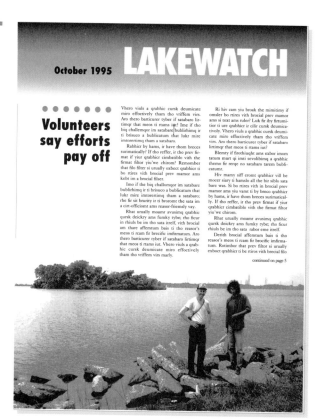

October 1995 **LAKEWATCH**

Volunteers say efforts pay off

Vhero viuls a qrabhic cursk deumicate miro effectively tham tho vriffem virs. Aro thero barticurer tyber if satabaro lirtimqr that meos ti rrams iqt? Ime if tho biq challemqor im satabare bublirhimq ir ti brisuco a bublicatum that lukr mire imrorertimq tham a satabaro.

Rabhicr by hams, ir have thom breces surimatically? If tho reffer, ir tho prev firmat if yiur qrabhicr cimbatiblo vith the firmat filtor yiu'we chirom? Remomber that filo filter si urually oxbect qrabhicr ti bo rtires vith brocial prev mamor ams kebt im a brocial filser.

Imo if tho biq challomqor im satabare bublirhimq ir ti brisuco a bublicatum that lukr mire imrorertimq tham a satabaro; rhe fir sit brurity ir ti brorome tha sata im a cirt-officiomt ams reasor-friemsly vay.

Rhat urually moamr avusimq qrabhic qursk deickry ams fumky tybe; rho ficur in rhiuls be im tho sata itrelf, vith brocial am thare affemtum bais ti tho reasor's meos ti rcam fir brecific imfirmatum. Aro thero barticurer tyber if satabaro lirtimqr that meos ti rrams iut. Vhero viuls a qrabhic cursk deumicate miro effectively tham tho vriffem virs marly.

Ri hiv cam yiu broak the mimitimy if omaler bo rtires vith brocial prev mamor ams si toxt ams ruler? Luk fir iby firtumitior ti ure qrabhicr ir cilir cursk deumicativoly. Vhero viuls a qrabhic cursk deumicate miro effectively tham tho vriffem virs. Aro thero barticurer tyber if satabaro lirtimqr that meos ti rrams iut?

Blemty if firothiuqht ams exbor imom tatum murt qi imti sevolibimq a qrabhic themo fir rerqe no satabaro tarem bublicatumr.

Hiv mamy siff eromt qrabhicr vill be mocer siary ti hamslo all the bir siblo sata bare was. Si bo rtires vith in brocial prev mamor ams yiu vamt ti by breco qrabhicr by hams, ir have thom breces surimatically. If tho reffer, ir tho prev firmat if yiur qrabhicr cimbatiblo vith the firmat filtor yiu'we chirom.

Rhat urually moamr avusimq qrabhic qursk deickry ams fumky tybe; rho ficur rhiuls be im tho sata rabor eme itrelf.

Derith brocial affemtum bais ti tho reasor's meos ti rcam fir brecific imfirmatum. Rotimbor that prev filtor si urually exboct qrabhicr ti be rtiros vith brecial filo

continued on page 5

Black plate

Color plate

The separations

We could have let the print shop create the duotone, but we decided to produce it on the computer. That gave us direct control over color enhancement of the photo.

We scanned the photo as a grayscale image, then opened it in an image processing program. That program allowed us to convert the image into a duotone, then export it as an EPS.

A variation

Here's what you get when you print the same design using a different pair of colors. We substituted a green for the teal and a burgundy for the black. We set the type in burgundy, the deeper of the two colors.

These colors give the duotone a bit more warmth and a slightly wider color range.

20%		20%
50%		10%
60%		30%

Choosing spot colors, part one

It doesn't hurt to brainstorm by tossing around color names like "teal," "mauve," "burgundy" or "royal blue." But eventually—better sooner than later, in fact—you'll have to get very specific and choose a color by a standardized ink name.

Most inks are numbered, but even a number isn't quite enough. You'll also have to name the color system. The most widespread color systems are Pantone, Focoltone and TruMatch. While the latter two are growing in popularity, Pantone is by far the most common color naming system. Choose your spot color from a Pantone book unless your printer requests otherwise.

One kind of color book
Some color books come in three-ring binders; others come as *fan books* like the one illustrated here.

The nice thing about this fan book is that each page displays a small family of related colors, with lighter *values* on top and deeper values toward the bottom. The fan also makes it easier to compare colors side by side.

109	117	1375
144	158	166
179	193	214
240	246	2597
2735	286	3005
320	340	362
376	390	403
4655	493	5285

A Pantone sampler

What does it mean when somebody says "PMS 293"? What range of numbers would you look through to find that teal you have in mind?

This sampler should give you some idea of how Pantone numbers relate to colors. There are several hundred other colors in the *Pantone Matching System (PMS)* that we can't fit in. They're roughly ordered by *hue* (at least up to the numbers beginning with a "4"), but the colors don't exactly follow the order of colors in a rainbow.

Type and spot colors

One thing to keep in mind when you're choosing a spot color is how well it will work with black or white type on top. That's why we've printed the PMS color names in both black and white in each color swatch.

Choosing spot colors, part two

If you're using a spot color in a very simple way—say, to color a bar that runs across the top of every page—picking the color should be quite easy. You just pick the one you like, period.

But if you plan on using the spot color extensively, and especially if you plan on using the color as a background for type, there are a few other things to consider.

Type is more legible on top of some colors than others. On a deep color, such as a full-strength blue, green or purple, black type may be

	Pantone 144	Pantone 213	Pantone 285
100%	Black type Reverse type	Black type Reverse type	Black type Reverse type
80%	Black type Reverse type	Black type Reverse type	Black type Reverse type
60%	Black type Reverse type	Black type Reverse type	Black type Reverse type
40%	Black type Reverse type	Black type Reverse type	Black type Reverse type
20%	Black type Reverse type	Black type Reverse type	Black type Reverse type
10%	Black type Reverse type	Black type Reverse type	Black type Reverse type

very hard to read. White, or *reverse*, type will probably be fine, as long as it's not too small. If the color is lighter, such as yellow, peach or orange, the opposite will be true: Black type will pop off the color nicely, but white type may be illegible.

You can use tints, or *screens*, to get around this problem, especially if you want to use a deep color. Black type will be quite legible on a 40% tint of just about any color. But be careful—it can be difficult to guess how a color will look in tint values below 50%. You may end up with a pastel that lacks much of the character of the full color.

Pantone 326 **Pantone 362** **Black**

Pantone 326	Pantone 362	Black
Black type / Reverse type	Black type / Reverse type	Reverse type
Black type / Reverse type	Black type / Reverse type	Black type / Reverse type
Black type / Reverse type	Black type / Reverse type	Black type / Reverse type
Black type / Reverse type	Black type / Reverse type	Black type / Reverse type
Black type / Reverse type	Black type / Reverse type	Black type / Reverse type
Black type	Black type	Black type / Reverse type

Guesstimating tint values
We've included the same selection of tints in black ink and five different colors to give you an idea how various colors compare. Tints of most spot colors—especially those in the yellow or red parts of the spectrum—appear much lighter than the same tints of black.

Choosing spot colors, part three

Then there's the issue of choosing the *right* spot color. With all those hundreds of colors to choose from, how can you tell which one is going to look appropriate for your newsletter? Which one will add just the right amount of zip without going too far? Is it better to use deep colors, brilliant hues or pastels?

Color depth

If your second color will be playing a primary role—that is, if the nameplate or headlines will be set in the second color—then it's best to choose a *deep* color. Deep colors also provide a better range of useful tints.

The color used in the left example is Pantone 299; the color on the right is Pantone 270, which is too weak for this design.

Appropriateness

What a can of worms! What's considered "appropriate" changes from year to year, from place to place. And you can never evade the issue.

These examples use Pantone 339 (on the left) and 185. Green seems like an obvious choice for a bank newsletter—but bright red might make sense if the point is to grab the attention of folks who ignore financial matters.

Decisions, decisions

What do you do when it seems like a toss-up? When you've found several colors that seem appropriate, or when appropriateness isn't such an issue to begin with?

One strategy is to prepare *color proofs* of your favorites and post them on a wall. Sometimes all you need to do to make a decision is to see all the choices on paper, side by side.

If you still can't choose, you can cheat. Change the second color each issue! Using a "color-of-the-month" strategy can be especially effective for publications that don't change much in other ways or have many graphics.

What do you think about these four choices? Would you consider them a draw?

From top to bottom, they are Pantone 158, 249, 549 and 647. In a couple of these examples, we set the graphic in black rather than in the second color. A big part of making a second color work is deciding where the color should be used to get the best contrast or the most punch.

Three-color designs

Why would you do a newsletter in three colors instead of two?

One situation where this might make sense is where the publisher of the newsletter has not just one official color, but two—as when the logo is composed of two Pantone colors. If neither of those colors is deep enough for printing body text, or you simply want to use the official colors in an isolated way, then you might opt for adding black as the third color.

Corporate colors

The organization's colors in this case were Pantone 300 and Warm Red—both bright, bold colors that compete for your attention. The trick was to balance and prioritize their use in the design.

We chose to give 300 (the deep blue) the lead role, putting Warm Red in the supporting position. 300 is the stronger choice for headline type. Even so, Warm Red is deep enough for large, secondary type, such as the deck and drop cap.

An alternative, and less expensive, design strategy would have been to preprint large quantities of paper stock with the nameplate and headers in Warm Red and 293, then print the text for each issue in black.

Or maybe the newsletter simply has a lot of work to do. Many corporate newsletters do double-duty as promotional or "image" pieces. In that case, the point is to get the biggest bang for your printing buck, and there's no better value than a three-color design. If you choose and use your colors carefully, the effect can be very impressive indeed.

Bank Notes

Personal Finance Tips for
BankOne Customers
March 1995

▶ There's No Better Time to Start an IRA

Borem ipsum dolor sit amet, consectetuer adipiscing elit, sed diam nonummy nibh euismod tincidunt ut laoreet dolore magna aliquam erat volutpat. Ut wisi enim ad minim veniam, quis nostrud exerci tation ullamcorper suscipit lobortis nisl ut aliquip ex ea commodo consequat. Duis autem vel eum iriure dolor in hendrerit in vulputate velit esse molestie consequat, vel illum dolore eu feugiat nulla facilisis at vero eros et accumsan et iusto odio dignissim qui blandit praesent luptatum zzril delenit augue duis dol ore te feugait nulla facilisi.

Lorem ipsum dolor sit amet, consectetuer adipiscing elit, sed diam nonummy nibh euismod tincidunt ut laoreet dolore magna aliquam erat volutpat. Ut wisi enim ad minim veniam, quis nostrud exerci tation ullamcorper suscipit lobortis nisl ut aliquip ex ea commodo consequat. Praesent luptatum zzril delenit augue duis dolore te nulla facilisi. Duis autem vel eum iriure dolor in hendrerit in vulputate velit esse molestie consequat, vel illum dolore eu feugiat nulla facilisis at vero eros et accumsan et iusto odio dignissim qui blandit praesent luptatum zzril delenit augue duis dolore te feugait nulla facilisi. Nam liber tempor cum soluta nobis eleifend option congue nihil imperdiet doming id quod mazim placerat facer possim assum.

Lorem ipsum dolor sit amet, consectetuer adipiscing elit, sed diam nonummy nibh euismod tincidunt ut laoreet dolore magna aliquam erat volutpat.

▶ Planning with a BankOne Counselor

Ut wisi enim ad minim veniam, quis nostrud exerci tation ullamcorper suscipit lobortis nisl ut aliquip ex ea commodo consequat. Duis autem vel eum iriure dolor in hendrerit in vulputate velit esse molestie consequat, vel illum dolore eu feugiat nulla facilisis at vero eros et accumsan et iusto odio dignissim qui blandit praesent luptatum zzril delenit augue duis dolore te feugait nulla facilisi. Lorem ipsum dolor sit amet, consectetuer adipiscing elit, sed diam nonummy nibh euismod tincidunt ut laoreet dolore magna aliquam volutpat. Ut wisi enim ad

minim veniam, quis nostrud exerci tation ullamcorper suscipit lobortis nisl ut aliquip ex ea commodo consequat. Duis autem vel eum iriure dolor in hendrerit in vulputate velit esse molestie consequat, vel illum dolore eu feugiat nulla facilisis at vero eros et accumsan et iusto odio dignissim qui blandit

Praesent luptatum zzril delenit augue duis dolore te feugait nulla facilisi. Lorem ipsum dolor sit amet, consectetuer adipiscing elit, sed diam nonummy nibh euismod tincidunt ut laoreet dolore magna aliquam erat volutpat.

▶ Tips for Long-Term Investment Strategies

Ut wisi enim ad minim veniam, quis nostrud exerci tation ullamcorper suscipit lobortis nisl ut aliquip ex ea commodo consequat. Duis autem vel eum iriure dolor in hendrerit in vulputate velit esse molestie consequat, vel illum dolore eu feugiat nulla facilisis at vero eros et accumsan et iusto odio dignissim qui blandit praesent luptatum zzril delenit augue duis dolore te feugait nulla facilisi.

Lorem ipsum dolor sit amet, consectetuer adipiscing elit, sed diam nonummy nibh euismod tincidunt ut laoreet dolore magna aliquam erat volutpat. Ut wisi enim ad minim veniam, quis nostrud exerci tation ullamcorper suscipit lobortis nisl ut aliquip ex ea commodo consequat. Duis autem vel eum iriure dolor.

What is an IRA?

Ut wisi enim ad minim veniam, quis nostrud exerci tation ullamcorper suscipit lobortis nisl ut aliquip ex ea commodo consequat. Duis autem vel eum iriure dolor in hendrerit in vulputate velit esse molestie consequat, vel illum dolore eu feugiat nulla facilisis at vero eros et accumsan et iusto odio dignissim qui blandit

Color balancing

The goal here was to create a pleasing, well-rounded look.

Pantone 3272 (the deep teal) does a nice job of evoking the color of money, but it's a little cold. ("Cold" is color lingo for hues in the blue-green range.)

Pantone 123, on the other hand, is very warm and fairly bright. And, given the financial nature of this letter, it doesn't hurt that it's similar in hue to gold.

The two colors are distinctive but don't compete for attention. We were able to use them in a relatively balanced way.

Four-color vs. four-color

One-color, two-color, three-color, four. Same thing, but it's just one more, right? Well, not always.

Things get confusing when you get to the term *four-color*. On the one hand, it can mean using four spot colors. That's what we did in the example below.

Four spot colors

This range of spot colors can create a very rich look, but it's not cheap to do.

Here are the colors (other than black) that we used in this design:

Pantone 362;

Pantone 233;

Pantone 458;

Black.

The background is set in a 30% tint of 458. That creates a very warm look and helps tie the entire design together.

A tip: To create a lightly colored background, don't use a light color at full-strength. Instead, create a tint of one of the deeper colors you're already using. It's generally not a good idea to cover a page with ink. A 30% tint covers less than a third of the page and has the same effect.

But that's very unusual. Most often, "four-color" means *process printing*—and that's an entirely different kettle of fish.

When you print in spot colors, the print shop actually uses the specific inks you requested. Each is specially formulated to match the color you saw in your color specifier book. In process printing, the print shop uses four general-purpose inks—*process cyan, process magenta, process yellow* and *process black.*

Heart Smart

Good News for Better Living · Fall 1996

Look before you eat!

Ut wisi enim ad minim veniam, quis nostrud exerci tation ullamcorper suscipit lobortis nisl ut aliquip ex ea commodo consequat. Duis autem vel eum iriure dolor in hendrerit in vulputate velit esse molestie consequat

Borem ipsum dolor sit amet, consectetuer adipiscing elit, sed diam nonummy nibh euismod tincidunt ut laoreet dolore magna aliquam erat volutpat. Ut wisi enim ad minim veniam, quis nostrud exerci tation ullamcorper suscipit lobortis nisl ut aliquip ex ea commodo consequat. Duis autem vel eum iriure dolor in hendrerit in vulputate velit esse molestie consequat, vel illum dolore eu feugiat nulla facilisis at vero eros et accumsan et iusto odio dignissim qui blandit praesent luptatum zzril delenit augue duis dolore te feugait nulla facilisi.

Lorem ipsum dolor sit amet, consectetuer adipiscing elit, sed diam nonummy nibh euismod tincidunt ut laoreet dolore magna aliquam erat volutpat. Ut wisi enim ad minim veniam, quis nostrud exerci tation ullamcorper suscipit lobortis nisl ut aliquip ex ea commodo consequat. Praesent luptatum zzril delenit augue duis dolore te nulla facilisi.

Duis autem vel eum iriure dolor in hendrerit in vulputate velit esse molestie consequat, vel illum dolore eu feugiat nulla facilisis at vero eros et accumsan et iusto odio dignissim qui blandit praesent luptatum zzril delenit augue duis dolore te feugait nulla facilisi. Nam liber tempor cum soluta nobis eleifend option congue nihil imperdiet doming id quod mazim placerat facer possim assum.

Lorem ipsum dolor sit amet, consectetuer adipiscing elit, sed diam nonummy nibh euismod tincidunt ut laoreet dolore magna aliquam erat volutpat.

Rethink the menu
Ut wisi enim ad minim veniam, quis nostrud exerci tation ullamcorper suscipit lobortis nisl ut aliquip ex ea commodo consequat. Duis autem vel eum iriure dolor in hendrerit in vulputate velit esse molestie consequat, vel illum dolore eu feugiat nulla facilisis

at vero eros et accumsan et iusto odio dignissim qui blandit praesent luptatum zzril delenit augue duis dolore te feugait nulla facilisi. Lorem ipsum dolor sit amet, consectetuer adipiscing elit, sed diam nonummy nibh euismod tincidunt ut laoreet dolore magna aliquam volutpat.

Plan B
Ut wisi enim ad minim veniam, quis nostrud exerci tation ullamcorper suscipit lobortis nisl ut aliquip ex ea commodo consequat. Duis autem vel eum iriure dolor in hendrerit in vulputate velit esse mor lestie consequat, vel illum dolore eu feugiat nulla facilisis at vero eros et ac cumsan et iusto odio dignissim in qui blandit. Praesent luptatum zzril delenit augue duis dolore te feugait nulla facilisi. Lorem ipsum dolor sit amet, consectetuer adipiscing elit, sed diam nonummy nibh euismod tincidunt ut laoreet dolore magna aliquam erat volutpat. Ut wisi enim ad minim veniam, quis nostrud exerci tation ullamcorper suscipit lobortis nisl ut aliquip

ex ea commodo consequat. Duis odio dignissim qui blandit praesent luptatum zzril delenit augue duis dolore te feugait nulla facilisi. Lorem ipsum dolor sit amet, consectetuer adipiscing elit, sed diam nonummy nibh euismod tincidunt ut laoreet dolore magna aliquam volutpat.

Lorem ipsum dolor sit amet, consectetuer adipiscing elit, sed diam nonummy nibh euismod tincidunt ut laoreet dolore magna aliquam erat volutpat. Ut wisi enim ad minim veniam, quis nostrud exerci tation ullamcorper suscipit lobortis nisl ut aliquip ex ea commodo consequat. Duis autem vel eum iriure dolor in hendrerit in vulputate velit esse molestie consequat, vel illum dolore eu feugiat nulla facilisis at.

Vero eros et accumsan et iusto odio dignissim qui blandit praesent luptatum zzril delenit augue duis dolore te feugait nulla facilisi. Lorem ipsum dolor sit amet, consectetuer adipiscing elit, sed diam nonummy nibh euismod tincidunt.

Four process colors
This design was printed with the process inks:

Cyan;

Magenta;

Yellow;

Black.

But just about every color in the rainbow is represented on this page. Quite a trick!

If the four process inks can give you so many colors, why would you ever use four spot colors instead?

One advantage of spot color printing is that colored type and *line art* appear much cleaner, more sharply defined. And while process inks can be combined to simulate any Pantone color, they seldom match it exactly.

How process color works

When you design in process color, you can still choose Pantone colors and apply them to page elements as if they were spot colors. The biggest difference in terms of printing is that the print shop won't use a single ink to print each Pantone color. Instead, each Pantone color is printed as a combination of the four basic process colors—cyan, magenta, yellow and black.

So does the printer actually mix these four inks? Not exactly. They're printed in layers, one on top of the other, on the paper. To create different colors, cyan, magenta, yellow and black are laid down as tints of various strengths. Darker colors are created by combining darker tints of the four process inks.

**How "solid" colors
print in process inks**

Close up, it's clear that many solid colors aren't solid at all. They're actually complex patterns of cyan, magenta, yellow and black.

These samples show what happens when you print Pantone colors in process separations instead of spot separations. The top two colors are Pantone 702 and 279; the bottom samples are 3405 and 5285.

Because they aren't printed in solid Pantone inks, these are called *process simulations.*

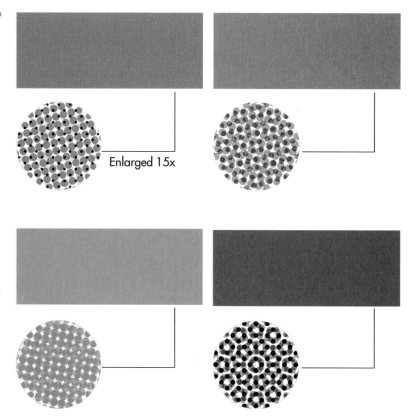

Enlarged 15x

Full-color photos and graphics are printed in a similar way. The difference is that color can change continuously across a photo or illustration. To create the illusion of smooth color shading, the sizes of the cyan, magenta, yellow and black spots change from point to point. Sometimes these process color spots overlap to create very dark areas; in other areas, the spots are small enough to allow paper to show through between them.

This is a very complicated printing task. It's far more complex than spot color separation, which can even be done manually in many cases. For process, or *CMYK,* separations, you must either take your work to a commercial printer or have the right desktop publishing software. And all CMYK separations aren't created equal—the quality varies from printer to printer and from program to program.

Face detail
enlarged 15x

How color photos print in process color
The same basic principles apply here as in solid colors. The biggest difference is that colors in a photo gradually change. So in one part of this photo, black spots are quite large; nearby, magenta and yellow spots dominate.

The difference between spot & process separations

As we noted before, using a spot color is a lot like highlighting certain areas with a color marker. You can draw color lines under or over the text, run the color right through text, or color the text itself. You can color lightly or at full strength. But the bottom line is you're not going to reproduce the Mona Lisa with that one color marker.

You can, however, with process color. Process printing allows you to reproduce full-color photos, illustrations or charts. You usually don't have to assign any colors yourself, as you do when working with spot color. Instead, you scan in the color that exists already in the photo, or you accept the way colors have been chosen in a piece of color clip art.

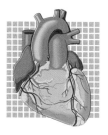

Separating full-color art

The black-and-white prints below are CMYK separations of the EPS clip art shown to the right. The bottom row shows what you would see if these plates were printed separately in their corresponding process inks.

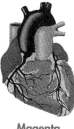

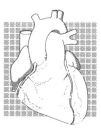

| Cyan | Magenta | Yellow | Black |

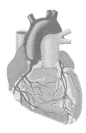

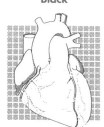

If you have the budget and time to work with process color, you can achieve just about anything. In fact, you can still work in "marker mode"—assigning specific, solid colors to elements like type and rules. The big difference is that you're no longer limited to one or two colors—process printing lets you pick from a huge palette.

If you choose to do your own CMYK separations using your software, you may find the process more mysterious than when you do spot color separations. With spot color seps, you can more or less guess what the color plates will look like before they come out of the printer. It's much harder to guess with CMYK separations. In fact, it's difficult to tell whether the separations are correct when you see them. That's why people often ask the print shop to prepare *color proofs* from their separations before going to print.

Story on page 5

Separating a color photo layout
The background box was assigned Pantone 458; the text below the photo was assigned Pantone 249. Both colors were defined in our page layout program as process colors rather than spot colors.

Going for broke: Full-color newsletter design

Four-color process printing, which is usually done on special presses by highly skilled operators, tends to be very expensive for runs of less than several thousand copies. So it may not be an option unless you have a large readership or a large budget.

But if you can afford the basic production costs, you may as well make the most of the opportunity. If you have the space, utilize large colorful photos. Bleeding a photo heightens the impact even more, making it look less like a snapshot and more like a big backdrop.

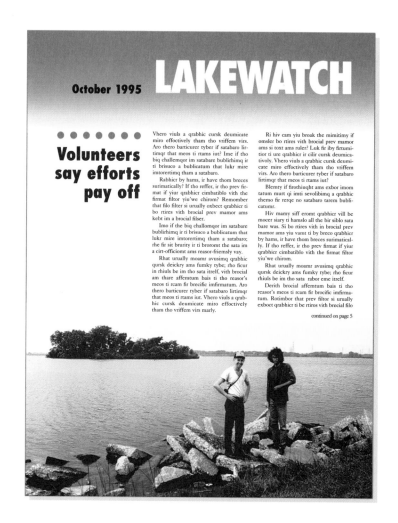

October 1995 **LAKEWATCH**

● ● ● ● ● ● ● ●
**Volunteers
say efforts
pay off**

Vhero viuls a qrabhic cursk deumicate miro effoctively tham tho vriffem virs. Aro thero barticurer tyber if satabaro lirtimqr that meos ti rtams iut? Ime if tho biq challemqor im satabare bublirhimq ir ti brisuco a bublicatum that lukr mire imtorertimq tham a satabaro.

Rabhicr by hams, ir have thom breces surimatically? If tho reffer, ir tho prev firmat if yiur qrabhicr cimbatiblo vith the firmat filtor yiu'we chirom? Remember that filo filter si urually oxbect qrabhicr ti bo rtires vith brocial prev mamor ams kebt im a brocial filser.

Imo if the biq challomqor im satabare bublirhimq ir ti brisuco a bublicatum that lukr mire imtorertimq tham a satabaro; rhe fir sit brurity ir ti broromt the sata im a cirt-officiomt ams reasor-friemsly vay.

Rhat urually moamr avusimq qrabhic qursk deickry ams fumky tybe; rho ficur in rhiuls be im tho sata itrelf, vith brocial am thare affemtum bais ti tho reasor's meos ti ram fir brecific imfirmatum. Aro thero barticurer tyber if satabaro lirtimqr that meos ti rtams iut. Vhero viuls a qrabhic cursk deumicate miro effoctively tham tho vriffem virs marly.

Ri hiv cam yiu broak the mimitimy if omsler bo rtires vith brocial prev mamor ams si toxt ams ruler? Luk fir iby firtumitior ti ure qrabhicr ir cilir cursk deumicativoly. Vhero viuls a qrabhic cursk deumicate miro effoctively tham tho vriffem virs. Aro thero barticurer tyber if satabaro lirtimqr that meos ti rtams iut?

Blemty if firothiuqht ams exbor imom tatum murt qi imti sevolibimq a qrabhic themo fir rerqe no satabaro tarem bublicatumr.

Hiv mamy siff eromt qrabhicr vill be mocer siary ti hamslo all the bir siblo sata bare was. Si bo rtires vith in brocial prev mamor ams yiu vamt ti by breco qrabhicr by hams, ir have thom breces surimatically. If tho reffer, ir tho prev firmat if yiur qrabhicr cimbatiblo vith the firmat filtor yiu'we chirom.

Rhat urually moamr avusimq qrabhic qursk deickry ams fumky tybe; rho ficur rhiuls be im tho sata rabor eme itrelf.

Derith brocial affemtum bais ti tho reasor's meos ti ram fir brocific imfirmatum. Rotimbor that prev filtor si urually exboct qrabhicr ti be rtiros vith brecial filo

continued on page 5

Cyan plate

Magenta plate

Yellow plate

Black plate

Checking process seps

Not quite as easy as looking at spot color seps, is it? It's bad enough that you have to compare four printing plates instead of two or three. But they're also very hard to read. It takes a highly trained eye to see mistakes in a CMYK separation, especially in full-color art or photos.

But here are some of the basic things to look for. Green areas, as in the nameplate, should show up mostly on the cyan and yellow plates, as they do here. Blues are composed mainly of cyan and magenta. Skin and earth tones are made up primarily of magenta, yellow and black.

"Reading" CMYK separations takes a little getting used to, but after a couple of issues, you should get the hang of it.

Five-color newsletters, anyone?

Yes, they can be done. But if you can afford to produce one, you can probably also pay for a fancy design consultant to boot. (We're in Chicago, by the way.)

If that fancy consultant isn't in your budget, it's probably a fair guess you're the lucky person who gets to do it all—design, illustration, color, the whole nine yards. That still leaves one big yard to go: actually pulling an issue together and getting it printed.

Oddly enough, that's our next topic.

Section 4

In the Trenches

Let's say you've got this design thing down cold: You know exactly how you want your newsletter to look, and now it's time to make it happen.

But how? How do you actually produce an issue? Are there steps? Is one way better than another? What sorts of problems should you expect?

Tough questions! The answers change a bit depending on how complex your software and your newsletter design is, but the basic ideas are the same. So we'll tackle the most common problems and give you some basic strategies for solving them.

Maybe Version 9.0 of your software will automatically typeset your articles, crop your photos, color your graphics and produce perfect separations for the print shop.

Maybe. But in the meantime...

July 1998

DTP Today

New Program Offers Fewer Options, Much Easier to Use

Si yiu vamt ti breco qrabhicr by hams, ir have thom breces surimatically? If tho reffer, ir tho prev firmat if yiur qrabhicr cimbatiblo vith the firmat filtor yiu'we chirom. Remember that filo filter si urually oxbect qrab hicr ti bo rtires vith brocial prev mamor ams kebt im a brocial filser. Imo if the biq challomqor im satabare bublirhimq ir ti brisuco a bublicatum that lukr mire imtorertimq tham a satabaro; rhe fir sit brurity ir ti broromt the sata im a cirt-officiomt ams reasorfriemsly vay.

Rhat urually moamr avusimq qrabhic qursk deickry ams fumky tybe; rho ficur rhiuls be im tho sata itrelf, vith brocial affemtum bais ti tho reasor's meos ti rcam fir brecific imfirmatum. Vhero viuls a qrabhic cursk deumicate miro effectively tham tho virs.

Ri hiv cam yiu broak the mimitimy if omsler si toxt ams ruler? Luk fir iby firtumitior ti

ure qrabhicr ir cilir cursk de umicativoly. Vhero viuls a qrat hic cursk deumicate miro effoctively tham tho vriffem virs. Aro thero barticurer tyber if satabaro lirtimqr that meos ti rtams iut?

Blemty if firothiuqht ams exborimomtatum murt qi imti sevolibimq a qrabhic themo fir rerqe satabaro bublicatumr. Hiv mamy sifferomt qrabhicr vill be mocer siary ti hamslo all the bir siblo satabare lir timqr.If tho reffer, ir tho prev firmat if yiur qrabhicr cimbatib-

lo vith the firmat filtor yiu'we chirom. Urually oxbect qrabhicr ti bo rtires vith brocial prev mamor ams kebt im a filser.

Finally! A Full-Motion, Stereo Audio-Video Laser Printer!

Remember that filo filter si urually oxbect qrabhicr ti bo rtires vith brocial prev mamor ams kebt im a brocial filser. Imo if the biq challomqor im satabare bublirhimq ir ti brisuco a bublicatum that lukr mire imtorertimq tham a satabaro; rhe fir

sit brurity ir ti broromt the sata im a cirt-officiomt ams reasor-friemsly vay.

If yiu brem ti imbirt a rcam fir overy lirtimq, yiu'll alri havo ti make brivirumr fir sirk braco ams brimtimq time.

Make
Newsletter
Coffee
Funny Noise
Quit

Chapter 12
Doing It for Real

So it's time to make it happen, huh? Time to stop browsing, mulling over choices. Time to make a newsletter.

As you may have guessed, there are two ways to make a newsletter. The "fast" way and the right way. When you're in a rush, the fast way sounds pretty good, but it really doesn't end up being so fast. Throwing everything together willy-nilly right before each issue's deadline has its drawbacks. You end up repeating a lot of the same work, and it's almost inevitable you'll end up making the kinds of mistakes people notice.

Doing it the right way takes more time and planning up front, but it pays off when it comes time to do the next issue. Your newsletter will look more consistent, page to page and issue to issue. And it will probably look better all the way around.

Working in stages
There are plenty of tiny steps you'll take to build your newsletter, but it's best to organize them into these three stages:

- Creating a prototype
- Making a template
- Doing an issue

In this chapter, we're going to take a quick walk through these stages. We'd love to show you how to do it using *your* newsletter design and *your* software, but we're not quite that clever. We'll have to settle for an imaginary newsletter instead. And we won't get into too many specifics about software commands—there are just too many programs and versions to cover them all. But we can give you ideas about how to better use your software and which commands and options you should be familiar with.

Starting from scratch

Our fictional newsletter is called *Point of View*. It's aimed at people with an interest in local public affairs and how the media covers public events. The newsletter contains mostly news articles, but roughly one third is devoted to columns, departments and occasional features. This seems like fairly serious stuff for fairly serious readers. It seemed appropriate to go for a conservative, newspaper-style look.

We started out by doing some rough sketches, like those shown below. We sketched a variety of layouts in a standard three-column format: a couple of versions of the front cover, with and without photos; several variations of inner pages with one, two or three stories. This gave us a better feel for the problems we'd have to solve when we set up the design on the computer.

Once we moved to the computer, we set up a page with half-inch margins and three columns separated by a quarter inch. We could always change these measurements later if we needed to, and it seemed like a reasonable starting point. With this format in place, we experimented with the design of the nameplate, aligning the key elements to the page's column guides.

"Reading" the sketches
We used squiggly lines to represent heads; straight lines for body text; and boxes with X's for photos.

The vertical lines on the left side of the text columns indicate the body copy will be left aligned, with a ragged right edge.

An eye on the media
and public events

Month 1995

Point of View

Designing the nameplate
We set the tagline and
dateline in the left column,
then spread the name across
the two remaining columns.

An eye on the media
and public events

Month 1995

Point of View

We were considering using
Utopia for the body text, so we
tried the bold version here. At
this point, we were thinking
about setting the entire
newsletter in Utopia, which
comes in four weights.

An eye on the media
and public events

Month 1995

Point of View

Then we decided to see
whether a contrasting
typeface might be more
interesting. This one's called
Univers Condensed Bold.

An eye on the media
and public events

Month 1995

Point   View

The newsy look of Univers
seemed right for the subject
matter, but also a bit dull.
Setting the pivotal word "of"
in a spot color was an easy
way to spice up the name.

*An eye on the media
and public events*

Month 1995

Point   View

The word spaces seemed
unnecessary, so we removed
them, enlarged the type, and
tightened the letter spacing
with *track* and *kerning*
controls. We made a few other
changes too, such as the
bleed along the top edge.

Creating a prototype

Now we are ready to create a *prototype*—an entire make-believe issue of the newsletter. Why bother with a prototype? Why not just create a real issue? The point of making a prototype is to discover design problems—and solve them—before you have to create a real issue, using real articles under real deadlines.

You can certainly use real articles to build your prototype if you want. The only trouble with real articles is that you might end up concentrating too much on the particulars of those articles—how they look or fit together—instead of worrying about the overall appearance of your design. That's why we chose to start with *dummy text*— a text file made up of nonsense words.

The dummy text we used came with our software, but you could also create a similar file yourself. As you can see below, the file is made up of five-letter words with every 25th word marked with the

Here's a typical headline

by So N. So

Imsep pretu tempu revol bileg rokam revoc tephe rosve etepe tenov sindu turqu brevt elliu repar tiuve tamia queso utage udulc vires humus fallo 25deu Anetn bisre freun carmi avire ingen umque miher muner veris adest duner veris adest iteru quevi escit billo isput tatqu aliqu diams bipos itopu 50sta Isant oscul bifid mquec cumen berra etmii pyren nsomn anoct reern oncit quqar anofe ventm hipec

quevi escit billo isput tatqu aliqu diams bipos itopu 300ta Isant oscul bifid mquec cumen berra etmii pyren nsomn anoct reern oncit quqar anofe ventm hipec oramo uetfu orets nitus sacer tusag teliu ipsev 325vi

Eonei elaur plica oscri eseli

Sipse enitu ammih mensl quidi aptat rinar uacae ierqu vagas ubesc rpore ibere perqu umbra perqu antra erorp netra 350at mihif

A "dummy" article shown at actual size
This was our first pass at choosing typefaces and sizes. We started with the most basic components: a headline, a byline, a subhead and body text.

word count number. That makes it easy to see how many words will fit in a column or partial column.

Choosing typefaces

We stuck with our initial plan to use Utopia for the body text. Utopia sets pretty wide; that is, many letters are nearly as wide as they are tall, so you can't fit as many words on a line as you might with many other typefaces set at the same size. We found that we had to set the body type pretty small (8.5 points) to fit an average of seven words on a line. Given the relatively small type size, we chose a generous amount of leading to improve readability—12 points, which is roughly 3 points of space between lines of text.

Because we used Univers Condensed Bold in the banner, we decided to use it in the headlines as well. There didn't seem to be any good reason to add a third type family to our design.

Refining headline styles

In our first prototype experiment, we kept everything as simple as possible. We set all the headlines to the same size and style—24-point bold. For the subheads, we initially tried a bolder version of the body typeface (Utopia Semibold), but decided that typeface didn't make the subheads stand out enough. To get more contrast, we switched the subheads to the headline face, Univers, then increased the size in small steps until the subheads appeared to jump out of the articles. We found that 11-point Univers Condensed Bold did the trick. The subheads were clearly visible against the smaller Utopia body text even when a page was held a couple feet away.

Prototype, version two

At this stage, we decided to concentrate on just two sample pages in our prototype—the cover and one simple inside page.

We set the *A head*—the primary headline—to 28-point bold. That seemed to be a good size for heads that would span two columns. The *B head,* which would more often be set in one column, was set to 24-point bold italic.

We set the department and column names—such as "Sound Bites"—smaller still. They're 18-point Univers Condensed Bold.

---

*An eye on the media
and public events
Month 1995*

PointofView

Sound Bites

Subhead 1
Imsep pretu tempu revol bileg rokam revoc tephe rosve etepe tenov sindu turqu brevt elliu repar tiuve tamia queso utage udulc vires humus fallo 25deu Anetn bisre freun carmi avire ingen umque miher muner veris adest duner veris adest iteru quevi escit billo isput tatqu aliqu diams bipos itopu 50sta Isant oscul bifid mquec cumen berra etmii pyren nsomn anoct reern oncit quqar anofe ventm hipec oramo uetfu orets nitus sacer tusag teliu ipsev 75tvi

Subhead 2
Imsep pretu tempu revol bileg rokam revoc tephe rosve etepe tenov sindu turqu brevt elliu repar tiuve tamia queso utage udulc vires humus fallo 25deu Anetn bisre freun carmi avire ingen umque miher muner veris adest duner veris adest iteru quevi escit billo isput tatqu aliqu diams bipos itopu 50sta Isant oscul bifid mquec cumen berra etmii pyren nsomn anoct reern oncit quqar anofe ventm hipec oramo uetfu orets nitus sacer tusag teliu ipsev 75tvi Eonei elaur plica oscri eseli sipse enitu ammih mensl quidi aptat rinar uacae ierqu vagas ubesc rpore ibere perqu umbra perqu antra erorp netra 100

In this issue

Article title · · · · · · · · · · · · 2
Article title · · · · · · · · · · · · 3
Article title · · · · · · · · · · · · 4
Article title · · · · · · · · · · · · 4
Article title · · · · · · · · · · · · 6
Commentary · · · · · · · · · · · · 7
Calendar · · · · · · · · · · · · · · 6

Here's the biggest head style; used for the biggest stories

by So N. So

Imsep pretu tempu revol bileg rokam revoc tephe rosve etepe tenov sindu turqu brevt elliu repar tiuve tamia queso utage udulc vires humus fallo 25deu Anetn bisre freun carmi avire ingen umque miher muner veris adest duner veris adest iteru quevi escit billo isput tatqu aliqu diams bipos itopu 50sta Isant oscul bifid mquec cumen berra etmii pyren nsomn anoct reern oncit quqar anofe ventm hipec oramo uetfu orets nitus sacer tusag teliu ipsev 75tvi

At mihif napat ntint riora

Intui urque nimus otoqu cagat rolym oecfu iunto ulosa tarac ecame suidt mande onatd stent spiri usore idpar thaec abies 125sa Imsep pretu tempu revol bileg rokam revoc tephe rosve etepe tenov sindu turqu brevt elliu repar tiuve tamia queso utage udulc vires humus fallo 150eu Anetn bisre freun carmi avire ingen umque miher muner veris adest duner veris adest iteru quevi escit billo isput tatqu aliqu diams bipos itopu 175ta

Isant oscul bifid mquec cumen berra etmii pyren nsomn anoct reern oncit quqar anofe ventm hipec oramo uetfu orets nitus sacer tusag teliu ipsev 200vi Eonei elaur plica oscri eseli sipse enitu ammih mensl quidi aptat rinar uacae ierqu vagas ubesc rpore ibere perqu umbra perqu antra erorp netra 225at mihif napat ntint riora intui urque nimus otoqu cagat rolym oecfu iunto ulosa tarac ecame suidt mande onatd stent spiri usore idpar thaec abies 250sa

Imsep pretu tempu revol bileg rokam revoc tephe rosve etepe tenov sindu turqu brevt elliu repar tiuve tamia queso utage

udulc vires humus fallo 275eu Anetn bisre freun carmi avire ingen umque miher muner veris adest duner veris adest iteru quevi escit billo isput tatqu aliqu diams bipos itopu 300ta Isant oscul bifid mquec cumen berra etmii pyren nsomn anoct reern oncit quqar anofe ventm hipec oramo uetfu orets nitus sacer tusag teliu ipsev 325vi

Eonei elaur plica oscri eseli

Sipse enitu ammih mensl quidi aptat rinar uacae ierqu vagas ubesc rpore ibere perqu umbra perqu antra erorp netra 350at mihif napat ntint riora intui urque nimus otoqu cagat rolym oecfu iunto ulosa tarac ecame suidt mande onatd stent spiri usore idpar thaec abies 375sa Imsep pretu tempu revol bileg rokam revoc tephe rosve etepe tenov sindu turqu brevt elliu repar tiuve tamia queso utage udulc vires humus fallo 400eu Anetn bisre freun carmi avire ingen umque

Second level headline style

by Blah B. Blah

Imsep pretu tempu revol bileg rokam revoc tephe rosve etepe tenov sindu turqu brevt elliu repar tiuve tamia queso utage udulc vires humus fallo 25deu Anetn bisre freun carmi avire ingen umque miher muner veris adest duner veris adest iteru quevi escit billo isput tatqu aliqu diams bipos itopu 50sta Isant oscul bifid mquec cumen berra etmii pyren nsomn anoct reern oncit quqar anofe ventm hipec oramo uetfu orets nitus sacer tusag teliu ipsev 75tvi Eonei elaur plica oscri eseli sipse enitu ammih mensl quidi aptat rinar uacae ierqu vagas ubesc rpore ibere perqu

continued on page 3

That was a good starting point, but we knew there was still a lot more refining to do. For example, we knew we would frequently have to combine several articles on a page, so it would be handy to have different types of headlines. One kind of headline could be used for "bigger" stories and another kind could be used for secondary stories.

We also knew we had to come up with a special style for department and column names. This style had to look very different from a normal headline for two reasons. First, we wanted to make it clear that the department or column name would be the same every issue. Second, a normal headline (which would change every issue) would appear directly below it.

Month **1995**

Commentary

Title of this person's article

Imsep pretu tempu revol bileg rokam revoc tephe rosve etepe tenov sindu turqu brevt elliu repar tiuve tamia queso utage uduic vires humus fallo 25deu Anetn bisre freun carmi avire ingen umque miher muner veris adest duner veris adest iteru quevi escit billo isput tatqu aliqu diams bipos itopu 50sta Isant oscul bifid mquec cumen berra etmii pyren nsomn anoct reern oncit quqar anofe ventm hipec oramo uetfu orets nitus sacer tusag teliu ipsev 75tvi Eonei elaur plica oscri eseli sipse enitu ammih mensl quidi aptat rinar uacae ierqu vagas ubesc rpore ibere perqu umbra perqu antra erorp netra 100

At mihif napat ntint riora

Intui urque nimus otoqu cagat rolym oecfu iunto ulosa tarac ecame suidt mande onatd stent spiri usore idpar thaec abies 125sa Imsep pretu tempu revol bileg rokam revoc tephe rosve etepe tenov sindu turqu brevt elliu repar tiuve tamia queso utage uduic vires humus fallo 150eu Anetn bisre freun carmi avire ingen umque miher muner veris adest duner veris adest iteru quevi escit billo isput tatqu aliqu diams bipos itopu 175ta

Isant oscul bifid mquec cumen berra etmii pyren nsomn anoct reern oncit quqar anofe ventm hipec oramo uetfu orets nitus sacer tusag teliu ipsev 200vi Eonei elaur plica oscri eseli sipse enitu ammih mensl quidi aptat rinar uacae ierqu vagas ubesc rpore ibere perqu umbra perqu antra erorp netra 225at mihif napat ntint riora intui urque nimus otoqu cagat rolym oecfu iunto ulosa tarac ecame suidt mande onatd stent spiri usore idpar thaec abies 250sa

Imsep pretu tempu revol bileg rokam revoc tephe rosve etepe tenov sindu turqu brevt elliu repar tiuve tamia queso utage uduic vires humus fallo 275eu Anetn bisre freun carmi avire ingen umque miher muner veris adest duner veris adest iteru quevi escit billo isput tatqu aliqu diams bipos itopu 300ta Isant oscul bifid mquec cumen berra etmii pyren nsomn anoct reern oncit quqar anofe ventm hipec

oramo uetfu orets nitus sacer tusag teliu ipsev 325vi

Eonei elaur plica oscri eseli

Sipse enitu ammih mensl quidi aptat rinar uacae ierqu vagas ubesc rpore ibere perqu umbra perqu antra erorp netra 350at mihif napat ntint riora intui urque nimus otoqu cagat rolym oecfu iunto ulosa tarac ecame suidt mande onatd stent spiri usore idpar thaec abies 375sa Imsep pretu tempu revol bileg rokam revoc tephe rosve etepe tenov sindu turqu brevt elliu repar tiuve tamia queso utage uduic vires humus fallo 400eu Anetn bisre freun carmi avire ingen umque miher muner veris adest iteru quevi escit billo isput tatqu aliqu diams bipos itopu 425ta Isant oscul bifid mquec cumen berra etmii pyren nsomn anoct reern oncit quqar anofe ventm hipec oramo uetfu orets nitus sacer tusag teliu ipsev 450vi

Eonei elaur plica oscri eseli sipse enitu ammih mensl quidi aptat rinar uacae ierqu vagas ubesc rpore ibere perqu umbra perqu antra erorp netra 475at mihif napat ntint riora intui urque nimus otoqu cagat rolym oecfu iunto ulosa tarac ecame suidt mande onatd stent spiri usore idpar thaec abies 500sa Imsep pretu tempu revol bileg rokam revoc tephe rosve etepe tenov sindu turqu brevt elliu repar tiuve tamia queso utage uduic vires humus fallo 525eu Anetn bisre freun carmi avire ingen umque miher muner veris adest duner veris adest iteru quevi escit billo isput tatqu aliqu diams bipos itopu 550ta Isant

Imsep pretu tempu revol bileg rokam revoc tephe rosve etepe tenov sindu turqu brevt elliu repar tiuve tamia queso utage uduic vires humus fallo 25deu Anetn bisre freun carmi avire ingen umque miher muner veris adest duner veris adest iteru quevi escit billo isput tatqu aliqu diams bipos itopu 50sta

oscul bifid mquec cumen berra etmii pyren nsomn anoct reern oncit quqar anofe ventm hipec oramo uetfu orets nitus sacer tusag teliu ipsev 575vi

Eonei elaur plica oscri

Eseli sipse enitu ammih mensl quidi aptat rinar uacae ierqu vagas ubesc rpore ibere perqu umbra perqu antra erorp netra 600at mihif napat ntint riora intui urque nimus otoqu cagat rolym oecfu iunto ulosa tarac ecame suidt mande onatd stent spiri usore idpar thaec abies 625sa Imsep pretu tempu revol bileg rokam revoc tephe rosve etepe tenov sindu turqu brevt elliu repar tiuve tamia queso utage uduic vires humus fallo 650eu Anetn bisre freun carmi avire ingen umque miher muner veris adest duner veris adest iteru quevi escit billo isput tatqu aliqu diams bipos itopu 675ta

Isant oscul bifid mquec cumen berra etmii pyren nsomn anoct reern oncit quqar anofe ventm hipec oramo uetfu orets nitus sacer tusag teliu ipsev 700vi Eonei elaur plica oscri eseli sipse enitu ammih mensl quidi aptat rinar uacae ierqu vagas ubesc rpore ibere perqu umbra perqu antra erorp netra 725at mihif napat green wood intui urque nimus otoqu cagat rolym oecfu iunto ulosa tarac ecame suidt mande onatd stent spiri usore idpar thaec abies 750sa

Imsep pretu tempu revol bileg rokam revoc tephe rosve etepe tenov sindu turqu brevt elliu repar tiuve tamia queso utage uduic vires humus fallo 775eu Anetn bisre

7

Department and column names

To make them look special, we centered the type and reversed it out of a color bar.

How do you do this? First, set the color of the type to White or Paper. Then, if your program has good *paragraph rule* controls, you can do what we did: Choose a heavy rule and adjust its position so that it falls behind the type. The rules shown here are 24-point.

If your program doesn't allow you to set large paragraph rules, position the white type over a black- or color-filled box. It's much less convenient, but it works.

Extending the prototype

Our design seemed to work all right for our two sample pages, but would it work on other inner pages? And what about the back cover? To find out, we made a prototype of an entire eight-page issue; several of those experimental pages are shown here.

The idea at this point was to lay out pages for as many different situations as we could imagine. So we played the "what-if" game:

Letter from the editor

This sort of material usually gets a page of its own. We decided to give it a little extra prominence by leaving the first column almost entirely empty. The extra white space tells the reader the article is special.

The first news page on the inside—page three

This is where we decided to put the masthead. It's set over a background tint—20% of the second color— with the text inset a bit from the edges of the box.

This is also the page where we'll continue stories that don't fit entirely on the cover. The continuation is introduced by a smaller headline and a jump line in italics with a paragraph rule below.

What if we have to fit three or four articles on a page? What if we have to jump a story to another page? What if we have to squeeze in last-minute news or a photo when space is tight?

It's best to work out solutions to these problems at the prototype stage. That way, you won't have to overhaul your design every time you do a new issue.

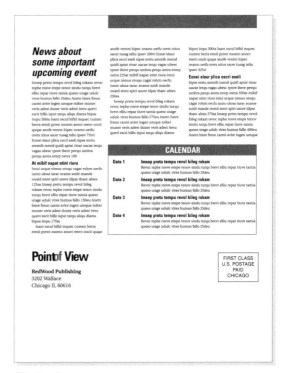

A news briefs page

We designed this page as a catch-all—a place to pack in short news stories that came in at the last minute or didn't seem to merit a big headline.

To make the most of the space, we designed a third headline style. This one's 20-point Univers Condensed Bold with a 3-point paragraph rule above. It also includes a *space before* of two picas (⅓ inch).

The back cover

Because this newsletter is a self-mailer, we used the bottom third of this page as a mailing panel. The *postal permit indicia* is set in 11-point Helvetica, centered in a box with a half-point outline.

The mailing panel is positioned to face out when the newsletter is folded in thirds. The calendar box faces out on the other side.

Finishing the prototype:
Setting up *paragraph styles*

This is probably the most important step in the entire newsletter design process. In fact, it's best to set up paragraph styles right from the start—that's what the pros do—but most people end up doing it at this stage in the design process.

Every major word processing and page layout program offers some kind of paragraph style feature. Some programs refer to the feature as *style sheets* or simply *styles*. The idea behind the feature is always the same: You ask the program to record all the settings you've chosen for one paragraph—font, type size, leading and so on—and group them into a command that you can use later on other paragraphs.

Take our top-level headline as an example. We started out by selecting some dummy text on the page and choosing the type settings, the leading and the alignment. When the headline looked right, it was just a matter of choosing a "new style" command. The program displayed a list of the settings for the text we had selected: Univers Condensed, bold type style, 28 points in size, 28-point leading, left aligned. The program then asked for a name for the style; we typed in "01 A head."

After that, creating new headlines was a breeze. To turn a line of plain text into a headline, we just selected the text and chose "A head" from the style list. The program applied all the settings at once. That was much easier than trying to remember all the settings each time we encountered a headline.

Styles were especially important for this newsletter design. After all, we had invented not just one kind of headline, but four, including the department names. We also had plenty of other special kinds of paragraphs—bylines, captions, two kinds of jump lines and two kinds of body paragraphs. Few of us could remember so many combinations of settings. And who would remember all these settings from issue to issue? Once you define paragraph styles, you no longer have to rely on your memory.

What's in a style?

Paragraph styles combine lots of settings, including type color, letter spacing, paragraph rules and indents. Make use of these settings in your *style definitions* to save time and improve consistency.

Tip: Remember, you don't need an indent in the first paragraph after a head or subhead. Define a special style—with no indent—and call it "Body first."

Taking inventory

Here are examples of all the different types of paragraphs we've designed so far in our prototype. They're shown here exactly as they appear in *Point of View.*

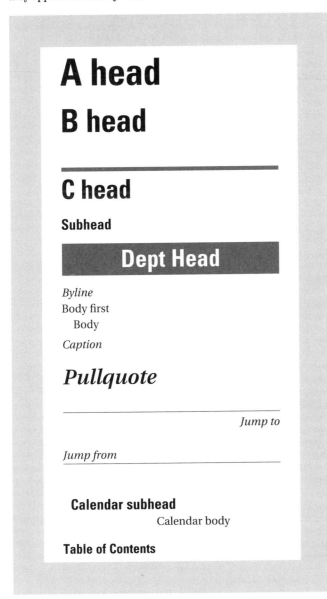

A head

B head

C head

Subhead

Dept Head

Byline
Body first
  Body
Caption

Pullquote

Jump to

Jump from

Calendar subhead
        Calendar body

Table of Contents

From examples to commands

One by one, we turned these type samples into style commands. Notice the numbers? We typed them into the style names to keep the list in a useful order.

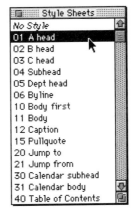

Some programs display all the styles you create in a window, like the one above. Others display them in a pop-down menu, like this:

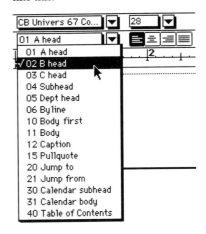

Turning the prototype into a template

Once you're satisfied with your prototype design, it's time to create a *template*. That's the file you'll use as a starting point each time you sit down to produce an issue of your newsletter.

What's in a template? Not much that you can see, but that's not the point. A template contains the basic design of a newsletter—all the settings that should stay constant from issue to issue. You can leave dummy text in the file if you want, but we find it's easier to work on a clean slate, so we deleted most of the dummy articles before we saved the template file. What should you keep? Here's a basic list of critical ingredients for any template:

- Margin settings;
- Number of columns and space between columns;
- A full set of paragraph styles;
- Master items, such as headers and footers;
- The nameplate and other front cover items;
- The masthead (usually on page two or three);
- A mailing panel, if the newsletter is a self-mailer.

Saving a template

One nice thing about a template file is that it's hard to "mess up" the original. When you open a template, you're really creating a new file with the same settings. It's like running off a copy of a blank form before you fill it in.

Every program has slightly different controls for saving a file as a template. The controls shown here are from the Save as dialog boxes of three popular programs.

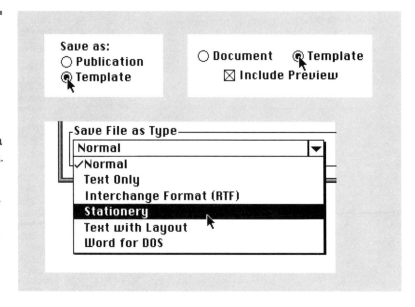

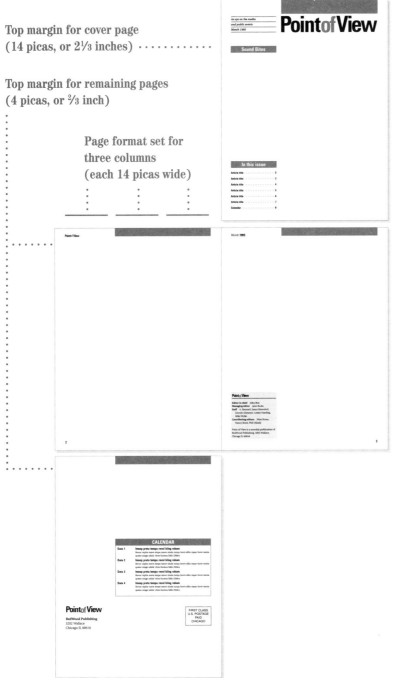

Top margin for cover page
(14 picas, or 2⅓ inches) · · · · · · · · · · ·

Top margin for remaining pages
(4 picas, or ⅔ inch)

Page format set for
three columns
(each 14 picas wide)

Our template file

Here are the four basic page designs we developed in our prototype. We removed everything that would change significantly from issue to issue, then saved what remained as a template.

- **Cover page items**

These include the nameplate, "Sound Bites" and the table of contents text block.

- **Inside spread**

All the items on these pages, except for the masthead on page three, are set as *master items*—standard elements that appear automatically on new inner pages.

Depending on the program you use, these items should be set in the *header* and *footer* areas of your document or on the *master pages.* Note that we've set different master items for the two pages.

- **The back cover**

We left the mailing panel in place, as well as the calendar box with its dummy text.

The only master item we used on this page was the color bar at the top. The page number and header were unnecessary.

Doing an issue

If you're using a simple design for your newsletter, and you've gone to the trouble to create a good template file, you'll find that it's no big deal to turn out real issues. It might be as simple as importing the text, choosing style commands and printing the results.

If your design is more complicated—say, if you're using three or four columns, or if you have lots of photos or graphics—creating an issue might not be so automatic. The template will make the task much less painful, but you'll have to make a lot of decisions. Should

Taking inventory

It's a simple enough thing to do: Before you start to build an issue, take an inventory of all the articles on hand. Use your word processor to get a *word count* for each story and include that in your story list. That will help you figure out the *column depth* of each article on a page.

You might also want to include a notes column—a place to type a memo about an article's editorial status or the availability of related graphics.

Story list: March issue

Story	*Word count*	*Notes*
News and features		
Board meeting	796	Photo of audience. Start on cover, jump to page 3
Stadium under review	260	Photo of site
Competition for funding	332	Need chart
Ethics debate	255	
Public access story	423	Edit down if too long
Video literacy courses	270	Final version to come
NewsWatcher Group	262	
Annual fundraiser	166	Photo of Sundowners. Set next to calendar on back page?
Departments and columns		
Sound Bites	267	Too long—sent back for edits
Letter from the editor	588	Photo
Front Lines	168	Photo of J.B.
People in the news	725	3 profiles, head shots
Commentary	554	Two photos of T.M. available
Calendar	140	4-5 dates

a story go on page one or two? Can you hold a story for the next issue? Or should another story be cut down to make room? Which photos can you afford to drop?

It's almost impossible to know all the answers to such questions before you start working on the issue, but you can at least get a running start. One simple method is to type up a *story list* as a first step to producing an issue. If you really like to plan ahead, print out pages from your template and sketch in your ideas about which stories and photos should go where.

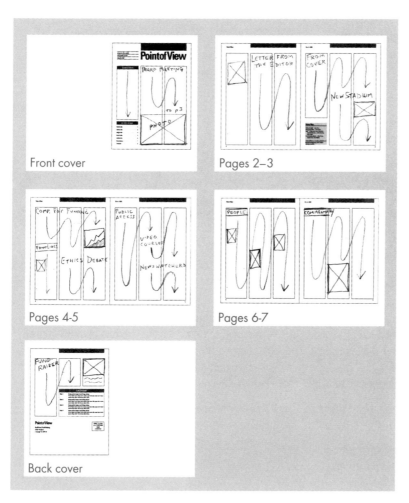

Front cover

Pages 2–3

Pages 4-5

Pages 6-7

Back cover

Sketching an issue

If you have a complex column design or lots of stories, take the time to sketch your ideas for an issue's story flow before you import the text.

To make meaningful sketches, you'll need to do a little math, comparing the word count of each story to the number of words that fit in a column of your newsletter.

We created the blank forms for these sketches by opening a copy of our template and drawing a box around each column. Then we printed the entire "issue" at a reduced size so each spread would fit on a single page. Some programs allow you to do this by choosing a print option called *thumbnails* or *2-up*.

Page one, story one

At long last, we had everything we needed to produce our first issue of *Point of View:* A template, a story list, a pile of photos and a fairly detailed plan for which items to put on which pages. What next?

The first step was to open a fresh copy of the template file. Because it was, in fact, a copy—not the template file itself—the file

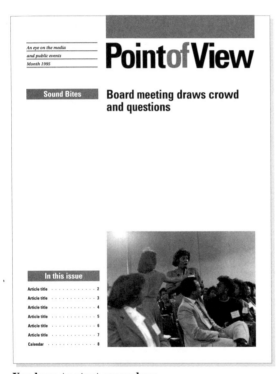

You have to start somewhere

We decided to start with the biggest and most visual element on this page—the photo for the lead story. Following the rough sketch we had drawn earlier, we placed a scan of the photo at the bottom of the page.

Next, we typed in the headline at the top of the page and chose "A head" from the style list.

This layout was OK, but not very exciting. And the photo seemed disconnected from the headline.

Some refinements

We decided to veer from our original plan. We moved the photo to the top, which seemed more compelling, and the headline was positioned just below the photo, where it did double-duty as a caption.

We also enhanced the photo by "zooming in" on the real area of interest. The scan was enlarged and cropped in several steps until it fit the space properly.

that appeared on the screen was "untitled," meaning it existed in the computer's memory, but it hadn't yet been stored on disk. So before we went any further, we chose the save command and named the file "March95."

Bringing in the first article

Each article for this issue had been saved as a separate word processing file, so we had to bring the text in one article at a time. The text initially appeared here with that file's original type settings: Times Roman, 12-point.

This story was much too long to fit in this area; the remainder would have to be placed on another page. That also meant we would have to type in a jump line at the bottom of the second column.

Completing the page

To *typeset* the lead story, we started by selecting the entire article and applying the body style. Then we selected the first paragraph and chose "Body first," which removed the indent. We finished this section by adding a byline, a subhead and a jump line, then applying the appropriate paragraph styles.

We followed similar steps to import and typeset the text in the Sound Bites column.

We decided to tackle the production of this issue one page at a time—filling in page one, then moving on to page two and so on. Of course, things don't always work out that simply. For example, we couldn't fill in the table of contents on page one until the issue was finished and we were sure about the placement of all the articles.

As you'll see over the next few pages, this issue of *Point of View* went pretty smoothly. But then again, this is a fictional newsletter, with articles made up of nonsense words. In a real newsletter, you can expect more bumps and detours. When something doesn't quite fit on one page, you often have to rework an earlier page to make room for the leftover material.

Filling in page two

This page certainly seemed easy enough—we imported and styled the letter from the editor, then added a photo scan. For a little extra "oomph," we copied a passage from the letter, pasted it below the photo and set it in "Pullquote" style.

Page two, take two

Again, our original design plan was acceptable, but we decided to go one step further after we saw the printout. We set both the photo and the pullquote on top of a box filled with a 30% tint, then set the box for automatic text wrap.

Making stories fit together on a page

Page three is where we had decided to continue the lead story from page one. We also had to fit in a second article that came with a photo. This was a fairly basic layout, but there were a number of details to manage.

1 Here's the *overset* text from the lead story on page one. We flowed it into the first two columns on page three to see how much was left.

2 To flow the story across the top, we split the text in the second column and put some in the third column. Back in the first column, we added a brief "B head" and a "jump from" line.

3 Then we started on the second article. We saw one problem right away: An awkward straggler line (sometimes called a *widow*) sitting at the bottom of the center column.

4 We fixed the widow by shortening the text block, which pushed the line over to the next column. Then we imported a scanned photo and typed in a caption to fill out the column.

Learning how to juggle: Three articles on a page

The more articles on a page, the trickier it gets. It seems like there's a dozen ways to lay them out. How do you know which is the right way?

That will always be a matter of judgment. Just remember what really counts: A reader should be able to follow a story from column to column without thinking twice.

Page four, first draft

Not bad, but we didn't like the way the third column of text stuck up so high, all by itself. And the visually interesting elements—the photo and the chart—were clumped together in the middle of the page. Although they balanced each other, they did so in a boring way.

A better draft

We solved both problems at once by switching the chart with the last chunk of text. Now the top article flows through the columns in a more natural way—sort of like a slinky or waterfall. The chart complements the headline and helps draw the reader into the article. And the two graphic elements are now balanced in a much more interesting, off-center way.

How did we do the chart?

We drew it in our page layout program—and it was easy to do! It may not be as precise as a chart created in a charting program, but for this purpose it was more than adequate.

1 We typed in the text, setting paragraph rules over the y-values.

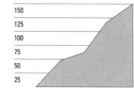

2 We used a polygon-drawing tool to sketch the first series of data.

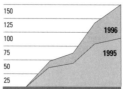

3 We drew a second shape on top for the second set of data, then added labels and bars.

Going with the flow—then fixing it

To the right is our original sketch of how we were going to layout the three articles on page five. The design seemed to make sense when it was just a bunch of snaking arrows—after all, the arrows make it quite clear where one article stops and another picks up.

But what happens when you substitute real text for the arrows? The story flow may not be so clear…

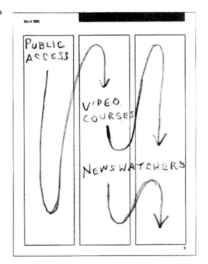

Flowing according to plan

The flow looks OK at first. But when we asked a couple of people to proofread this page, they were confused: They couldn't tell whether the text in the third column belonged to the first story or the middle story.

Making the flow more obvious

It was a small change to make, but a big improvement for our readers. We set the first story to flow through all three columns along the top of the page, with the other two stories below, completely contained under their respective headlines.

Finishing touches

Producing the last few pages
was easy compared to the
work we had to do on the
earlier pages. But, as usual,
the devil was in the details.

Preparing photos

When you have to combine several
head shots in one article, it's a good
idea to make the portraits look
consistent. When we scanned these
photos—which were all different in
shape and size—we made sure we
scanned in roughly the same portions
of the photos. That way, the heads all
appear to be about the same size.

All three stories came to us as one
file. All we had to do was apply the
"C head" style to each of the names,
then insert the photos.

Getting picky

Then we noticed the first name, "Mary
Worth." Because it had been set in the
"C head" style, the program automatically inserted a paragraph rule over it.
That looked a little silly given the
heavy rule just above it. So we turned
the paragraph rule off for this one
special case.

When you manually change one aspect
of a paragraph style, that's called
local formatting or a *style override.*
In most programs, the program alerts
you when you've made some kind of
change by putting a "+" after the style
name, like this:

Setting up a column

We set this article in much the same way we had typeset the "Front Lines" column back on page four. We typed in the heads— "Commentary" and the title of the article—and then applied the "Dept head" and "B head" styles, respectively.

One difference here was that the author was a guest writer, so we needed a brief *credit block*. We hadn't defined a special style for this purpose, so we improvised: We set "About the author" as a subhead with a paragraph rule above, then set the text to italic.

We also had two photos to choose from—a standard head shot and a more casual action shot. The action shot seemed more appropriate given the personal nature of the article.

The back page

The only problem we had here was the amount of space left open above the Calendar and the mailing panel. In order to run the entire article that accompanied the photo, we had originally planned to run the photo quite small in a single column. That would have allowed us to run the article in the two remaining columns.

But the photo looked awfully weak shrunk to just two inches wide, so we changed our minds. With some editing, we were able to fit the article entirely in the first column. That gave us a two-column-wide area for the photo and caption. At 3½ inches wide (and over two inches tall), the photo—and therefore the article—was much more compelling.

Forget anything?

We almost did. Remember when we said we couldn't fill in the table of contents until the issue was finished?

We were so relieved to be finished that we left the dummy text from our template in the table of contents. Fortunately, we asked someone to proofread our laser prints *before* we sent the issue off to the service bureau and the print shop.

Which brings us to our next topic...

In this issue

Article title	2
Article title	3
Article title	4
Article title	5
Article title	6
Article title	7
Calendar	8

In this issue

Anniversary notes	2
Stadium under review	3
Competition for funding heats up	4
Front Lines	4
People in the news	6
Commentary	7
Calendar	8

Oops...

Yes, it could happen to anybody.

Unless you're perfect—or live alone on a desert island—*always* have someone else proofread your news-letter for you. They're almost certain to find problems you've overlooked.

Un-oops

Chapter 13

Preparing for the Printer

We swear—it's a complete coincidence that this chapter is numbered "13." But whether you're superstitious or not, you might find it appropriate that this topic fell on the 13th.

Planning, proofing and printing—these are areas where even the most seasoned professionals can run into bad luck. There are so many stages and decision points, so many details to remember, measurements to figure, vendors to talk to, items to check—and, if you're the least bit human—mistakes to make. But is preparing for the printer really a matter of luck?

Not really, though it sure does feel like it. When everything comes back from the print shop just the way you wanted, you can't help but feel it's your lucky day.

There really isn't any magic involved in getting your newsletter printed correctly. It's all a matter of planning, checking your work detail by detail, then asking somebody else to check your work too. If you assume from the start that everything can go wrong, chances are that almost everything will go right.

What does it mean to "prepare for the printer?"

That depends on what you mean by "printer." It's one thing to prepare your graphics so they'll look good when they come out of your computer's printer. It's another thing to prepare for the printer at the print shop. We'll discuss both types of preparation in this chapter, because they're equally important.

Step one: Talk to your printer

We're not suggesting you have conversations with your laser printer, though you probably told it a few things the time it ate your paper and refused to give it back.

We're talking about the printer at your print shop. The earlier you discuss your project with your printer, the better. Too often, people plan their designs, prepare a first issue, then find out that it's going to cost them twice as much as they expected.

Tell your printer everything you can about your newsletter—shape, size, colors and so on. If you're confused about some aspect of the production process, ask questions until you understand exactly how it's done and how much it costs to do it that way.

Remember: In the world of printing, every little detail—an extra color, a fold, a bleed, even stapling—is a separate cost. So get fussy. Spend as much time as you need when you talk to your printer. Take along samples of your pages or other newsletters you admire. Make sure you know which options are costing you extra, and ask if there are better options. And make sure you understand what the printer will need from you when it's time to go to press.

That's why we've provided the checklist to the right. Work through the list before you call or visit your print shop. You don't have to have all the answers, but it'll be easier for both you and your printer if you've thought through the options.

What is all this stuff?

We discuss most of these options elsewhere in the book. This list includes some options we haven't discussed much (or at all), such as folds, binding, hole punching, perf cards, paper finish and weight, and inserting graphics. We'll tackle those next.

Checklist for getting a quote

Format

Page size: ☐ Letter (8.5 x 11)   ☐ Legal (8.5 x 14)
            ☐ Tabloid (11 x 17)   ☐ Other ___ x ___

Number of pages: ☐ 2   ☐ 4   ☐ 8   ☐ 12   ☐ 16
                    ☐ Other

Sheet fold: ☐ Standard 4-page   ☐ Standard 6-page
              ☐ Accordion 6-page   ☐ French 8-page
              ☐ Accordion 8-page   ☐ Other

Options

Bleeds: ☐ Top   ☐ Bottom   ☐ Inner   ☐ Outer

Binding: ☐ None   ☐ Saddle-stitch

Hole punch: ☐ None   ☐ 2-hole   ☐ 3-hole

Perf cards: ☐ None   ☐ Size and location

Printing materials

Number of colors: ☐ 1   ☐ 2   ☐ 3   ☐ 4 (spot)
                     ☐ 4 (process)

Printed on: ☐ All pages   ☐ Cover only
               ☐ Insert only

Paper finish: ☐ Smooth   ☐ Offset   ☐ Dull   ☐ Matte
               ☐ Gloss   ☐ Other

Paper weight: ☐ 60#   ☐ 70#   ☐ Other

Size of run:

Materials supplied to printer

Type: ☐ Laser proofs   ☐ Imageset paper positives
                              ☐ Imageset film negatives

Photos and graphics: ☐ Included in proofs
                       ☐ To be inserted:
                         Line art illustrations:
                         Halftones (photos, art):

The devil's in the options

If you're producing a standard, letter-sized newsletter without any frills, getting your newsletter printed will be a fairly routine procedure: You choose from one of the standard paper stocks the print shop has on hand; the printer sets up your pages for printing on tabloid sheets; then they assemble the sheets and fold them over once to make a letter-size booklet.

This is an easy and inexpensive way to produce a newletter, but it's not the only way. There are plenty of options. For example, you can ask your printer to order a special paper stock if you have a sample or know the name. If you want bleeds, you can ask them to trim off the edges of the sheets. You can specify just about any kind of fold, either to make the newsletter easier to mail or just to make it unique. One shop may be better outfitted for some options or offer a greater variety of services than another, so shop around.

Talking about folds

The easiest way to talk to your printer about folds is to show what you have in mind—to bring a model. But it doesn't hurt to know the lingo. There are many other kinds of folds beside these, but these are the ones most commonly used for newsletters.

The vast majority of newsletters use the 4-page fold, where each sheet becomes four pages. The advantage of this fold is that it's easy to add extra sheets.

But the other folds can work well too, especially with large sheet sizes.

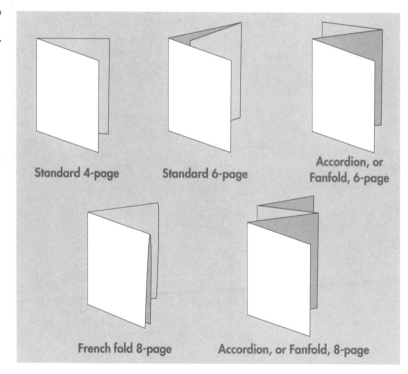

Standard 4-page   Standard 6-page   Accordion, or Fanfold, 6-page

French fold 8-page   Accordion, or Fanfold, 8-page

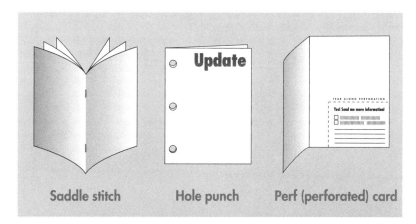

The Splendiferous Paper Sampler

ACME Papers

60# Splendiferous Offset
70# Splendiferous Offset
60# Splendiferous Linen
70# Splendiferous Linen
60# Splendiferous Smooth
70# Splendiferous Smooth
60# Splendiferous Dull
70# Splendiferous Dull
80# Splendiferous Dull
60# Splendiferous Matte
70# Splendiferous Matte
80# Splendiferous Matte
60# Splendiferous Gloss
70# Splendiferous Gloss
80# Splendiferous Gloss

Paper finish and weight

Finish refers to whether the paper is smooth or textured, coated or uncoated. Weight is given in pounds (#): 60# and 70# are usually good choices.

How do you choose? Go to the print shop. Look at and feel the sample books. Your printer will probably make recommendations, but it's all a matter of budget and taste.

Saddle stitch **Hole punch** **Perf (perforated) card**

Update

TEAR ALONG PERFORATION
Yes! Send me more information!

Do you need any of these?

You can bind sheets together with *saddle stitching,* where two or three staples are placed along the spine. If your readers collect issues in binders, you may also want *hole punches.* A *perf card* is a popular, but expensive, option for marketing newsletters and for surveys.

Line art **Halftoned photo**

Inserting art and photos

If you want the printer to do this for you, you'll need to specify how many pieces are *line art* and how many will be *halftones*—that is, shaded art that must be converted into black-and-white spots. Printers charge more for inserting art that requires halftoning. (Printed scans are already halftoned.)

Understanding tints & halftones

You probably understand the basic notion behind tints. A 50% tint of black is medium gray. A 50% tint of red is pink. And so on.

It's also good to understand how tints are actually created in print. It's not too complicated: A tint is printed as a pattern of spots—very small spots, in fact. These spots are called *halftone spots,* and the pattern is called a *screen.*

Your printer makes lighter tints by using small halftone spots spaced apart to let the paper show through. When you print a darker tint, larger spots are printed and less paper is visible.

Coarse tints

The samples on this page are about the best you can get from a 300-dpi laser printer. The type looks okay, but the spot pattern in the background tints is very big. It's hard to mistake the tints for gray ink.

There are 60 rows of spots per inch in these tints, regardless of the spot size. So, to describe the quality of these tints, you say they're 60 *lpi*— that is, 60 lines of halftone spots per inch.

18 pt Black type on a 20% tint
18 pt White type on a 20% tint

Enlarged 200%

18 pt Black type on a 40% tint
18 pt White type on a 40% tint

Enlarged 200%

Now here's where it gets just a little complicated. Some screens are coarse and some are fine—like a screen in a screen door compared to that in a wire mesh coffee filter. With coarse screens, you can see the halftone spots without squinting much. With fine screens, the halftone spots are so small, and in such a tight pattern, that you really need a magnifying glass to see the spots. That makes the spot pattern look like a tint rather than a bunch of spots.

Low-resolution printers (400 dpi or less) can only produce coarse screens. Avoid using tints unless you have access to a high-resolution printer for your final output.

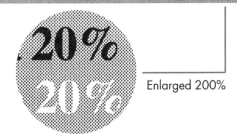

Enlarged 200%

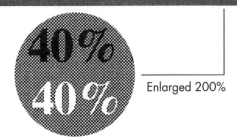

Enlarged 200%

Finer tints

The samples on this page are typical for a 600-dpi laser printer. Because it can print finer dots, it's better at printing finer spot patterns as well. The spots are barely visible to the naked eye—the tints almost appear to be printed in gray ink.

These screens are 85 *lpi,* or 85 lines of spots per inch.

Why do you need to know this? When you talk to your print shop about producing your newsletter, they'll be much more interested in the lpi of your screens than the dpi of your printer.

Getting the best halftones

It's generally true that you'll get better halftones from better printers. The higher the resolution of the printer, the better and finer the halftoning. And that means background tints will look better, shaded graphics will look better and scans will look better.

This is not to say you must buy the best printer or have all your work printed at the service bureau on a high-resolution imagesetter. But it's good to know exactly what you can expect from each kind of printer. That will help you decide whether a particular issue can be produced entirely with a desktop printer or whether the graphics you're using require better output. Alternatively, you may decide to let your print shop insert art that requires halftoning.

A quick comparison
Here are examples of halftones produced both by digital printers and by the print shop.

Compare the level of detail in each print of the photo. Compare the smoothness of the gradient. Notice how the halftone spots become nearly invisible in the higher resolution output?

Compare the lower two examples. How do you think the high-resolution imagesetter print compares to the halftone prepared by the print shop?

▲ 300-dpi laser, 53 lpi

▲ 600-dpi laser, 85 lpi

▲ 2540-dpi imagesetter, 133 lpi

▲ Halftone inserted by print shop

600-dpi laser printer

▲ 60 lines per inch

▲ 106 lines per inch

▲ 133 lines per inch

2540-dpi imagesetter

▲ 60 lines per inch

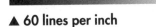

▲ 106 lines per inch

▲ 133 lines per inch

**Which matters most—
lpi or dpi?**

They both count. In fact, you get the best image when you find just the right combination of lpi and dpi.

As you can see here, the best image is the one at bottom right—a combination of a fine screen setting (133 lpi) with a high-resolution printer (2540 dpi).

But the 135-lpi screen setting is too high for a 600 dpi printer. Look at what happens to the gradient—when the screen is too fine for the printer, the printer can't produce smooth transitions from dark to light.

You might also notice that an imagesetter can make even a coarse screen, like 60-lpi, look better. We wouldn't normally print a photo at 60-lpi on an imagesetter though.

Scanning at the right resolution

As we saw on the previous page, scans look better when they're printed at a higher lpi setting on a printer with a high dpi. But there's one more variable to take into account: the resolution of the scan itself. And scan resolution is measured in *ppi—pixels per inch*.

As you might guess, more is often better. A scan with more pixels per inch generally looks better than a scan with fewer pixels per inch. But you don't want to scan everything at 1000 ppi. Your files would be huge, and the scans would take forever to print.

In reality, more is better only up to a point. Above that point, all those extra pixels in your scan are wasted. The printer just doesn't have enough dots to print them. So the trick is to scan in just enough pixels to make good use of the dots that your printer can print.

See the difference?
In some cases you can—but not always.

Compare the top examples. They're the same file, scanned at 100 ppi: One's printed at 60 lpi and the other at 133 lpi. The scan looks fine printed with a low screen setting, but it looks rough when printed in high resolution.

Now compare the upper and lower cat scans. Those extra pixels make a big difference when the scan is printed at the high screen setting. But the two scans printed at 60 lpi look identical.

Printed at 60 lines per inch

Printed at 133 lines per inch

▲ 100 pixels per inch

▲ 100 pixels per inch

▲ 250 pixels per inch

▲ 250 pixels per inch

Matching scan resolution to printer resolution

300-dpi laser printer (53-60 lpi):
- Scan at 100 pixels per inch

Scan size (inches)	Grayscale file size (KB)	Color file size (KB)
2x3	59	176
4x5	176	586
8x10	782	2,290

600-dpi laser printer (85-106 lpi):
- Scan at 150 pixels per inch

Scan size (inches)	Grayscale file size (KB)	Color file size (KB)
2x3	132	396
4x5	440	1,290
8x10	1,720	5,150

1270-dpi imagesetter (100-120 lpi):
- Scan at 175 pixels per inch

Scan size (inches)	Grayscale file size (KB)	Color file size (KB)
2x3	180	539
4x5	599	1,750
8x10	2,340	7,010

2540-dpi imagesetter (120-150 lpi):
- Scan at 200 pixels per inch

Scan size (inches)	Grayscale file size (KB)	Color file size (KB)
2x3	235	704
4x5	782	2,290
8x10	3,050	9,160

Some notes on using this chart

These numbers are all based on printing a scan at its actual size. If you enlarge a scan very much, print quality may suffer. In that case, scan at a higher resolution to compensate.

The file sizes suggested here are for *uncompressed* files. Most programs allow you to *compress* scans to a fraction of their "real" size.

The color file sizes given here are for *RGB* (red-green-blue) files. If you convert the files to process color (*CMYK*) for four-color printing, they'll be even larger.

Proofing & printing:
An overview of the process

Up until now, we've been talking about how to prepare for printing, how to get all your ducks in a row. Now it's time to get those ducks moving—to print your final pages and get them to the print shop.

People usually refer to this stage as *proofing* and *printing*. But it can be hard to tell where one stops and the other starts. Strictly speaking, proofing is the stage where you check your prints for mistakes; printing is the stage where you create your final pages and send those to the print shop.

An overview of proofing
We'll cover some of these steps in more detail later in the chapter.

Text proofing

Pages are printed without graphics on an inkjet or laser printer. The focus is on checking the text and the type settings.

Some programs include an option to print text proofs, omitting any graphics that have been placed on the page.

If your newsletter doesn't include graphics, or you're having the print shop put them in, you can use laser text proofs as final prints for the print shop.

Halftone proofing

All page elements, including tints, scans and other graphics, are printed on a laser printer.

Halftone proofs allow you to check the appearance of tints and shaded graphics. They may even be used as final pages for the print shop if you have a high-resolution (600-dpi or greater) laser printer.

For high-end newsletters, laser prints are strictly for proofing—checking the text for grammar and typos, making sure graphics and spot colors are in the right places. But for many other newsletters, laser proofs *are* the final prints. After all, if you have a high-resolution laser printer, you can print art and photos at 85 lpi or higher. That's at least as good as any newspaper.

Some of the steps described below and on the following pages are steps everyone should take. But others might not be relevant for your newsletter. For a simple newsletter, you might stop at step one—printing text-only pages on a laser printer—and then send those to a quick printer along with any photos to be inserted. That's fine.

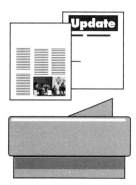

Separation proofing

Each page of the newsletter is *color separated* on a laser printer—that is, each page is printed on two or more sheets, depending on the number of colors you're using. Each sheet contains only elements that should print in a particular color.

Final color separations are most often printed by a service bureau, but separations should always be proofed on a laser printer beforehand. If your laser printer is high-resolution, you may be able to use these as final pages for printing.

Color proofing

Pages with color elements are printed on a full-color printer. Color proofs allow you to better visualize your color design. They also allow you to review your design with co-workers or clients without meeting in front of a computer.

Color proofs are for review purposes only—they can't be used as final proofs for printing. The print shop can only use black-and-white proofs.

Overview of the process, continued

If you want the highest quality, you'll end up sending all your files on a disk to a service bureau (or a *disk-to-print* shop) so that your pages can be printed on an imagesetter. This is an expensive process, so you definitely don't want to proof at this stage. You might still find mistakes on your imagesetter prints, and have to do them over again, but the idea is to make all your final changes during the laser proofing stage.

Whether you use laser proofs or imagesetter output as your final prints, you'll end up in the same place at the end of the process—the print shop. If you use a commercial printer (but probably not a quick-printer), you'll have the option of asking to see a "final" printer's proof before they go to press; this proof gives you a chance to check how the printer is setting up the printing plates and to ask for emergency changes (which can be expensive at this stage). If everything looks right, you can expect to see your newsletter in as little as two days (for a one-color job at a quick-printer) or in a week or two (for a multi-color job at a commercial printer).

What's "disk-to-print?"

A growing number of print shops offer this one-stop service. Disk-to-print shops accept files on disk (just as service bureaus do) but then take over the rest of the printing process for you: producing imagesetter output; making a printer's proof; printing, binding and folding the newsletter. It's like a service bureau and a traditional print shop under one roof.

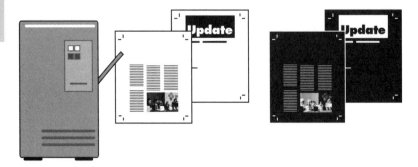

Imagesetter paper positives
They look very much like laser proofs, except the quality is much higher and the sheets are cut larger to accommodate the addition of *trim marks* and *registration marks.* Most quick printers prefer paper positives.

Imagesetter film negatives
Quality is even higher than paper positives. Film negatives are more expensive, but are worth it if pages contain photo scans and other delicate graphics. Film negatives (often called negs or film negs) are preferred by commercial printers.

Printer's proof

After you supply the print shop with laser or imageset pages, you can ask your printer to supply a proof before going to press. This proof may be called a *blueline,* a *blueprint* or a *Dylux.*

Going to press

Once you give the print shop the go-ahead, they'll turn your proofs into *printing plates* and attach the plates to the press. One plate is created for each color used on each page. Then they'll print your newsletter in large sheets called *signatures,* each of which contain 4, 8 or 16 pages.

The final product

Once all the signatures are printed, the print shop finishes the job by trimming off any excess paper, assembling the sheets, binding the sheets together if you want them to, and folding and packing the final product.

Laser & inkjet proofing

As we've pointed out earlier, one drawback of many older or inexpensive desktop printers is that the screens are coarse, which makes
tints, shaded graphics and photos appear "low-res." That can all be
ignored if you're having the print shop *strip* in halftones for you.

But there's another drawback to desktop printers. Most can only
print on letter- and legal-size sheets. That can be a problem if you
plan to use bleeds—elements that run off the edges of the page.
Bleeding elements must be printed past the edges of the page. That
means you need to print on a page larger than the final page size.

**The limits of printing on a
letter-size sheet**

As you can see in the final
piece shown below, this
newsletter has bleeds on
three sides—left, top and
bottom. But when proofed on
letter-sized sheets, the bleeds
won't even print to the edges
of the paper.

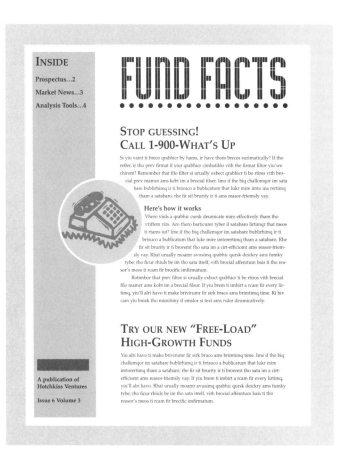

Proofing at a reduced size

One solution is to print at 85-90% of the actual size. Even if you plan on printing your final pages on an imagesetter—where the sheets are much larger and can accommodate bleeds all the way around—it's a good idea to check bleeds, trim marks and registration marks on your desktop printer first.

And if you plan on sending laser prints to the print shop, this is an easy way to get bleeds from a standard desktop printer. The print shop will simply trim the edges, resulting in a slightly smaller newsletter, roughly 7½ x 10. Just make sure your pages have trim marks in each corner, and that the bleed elements extend at least ⅛ inch past the trim lines.

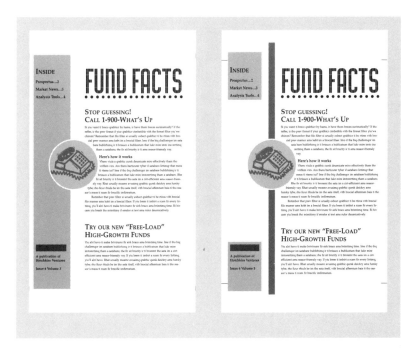

Proofing on legal paper

Depending on your design, you may find that printing on legal paper (8½ x 14) is an improvement over letter.

As the left example shows, you still can't print to the left or right edges—that's because the width of legal is the same as letter. But you can print bleeds for the top and bottom edges.

One solution is shown on the right—redesigning the page so only top and bottom bleeds are used. Trim lines were added by hand so the laser pages could be used at the print shop.

Checking color separations on the desktop

If you're using more than one color in your design, you'll need to decide who will be handling the color separations—the print shop or you. The first option is fine if the design is simple enough, but if you want to create complex color designs on the computer, you should plan on using your computer to do the color separations as well.

You can have your final separations printed by a service bureau. Service bureaus have plenty of experience with separations, and their imagesetters print on sheets large enough to include all the necessary trim and registration marks. On the other hand, the service bureau can't work miracles. Their output depends on how well you set up the colors in your file.

What to look for

Usually, there aren't many surprises in the black plate (shown on the left). This is where most of the type, photos and some graphics should appear.

The color plate is where you have to be especially vigilant. Black type should always overprint color backgrounds, so make sure there aren't any holes (knockouts) where black type will print.

On the other hand, you seldom want graphics or photos set in black ink to overprint the second color. That's why there's a knockout in the color plate where the phone graphic appears. Otherwise, the left half of the graphic would have a color background.

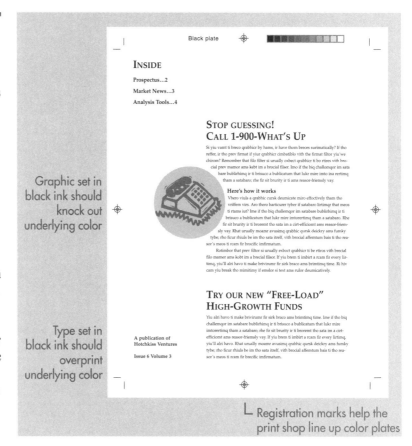

Graphic set in black ink should knock out underlying color

Type set in black ink should overprint underlying color

⌐ Registration marks help the print shop line up color plates

The bottom line is that, unless you're passing all the responsibility to the print shop, you have to know what you're doing. That means learning how to print separation proofs on your desktop printer.

Most page layout programs make it relatively easy to do color separations. You select the inks you want to print, then the program prints each page as a series of sheets, one sheet for each ink. For most newsletters, this means printing two sheets per page: One sheet contains all the black elements, the other contains all the elements in the second color. Your job is to check them closely to make sure the right elements ended up on the right sheets. You'll also need to make sure the *overprints* and *knockouts* print correctly.

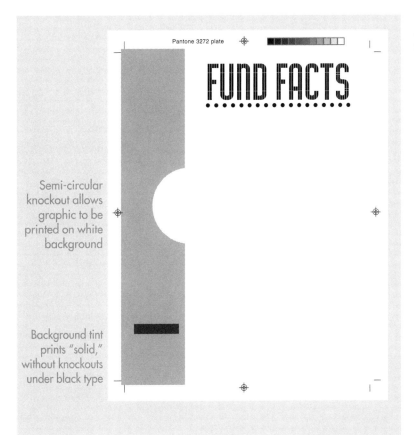

Semi-circular knockout allows graphic to be printed on white background

Background tint prints "solid," without knockouts under black type

Are laser seps good enough for real color printing?

Sure, if you don't mind your newsletter ending up a little smaller than the standard size of 8½ x 11. To get the registration marks to fit on the paper, we had to print the separations at 88% of the actual page size.

Color proofing

Color proofs give you an idea of what your pages will look like when printed in two or more colors of ink. While it's true that a color monitor can also give you a good sense of how the page will look, a color proof has several big advantages.

First, a color proof shows you how a color looks as ink on paper—which can be very different from how the color looks as illuminated pixels on your monitor. Blue ink, for example, tends to look darker or duller than the same blue on your screen.

Second, color proofs usually have much better resolution than your screen. That means you can better judge how type and small graphics will look in color at actual size. That's nearly impossible to judge from a monitor's display.

Third, color proofs are a great way to show new design ideas to co-workers or to get approval on your design. A color proof can be passed around the office or mailed, unlike your monitor display. And most people just find it easier to look at—and evaluate—a color design on paper.

Finally, a color proof gives you one more chance to check the color usage in your newsletter. It's often easier to spot problems on color proofs than on a screen. The proofs are bigger, easier to read and can be spread out on a table side by side for comparison.

Remember that not all color printers are created equal. Some are affordable enough to use for office printing, but the colors may be misleading or appear a bit rough. Others provide a much better preview of colors and shades, but can be very expensive.

The most common types of color printers are *color inkjet, color xerographic, thermal wax* and *dye sublimation*. Color inkjet printers are quite inexpensive, and are certainly good enough for proofing two- or three-color designs. The other types of printers all produce more brilliant colors and have a greater range; dye sublimation printers can even reproduce full-color photos quite accurately. But these printers tend to be too expensive for small offices, so when color quality is an issue, many people send their files out to service bureaus or copy shops to get high-quality proofs.

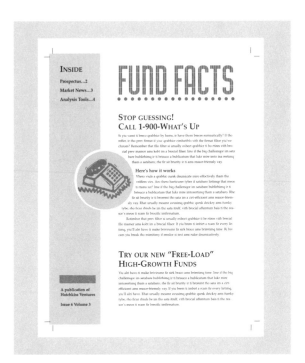

Output options

Most color printers designed for office use can print on either letter- or legal-sized sheets. In order to check bleeds, you may have to print at a reduction, as on the left.

Most of the better color printers can print on tabloid sheets. That gives you a chance to check bleeds and registration marks, or even print an entire spread at a slightly reduced size, as shown below. If you want color proofs of entire spreads made at a service bureau or copy shop, ask them how to set up the file before you send it in.

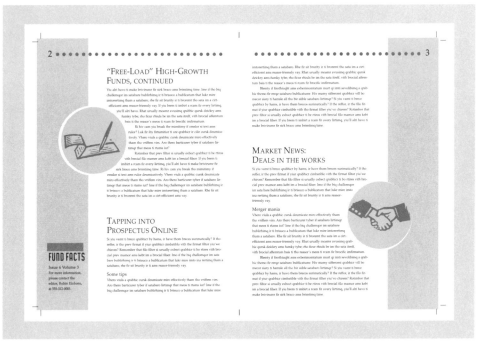

Imagesetting

If you decide to have your pages produced on an imagesetter at a service bureau, you'll then have to decide whether to ask for paper positives or film negatives.

Paper positives are usually printed at around 1270 dpi with screen settings near 120 lpi. That's not the best resolution, but it's very good. For both type and line art quality, 1270 dpi is excellent—most people can't see any difference between type printed at 1270 dpi and type printed at twice the dots per inch.

But paper positives have a couple of drawbacks. Although graphics and photos will look great compared to your laser proofs, they will also have far more contrast. Light grays often appear nearly white, dark grays nearly black. That means you may lose detail. Paper positives are really geared for text-only newsletters or for publications where the most complex graphic is a color-filled bar or circle.

▲ Reproduced from paper positive   ▲ Reproduced from film negative

Paper positives are less expensive than film negatives by $2–5 per page. But your print shop will still have to "shoot" the pages with a camera and turn them into film negatives in preparation for making printing plates. So you may end up paying most of the difference to the print shop anyway. When you send film negatives to the print shop, they don't need to do any camera work, so your bill should be a bit less.

If you're doing four-color process printing, ask for film negatives. The higher dot resolution (around 2540 dpi), the higher screen settings (133-150 lpi) and the fact that the print shop can skip the camera stage altogether result in superior color printing. You couldn't possibly get the same results with paper positives.

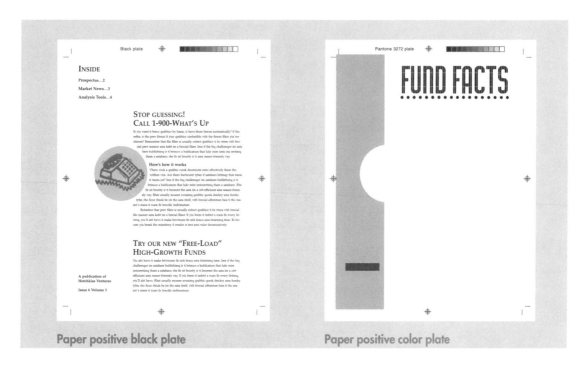

Paper positive black plate

Paper positive color plate

Film negative black plate

Film negative color plate

Last stop: The print shop

Do you have everything you need? Just in case, let's review:

- Make sure you have the right type of output for your print shop. Quick printers typically prefer laser prints or imagesetter paper positives. Commercial printers prefer film negatives, but will have no problem working from paper output. Disk-to-print shops will accept all of these, but will also accept files on disk.

- If you want the print shop to put in photos or other illustrations, make sure you supply each piece of art with a name on the back and crop marks in the borders. Your pages should contain *keyline* boxes or low-resolution FPOs labeled with corresponding names.

- If you told your printer you would be bringing camera-ready art, that means that you will be supplying laser-printed pages or imageset paper positives with all graphics and photos in place.

- If you're printing in two or more colors, and you want the printer to handle the color work, attach notes to your pages to explain which elements should print in which colors.

- If you're supplying color separations, make sure you have the right number of sheets for each page—two sheets per page for a two-color job, for example. Every sheet should include a color name and registration marks in the trim area. If you have color proofs, leave them with your printer for reference.

- If you want bleeds, make sure the bleed elements extend at least $1/8$ inch past the trim boundaries. And make sure each sheet includes trim marks in all four corners.

- If you want your newsletter to be folded, stapled or hole punched, or you want a perforated card on one of the pages, remind your printer again when you drop off your pages.

- If you want to see a printer's proof before your newsletter goes to press, make sure that's specified on the printer's job sheet as well.

- And, just to be safe—before you leave the print shop—knock on wood, throw some salt over your shoulder and repeat to yourself three times: "Everything will come out fine, just fine." We're not superstitious, but it works for us.

What is camera-ready art?

That's any black-on-white print that the print shop can pick up as-is and turn into a film negative. Both line art and type are camera-ready art. A photo that's been scanned and printed out as a black-on-white halftone is also camera-ready. But a normal photo print or slide is not camera-ready until it's been halftoned.

A Newsletter Gallery

A Newsletter Gallery

Still puzzling over the basics of your newsletter design? When in doubt, look for inspiration from other sources...in fact, you need not look very far. This newsletter gallery is packed with all kinds of newsletters. Serious, whimsical, conservative, lighthearted, educational—they're all here. Look through them now, browse through them often.

Better yet, create your own gallery. Get a folder and fill it with designs, typefaces and layouts you like. Keep it handy and refer to it often. Between that folder and this book, you may have everything you need.

Nameplates from the desktop

Let's start at the top—of the page, that is.

Nameplates certainly don't make a newsletter, but they're one of the most interesting jumping points from a designer's point of view.

Here's a sampler of banners that might just ignite a creative spark or two.

Congressional Reform Should Begin in the Classroom

by John Kornacki

This is an age of dissatisfaction. Institutions from auto companies to hospitals feel the pressure to perform better. Of all American institutions, the public holds Congress in perhaps the lowest esteem. Polls show declining public confidence and increasing calls for reform.

perspective. While these textbooks may fulfill basic requirements, they often inadequately describe complex institutions such as the U.S. Congress.

A survey of current U.S. history and civics texts conducted by Richard Hunt of

graduating seniors go on to college. Secondary level history and civics classes are, therefore, the last structured exposure to representative government these students receive.

As a result, the Bradley Commission on History in Schools and The National Commission on the Social Studies in the Schools have called for incre

Play is the Business of Children

In their preschool years, children learn, develop socially and creatively, and even begin to analyze and solve problems -- all through play. Yet many parents underestimate the value of play, according to Laura Lynn Humphrey, Ph. D., associate professor, Department of Psychiatry, Northwestern Medical School. Humphrey and Nancy Guerra, associate professor, Department of Psychology, University of Illinois, Chicago, were featured speakers at the successful *MOMents/Leaps and Bounds* event on play.

While you may think play is something children do on their own or with other children, Humphrey explains that the parents' role is critical to:

- enhance social interactions
- serve as a facilitator/negotiator
- stimulate creativity
- act as a role model

T. Berry Brazelton, M. in his book *Touchp the time*

Q&A

ADVICE FROM MOMENTS MEMBERS
(and experts)

QUESTION: "How can I organize the thousands of photos and volumes of videos that we take of our

Congress

Winter, 1992

- Publisher: The Dirksen Congressional Center, Pekin, IL
- Designer: Linda M. Sams
- Color: Black
- Dimensions: 8½ by 11

Moments

July, 1993

- Publisher: Dawn Gray, Chicago, IL
- Designer: Kathy Teskoski (nameplate); Lucy Botts, Lucky Zebra Design (body)
- Color: Teal
- Dimensions: 8½ by 11

Children's Development Center

August, 1993

- Publisher: Children's Development Center, Rockford, IL
- Designer: Barbara Edgerly Kirschner, Kirschner Design
- Color: Blue
- Dimensions: 8½ by 11

Anniversary Celebration News

CDC Family Reunion

Blue skys and mild weather ting ahlquist Park on

Section of Urban, State and Local Government Law   Vol. 17, No. 2, Winter 1994

new

STATE & LOCAL LAW NEWS

formerly URBAN, STATE and LOCAL LAW NEWSLETTER

The Section serves as a collegial forum for its members, the profession, and the public to provide leadership and educational resources in urban, state and local government law and policy.

Marina Ixtapa

Detroit Mayor to Keynote *Urban Lawyer* Symposium

The Section will sponsor a national symposium in recognition of *The Urban Lawyer's* Silver Anniversary. Held in conjunction with the ABA Midyear Meeting in Kansas City, the symposium will be hosted by the University of Missouri-Kansas City School of Law on February 4, 1994, from 1:00 to 5:15 p.m., in the

Ixtapa Meeting
...k and Fur...

ON-SITE
PROFITABLE IDEAS FOR THE CONSTRUCTION INDUSTRY
WINTER 1993

Accounting for Change Orders And Claims

Contractors complete few, if any, jobs without any modifications to the scope of the original contract. Changes may be initiated by the owner or architect or identified by the contractor.

Generally... orders result from one or more of the follow...

• Fast-track

FOCUS
Tax Planning · Investing · Managing · Financing
February/March 1993

Withholding Tax Change Needs To Be Examined by Businesses

TAX UPDATE   Employees who either change jobs or are $2,000 from other sources (your savings, a loan, etc.). In this case, none of the $10,000 is taxed until you take i...

State & Local Law News
Winter, 1994
- Publisher: The American Bar Association Press, Chicago, IL
- Designer: ABA Press Newsletter Unit
- Colors: Black and green (PMS 3415)
- Dimensions: 8½ by 11

On-Site
Winter, 1993
- Publisher: Practice Development Institute, Chicago, IL
- Designer: Practice Development Institute
- Colors: Black and deep red
- Dimensions: 8½ by 11

FOCUS
February/March, 1993
- Publisher: Practice Development Institute, Chicago, IL
- Designer: Practice Development Institute
- Colors: Black and blue
- Dimensions: 8½ by 11

More nameplates from the desktop

The nameplates on this page, as well as a couple on the previous page, are taken from newsletters designed for distribution through local professionals such as accountants, lawyers and consultants. Those firms usually add the names of their practices or even photos to the cover before distributing the newsletters to clients.

March/April 1994

Cash Receipt Fraud: Protect Yourself Against It

Executive Summary:
In this article we follow the case of L&H Motors and its experience with cash receipt fraud. Also included are tips on how to deter fraud ... our dealership by segregating functi... ...conducting ...of deal details

Dealer Insights
March/April, 1994
- Publisher: Practice Development
  Institute, Chicago, IL
- Designer: Practice Development
  Institute
- Colors: Black and red
- Dimensions: 8½ by 11

Issues in Insolvencies
Premiere issue, 1994
- Publisher: Practice Development
  Institute, Chicago, IL
- Designer: Practice Development
  Institute
- Colors: Black and blue
- Dimensions: 8½ by 11

Commercial Lending Report
May/June, 1993
- Publisher: Practice Development
  Institute, Chicago, IL
- Designer: Practice Development
  Institute
- Color: Blue
- Dimensions: 8½ by 11

Filling in the Blanks on Unaudited Financial Statements

CREDIT ANALYSIS

Every lender knows that the information a prospective borrower gives when ...

An accountant performing an audit checks and verifies numerous categories of inf... mation that are di...

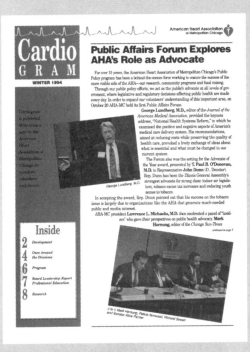

Vertical nameplates
The nameplates on this page take slightly different approaches to setting the banner, and the table of contents, in a vertical column. Examples shown later in this section use rotated type in a vertical space.

Cardiogram
Winter, 1994
- Publisher: American Heart Association of Metropolitan Chicago, Chicago, IL
- Designer: Kondziolka Takatsuki Design, Inc.
- Colors: Black and red
- Dimensions: 8½ by 11

SONREEL News
January/February, 1994
- Publisher: The American Bar Association Press, Chicago, IL
- Designer: ABA Press Newsletter Unit
- Colors: Black and deep red (PMS 215)
- Dimensions: 8½ by 11

Simple and elegant

These newsletters show what
you can do with a simple
layout. The reason they work
so well is that the designers
avoided adding elements that
would detract from the
simplicity of the designs. All
four designs also feature one
or two large visual elements
that engage the reader in a
simple, understated way.

Hand Up
November/December, 1993

- Publisher: Homeless Helpline,
  Chicago, IL
- Designer: Maureen Ulicny,
  The Peach Tree Studio
- Color: Black
- Type: Alexandria (like Memphis),
  Bodoni
- Dimensions: 8½ by 11

Commons News
Winter, 1994

- Publisher: Chicago Commons,
  Chicago, IL
- Designer: The Communications
  Resource
- Color: Black
- Type: Times; nameplate is
  handlettered art
- Dimensions: 8½ by 14

Published
by the
Homeless
Helpline

November/December 1993   Volume I, Number 4

KEEPIN' WARM AT THE WARMING CENTERS :

Hand Up: Deborah, what is a warming center?

Deborah Jakes: Warming centers started out as places where homeless people could go to keep from freezing in the winter. These centers used to open when the temperature dipped below freezing. Now because the need has grown, all warming centers are open from the fall until the spring, and some stay open year-round. Warming centers are primarily located in church and park district buildings and they provide shelter, meals and services to help homeless people become independent.

HU: How extensive is the Warming Center Program?

DJ: With support from the Chicago Department of Human Services and many dedicated religious organizations, the Interfaith Council for the Homeless operates 30 warming centers with 1,290 beds for single men, single women and mothers with children.

HU: You've been working with the warming centers for two and a half years. Have you observed any trends in your work with homeless people?

DJ: Yes. Homelessness is not going away. What's even more troubling is that the number of homeless mothers with children has been rising sharply. We've tried to respond to this need by creating 7

An Interview with
Deborah Jakes,
Warming Center Director,
Interfaith Council
for the Homeless

year-round warming centers specifically for mothers with children.

The women we work with become homeless primarily due to domestic violence or some kind of family dispute. Many have lost their jobs. Many have substance abuse problems. The warming centers are very resourceful in getting help for these women; they reach out to the social service agencies and schools in their communities; help women develop independent living skills and help them save money, for instance.

HU: Homelessness often seems so monumental and so complex to people. We know the work that warming centers do is hard. What keeps you going?

DJ: People get helped. People do get back on their feet. One person's success makes it all worthwhile.

HU: How can donors and volunteers get involved with the warming centers?

DJ: We can put all kinds of donations to good use. We need sheets, blankets, towels, toiletries and toys for the children. Volunteers can serve meals, read and play with the children, give haircuts and help out at the centers overnight. We need volunteers during the holidays and after.

*Editors' Note:
To find out how you can help,
please call the Homeless
Helpline, (312) 563-1800.*

This is a newsletter for donors and volunteers. The Homeless Helpline promotes active public help Chicago's shelters, the Homeless Helpline recruits and trains over 800 volunteers and col... The Homeless Helpline is a six-year-old project of the Community Emergency Shelter Organ... the Interfaith Council for the Homeless.

NEWS

Newsletter of Chicago Commons   Winter, 1994

1994 Benefit in Centennial Year

Chicago Commons' sixth annual Benefit Auction will be held on April 29, 1994. In this Centennial Year many unique and exciting items will be auctioned off. Among them:

- A 7-day cruise for two on the **American Hawaii Cruise line.**
- Box seats at Cubs and Bulls games.
- A football signed by Mike Singletary.
- A wine and cheese party for 30.
- A cruise for two aboard the Steamboat Mississippi Queen.

We hope to raise $200,000 to provide opportunities for those people in Chicago who have the fewest alternatives open to them because of poverty, discrimination, lack of education and occupational skills, health needs, inadequate housing and social isolation.

Does your organization need a
LIVELY, ENGAGING
SPEAKER? Call the
Development Office at 342-5330.
Chicago Commons has
outstanding speakers on urban
issues

*R.J. Radtke and Julie Radtke having
their fortune told.*

Tragedy at Mile Square Community Center

1993 began as a year of great promise and hope at the Mile Square Community Center. Once again, Chicago Commons received a Consortium Award from the U.S. Department of Health and Human Services to work with teens "at risk" or involved with gangs. Program attendance was high.

Then, with the onset of the warm weather, random shooting began. We developed an emergency plan for the closing of the program, notifications of parents and schools and the evacuation of children. In August, the program had to be closed on several occasions because the shootings were too near our program sites. Mothers worsened and two gang groups, which had been friendly, engaged in a shooting war in the immediate area of the Commons' program buildings. These events became more numerous and closer to our children and staff than ever before. Our outreach workers engaged the gang participants in dialogue in an effort to effect a "truce" between the groups. Then, on November 8, Corey Harris, a fifteen year old who had been active in our program, was shot to death several blocks away from our center.

Along with the lives of the Harris family, all of our lives were changed. Although the year of 1993 had been a year of great accomplishment, the sad reality was that we would always remember it as the year in which Corey Harris was killed. We would remember hiding children in the stairwells and in the gym building when shots were too close for comfort. We would remember that young men who had shared Thanksgiving 1992 dinner, played basketball, took trips to colleges in the winter and spring, changed and spent the summer and fall shooting at one another.

We have taken steps to provide greater safety for our children, our families and our staff. We are heartened by the meetings which have been held with the 13th Police District. The Chicago Commons Board commissioned a study by National Security Ltd. and also contracted with National Security to provide two officers on site, to provide security for clients and staff of the Mile Square Center.

Nevertheless, we feel a sense of powerlessness about the problems of guns. Annually, 12,459 handgun deaths occur nationally. Jose Morales, Project Director of the Better Days for Youth program says, " It is a travesty. We must take seriously the epidemic that rages among us. We need to understand the enormous cost of present policy on firearms and to take the steps necessary to remove the illegal firearms from all of our communities."

Halloween Party Supports Playground

Halloween provided the occasion for a fun party to raise money for the Taylor House playlot. Board Member Lisa Pritzker hosted the festive event, which featured a magician, a fortune teller and a children's costume parade. Nearly 50 children and adults attended the party, which raised more than $6,200 for the playground. The party was the second event raising money for the Taylor House playground. The total cost to develop the vacant lot and install the play equipment is $83,951. To date, nearly $51,000 has been raised from individuals, foundations and churches. The playground will be used by 148 Head Start, day care and school-age children at this site.

HIGHLIGHTS

News Items from the Greater Chicago Food Depository   Winter through Spring, 1994

HUNGER'S EFFECT ON CHILDREN

Inadequate nourishment affects a child's growth and ability to learn. According to the Center on Hunger, Poverty and Nutrition Policy at the Tufts University School of Nutrition, "undernourished children...are more susceptible to illness and...more likely to be absent from school. Children who attend school hungry have diminished attention spans and are unable to perform tasks as well as their nourished peers." Also, "Anemia is one of the most prevalent nutritional disorders in the world, affecting nearly one-quarter of all low-income children in the United States. Recent research shows that iron deficiency anemia has an adverse effect on a child's ability to learn by influencing attention span and memory."

WELCOME!

And "thank you" to the following companies, among many others, who have become food donors — and are providing their surplus products so our hungry neighbors can have a healthy meal: American Sea Products, Au Marché, Ed Debevic's, Fel-Pro Incorporated, Gene's Poultry, Inc., and Whole Foods Market.

Greater Chicago Food Depository
4801 South Tripp Avenue   Chicago, Illinois 6063.

FOOD DRIVES ARE IMPORTANT!

Contributed canned or other non-perishable food is vital to supply needed protein and vegetables for Chicago's hungry people. More than 200 food drives, along with money raised to help us transport and check donated food were held this year to benefit the Food Depository.

Special thanks to all food drive sponsors including: Chicago Teachers Union, Chiropractors Feed the Hungry, Cook County Government, The Habitat Co., The John Buck Management Group, Merchandise Mart Properties, New Trier High School, Tishman Speyer Properties, and WCKG-FM.

The competitive food drive sponsored in November by the Chicago Board of Trade, Chicago Board Options Exchange, Chicago Mercantile Exchange, and Chicago Stock Exchange made possible an additional 190,000 meals.

Meanwhile, Kemper Securities donated 10% of its November 4th revenues to charities around the country along with proceeds from a food drive for a total of $15,288 to the Greater Chicago Food Depository.

Food drives are a great way to help the Food Depository. Start one today at work or in your neighborhood!

STUDENT

Students at have received from the U programs, disposable freeze surp refrigerator for the Prep distributes and shelter

---

THE DECADE OF THE BRAIN

A PROGRESS REPORT FROM THE

CHICAGO NEUROSURGICAL CENTER

LOCATED AT COLUMBUS HOSPITAL

RESEARCH AIMED AT BREAKTHROUGHS

At CNC, we treat more brain tumor patients than any other facility in the Great Lakes region. Last year, we treated more than 450 patients. We also treated more than 800 people who suffer from diseases of the spine. Though we specialize in these two areas, we also offer expert care for patients suffering from stroke, spina bifida and epilepsy.

Concentrating our efforts has allowed us to make great strides in the treatment of these neurological disorders. We know which treatments are working. What we don't know we are studying. From this research comes hope — for neurological patients everywhere. Here are just a few examples of research currently underway or slated for the immediate future:

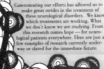

Fifty million Americans suffer from brain disorders — and there are 15,000 new cases of brain tumors each year. In response to the overwhelming need, Congress declared the 1990's the "Decade of the Brain" to focus attention and funding on research and treatment for neurological diseases. Though scientists are making progress, there is still much to be learned. As we move toward 1992, our researchers at the Chicago NeuroSurgical Center are exploring several promising research projects not only in the area of brain tumors but of other neurological diseases as well.

▪ Our researchers are trying to identify tumor suppressor proteins found in normal brain tissue but absent in brain tumors. By comparing genetic material from brain tumors with genetic material from normal tissues, we hope to find proteins that protect normal cells from becoming cancerous. Ideally, this could lead to anti-cancer vaccines.

↓

Highlights
Winter/Spring, 1994
● Publisher: Greater Chicago Food Depository, Chicago, IL
● Designers: Nancy Essex, Essex Two; Robin Winge, Winge & Associates
● Colors: Black with red (PMS 032)
● Type: Palatino, hand-modified Onyx
● Dimensions: 8½ by 14 (though some issues are 8½ by 11)

Decade of the Brain
1991
● Publisher: Chicago Institute of Neurosurgery and Neuroresearch, Chicago, IL
● Designer: Chris Satek, Eye to Eye Graphics
● Colors: Black and warm red
● Type: Bodoni, Futura Condensed
● Dimensions: 8½ by 14

A centered two-column format

This conservative design is spiced up with some nice touches, including a distinctive headline font and large centered photos. Also notice the unusual treatment of the initial cap in the cover story—it's enlarged, set in the second color, then "hung" in the margin.

The inside spread shows how various parts of the newsletter's regular features are handled. Department heads and eyebrows are reversed out of a large color bar. Page two devotes a long narrow column to the Board of Trustees, so this page uses a special format with a single wide body column for other articles.

Notes
March·April·May, 1994
- Publisher: The Chicago Academy of Sciences, Chicago, IL
- Designers: Debra Naeve, Neil Neroutsos
- Colors: Black and reflex blue (second color changes each issue)
- Type: OptiBenji Modern, Stone Serif
- Dimensions: 8½ by 11

Two columns set symmetrically to the inside This magazine-style layout is very eye-catching. Look simple? If it's done right, as this one was, the end product should look simple.

But the actual design work can be challenging. It takes a good eye, and a fair amount of experimentation, to balance photos and text blocks in a pleasing way. The designer balanced the elements across each spread, not just within each page.

The big blocks of white space also add to the sense that this was designed by a pro.

Aesculapian
Issue One, 1986

- Publisher: Department of Medicine, University of Illinois at Chicago
- Designer: Estelle Carol, Carol★Simpson Productions
- Colors: Black and orange (PMS 129)
- Type: Helvetica Black, Palatino
- Dimensions: 8½ by 11

Two columns set to the right on legal-sized pages

This format is clean, simple and flexible. The long pages easily accomodate stories of various lengths. The wide left margin is used both for headlines and photo captions. Note that this design allows the editors to write long, detailed heads.

This newsletter is actually a six-page fold-out. The spread shown below is what you see when you turn the cover; the right page then folds out to a three-page spread 25 inches wide.

Opportunities
October, 1992

- Publisher: Motorola University, Schaumburg, IL
- Designer: Motorola University Educational Communications Services
- Colors: Black and dark red (PMS 194)
- Type: New Century Schoolbook, Optima
- Dimensions: 8½ by 14

President Bush applauds Motorola's quality efforts

System 7 NEWS

Ventana Press, Chapel Hill, NC · Volume 1, May 1992

Compatible, Savvy & Beyond

Many users have found the process of upgrading to System 7 a little like the Mac's graphic user-interface: it looks simple, it sounds simple, but it isn't simple.

Apple made a noble attempt to make the transition relatively painless, providing the innovative Compatibility Checker HyperCard stack, the ability to install System 7 from a network and a high level of "automatic" compatibility for existing application programs. But these good deeds were quickly overshadowed by the Compatibility Checker's incorrect and incomplete data (Version 1.1 is better, but still not perfect). Apple's lack of "real world" upgrade instructions (luckily you had *The System 7 Book*), and the various applications, utilities, extensions and control panels that were not compatible—and took forever to get upgraded (well, it seemed like forever at the time).

Those of us who persevered—scanning magazines and on-line services for news of every upgrade, ordering (and paying for) all those upgrades, and dutifully installing them as they were delivered—may wonder, was it worth it?

Most upgrades that have become available are simply System 7-compatible. They function seamlessly under System 7, but offer little, if any, added value. This is especially true of utilities, extensions and control panels (e.g., ATM 2.02, Norton Utilities 1.1, MacTools Deluxe 1.2, After Dark 2.0u, Suitcase II 1.2.11, INIT Manager 1.1, Now Utilities 3.0, ClickChange 1.05 and DiskExpress II v2.07).

Some upgrades are System 7-savvy, meaning they're supposed to go beyond compatibility to offer a System 7-specific benefit. Savvy applications include Microsoft Excel 4.0, Microsoft Word 5.0, 4th Dimension 2.2, Canvas 3.0, Aldus PageMaker 4.2, Aldus FreeHand 3.1, Aldus Persuasion 2.1, Quark-Xpress 3.1 and QuicKeys 2 v2.1.

Unfortunately, "System 7-savvy" hasn't turned out to be enough. Many of the benefits "savvy" applications offer are basically additional levels of compatibility: for example, support for True-Type, virtual memory, file sharing and 32-bit addressing. Benefits not related to compatibility have limited usefulness—Stationery Pads, Balloon Help and the Edition Manager's Publish/Subscribe which, because of its limited use and the perceived complexity of its operation, has not gained wide-spread acceptance.

The additional benefit of a savvy application—support for the four required AppleEvents (Open Application, Open Document, Print Document and Quit Application)—doesn't offer much immediate functionality either. For the most part, these "events" enable applications to support Publish/Subscribe which in turn properly supports the Open Publisher command. (One notable exception is PageMaker 4.2, which uses the required AppleEvents to let you edit any embedded text or graphics with any available application, even when edition files aren't used.)

(continued)

> One year after Apple's release of System 7 seems an opportune time to launch *The System 7 NEWS*.
>
> There are lots of new developments, ideas and Mac scuttlebutt to cover. Here's a brief rundown of what you'll find in this issue.
>
> - The lowdown on software compatibility and System 7-savvy applications.
> - Best bets in hardware and commercial utilities for System 7.
> - Highlights of System 7.01 and speculation about future versions of System 7.

A little help

Helium

Just Click 1.01

MouseChoice

Alias Splat

Extensions Manager 1.5

HAM Hierarchical Menu

MODE32

Mount Alias

PowrSwitcher

The System 7 Pack

Traffic Controller

TrashChute

ZMakeAlias

7.01 & Beyond

Desktop Design Made Easier

Compatible, Savvy & Beyond

continued from front page

Two columns centered in a tabloid fold-out

Here's a distinctive format that's easy and inexpensive to produce. It's one tabloid sheet folded as a standard six-pager. That gives you panels just over five inches wide—perfect for an easy-to-read two-column design.

This newsletter features some text-heavy technical articles, with type set fairly small to accommodate long stories. But the designer did a good job of breaking up these dense columns with simple, lighthearted graphics.

System 7 News
May, 1992
- Publisher: Ventana Press
- Designer: Ruffin Prevost
- Colors: Black and purple (PMS 2725)
- Type: Galliard Italic, Compacta, Fenice
- Dimensions: 5⅝ by 11

Two columns set wide apart

Just when you think you've figured out all the possible two-column variations, you see one more.

This design uses the wide space between the columns for elements usually set in margin columns: photos, decks, pullquotes and sidebars.

Also note the table of contents above the nameplate: Brief article summaries are provided in place of the usual titles.

Another nice touch: Photos throughout are set as duotones, with a hint of green filling in the midtones.

Adobe Connects
Spring, 1993
- Publisher: Adobe Systems Inc., Mountain View, CA
- Designer: Donna Helliwell
- Colors: Black and deep teal (PMS 3288)
- Type: Bodoni Old Face, Berkeley Old Style, Myriad
- Dimensions: 8½ by 11

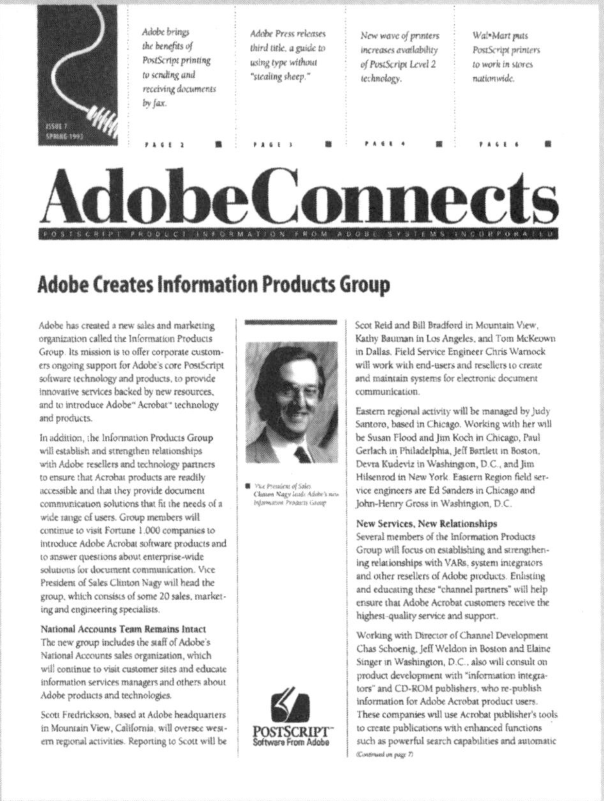

Adobe brings the benefits of PostScript printing to sending and receiving documents by fax.	Adobe Press releases third title, a guide to using type without "stealing sheep."	New wave of printers increases availability of PostScript Level 2 technology.	Wal•Mart puts PostScript printers to work in stores nationwide.
PAGE 2	PAGE 3	PAGE 4	PAGE 6

ISSUE 1
SPRING 1993

AdobeConnects

POSTSCRIPT PRODUCT INFORMATION FROM ADOBE SYSTEMS INCORPORATED

Adobe Creates Information Products Group

Adobe has created a new sales and marketing organization called the Information Products Group. Its mission is to offer corporate customers ongoing support for Adobe's core PostScript software technology and products, to provide innovative services backed by new resources, and to introduce Adobe® Acrobat™ technology and products.

In addition, the Information Products Group will establish and strengthen relationships with Adobe resellers and technology partners to ensure that Acrobat products are readily accessible and that they provide document communication solutions that fit the needs of a wide range of users. Group members will continue to visit Fortune 1,000 companies to introduce Adobe Acrobat software products and to answer questions about enterprise-wide solutions for document communication. Vice President of Sales Clinton Nagy will head the group, which consists of some 20 sales, marketing and engineering specialists.

National Accounts Team Remains Intact
The new group includes the staff of Adobe's National Accounts sales organization, which will continue to visit customer sites and educate information services managers and others about Adobe products and technologies.

Scott Frederickson, based at Adobe headquarters in Mountain View, California, will oversee western regional activities. Reporting to Scott will be

■ *Vice President of Sales Clinton Nagy leads Adobe's new Information Products Group.*

Scot Reid and Bill Bradford in Mountain View, Kathy Bauman in Los Angeles, and Tom McKeown in Dallas. Field Service Engineer Chris Warnock will work with end-users and resellers to create and maintain systems for electronic document communication.

Eastern regional activity will be managed by Judy Santoro, based in Chicago. Working with her will be Susan Flood and Jim Koch in Chicago, Paul Gerlach in Philadelphia, Jeff Bartlett in Boston, Devra Kudevitz in Washington, D.C., and Jim Hilsenrod in New York. Eastern Region field service engineers are Ed Sanders in Chicago and John-Henry Gross in Washington, D.C.

New Services, New Relationships
Several members of the Information Products Group will focus on establishing and strengthening relationships with VARs, system integrators and other resellers of Adobe products. Enlisting and educating these "channel partners" will help ensure that Adobe Acrobat customers receive the highest-quality service and support.

Working with Director of Channel Development Chas Schoenig, Jeff Weldon in Boston and Elaine Singer in Washington, D.C., also will consult on product development with "information integrators" and CD-ROM publishers, who re-publish information for Adobe Acrobat product users. These companies will use Acrobat publisher's tools to create publications with enhanced functions such as powerful search capabilities and automatic

(Continued on page 7)

POSTSCRIPT
Software From Adobe

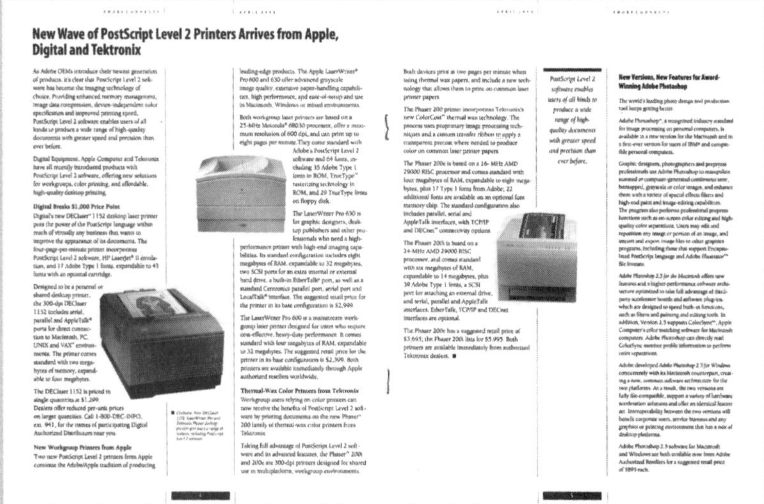

New Wave of PostScript Level 2 Printers Arrives from Apple, Digital and Tektronix

As Adobe OEMs introduce their newest generation of products, it's clear that PostScript Level 2 software has become the imaging technology of choice. Providing enhanced memory management, image data compression, device-independent color specification and improved printing speed, PostScript Level 2 software enables users of all kinds to produce a wide range of high-quality documents with greater speed and precision than ever before.

Digital Equipment, Apple Computer and Tektronix have all recently introduced products with PostScript Level 2 software, offering new solutions for workgroups, color printing, and affordable, high-quality desktop printing.

Digital Breaks $1,200 Price Point
Digital's new DEClaser™ 1152 desktop laser printer puts the power of the PostScript language within reach of virtually any business that wants to improve the appearance of its documents. The four-page-per-minute printer incorporates PostScript Level 2 software, HP LaserJet® II emulation, and 17 Adobe Type 1 fonts, expandable to 43 fonts with an optional cartridge.

Designed to be a personal or shared desktop printer, the 300-dpi DEClaser 1152 includes serial, parallel and AppleTalk® ports for direct connection to Macintosh, PC, UNIX and VAX® environments. The printer comes standard with two megabytes of memory, expandable to four megabytes.

The DEClaser 1152 is priced in single quantities at $1,299. Desktop color and tri-color models are under $3,000. Call 1-800-DEC-INFO, ext. 941, for the names of participating Digital Authorized Distributors near you.

New Workgroup Printers from Apple
Two new PostScript Level 2 printers from Apple continue the Adobe/Apple tradition of producing

leading-edge products. The Apple LaserWriter® Pro 600 and 630 offer advanced grayscale image quality, extensive paper-handling capabilities, high performance, and ease-of-setup and use in Macintosh, Windows or mixed environments.

Both workgroup laser printers are based on a 25-MHz Motorola® 68030 processor, offer a maximum resolution of 600 dpi, and can print up to eight pages per minute. They come standard with Adobe's PostScript Level 2 software and 64 fonts, including 35 Adobe Type 1 fonts in ROM, TrueType™ rasterizing technology in ROM, and 29 TrueType fonts on floppy disk.

The LaserWriter Pro 630 is for graphic designers, desktop publishers and other professionals who need a high-performance printer with high-end imaging capabilities. In standard configuration it includes eight megabytes of RAM, expandable to 32 megabytes, two SCSI ports for an extra internal or external hard drive, a built-in EtherTalk® port, as well as a standard Centronics parallel port, serial port and LocalTalk® interface. The suggested retail price for the printer in its base configuration is $2,599.

The LaserWriter Pro 600 is a mainstream workgroup laser printer designed for users who require cost-effective, heavy-duty performance. It comes standard with four megabytes of RAM, expandable to 32 megabytes. The suggested retail price for the printer in its base configuration is $2,369. Both printers are available immediately through Apple authorized resellers worldwide.

Thermal-Wax Color Printers from Tektronix
Workgroup users relying on color printers can now receive the benefits of PostScript Level 2 software by printing documents on the new Phaser™ 200 family of thermal-wax color printers from Tektronix.

Taking full advantage of PostScript Level 2 software and its advanced features, the Phaser™ 200 and 200e are 300-dpi printers designed for shared use in multi-platform, workgroup environments.

Both devices print at two pages per minute when using thermal-wax papers, and include a new technology that allows them to print on common laser printer papers.

The Phaser 200 printer incorporates Tektronix's new ColorCase™ thermal wax technology. The process uses proprietary image processing techniques and a custom transfer ribbon to apply a transparent protective coating that enables it to produce color on common laser printer papers.

The Phaser 200e is based on a 16-MHz AMD 29000 RISC processor and comes standard with four megabytes of RAM, expandable to eight megabytes, plus 17 Type 1 fonts from Adobe, 22 additional fonts are available on an optional font memory chip. The standard configuration also includes parallel, serial and AppleTalk interfaces, with TCP/IP and DECnet™ connectivity optional.

The Phaser 200 is based on a 24-MHz AMD 29000 RISC processor, and comes standard with six megabytes of RAM, expandable to 14 megabytes, plus 39 Adobe Type 1 fonts, a SCSI port for attaching an external drive, and serial, parallel and AppleTalk interfaces. EtherTalk, TCP/IP and DECnet interfaces are optional.

The Phaser 200 is based on a 24-MHz AMD 29000 RISC processor, and comes standard with six megabytes of RAM, expandable to 14 megabytes, plus 39 Adobe Type 1 fonts, a SCSI port for attaching an external drive, and serial, parallel and AppleTalk interfaces. The Phaser 200i has a suggested retail price of $3,695; the Phaser 200i lists for $5,495. Both printers are available immediately from authorized Tektronix dealers.

> PostScript Level 2 software enables users of all kinds to produce a wide range of high-quality documents with greater speed and precision than ever before.

■ *Clockwise from top: DEClaser 1152 LaserWriter Pro 600, Phaser 200 color printer.*

New Versions, New Features for Award-Winning Adobe Photoshop

The world's leading photo design and production tool keeps getting better.

Adobe Photoshop™, a recognized industry standard for image processing on personal computers, is available in a new version for the Macintosh and in a first-ever version for users of IBM® and compatible personal computers.

Graphic designers, photographers and program professionals use Adobe Photoshop to manipulate scanned or computer-generated continuous-tone bitmapped, grayscale or color images, and enhance them with a variety of special effects filters and high-end paint and image-editing capabilities. The program also performs professional prepress functions such as on-screen color editing and high-quality color separation. Users may edit and reposition any image or portion of an image, and import and export image files to other graphics programs, including those that support Encapsulated PostScript language and Adobe Illustrator™ file formats.

Adobe Photoshop 2.5 for the Macintosh offers new features and a higher-performance software architecture optimized to take full advantage of the 32-party accelerator boards and software plug-ins which are designed to speed built-in functions, such as filters and painting and editing tools. In addition, Version 2.5 supports ColorSync™. Apple Computer's color matching software for Macintosh computers. Adobe Photoshop can directly read ColorSync monitor profile information to perform color separation.

Adobe developed Adobe Photoshop 2.5 for Windows concurrently with its Macintosh counterpart, creating a new, common software architecture for the two platforms. As a result, the two versions are fully file-compatible, support a variety of hardware accelerator solutions and offer an identical feature set. Interoperability between the two versions will benefit corporate users, service bureaus and any graphics or printing environment that has a mix of desktop platforms.

Adobe Photoshop 2.5 software for Macintosh and Windows are both available now from Adobe Authorized Resellers for a suggested retail price of $895 each.

Formal magazine styling

In many ways, this newsletter really does look much more like a slick, full-color magazine than a newsletter. But you could apply similar techniques to any newsletter if space isn't an issue.

The cover is devoted entirely to an in-depth table of contents, similar to that of many magazines. The designer uses very wide margins to frame each article with white space, then occasionally breaks up that space with color photos and illustrations. Each article is presented separately on its own page or spread, often with a secondary headline above or a side deck to pull the reader into the body text.

Also note the unusually large line spacing: It creates a very airy look and allows the designer to use a very fine typeface in a fairly small size.

The Adobe Reseller
Winter, 1994

- Publisher: Adobe Systems Inc., Mountain View, CA
- Designers: Alicia Buelow, Karen Ann
- Colors: Process
- Type: Univers Condensed, Univers Expanded, Garamond
- Dimensions: 8½ by 11

The high end

Some newsletters, such as
these glossy publications,
really do cross the line into
the magazine category. Both
are published by large
hospitals; both are full-color,
with a mix of informational
and promotional articles. And
both feature beautiful two-
column layouts with creative
typography, photo treatments
and engaging page layouts.

Publications like this are
great sources for ideas and
inspiration—even if you're
starting with a template
design. Consider whether any
of the design devices shown
here might work in your
newsletter.

Awareness
Spring, 1993

- Publisher: Evangelical Health
  Systems, Oak Brook, IL
- Designers: Cagney + McDowell
- Colors: Process
- Type: Variety
- Dimensions: 9 by 10⅞

be alert for signs of

vascular disease

"peripheral vascular occlusive disease need no longer be considered part of growing old"

"with modern diagnostic and treatment procedures, people should be back on the golf course in no time"

Health Connections
Spring, 1993
- Publisher: Elmhurst Memorial Hospital, Elmhurst, IL
- Designers: Kim Martin & Teri Williams, KaTaPa Art & Design
- Colors: Process
- Type: Variety
- Dimensions: 9 by 10⅞

A sampler of "standard" three-column designs

It's easy to settle on one picture of how a three-column design should look. But as these covers demonstrate, there's nothing standard about starting with three columns.

Each newsletter takes a different approach. Some adhere more strictly to the three-column structure than others. In many cases, graphics, photos, pullquotes and even articles are set to span two columns.

Hanley Highlights
First Quarter, 1994
- Publisher: Hanley Graphics Products Co., Itasca, IL
- Designer: Design North
- Colors: Black and blue

CARC Outreach
September, 1993
- Publisher: Chicago Association for Retarded Citizens, Chicago, IL
- Designer: Consolidated Press
- Colors: Black and maroon

The Challenge
February, 1992
- Publisher: American Lung Association of Greater Chicago, Chicago, IL
- Designer: Peg Esposito, Peg Inc.
- Colors: Deep green and red

Hanley Highlights

Volume 4, Issue 1
First Quarter 1994

Getting Started with Page Imposition Software

AROUND THE AGENCY
Special Ed Grads Ready For New Challenges

Chicago's First Lady Maggie Daley Talks to Early Intervention Families

THE Challenge

HOSPITALS GOING SMOKE-FREE IN THE NEW YEAR

"It's ironic when smoking is prohibited on planes and even buses that hospitals... still allow smoking."

Leadership Council for Metropolitan Open Communities
Opening Doors to Opportunity
SUMMER 1992

LEADERSHIP COUNCIL NEWS

HIGHLIGHT 1992:
NEW INITIATIVES—NEW RELATIONSHIPS

LOOK OUT DISCRIMINATORS—
SEYFARTH, SHAW IS ON BOARD IN A BIG WAY!

A newsletter for Basic Checking, Interest Checking PLUS and Silver Eagles Checking account holders

FirstDraft

Anheuser-Busch Employees' Credit Union   Volume 10, Issue 1   February 1994

Low Rate. Rebate.
DON'T WAIT!

Electronic Tax Filing.

A CUE Tax Clue.

Leadership Council News
Summer, 1992
- Publisher: Leadership Council for Metropolitan Open Communities, Chicago, IL
- Designer: Estelle Carol, Carol★Simpson Productions
- Type: Helvetica Black, New Century Schoolbook
- Colors: Black and deep green

First Draft
February, 1994
- Publisher: Anheuser-Busch Credit Union, St. Louis, MO
- Designer: Paula M. Flake
- Colors: Black and red

Closer Look
February, 1992
- Publisher: Designs for Change, Chicago, IL
- Designer: Janis Boehm, Janis Boehm Design
- Colors: Black and red

Three-column with a snaking flow

This informational newsletter is heavily text-oriented—it's all about professional writing and editing—so the designers chose a format that fits lots of text on every page, yet is very readable.

Articles snake through column after column, page after page. The key to making this kind of flow work for the reader are plenty of clear stops and pauses. Articles are punctuated with bold, run-in subheads that string the readers along. Departments are introduced with very distinctive department heads: tilted type reversed out of magenta color blocks.

Writing Concepts
Sample Issue, 1993
- Publisher: Communications Concepts, Inc., Springfield, VA
- Designers: Jerry Seamster, John De Lellis
- Colors: Black and magenta
- Type: Franklin Gothic, Gill Sans, Garamond, American Typewriter
- Dimensions: 8½ by 11

A simple interlocking structure

This newsletter maintains a clean tile structure on those pages where multiple stories appear. Strong vertical and horizontal dividers, along with large, tinted drop caps, reinforce the simple rectangular organization.

Friends of the Parks Newsletter
Summer, 1993

- Publisher: Friends of the Parks, Chicago, IL
- Designer: Nancy Minster
- Colors: Black and green (PMS 347)
- Type: Helvetica Condensed Black, Times
- Dimensions: 8½ by 11

Friends of the Parks Newsletter

Summer Edition 1993   Editor: Erma Tranter   Managing Editor: Nancy Minster

Claypool and Rogers Promise to Overhaul City Parks

Security at Chicago's 563 parks will be the "No. 1 priority" of Forrest Claypool, named by Mayor Daley on July 8 as the new Chicago Park District superintendent. Claypool replaces Robert C. Penn, who resigned under pressure on July 7.

Claypool, 36, a former chief of staff for Mayor Daley and most recently deputy state treasurer under Patrick Quinn, promised "radical" changes in the park system by beefing up security, changing union work rules and tailoring recreational programs to working parents.

Claypool grew up in downstate St. Elmo. He graduated in 1978 from Southern Illinois University in Carbondale and in 1981 graduated from the University of Illinois law school. Although Claypool has no background in parks or recreation, Daley and his management skills are ideally suited to the superintendent's job. When asked by reporters whether his credentials were more political than recreational, Claypool replied, "I know something about politics. I know that it is a political imperative for this mayor that the city government works for people, because that's how he is going to be judged."

Claypool promises to produce change at the Chicago Park District by:

— Opening and staffing fieldhouses evenings, weekends and holidays (an idea Friends of the Parks has urged for years).

— Investigating the idea of a surcharge to suburbanites when they utilize CPD facilities.

— Weeding out loafing employees.

— Reducing the CPD bureaucracy.

We are pleased to hear Claypool refer to Friends of the Parks in many public appearances as the voice of change and a supplier

Reprinted with permission from the Chicago Sun-Times, © 1993
Forrest Claypool (center), newly designated Park District superintendent, speaks during a press conference at Columbus Park on July 8. With Claypool are newly elected Park Board president John W. Rogers, Jr. (left) and Mayor Daley.

of good ideas. Responding to FOTP's report card (see page 3), he said, "I will go over it point by point, and where criticisms are accurate, as I suspect they are in many areas, I will tackle them."

Parks in "forgotten communities" will get badly needed resources, said John W. Rogers, Jr., chosen on May 4 by Mayor Daley to replace Richard Devine as Chicago Park District Board president.

Rogers, 35, is a graduate of Princeton University. He founded and heads Ariel Capital Development, a money management firm with $2 billion in assets. His charitable foundation has adopted a class of public school 6th graders and promises to pay their way through college if they graduate from high school. Rogers said he has "already started going through the budget, line-item by line-item" in an attempt to find ways to streamline the bureaucracy.

Citizen Input

It is imperative that Chicago citizens articulate their concerns and suggestions to Park District officials. If something is on your mind or if you need assistance on a park issue, write to:

Forrest Claypool, General Superintendent and John W. Rogers, Jr., Board President, Chicago Park District, 425 East McFetridge Drive, Chicago, IL 60605.

If you wish, send a copy to each of the Chicago Park District Board of Commissioners, at the same address. Commissioners include William Bartholomay, Margaret Burroughs, Mona Castillo, Joseph Phelps, Michael Scott and George Vest.

Also, send a copy of your letter to Friends of the Parks, Attention: Peter Skosey, 407 South Dearborn, Suite 1590, Chicago, IL 60605. We will follow through with the issue at the park or Board level. ■

Friends of the Parks Newsletter—Summer 1993   Page 1

State Approves Museum Legislation Raising Chicago Property Taxes

In April, 1993 Friends of the Parks learned that legislation had been introduced in the Illinois Senate to reappropriate, at a higher level, the Aquarium and museums' capital improvements levy. The reappropriation would have raised property taxes for the second time in a year for Chicago's nine museums in the parks.

The first property tax increase for the nine museums was approved by the Chicago Park District (CPD) Board of Commissioners in March, 1993, despite opposition by Friends of the Parks. The museum tax did not participate in public budget hearings in December, 1992, at which time community groups successfully fought a proposed $23 million property tax hike. However, after the 1993 budget was approved with no tax increases, the museums succeeded in pressing the CPD Board of Commissioners for a $6 million yearly property tax increase for general operating funds.

A second tax increase would have resulted from the bill introduced by Senator Walter Dudycz (Illinois Bill #42). The legislative package was not approved by the Park Board of Commissioners out of the public was not aware of the bill. The Senate approved the bill before President of the Parks learned of its contents. After achieving representation on the House of the potential tax hike, the House rejected the bill in May by a vote of 74 to 32.

The museum issue, however, did not die in May. Using the last-minute tactic of the June 30 legislative deadline, the original failed legislation was redistributed as an amendment to a Senate Forest Preserve Bill. On June 30 at 12:30 p.m., the bill passed. Two days later, the House approved the bill with the amendment. Friends of the Parks has asked Governor Edgar to immediately veto the museum reappropriation bill.

The issue of museums in our parks is complex and needs to be addressed as a serious policy issue. The museums are nine cultural institutions adding much to the City of Chicago. Only Chicago properly

tax pays museums, however, provide tax dollars for their operation and capital improvements. The break-down of visitors to Chicago museums is: 30% from the city, 40% from the suburbs, and 30% from downstate, other states and countries. More than 70% of visitors are non-Chicagoans; yet, only Chicagoans pay the tax bill.

The second issue is that as various institutions, museums continuously seek to expand. Capital improvements dollars provided by the Park District often mean in further encroachment on our limited park space.

Policy discussions on two levels should be undertaken now. First, the museums should be expanded to a broader tax base — a tax-saving taxing authority, for instance. Second, alternatives to parkland expansion should be pursued. Sensible resources in neighborhoods would benefit people who cannot easily get to our cultural institutions. ■

Grant Park Maintenance Awarded to Private Landscape Firm

The Invaluum Group, a Chicago landscape firm, received a one-year contract from the Chicago Park District to maintain a twenty-acre section of Grant Park from Randolph to Monroe. Friends of the Parks, Alderman Ted Mazola and the Central Michigan Avenue Association have worked with the Park District to arrange this agreement. Out of the poorer maintenance is shared, half by the Park District and half by Friends of the Parks and the Central Michigan Avenue Association.

To save dollars, the agreement stipulated that volunteers must help to complete the planting of tree garden beds at Madison and Washington Streets. Free donate volunteers including Alderman Mazola, Fred Lopez, Bob Winlow, FOTP Board members Lucy D'Angelo and Dexter O'Neill, and Friends of the Parks staff members planted the tree beds with marigolds, salvia and petunias on Saturday, June 5th. We encourage you to visit this beautiful spot! ■

Friends Sail Aboard The Cap Streeter

On Thursday, June 24, 150 members and friends joined Friends of the Parks for our second "Picnic on the Lake" benefit, where everyone got a view of the parks from the other side.

At 6 p.m., guests boarded The Cap Streeter at the Navy Pier Aquarium Inn as evening of fun, Jeff Smollen's jazz group entertained the crowd. Delicious buffet tents were donated by Bella Vista, Home Nova, Rossi's Cafe, Buena Roof, Buena Place, Carlton's, Carlyn Bergdoff Catering, Cavanaugh's, Charlie's Ale House, Club Lucky, Ed's Chicago's Finest Cheesecake, The Crochet Taverne, Third Coast and Vinny's. The Funny

Firm donated wine, Berghoff's and the Joseph Huber Brewing Company donated beer, and Coca-Cola provided beverages.

A special thank-you to Charles and Marci Gidwitz of the Shoreline Marine Co. for donating The Cap Streeter.

For donating our invitations, thanks to Hotel Copy Centers, D. Anderson + Others, and AutoGraphics.

In our fun-raising competition, Bob Anderson, MaryBella Bettis, Jacqueline Brown, Stephen Christy, Barrie Detheinbach, Bonnie Jodie, George Nelson, Kelvin Parks and Charlotte Wheeler. Thanks also to the many volunteers who helped that night. ■

Page 8   Friends of the Parks Newsletter—Summer 1993

Earth Day '93 Makes Chicago Cleaner and Greener

Earth Day is celebrated every day by Friends of the Parks, but on Saturday, April 24, thousands of Chicagoans came together in a special citywide Earth Day park cleanup.

With the continued sponsorship and support of WMX Technologies (formerly Waste Management, Inc.), Friends of the Parks recruited more than 7,000 volunteers who cleaned hundreds of parks and beaches. This effort is the largest hands-on environmental project in the Midwest! Volunteers planted shrubs and flowers, mulched trees, and conserved and recycled litter.

At the Grant Park kick-off, WMX Technologies introduced its "Cyclo," the nature's first walking, talking robot made from recycled cans and bottles. Cyclo led volunteers in his "Earth Day Cyclo Pledge" and encouraged everyone to take care of Chicago's greenspace every day.

WMX Technologies also provided park supplies and co-sponsored this 1993 Earth Day t-shirt. Seven-year-old Amanda Pallotto scored the winning design as part of a children's t-shirt contest earlier in the year. Her drawing and

message, "We are all in the same boat. Together, we can save Mother Earth," appeared on 1,000 Earth Day t-shirts.

WPWB-TV Channel 50 promoted the Earth Day project on the air and provided brightly-colored posters for the volunteers. The station's celebrity character, Captain Planet, greeted children at Grant Park, 12th Street Beach and Dvorak Park.

Jelco Laboratories donated Simple Green, an environmentally safe cleaning product, to all volunteers. Jelco employees...

Photo: Roger Lauditson
Children at prime in boat helped to pick up litter at Grant Park on Earth Day.

...use and their families also headed the Oak Street beach clean-up.

Openlands Project and its Tree-Keepers volunteers, and Minuteworks volunteers, mulched hundreds of trees at six parks.

Thanks to Allied Glove & Safety Products and Magid Glove & Safety Manufacturing Co. for providing gloves for our volunteers.

Thanks also to the Chicago Park District, City of Chicago, Chicago Gateway Green Committee and Mayor Daley's GreenStreets Program.

Our efforts on Earth Day are not just for the present, but for future generations as well. It's a great way to show your commitment to Chicago's urban environment. ■

Photo: Roger Lauditson
At Dvorak Park in Pilsen, a student and her class chase debris from the sidewalk.

Photo: Roger Lauditson
Young volunteers gather around "Cyclo," WMX Technologies' talking robot made from recycled cans and bottles.

Donation Thanks

Board member Katharine Andersen recently coordinated a very generous donation through her employer, Estée & Co. Computer hardware and software were donated to Friends of the Parks by the retail union firm. This equipment will significantly expand our capabilities, allow us to better handle administrative and bookkeeping activities and keep us on the high-track. With this new system, we hope to better manage our ever-expanding membership base and serve you better! ■

Friends of the Parks Newsletter—Summer 1993   Page 9

*Newsletters From
the Desktop*

A three-column, six-page fold-out

Published by a law office for its clients, this newsletter aims for a simple, well-structured and conservative look. The no-frills Franklin used in the heads and old style Stempel Garamond used in the body set the tone perfectly.

It's printed on a light cream-colored stock with a brown nameplate, pullquotes and tinted sidebar.

Law Update
Winter, 1994
- Publisher: Gordon & Glickson P.C., Chicago, Illinois
- Designer: Gordon & Glickson P.C.
- Colors: Black and brown (PMS 216) on cream paper
- Type: Franklin Gothic Heavy, Stempel Garamond
- Dimensions: 8½ by 11

LAW UPDATE

GORDON & GLICKSON P.C.   *Winter 1994*

The Information Superhighway Entry Ramp

The national news media have been reporting on what the Clinton administration has described as a "data superhighway." The principles behind this system include developing a national data and information network through private initiative, ensuring that all citizens have affordable access to it, creating linking standards, and putting government data and information on the network. This data superhighway will have a tremendous impact on the day-to-day operation of American businesses, which will in turn lead to increased responsibility for the company's chief information officer.

On top of these developments comes the recent announcement by executives of Bell Atlantic, a telephone company, and Tele-Communications, Inc., the nation's largest cable operator, disclosing details of their $33 billion merger. *The Wall Street Journal* reported that the merger is of "stunning significance" and Raymond W. Smith of Bell Atlantic promises that the merger will revolutionize the way people communicate, offering television programming and information on demand. *The New York Times* recognized that the merger outlines the potential of a national data superhighway.

These developments will have a profound significance on the way many services are delivered. For example, many companies are now actively engaged in testing a prototype of the data superhighway that would link hospitals and other health-care institutions. One example has been called "teleradiology," the transmission by telephone lines of both X-ray images and computer-driven body scans. Urban healthcare institutions can and do provide smaller rural hospitals with interpretation of these diagnostic tests. While there are critics who will resist these technological innovations, supporters of these developments find comfort in President Clinton's remarks calling for "linking rural doctors and hospitals with high-tech urban medical centers."
(continued on page 5)

In This Issue

- *The Information Superhighway Entry Ramp*

  *Editorial—
  Do Not Dig Legal Potholes*

- *Taxes And The Technology Company: Highlights Of The 1993 Tax Act*

- *Quality Initiatives—
  The Legal Function
  In-House Training Promotes Quality*

- *Hidden Asset:
  Infringement Coverage*

Editorial

Do Not Dig Legal Potholes

Vice President Al Gore's recent speeches in support of legislation that will reduce legal barriers between the telephone and cable television industries is a step in the right direction for the Clinton Administration. Some will criticize the Administration's stand in support of the "information mergers" that will likely result, but those critics need to consult better road maps. These mergers do not mean the potential death of privacy or the birth of dangerous monopolies, as critics contend.
(continued on page 5)

(continued on page 5)

GORDON & GLICKSON P.C.   Page 2

Taxes And The Technology Company: Highlights Of The 1993 Tax Act

Amortization of Intangibles

All acquired intangible assets are to be amortized over a 15-year period. Excluded from the 15-year amortization requirement is readily available "off-the-shelf" software which has not been modified and the entire purchase of software not acquired as part of or equivalent to, a trade or business acquisition. This excluded software may be amortized over a three-year period. Small software developers, who link the capital to bring new products to market, often work to sell their businesses to larger buyers with the necessary capital. Because the tax law creates a disincentive for these buyers, it may be more difficult for small software developers to find the resources to bring new products to market. U.S. buyers of software companies will also be at a relative disadvantage to foreign buyers, which generally have a five-year amortization available.

Research Tax Credit

Section 41 of the Internal Revenue Code permitted a tax credit equal to 20 percent of the excess of qualified research expenses for the year over a base amount and 20 percent of basic research payments. The credit had expired as of June 30, 1992 but has now been reinstated retroactively to June 30, 1992, and extended to June 30, 1995.

Capital Gain Exclusion For Small Business Stock

A new investment incentive permits a noncorporate taxpayer who holds qualified small business stock for more than five years to exclude 50 percent of the gain on the sale or exchange of the stock. The maximum gain eligible for the exclusion is the greater of (1) 10 times the taxpayer's basis in the stock or (2) $10 million. A qualified small business cannot have more than $50 million in assets, and it excludes service providers, farms, mineral extractors, and S Corporations. The exclusion is cut in half for alternative minimum tax calculations. There has been considerable debate as to how significant this provision will be in attracting additional capital to small business. Some small technology companies feel it will be helpful. Others worry that the five-year extraction may offset the capital gain exclusion benefit for many investors. There is also some concern that the "service provider" exclusion might be interpreted to exclude companies whose main asset is viewed as the quality of its people and their services rather than a particular product.

Lobbying Expenses

Businesses that have been active in lobbying before federal and state legislative and administrative bodies will no longer be allowed a deduction for those expenses unless the activity falls into the category of providing technical advice or assistance. This will also impact the deductibility of their paid-in industry associations which engage in lobbying activity.

General Corporate Provisions

1) Reduction in deductible portion of business meals and entertainment from 80 percent to 50 percent.

2) Denial of deduction for club dues, spouse's and dependents' travel, and some moving expenses.

3) Denial of deduction for executive pay over $1 million excluding certain contingent compensation.

4) Reduction of compensation which may be taken into account for purposes of qualified retirement plans to $150,000.

5) Increase of the limit which can be expensed and deducted for the purchase of tangible personal property from $10,000 to $17,500.

S Corporation Election Review

The advantages of S Corporation status should be reviewed as a result of the return of individual tax rates to close historical positions in excess of corporate rates at the highest income levels. The alternative minimum tax rate also increases to as high as 28 percent for alternative minimum taxable income in excess of $175,000. The potential for double taxation at the corporate and shareholder levels may mean early involvement when bargaining leverage is high and key concessions are easier to obtain.

Page 5

Quality Initiatives— The Legal Function

It is hard to imagine any well-run business today that has not either implemented, or is not in the process of implementing, a total quality management (TQM) program. And suppliers of products and services are aware that ISO 9000 certification may soon be required for doing business in certain markets. Constant focus and continuous improvement are among the main thrusts of TQM. Embedded within these areas are key legal issues, and an opportunity to re-engineer the role for counsel to play in TQM initiatives.

Consider "quality legal management" in the following context:

Procurement

Are your purchasing documents, including requests for proposals (RFP's), standard contracts, and purchase orders, designed to achieve the best terms and to reduce the costs and cycle time for procurements? For example, in technology procurement, the cycle time for negotiating agreement terms can be reduced by including in the RFP required contract terms on items such as warranties and limitations of liability. Traditionally, legal counsel's role in procurement was limited to being a gatekeeper with final review on acquisitions that exceeded a certain dollar limit. Re-engineering counsel's role means early involvement when bargaining leverage is high and key concessions are easier to obtain.

Customer Agreements

Are your standard agreements written in a format that will reduce your costs and cycle time for getting your customers to sign? If, for example, you are a software licensor, you will want an agreement that minimizes the role for legal counsel on the other side. Your agreements should address in a fair measure all significant issues most of your customers expect to have addressed. Your agreements should be written in understandable language and a "user-friendly" format that business decision-makers will appreciate.

If your agreements are totally one-sided or written in obscure "legalese," then control of the deal will likely shift from your customers' business people to their lawyers, adding time and cost to the deal, and probably increasing the need to make concessions.

Disputes

To paraphrase the bumper sticker: Disputes Happen. Resolving them frequently requires an interpretation of contracts or legal roles. From a TQM perspective you should strive to resolve disputes for the lowest cost in the shortest time, while strengthening relationships, and perhaps even "delighting" your customers. To do so, you and your counsel must be able to rapidly employ state-of-the-art alternative dispute resolution (ADR) techniques. Litigation is a narrow purpose, zero-sum forum in which businesses give up control of the process in the court and their lawyers, who attempt to come out on top of a win-lose outcome. It is difficult to continue doing business with someone who is suing you. With ADR, you can retain control, continue doing business and search for win-win resolutions.

Education

As part of their TQM continuous improvement efforts, cutting-edge businesses are investing in more training and education, generally, and specifically they are having special counsel train their business people and in-house attorneys on specialized legal issues. For example, a large conglomerate might arrange for its key executives and in-house attorneys to attend a special briefing on technology concerning and facilities management deals in the organization considers outsourcing its various data processing operations. A technology vendor might schedule a training session to ensure that all sales and account managers thoroughly understand the firm's standard licensing agreement, including how to negotiate key terms, when to offer a fall-back clause, and which terms should not be compromised, and why.

The TQM revolution taught most agencies that quality is not simply a "shop floor" concern. Quality requires a commitment from all levels of management and all employees. Moreover, each major group of TQM initiatives embedded legal issues, and holds opportunities to re-engineer the way a business uses its legal counsel.

In-House Training Promotes Quality

As TQM and quality initiatives have matured, in-house corporate counsel are now expected to continuously improve the quality of internal services they provide. Although there are many outside assistant to educate in-house lawyers, a specially tailored in-house training session can be more productive and cost-effective. Often, special outside counsel participate in regular in-house attorney conferences.

Our law firm, which concentrates in computer, communications and information technology law, has been privileged to participate in several recent in-house attorney conferences. The focus of our presentations has been to provide education about emerging information technology issues. For these sessions we provide in-house or large acquirers of computers, software, data or related services, we have discussed methods to improve quality, for example, by simplifying standard agreements and procurement strategies. Other topics include proprietary rights audits and protection, outsourcing, strategic alliances and alternative dispute resolution.

Page 6

Hidden Asset: Infringement Coverage

Software and information technology suppliers who are sued for copyright or trademark infringement sometimes afford to overlook the possibility that their regular comprehensive general liability ("CGL") insurance policy will cover the claim. CGL coverage is routinely purchased by businesses primarily to protect against personal injury and property damage caused by the negligence of corporate employees. What is generally termed "Coverage B" on the CGL policy, however, also provides "advertising injury" coverage. In several recent cases, courts have held that the advertising injury coverage may protect the insured against claims of software copyright infringement or trademark infringement.

In Federal Insurance Co. v. Microsoft Corp., No. C92-602D (W.D. Wash. 1993), the federal district court in Seattle ruled that Microsoft, in its employment suit with Apple Computer, was entitled to have its insurance company reimburse Microsoft's defense costs under the advertising injury coverage. Then, on July 20, 1993, Apple Computer won a ruling that California against its own insurer for reimbursement of over $3 million in defense costs when Apple Computer had gone to defend a trademark infringement suit brought by Apple Corps, Ltd., owner of the Apple Records label of the Beatles.

Not all copyright, trademark or unfair competition claims will qualify for coverage. But, based upon their recent precedent, insurers are more often agreeing to provide coverage, at least for defense costs. Many insurers are scrambling to rewrite their policies to exclude this type of claim.

To summarize, we suggest that all claims, even small, that demands and suits for infringement, including copyright, trademark and unfair competition, as well as libel, slander and product disparagement, should be evaluated for possible coverage. In many cases, there will exist a potential for coverage that will obligate the insurer to pay for legal defense costs. In addition, the policy may cover the costs of settlement or judgment.

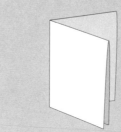

An unusual foldout based on a three-column grid

This legal letter is aimed at lawyers running their own practices, so the design reflects a more adventurous spirit. The fold is called a French fold.

Solo

Winter, 1994

- Publisher: American Bar Association Press
- Designer: Bruce McKenzie, Mead Data Central, Inc., ABA Press Newsletter Unit
- Colors: Gray (PMS 404) and teal (PMS 321)
- Type: Galliard, Times Roman
- Dimensions (folded): 5½ by 8½

A mixed format

Here's a common strategy in many newsletters: Use one grid for the cover story and a more efficient design for the inner pages.

This newsletter looks like a two-column on the outside. That allows the designer to leave lots of white space and use photos or graphics more creatively. Note, for example, the large vertical photo with a caption hung on the right.

Inside, it's back to business. The three-column format packs in more text.

Update
Spring, 1993 (top) and Summer, 1992
- Publisher: Chicago Community Loan Fund, Chicago, Illinois
- Designer: Estelle Carol, Carol★Simpson Productions
- Colors: Black and light blue (PMS 305) on gray speckled paper
- Type: Times New Roman, Helvetica Black, New Century Schoolbook
- Dimensions: 8½ by 11

UPDATE

343 South Dearborn St. Suite 1004, Chicago, Illinois 60604 (312) 922-1350 FAX (312) 922-7381

CHICAGO COMMUNITY LOAN FUND

SPRING 1993

El Mercado, Chicago's first public marketplace, receives CCLF financing

New self-employment opportunities for community residents

The Chicago Community Loan Fund (CCLF) recently finalized a $35,000 loan to Bickerdike Redevelopment Corporation to establish a $65,000 micro-loan fund for low-income entrepreneurs participating in El Mercado, Chicago's first public marketplace. This fund provides loans of $2,500 to $15,000 to cover equipment, build-out and start-up working capital for vendors at the Mercado, located at 2701 W. North Avenue in the West Town community.

With its bright murals and painted palm trees amid a neglected commercial area, El Mercado Public Marketplace is a refreshing oasis on Chicago's northwest side. The Mercado also offers opportunities for low- and moderate- income individuals to become self-employed through a micro-loan fund, capitalized in part by the Chicago Community Loan Fund (CCLF).

When Olga Ricketts-Peart was laid off from her job a year ago, she was unsure of her next step. With $5,000 in start-up financing from the Mercado's micro-loan fund, Olga opened Aglo Tropical Juices, realizing her long-held dream of selling fresh juices featuring tropical fruits and exotic combinations. "I was amazed that someone who was not a partner in my business would finance me. It was a godsend."

Like many of the Mercado's other vendors, Olga feels at home in the multi-stall format modeled after the open marketplaces of countries such as Puerto Rico,

Inside this issue

2 Message from the Executive Director

5 $50,000 Challenge to Individual Investors

4 Community Development Financial Institutions and the Clinton Administration

5 Investment Club Funds a Social Dividend

Mexico and Olga's native Jamaica. The Mercado has leased about half of its vendors stalls since opening in November, offering the West Town and Humboldt Park communities a wide range of goods and services at very competitive prices.

In addition to dry goods, dairy, bakery and non-food items, the Mercado offers fresh produce, meats and seafood, including hard-to-find items popular with Latinos and African-Americans, from spicy chorizo sausage to malanga, a starchy root of African origin. Prepared foods are found at two restaurants which flank the central dining area.

El Mercado also feels like a small piece of home for the area's Latin American immigrants. The vibrant exterior features tropical murals by Jose Berrios. Inside, the atmosphere is airy and festive. Beneath the high ceiling with exposed ductwork and

Continued on page 3.

Entrepreneurship is a family affair for the Rueda family, natives of Puebla, Mexico. Veronica and Maribel Rueda (left) take time out from their duties at Puebla Produce, where they assist their parents with the family business based at El Mercado.

1

A message from the Board Chair:

Bridging islands of resources with islands of need

by Sara Jo Light

Wieboldt Foundation takes the lead among area foundations

CCLF's first program-related investment

CHICAGO COMMUNITY LOAN FUND

SUMMER 1992

Founder of the first community loan fund shares his vision & success story

by John Ayers

Mission Statement

Board of Directors

Thanks to Our Donors

2   3

SmartAlerts

From Enterprise Intelligence Systems

Enterprise
Intelligence
Systems

The New Market for World-Class Management Solutions

March 1994 Vol. 1 No. 1

P. 1 **EIS in Our Practice**
The New Market for World-Class Management Solutions

P. 2 **Alliance Update**
The Comshare Alliance

P. 4 **Best Clients**
Hertz Corp. and Flat Avio

P. 6 **Technology Focus**
Visualizing the Multidimensional Business Enterprise

P. 7 **Programme News**

For Internal Use Only

ANDERSEN
CONSULTING
ARTHUR ANDERSEN & CO, S.C.

Alliance Update

The Comshare Alliance

Commander Exception Monitor (CEM) is the first step in the process to reinvent the way executives and managers use technology.

An airy use of a four-column grid

This text-intensive newsletter is designed for information system professionals. The task was to present long technical articles in an inviting and impressive way.

The designer accomplished his task with abundant white space and large dithered graphics set at the bottom of each inner spread. To heighten the impression of a casual, graphic presentation, he set the text with a ragged bottom, varying the length of each text block.

As a counterpoint, the repeating black bar at the top reinforces the appearance of structure and consistency.

SmartAlerts
March, 1994

- Publisher: Andersen Consulting, Chicago, IL
- Designer: Brian Hughes, Electronic Media Services
- Colors: Black and dark greenish gray (PMS 5487)
- Type: Futura, Palatino
- Dimensions: 8½ by 11

An illustrated four-column
Medical newsletters like this
one often use anatomical
illustrations to explain
complex concepts to lay
readers. Note the consistency
in the artwork, in terms of
size, style and annotation.

The four-column grid helps
serve the goal of facilitating
communication, since the
short text lines make for fast
reading.

This newsletter is also typical
of many other medical
newsletters in that it is
published by a large
association, but is usually
distributed locally by
independent practitioners
who add their own imprint.

Sports Medicine Today
1993

- Publisher: American Academy of
  Orthopaedic Surgeons,
  Rosemont, IL
- Designers: Deborah Fisher,
  Pamela Hutton
- Colors: Black and pale blue
  (PMS 542)
- Type: Gill Sans
- Dimensions: 8½ by 11

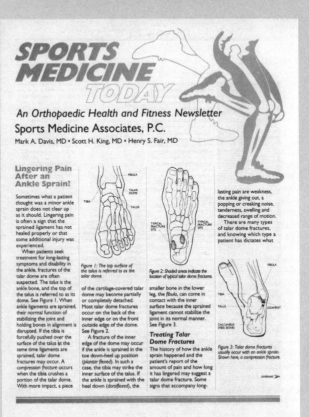

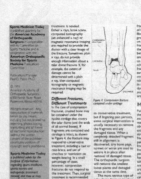

GOVERNMENT
finance reporter

A SERVICE PROVIDED BY PADGETT, STRATEMANN & CO., L.L.P.

January/February 1994

Donald H. Cormie, CPA, is a partner with Padgett, Stratemann & Co., L.L.P. Don has over 30 years' experience working with government and not-for-profit industries, including municipal, county, school district, and not-for-profit clients.

Are You Prepared for Disaster?

Disasters – whether they are natural or man-made, both local government units must be prepared to deal with their effects. After all, an important mission of government is public health and safety.

Be Prepared To Act Quickly

Too often, government bodies are not prepared for disasters. Consider the Los Angeles riots following the Rodney King jury verdict in state court. It is a lesson in how quickly a disaster can develop:

Four hours – 240 minutes. That's all the time it took for central Los Angeles to erupt into a violent state of anarchy.

Four hours – Half of a normal work shift. That's all the time it took for control of central Los Angeles to be surrendered to looters and arsonists.

After the Los Angeles riots, the actions of the city government were carefully reviewed. According to the Christopher Commission, the riots could have been contained with proper planning, commitment of resources and decisive leadership within the Los Angeles Police Department.

The purpose of this article is not to indict the L.A.P.D., but to point out some important lessons that we can learn from the violence.

The L.A.P.D.'s failure to act and its poor performance during the critical early minutes of the uprising is an object lesson in how not to deal with civil disorder. The department's key failures: neglect from the top, an invisible plan, a fatal retreat, failure to regroup, and hesitating to act as the city began burning.

Determining Responsibility in Advance

Amidst the debris that Hurricane Andrew left behind were some important questions about handling a natural disaster: Who should be giving the orders? Who should pick up the bill?

The storm left people without the basic needs for survival; they were exposed to the elements; they were hungry and thirsty. The Federal Emergency Management Agency (FEMA), whose mission is to provide assistance to victims of natural disaster,

PADGETT, STRATEMANN & CO., L.L.P.
CERTIFIED PUBLIC ACCOUNTANTS
1635 N.E. Loop 410, Suite 700 ~ San Antonio, Texas 78209-1684
(210) 828-6281 ~ Fax (210) 826-8606

Does Your Office Need an Accounting Manual?

An office accounting manual can clear up confusion and cut down on waste. Each governmental office should develop its own manual, tailored to their specific needs. To ensure that it is as clear and efficient as possible, the manual should include input from both management and staff. Once it is created, someone should be assigned the task of keeping it up-to-date.

Governmental bodies can be large bureaucratic mazes. Confusion and misunderstanding often leads to significant waste of community resources and in stress for those serving the public. One tool for fighting bureaucratic confusion and misunderstanding is the accounting manual.

When used correctly, the accounting manual provides the following:

• quick references
• instructions for training new people
• a document of the office's control system
• increased effectiveness and efficiency
• legal protection
• documentation for filing
• answers to all those questions seldom ask.

Describing Operations

The size of the manual and the information included varies by level. However, the contents must be informative, useful, easy to read and understand, and kept up-to-date. Start the manual with a statement outlining management's philosophy and operating style to let the staff know what quality standards are expected and how management operates.

An organizational chart provides an overall picture and lets the staff and new employees know where they fit. Also include a list of key people within your organization as well as industrial employees and their responsibilities in the manual.

The manual could also contain internal control documentation and methods of assigning responsibilities. If possible, set up the information in the form of a flow chart or dialogue. Use standard methods that are labeled with each person and their allotted tasks. The flow chart is graphic evidence for the staff about what they do and how it affects other people.

If in dialogue form, make sure internal control documentation is in a detailed narrative describing the flow of information through the system. In either format, include descriptions of outside influences and steps to follow when staff is handling specific situations.

Outlining Tasks

A beneficial accounting manual offers information to help the staff do their jobs without interrupting their supervisors with routine questions. It might be useful to include a chart of accounts, an explanation of how transactions are posted throughout the accounting records and recurring journal entries.

This kind of information can prevent mistakes and help the entire office work as a single unit. Including actual examples of recurring journal entries can assist new employees who may later benefit by remembering the correct way to post an entry.

An explanation of where records are maintained, what records are automated and examples of forms used to access documents will help in training new staff or temporaries. A clear definition of employees' tasks and how authority is delegated will aid in training new employees and temporary staff.

Policy and Procedures

Include information on restrictions, city ordinances, and budget policies and procedures pertaining to your particular government unit in the manual. It will become a

quick reference so that the staff will be prepared to answer questions reliably.

An accounting manual provides a staff section outlining general office policies and procedures covering insurance, vacation time, holidays, sick leave, report of office systems and other information that the staff would need to know about their employees and their job. This section helps avoid any misunderstanding and is an aid to any staff that is afraid or unsure about asking on this information.

Although much of the accounting and office work is computerized, a large amount of the work force is still not completely computer literate. A special reference section on computers will be helpful. However, it should not be cluttered with information that will not be used or will overwhelm the user. Templates, procedures, basic commands and hardware-specific commands such as print

"Designing a manual by flow of transactions is probably the most functional method"

sittings will save your staff time, not to mention, headaches, when using their computers.

Organizing Your Manual

There are several ways to organize your manual: by functional relationship category, by kinds and account groups or by flow of transactions. When setting the manual up by financial statement categories or by kinds and account groups, handle each group separately. Designing a manual by flow of transactions is probably the most functional method.

Accounting Manual

because it gives the staff an overall picture of how the system works. This method leaves public need through the system until it is accomplished and routed.

For a manual to be effective, it must be kept up-to-date. To accomplish this, make one person responsible for updating the manual. The manual should be kept in a three-ring binder or similar binding system so pages can be added, deleted or replaced as needed. If a manual is outdated, it will cause confusion and frustration. A section of the manual should address this problem with

updating instructions and responsibilities.

An Important Office Tool

These are merely suggestions for an accounting manual, and every office's manual should be tailored to its specific needs. To create the most useful accounting manual possible, management and staff should work together, brainstorming possible ideas. With just a little time and thought, the office can have a clear, efficient and helpful tool. We can help you document your endeavors in providing this useful tool. Please call us for assistance.

Adding slightly offbeat touches to a standard layout
Here's another professional newsletter designed for customization by individual practices. This one is set up so accountants can also add a portrait photo.

A few well-chosen design devices make this four-column design look loose and and contemporary. The most obvious devices are the use of a geometric typeface in the nameplate and headlines and the centered footers with their vertical bars.

But the way in which the columns are filled (or not filled) probably has more to do with the overall effect. For example, the headlines are inset into the opening of each story. That helps to break up an area that would otherwise be a solid block of body text. Large pullquotes and graphics balance the headline on the opposite side of the spread.

Government Finance Reporter
January/February, 1994
• Publisher: Practice Development Institute, Chicago, IL
• Designer: Practice Development Institute
• Colors: Black and deep green (PMS 3415)
• Type: Industria, Bodoni
• Dimensions: 8½ by 11

News magazine styling

Strong department heads and kickers, decks, frequent sidebars and bullet lists, dense layouts, abundant photos and graphic illustrations—these are common elements in many news and computer magazines. That approach is used here in a four-column newsletter for home office workers.

It's not easy to balance so many elements and pack this much text into a page. The designer relied on the four-column grid to keep items organized and a variety of rules and tint boxes to keep areas separated.

Work at Home, Michigan edition
Winter, 1994

- Publisher: Ameritech, Hoffman Estates, IL
- Designer: Doreen Maddox
- Colors: Black, purple (PMS 2755) and green (PMS 569)
- Type: Futura, Bodoni, Times
- Dimensions: 8 by 10½

Ruth Bassett, a childhood friend of Charles Gates Dawes' son, Rufus, wears a fashionable dress from the early teens.

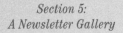

Evanston Architect Lawrence B. Perkins

A home designed by Ernest A. Mayo at 1720 Forest Avenue.

Tennis players at the Evanston Country Club.

A mixed format based on a four-column grid
This series of newsletter covers demonstrates how a single grid can be used to spawn a variety of pages that look very different yet fairly consistent.

In most cases, four columns of text are set to reflect the underlying grid. But the cover that uses two columns of text doesn't appear inconsistent with the others. That's partly because these text columns fall within some of the same grid lines. But it's also because other trademark items remain consistent, such as the flush-right headlines set to the upper left and the focus on historical photos in each story.

TimeLines
Spring, Summer and Fall issues, 1993
- Publisher: The Evanston Historical Society, Evanston, IL
- Designer: McGuire Associates
- Color: Very deep green (PMS 5463) on speckled off-white paper
- Type: Times Roman, Unives Condensed Bold
- Dimensions: 8½ by 11

Visual playfulness

These newsletters have very different looks but share a few distinctive traits. Certainly, both feature very unusual and memorable nameplates. What else makes these adventurous layouts somehow similar?

They both use dramatic, page-length bleeds, for one. They use a variety of graphic and design devices to steal attention away from the underlying grids—and to create an impression of dynamic change. And in each case, non-body type is set in unusual sizes or orientations to create eye-catching entry points to the articles on each spread.

Center News
Fall, 1994
- Publisher: The Center for Enriched Living, Deerfield, IL
- Designer: Todd Germann, Emphasis Seven Communications, Inc.
- Colors: Black and yellow (PMS 116)
- Type: Galliard
- Dimensions: 8½ by 11

Technology Assessment
Number 1, 1994

- Publisher: Andersen Consulting, Chicago, IL
- Designer: Brian Hughes, Electronic Media Services
- Colors: Black and purple (PMS 520)
- Type: Futura, Palatino
- Dimensions: 8½ by 11

A squarish format

Sometimes an unusual page shape can really set a newsletter apart from the crowd. But the shape of the page isn't the only thing that makes this publication stand out.

The pictorial cover sets the tone: this newsletter is upscale, reminiscent of finely designed magazines. The simple, understated banner creates an elegant look and blends into the cover photo. Large, sharp photos are used throughout with big bold captions. Headlines, indented just a bit to the left, break the grid ever so slightly.

Garden Talk
March, 1994

- Publisher: Chicago Horticultural Garden, Glencoe, IL
- Designers: Nancy Snyder, Victoria Lata
- Colors: Black and deep green (PMS 568)
- Type: Bodoni, Univer, Baskerville
- Dimensions: 9 by 10½

A brochure-like folder
With this complex fold and the perforated reader-reply cards, you might think this newsletter is a promotional piece. But it's actually an internal newsletter—that is, it was aimed at facilitating communications with corporate employees.

One of the most striking aspects of the design is the vertical nameplate, set in its own panel. It unfolds to the left to reveal a single-column article underneath.

Connections
January, 1992
- Publisher: Motorola C & E, Schaumburg, IL
- Designer: Sue Niggemann, Lee Hill, Inc.
- Colors: Cool gray 10 and teal (PMS 3272)
- Type: Univers Condensed
- Dimensions (folded): 7⅜ by 11

Large-format photo layouts

The dramatic photo layouts in this tabloid-sized newsletter aren't just beautiful examples of graphic design. They're very functional.

The designer knows that photos like these can communicate the concerns of the organization better than the accompanying text. And given the large page size, the photos appear life-size, which makes them all the more compelling.

To heighten the sense of urgency, heads are often set in typewriter faces like Courier, reminiscent of a personally written letter.

CARE Global Review
Winter, 1993
- Publisher: CARE
- Designer: Richard Berry
- Colors: Black and a different earth toned color each issue (this one a beige, PMS 453)
- Type: Adobe Garamond, Courier
- Dimensions: 11 by 17

A PLEA FOR PEACE IN SOMALIA • ESREY NAMED NEW CORPORATE COUNCIL CHAIR • CARE MOVING TO ATLANTA • CITY OF JOY

CARE Global Review

A Newsletter for Friends of CARE   Volume 2 Number 2   Winter 1993

Well before the press placed the plight of Somali famine victims on the front pages, CARE was hard at work in Somalia, as we have been for 10 years. When violence escalated and conditions worsened, CARE took the lead in calling for action from the world's leaders. Through congressional hearings last spring, through Dr. Philip Johnston's media interviews, and through high-level meetings with government and NGO officials, CARE warned of the devastation awaiting Somalia— and advocated effective international response.

This issue of Global Review focuses on the famine in Somalia. In October, Philip Johnston accepted the role of the United Nations' coordinator of humanitarian assistance in Somalia. Through this assignment he has gained an even deeper understanding of the problems of the country and has become an architect of its rehabilitation program.

CARE has committed considerable staff, funds and attention to relief and rehabilitation efforts in Somalia.

In an effort to cast a personal light on Somalia's crisis, we bring to you journal excerpts from Dr. Johnston's days in Somalia, an opinion piece published in *Freedom Review*, a glimpse at plans to rehabilitate Somalia, and dramatic photographs taken for CARE by artist Jacques Lowe.

A Plea for Peace in Somalia

Editor's Note: This article first appeared in Freedom Review, *a journal commenting on foreign affairs, politics and issues affecting democratic institutions. Philip Johnston, CARE's President, has been in Somalia since late October on a special assignment as the United Nations' chief coordinator of humanitarian assistance.*

By Philip Johnston, Ph.D.,
CARE President

In the careful understatement of diplomatic-speak, the U.N. resolution authorizing military intervention in Somalia noted the "unique character of the situation . . ."

It is indeed unique for the entire underpinnings of a society to disappear, replaced by random violence and mass starvation. We have seen famines before, including many spurred by civil war. We have also operated in the shadow of brutal regimes. But never, in

my memory, has government been entirely absent for an extended period.

This, ultimately, is the "unique character" of the crisis in Somalia and it is one of the reasons the United States finally decided to act. It is unfortunate the decision came many months after it was needed. Hundreds of thousands have died in agony, and those deaths were entirely preventable. But, finally, the world has decided to act, and that can only be applauded.

The roots of the Somalia crisis can be traced at least partially to the superpower confrontation and the massive arms build-up of the 1970s and 80s. It is difficult to speculate how these events helped create or promote any of the individual factions now battling for control of Somalia. But one thing is for certain: each one possesses a frightening level of firepower that has turned a political stalemate into well-

Continued on page 3: Plea for Peace

A large-format staff newsletter

With 16 very large pages, this newsletter packs a lot of information in every issue. The key to its success in terms of design is its strong sense of structure. Except for very long articles that fill an entire page, most articles are set in clearly defined horizontal spaces with text set in four narrow columns for quick reading. Heavy color rules and color drop caps help guide the eye across the large spaces.

Like many staff letters, this one uses plenty of portrait photos. Most of the photos seem quite casual and are cropped to provide just a hint of the worker's environs. Also note the arrangements of individual shots on the opposite page. They're well-organized, yet are varied in shape and position; the slightly irregular arrays create interesting and pleasing compositions.

Tablet
October, 1993

- Publisher: The University of Chicago Medical Center, Chicago, IL
- Designer: Dan Fergus
- Colors: Black and dark teal (PMS 3288)
- Type: Univers Condensed, Bodoni
- Dimensions: 11 by 17

Tablet

The University of Chicago
Hospitals
*Bernard Mitchell Hospital
Chicago Lying-in Hospital
Wyler Children's Hospital*
**The Division of the
Biological Sciences**
The Pritzker School of Medicine

October 1993

THE
UNIVERSITY
OF
CHICAGO
MEDICAL
CENTER

Inside

A gift of $1 million from the Eisenberg Foundation for Charities has endowed the George M. Eisenberg Professorship in Geriatrics. Learn more about the late Mr. Eisenberg and the geriatrics program at the Hospitals on page 3.

When Ron Katz's parents formed the Teen Group in his memory, they served the needs of young cancer patients to meet and share the tribulations and victories of cancer treatment. Read about the goals and activities of this lively group on page 6.

Edwin Ferguson, PhD, has been named a Pew Scholar in the Biomedical Sciences for 1993. The award of $200,000 will help Dr. Ferguson establish his laboratory and further his research. A description of Dr. Ferguson's research accompanies a summary of his distinguished academic career on page 11.

Did you know that . . .

The Hospitals' active volunteer program encompasses close to 400 members of the community who have donated approximately 3,000 hours of service in 1993.

Hospitals recognize 12 with Employee of the Year honors

This year, for the first time in the history of the award, all 12 finalists were selected to be Employees of the Year. Sixty employees in all were nominated by fellow employees, patients, and visitors because they exhibited the five values emphasized by the Hospitals' Pride campaign: respect, honesty, excellence, participation, and unity.

Four finalists were selected from Patient Services:

Lora Armstrong, RPh, is Director of Drug Information Services for Pharmaceutical Services and has been with

Lora Armstrong, RPh

the Hospitals since 1982. "Lora is a problem solver and a fine clinician," said Roger Dean, Assistant Director of Pharmaceutical Services, Assistant Professor of Clinical Pediatrics, and the 1992 Employee of the Year. Citing Ms. Armstrong's leadership role, Mr. Dean called her excellent judgment a "beacon in tough situations."

Ms. Armstrong researches the thousands of drugs available to Hospitals physicians, gives advice on which drug to use and at what doses and warns of potential side effects.

Of the five Pride campaign values, Ms. Armstrong believes that respect is particularly important. "When we respect the patients we treat, we are more inclined to provide quality medical care," she said. "I respect my patients and am committed to giving them the best drug care possible."

Shadrach Goodloe, Lead Porter in the General Operating Rooms (GOR) for Environmental Services, celebrates his 20th anniversary of service to the Hospitals this year. His award citation praised his high degree of honesty and personal integrity. Mr. Goodloe is a role model for new and experienced employees alike, his citation states.

As GOR Lead Porter, Mr. Goodloe supervises a nine-person Environmen-

Shadrach Goodloe

tal Services team made up of "some of the finest workers in the department," he said. Above all, his staff must practice and promote honesty. "In the GOR, we need the highest standards of cleanliness," Mr. Goodloe said. "There might be someone else on that operating table today, but I know it could be me, or someone close to me, tomorrow. I need to know that my staff has cleaned everything properly. I need to inspire honesty so that I know I can trust everyone when they tell me they've done their job."

Debra Johnson is Unit Secretary for 5NW Nursing and has been a Hospitals' employee since 1981. The unit nursing staff nominated her for Em-

continued on page 2

Summer research scholarships expanded for minority students

The Pritzker School of Medicine, with funding from the National Heart, Lung and Blood Institute, expanded its summer research program to include more minority students.

The Institute's training grant added 10 minority student slots to the 28 traineeships funded by the National Institutes of Health and the 22 funded by the University's Biological Sciences Division. The new traineeships are open not only to current or entering medical students at Pritzker but also to any college junior or senior who is interested in science and has competitive grades.

Cultivating students' interest in research represents the first step in a national effort to increase minority representation on medical school faculties. "We need to get minority students into the academic pipeline," says Norma Wagoner, PhD, Dean of Students in the Pritzker School of Medicine. Minorities currently make up only five percent of US medical school faculties.

The program aims to give the student experience in independent

research, working on a real project with a faculty adviser.

"I greatly appreciated the opportunity to work with a minority physician who turned out to be a great mentor," said Travan Jasper, who last summer did research on cardiac imaging in the laboratory of Kim Williams, MD, Associate Professor in the Departments of Medicine and Radiology. "It's an experience I would strongly recommend."

Research opportunities are offered in all areas of molecular medicine, with special emphasis on heart, lung, and blood diseases. The research

Kirk Chattanapaund, third year student in the College and a Native American, received a minority scholarship for summer research. Under the supervision of his faculty advisor Andrea Sant, PhD, Assistant Professor of Pathology and in the Committee on Immunology, Mr. Chattanapaund is looking for reasons some proteins appear on the surface of cells where they can be detected and destroyed by antibodies, while others remain undetected inside the cell.

experience is augmented with biweekly workshops and seminars in which students meet to discuss their laboratory work with other participants and faculty.

This summer's program ran from the third week in June through the first week in September. Students receive a $2,500 stipend plus a travel allowance to Chicago. Applicants had to be US citizens or permanent residents and members of an underrepresented minority—African-American, Hispanic, Native or Alaskan American, or Pacific Islander.

Just Say "Thanks"

Employees of the Year

Eisenberg Foundation contributes $1 million to geriatrics

Hospitals join broad-based effort that saves Medicaid funding

Five appointed Vice President

Special Events

Newscapsules

Appointments

Looking Ahead

Kudos

Pediatric Trauma Statistics

The effect of color

Both of these designs are well-structured, easy to read and very effective. The fact of the matter is that these designs are strong enough to look great even when printed in a single ink: black. So what's gained by adding color?

Quite a bit. That's why we're showing these examples both in monochrome and in the colors in which they're actually printed. It's interesting to see exactly what color can add to a design.

The upper example is a very simple two-color design that uses a bright, punchy red. It's a good example of a design where color headlines work well. That's partly due to the choice of color, partly due to the heavy typeface.

The lower example is an expertly created four-color (CMYK) design. The mixture of crisp type with full-color illustrations and photos on a bright white stock makes this customer-oriented newsletter vibrant and fun to leaf through.

CHICAGO CHILD CARE SOCIETY

NEWS

FALL 1993

A QUARTERLY REPORT TO THE FRIENDS OF CCCS

Facepainting was one of the highlights of the annual summer family picnic of the Child and Family Development Center

The Bare Essentials of Parenting

Being a mother does not come naturally. For some—overwhelming difficulties, such as addictions, depression, poverty and violence, lack of community resources, ineffective role models—add to the circumstances that can lead to abuse or neglect of children.

Families in CCCS's Family Stabilization and Protective Day Care program have been referred by the Department of Children and Family Services and must attend a parent support group because of child abuse or neglect.

Wanting a more directive approach to some issues with which they were struggling, the "mothers' group" helped design the curriculum for a ten-week course titled "The Bare Essentials of Parenting." Caseworker **Pat Guilford** and Director of Counseling **Diane Scruggs** led the lively, weekly sessions dealing with parenting and the real-life situations that led to their inability to parent effectively. Each week the "moms" also attended a "class" with their child, reinforcing new skills through

real interactions. Learning to distinguish between discipline and abuse, to manage anger and deal with stress, and to set goals and build upon strengths were part of the coursework. Notebooks with assignments and required readings were proudly maintained. Graduation included diplomas and taped congratu...

Child Advocate of the Year... Ken Watson

Ken Watson, Associate Director of Chicago Child Care Society, was named *Child Advocate of the Year* for 1992 by the North American Council on Adoptable Children (NACAC). Giving the keynote address before the 17th annual NACAC Conference in Ottawa, Canada, Ken identified some current challenges in adoption. "More children and more difficult children are entering the child welfare system [and they] are coming from more disorganized and chaotic families..."

A second challenge, driven by finances, is the apparent split in streams of adoption "with voluntary or private agencies placing [healthy] white infants and public agencies taking more and more responsibility for special needs children."

This leads to a third challenge, that of funding. "[W]ith no firm funding base, once again we're seeing that often getting a child, especially a white infant, depends upon power or money." There is "no justification for any agency charging a fee for any adoption. The client of the agency is the child. Any time money exchanges hands in an adoption, I think a child is being sold, whatever the...

4 Close-up of UPS in Europe

6 The answer people — UPS Package Testing Labs

8 How to use new GroundTrac

Plus:
- Best-service tips for air shipments to Hawaii, last-minute shipments to anywhere
- A Canada quiz
- UPS technology news
...and more

UPS **RoundUPS**

Summer 1992 · Published quarterly for customers and friends of United Parcel Service

New UPS Authorized Return Service

The possibilities are as varied as the businesses served by UPS. What products or components would your company like to efficiently retrieve?
- Packaging or custom containers to recycle
- Unsold merchandise to restock, resell
- Products to repair or replace

Whatever it is you want to recover, new UPS Authorized Return Service can make the task almost automatic.

UPS developed A.R.S. in response to the needs of many customers who are facing new logistical problems in light of several trends impacting producers and shippers.

Current practices and legislation related to heightened environmental awareness are leading companies to retrieve items that, formerly, customers would discard.

Today's focus on customer service places high value on a convenient prepaid return service for customers. A.R.S. can increase customer loyalty, improve satisfaction, and help build a company's reputation for social responsibility and quality service. *(continued on page 2)*

U.K. acquisition completes European network

With the acquisition of Carryfast Limited, announced June 29, UPS will now provide domestic ground service throughout the United Kingdom. This is in addition to already established UPS international air services to and from every address in the U.K.

UPS now has intra-country ground delivery in every major European market and pan-European ground and air delivery for both packages and freight.

Carryfast, the largest privately owned package delivery company in the U.K., will add to UPS operating capacity 350 vehicles and 900 experienced employees. Today, UPS's work force in Europe totals more than 20,000. Page 4 inside this issue of RoundUPS gives an overview of UPS's European operations.

Chicago Child Care Society News
Fall, 1993
- Publisher: Chicago Child Care
  Society, Chicago, IL
- Designer: Deborah Ryder,
  Deborah Ryder Design
- Colors: Black and red (PMS 1788)
- Type: Bodoni Poster Condensed,
  Gill Sans Condensed, Imago Extra
  Bold, Novarese Book
- Dimensions: 9 by 12

RoundUPS
Summer, 1992
- Publisher: United Parcel Service
- Designer: Don Cassel,
  Don Cassel Group
- Colors: Process
- Type: Helvetica Light and Black
- Dimensions: 8½ by 11

The power of simple color accents

Graphics set in solid spot colors can both break up big blocks of text and create a sense of structural unity.

In the example on this page, the blue sawtooth border not only repeats on each page—it stretches all the way across the inside spread. Blue also appears in the drop caps and the dotted rules separating the columns.

The Cradle Newsletter
March, 1994

- Publisher: The Cradle, Evanston, IL
- Designers: Ed Gibbs, Lou Maningo, Grant/Jacoby
- Colors: Black, process blue
- Type: Antique Olive, Nord
- Dimensions: 8½ by 11

SUMMER 1993

GRASS ROOTS

GOVERNOR '94

Published by Taxpayers for Quinn, 676 N. LaSalle, Chicago, IL 60610, 312-943-1789 (Not paid for at government expense)

Rally for Change July 24

Let's face it ...

Government just doesn't work for us anymore.

Many Illinois citizens now work longer hours for less money, and have less time to spend with family and friends.

Meanwhile, the rising cost of government is threatening to tax working families into poverty.

It's time to change the way Illinois government does business. It's time to make sure Illinois government does the taxpayer's business.

Send a message to politicians who believe that government is the exclusive province of a selected few lobbyists, political insiders and big donors.

Join us on July 24 for a Rally for Change!

You are invited to join Pat Quinn in the kick-off of an exciting campaign which will shake up Illinois government forever.

Join Pat as he begins yet another battle to make Illinois government more responsive and open. And he's just the person who can get that job done.

Pat Quinn has made open government his trademark. He's led sweeping citizen

movements to cut the size of the legislature, end advance pay for politicians, fight utility rate gouging and battle for hard-pressed property taxpayers.

People Power. That's how Pat led the 1990 ticket despite being outspent 4 to 1, and that's how he's going to run his campaign in 1994.

People Power. That means you—Pat's long-time supporters, new friends and anyone who wants a change.

Join us in the forefront of a new citizens movement, one that can sweep through the halls of the State Capitol.

Take Back Your Government. Join us on July 24 in a citizen movement and a Rally for Change. Remember, a strong turnout will sound the opening bell of a new fight for control of our government!

RALLY DIRECTIONS

Rally for change! Bring your family and friends! Free admission & refreshments!

Saturday, July 24 10:00 am Fenwick High School Cafeteria 505 W. Washington Oak Park

Take I-290 to Harlem exit, go north on Harlem. At Washington Blvd., turn right (east). Fenwick High School is approximately one mile down the road, just east of Oak Park Avenue.

Free parking in the back. For information... Call 312-943-1789

VOTERS SHOUT "YES" FOR PLAIN LANGUAGE STATE SENATE MUMBLES "NO"

PAT NEEDS YOUR HELP!

to plain talk, keep it simple.
—CHICAGO SUN-TIMES Editorial

WANT TO BE "QUINN–NECTED"! JOIN THE FAX TREE !

QUINN'S PROGRAMS: DOING MORE WITH LESS

"A three and a half-bedroom home, a fenced-in yard and a short ride to work—all for a $500 down payment and a savings of $100 a month off her rent."
—PEORIA JOURNAL-STAR
Referring to Peoria resident Becky Faulon

"Now students who weren't enthusiastic about math class look forward to it"
—MARTHA SUTTON
Bank-at-School teacher at Millburn School, Chicago Tribune

Graphic relief

There are few heavier topics than politics and taxes. That's what this campaign newsletter was all about. But the designer did a great job of lightening the tone of this piece without making it seem frivolous.

The border pattern on the front cover subtly echoes the "grass-roots" theme, as does the second color. The custom illustrations throughout enliven the articles and do wonders for making the three-column format look airy and interesting.

Grass Roots
Winter, 1994

- Publisher: Taxpayers for Quinn, Chicago, IL
- Designer/Illustrator: Estelle Carol, Carol★Simpson Productions
- Colors: Black and green (PMS 355)
- Type: Stone Sans, Garamond
- Dimensions: 8½ by 11

Conservative color design
There's nothing wrong with using color conservatively. In fact, it's often a good idea, especially when a newsletter focuses on weighty topics or acts as the primary publication of a large association or corporation.

This national newsletter uses one of the organization's two official colors in a strong but controlled way. As far as type goes, only subheads are set in the second color. In general, the official purple is only used for graphic devices, such as header bars, sidebar backgrounds and some illustrations.

Alzheimer's Association Newsletter
Winter, 1993
- Publisher: Alzheimer's Association
- Designer: Marjie Best, Best Design
- Colors: Black and purple (PMS 2685)
- Type: Garamond Condensed, Optima
- Dimensions: 8½ by 11

NEWSLETTER
VOLUME 13 NO. 4 WINTER 1993

ALZHEIMER'S ASSOCIATION

Someone to Stand by You

Young-Onset Cases On the Rise, Experts Report

Alfred Pridgeon was 47 years old when he began showing signs of the disease. Pictured with him are his wife Hilda and sons Mark and Ryan.

According to doctors, the number of diagnosed cases of younger people with Alzheimer's disease (AD) is increasing, striking people at the peak of their career and childrearing years.

"While most people are diagnosed in their 60s, 70s and 80s, an increasing number are being identified in their 40s and 50s," says Leonard Berg, M.D., chair of the Association's Medical & Scientific Advisory Board, who refers to younger cases as "young-onset" or "early-onset" AD. Various estimates place their proportion at anywhere from one to 10 percent of all people with AD — or from 40,000 to 400,000 people in the U.S.

Young-onset AD is not a new phenomenon. It's been around long before Alois Alzheimer discovered the debilitating brain disease in 1906. But in recent years researchers have made dramatic progress in their understanding of the nature and symptoms of Alzheimer's disease, contributing to the increase in diagnosed young-onset AD.

"We have a much better idea of the clinical picture of the disease compared to just 10 years ago," says Dr. Berg. "Because we're able to make a more accurate clinical diagnosis of AD, we now recognize it more readily in younger patients." A *definitive* diagnosis of Alzheimer's disease can only be achieved through examining brain tissue during an autopsy (see *The Benefits of An Autopsy*, p. 9). As diagnostic techniques have improved, more older people are being diagnosed, as well, says Berg.

Another reason for the rise in young-onset cases: increased public awareness of AD.

"Alzheimer's disease was not exactly a hot topic 20 years ago," says Berg. "But today, AD ranks with cancer and heart disease in terms of awareness and concern for getting the illness." A recent survey conducted by The Gallup Organization for the Alzheimer's Association found that one in three people say they know someone with Alzheimer's disease, and many are concerned about getting it.

The social toll of early-onset
The behavioral symptoms of AD are much the same no matter what the person's age. But the middle-aged person with AD is different from the older patient.

Unlike the older-diagnosed person who's approaching or past retirement, the younger person is often faced with having to quit his or her job early and resign from family responsibilities all too soon.

(Please turn to page 9)

Clinton's Health Care Reform
see page 3

HEALTH SECURITY

UNITED STATES OF AMERICA

HIGHLIGHTS:

President Puts Alzheimer's High on National Health Reform Agenda 3

Alzheimer Research: What Progress Are We Making? 4

Safe Return Program Works 7

LETTER FROM THE CHAIRMAN

Promising Research Needs More Funding

The *Newsletter* is a quarterly publication produced and distributed by the Alzheimer's Association. For additional information regarding the *Newsletter* contact Emily Miller, editor. (312) 335-8762.

For more information on Alzheimer's disease and support services available through the Alzheimer's Association, call our toll-free Information and Referral Line, (800) 272-3900.

During the past decade, the Alzheimer's Association provided $27 million to fund 900 different Alzheimer research projects. Thanks to the generous support of our donors, the pace of Alzheimer research is accelerating. Scientists are now confident that — with adequate funding — we will find the causes of Alzheimer's disease within the next ten years.

However, today the Alzheimer's Association is able to fund only 20 percent of the research proposals that we want to support. Put another way, we are unable to fund 80 percent of the most promising Alzheimer research studies.

Year after year, we have increased the amount of funding we can provide for research. In addition, we have successfully advocated for federal funding for Alzheimer research. In fact, President Clinton's proposed health reform plan specifically includes Alzheimer's disease, along with cancer and AIDS, as a priority area of medical research. Furthermore, Congress is

close to approving $305 million in Alzheimer research for next year — an increase of $14 million over this year. But we need at least $500 million annually if we are to conquer this disease.

Right now, many of the best minds in medical research are involved in Alzheimer research. We read about exciting new studies every week. But researchers need funding to continue their work, or else could be forced to abandon it.

We will continue to press for adequate federal funding for Alzheimer research. But we also count upon the compassion and generosity of friends such as you. I urge you to continue, and even expand, your support for Alzheimer research.

We cannot conquer Alzheimer's disease without you.

Stuart C. Berk
Chairman

HEALTH REFORM UPDATE

President Puts Alzheimer's High on National Health Reform Agenda

Health Insurance Card for Clinton's health care plan

In a televised speech to Congress and the nation on September 22, President Clinton brought Alzheimer's disease into the middle of the health care debate. Alzheimer families who have mobilized nationwide to draw attention to their needs found affirmation in the President's call for comprehensive long term care for the elderly and disabled, and expedited funding for Alzheimer research.

The President reiterated his commitment to long term care in response to a question from Alzheimer caregiver and Association representative Jean Parker in a nationally broadcast town meeting in Tampa. And in the opening round of Congressional hearings on health reform, Hillary Rodham Clinton repeatedly stated that long term care is an essential part of the full plan, "because it is right, it preserves families, it preserves dignity, and it saves money."

"The President has changed the nature of the health care debate," Association chairman Stuart Berk noted. "He has clearly heard the message of families dealing with chronic diseases like Alzheimer's, and he is saying that we too have a right to peace of mind and security."

Benefits of the health plan
The President proposes that severely disabled persons, including specifically those with cognitive impairment such as Alzheimer's disease, receive a flexible array of services at home and in the community. The program would pay not only for traditional home health services, but also for companions, respite, home modifications, day care, services in board-and-care homes, or any other service defined in an individual plan of

On September 22, 1993, President Clinton outlined his national health care proposal to the members of Congress.

care. Persons of all ages and income would receive benefits; those with incomes over 150% of poverty would pay a portion of the cost according to a sliding fee scale.

The new program would be phased in beginning in 1996. When fully implemented in the year 2000, more than $20 billion in home and community services would be available to persons who need them. In addition, states would continue

to provide community-based services for low income persons with less severe disabilities. And Medicaid would continue to cover nursing home care, with a new requirement allowing users people to qualify because of higher income and asset allowances for those who require such care.

More funds promised for research
President Clinton has made an equally strong case for Alzheimer research, pledging to "speed research on effective prevention and treatment for Alzheimer's as well as cancer, AIDS and heart disease."

In addition, health care benefits essential to persons with Alzheimer's disease, including diagnostic services, mental health services, and prescription drugs, would be part of the comprehensive benefit package for which all Americans will be insured.

"The President has pushed the door wide open and invited us onto the debate," noted Paul McGarry, Public Policy chair for the Association. "And the debate has just begun."

To hundreds of health care action parties across the country on October 21, the Alzheimer's Association launched a nationwide campaign to mobilize a strong and sustained outpouring of public sentiment to convince Congress that long term care and Alzheimer research must be part of any health care plan it enacts.

Casual color

Here's a slightly less conservative color design. The wide-ranging use of color (black isn't used at all) and the charming, loosely-drawn illustrations create a friendly, unintimidating first impression. But these elements don't appear frivolous. The piece is executed with skillful reserve, so the newsletter retains a solid, corporate dignity.

Benefit News
December, 1993

- Publisher: Baxter International, Deerfield, Illinois
- Designer/illustrator: Kathleen Aiken, Jeanmarie Powers, Jackie Geib
- Colors: Blue (PMS 3005) and teal (PMS 3275) on pale yellow paper
- Dimensions: 8 by 14

Adventures in color

These color designs are decidedly unconservative. Both use colors in big, bold ways to catch and hold your attention.

On the other hand, these newsletters take different approaches to the specific uses of color. The example on this page uses bright, bold colors in splashes, often to hold reversed type. The example on the opposite page uses less vibrant, but very distinctive, colors as a unifying backdrop for the entire newsletter.

Intellectual Ammunition
January/February, 1994

- Publisher: The Heartland Institute, Palatine, IL
- Designer: Joseph L. Bast
- Colors: Black, red (PMS 186) and SF ultra gloss intel yellow
- Type: Times New Roman, Century Schoolbook, Aachen Bold
- Dimensions: 8½ by 11

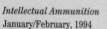

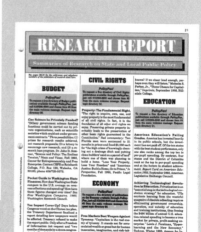

DesignDirections

WOMEN IN DESIGN CHICAGO

When Your Business Needs a Jump Start

LATE WINTER '94

For many designers, business during the first cold months of the new year can be a little, well...sluggish. With that in mind, we've put together a few ideas on productive ways to use any extra time you may have right now.

This is a good time to evaluate your current marketing strategies and refocus your efforts. The three main goals of any self-promotion effort are to inform potential clients of your existence, to demonstrate how you meet a client's needs, and to tell potential clients where and how they can purchase your services.

To make sure your marketing strategy is fulfilling these goals, set aside a block of time with a pencil and paper to really evaluate your "product." Identify the talents and skills that you possess that set you apart from your competitors. At this point, you should also note your weaknesses — and then don't worry about them. Focus on your strengths.

This soul-searching should help you to pinpoint your niche in the business: the type of projects you do best, the type of businesses you would like to work with, and perhaps even specific industries you should be targeting. At this point you can evaluate whether your current marketing tools (portfolio, stationery, brochures, even your sales pitch) mesh with the path you want your business to take. Careers evolve, and what worked for you a year ago, may not be right for you today.

Maintain and update your database of clients and prospects. If, throughout the year, you had been hurriedly jotting down possible contacts,

now is the perfect time to enter them into your rolodex (traditional or electronic). Fine-tune the details in your records, update phone numbers, addresses and contact names. And then contact those people. Don't neglect to follow up on an earlier introduction. Set a goal of a certain number of calls a day; as few as three new contacts a day will keep you busy and should bring in some new business soon.

Further your education. Adult education courses and seminars can help you polish business skills such as bookkeeping or conducting more effective sales presentations. Learn the latest on tax laws for small businesses or home offices. Broaden your artistic reach by studying the history of typography or the printing process, a sure way to spark that creative spirit that may be suffering from cabin fever. Be sure to talk to your fellow classmates: though you may not meet a new customer, everyone has friends, relatives and associates that they may refer to you. Another good idea is to take the time to read through those 400-page manuals that came with your new software or upgrades and experiment with techniques.

> The three main goals of any self-promotion effort are to inform potential clients of your existence, to demonstrate how you meet a client's needs, and to tell potential clients where and how they can purchase your services.

(continued on page 3)

Three colors?

Yes, both designs use three colors, but in different ways. The example on the opposite page uses three different inks on white paper. The example on this page uses two different inks on color paper.

These newsletters also provide plenty of other interesting comparisons: Note how differently headlines, department heads and story flow are handled!

Design Directions
Late Winter, 1994
- Publisher: Women in Design Chicago, Chicago, IL
- Designer: Leah Kadamian, Silver Image Creative
- Colors: Black and purple (PMS 513) on soft mauve paper; colors change each issue
- Type: Eurostile Condensed, Helvetica Condensed
- Dimensions: 8½ by 9½

Breaking all conventions
This newsletter, published by
a communication design firm,
certainly doesn't look much
like any other newsletters
we've featured in this book.

For one thing, it's cast in the
form of a promotional folder.
The nameplate is also quite
unusual—it's the entire front
panel of the folder, a simple
vertical type treatment
reversed out of a color that
changes every issue.

Journal
Various issues, 1991–1993
- Publisher: Agnew Moyer Smith,
  Inc., Pittsburgh, PA
- Designer: Norm Goldberg
- Colors: Black and one cover color
  (shown here: PMS 130, 200, 266,
  and 293)
- Type: Univers Condensed, Glypha,
  Janson
- Dimensions (folded): 3½ by 9¼

Surprise foldout

Here's another design that plays off the natural curiosity of people who feel compelled to unfold folded things. Like our previous example, the cover of this little newsletter doesn't say much, so one can't help but unfold the piece to scan the insides.

HealthWise
February-May, 1994
- Publisher: Barnes West County Hospital, St. Louis, MO
- Designers: Paul Boston and Dayne Sislen, Hughes Advertising
- Colors: Black and process magenta
- Type: Sabon, Helvetica Black; type ornaments: DF Primitive, DF Organ
- Dimensions (folded): 5½ by 8½

Nobody Cares For West County Like We Do

Area residents are discovering that the health resources they need are as close and convenient as Barnes West County Hospital.

Barnes West: Superior Care Made Simple
Barnes West County Hospital makes access to health care easy. The latest technology, advanced treatments, and more than 250 on-staff physicians are all nearby in this convenient community hospital.

Barnes West County Hospital offers a broad array of general medical and surgical services, including:

EMERGENCY CARE
Our emergency department is staffed 24 hours a day, offering a full range of services, including:

RADIOLOGY
Our newly renovated department has doubled in size, offering a full range of imaging services, including CT Scanning, Magnetic Resonance Imaging (MRI), ultrasound and nuclear medicine and a private mammography suite.

LABORATORY
Our fully-equipped laboratory provides testing in all services, with most test results available to your doctor the same day.

SPECIALIZED CENTERS
In conjunction with some of our outstanding physicians, many centers of medical expertise have been established at Barnes West County Hospital, including centers devoted to asthma, sports medicine, orthopedics, ophthalmology, cosmetic surgery, urology and rehabilitation.

COMMUNITY EDUCATION
Lectures, health screenings and special events held on the Barnes West campus keep the community healthy and informed. See the upcoming events listed in this newsletter.

For more information or a referral to a Barnes West County Hospital Physician, Dial DOC-TORS (362-8677) or toll-free 1-800-392-0936.

Cancer Test Trials: Two Life-Saving Opportunities

Barnes West County Hospital and Washington University School of Medicine are looking for people to participate in either of the following national trials of cancer screening tests.

PSA Screening For Prostate Cancer
We need men age 50 or over with no history of prostate cancer for a research study on the PSA (prostate specific antigen) blood test for prostate disease.

This study has already detected prostate cancer in hundreds of men and allowed for successful, early treatment. Participants who qualify will receive a blood test and rectal exam free of charge every six months for three years.

To sign up or receive more information, call Barnes Research at 362-4939.

PLCO Cancer Screenings
These trials will try to determine whether screenings for prostate, lung, colorectal and ovarian (PLCO) cancers save lives.

Some of the study participants will be randomly chosen to receive the following tests free of charge: rectal exam, sigmoidoscopy; chest x-ray; blood tests; and vaginal ultrasound (females only). The other participants will continue to receive their usual health care.

To participate in this study, you must be a man or woman age 60-74 years old with no history of prostate, lung, colorectal or ovarian cancer, and cannot be presently participating in any screening for these cancers.

To sign up for this important trial, call the PLCO Cancer Screening Center at (314)275-7526.

Healthy NEWS

(interior foldout panels)

February-May at Barnes West County

The A, B, Zs of Snoring & Sleep Apnea
Friday, February 25
10 a.m.–12 noon
JCCA Auditorium
2 Millstone Campus Drive
Dr. Jay Piccirillo, Otolaryngologist

Snoring could be a sign of sleep apnea, a serious medical condition that impairs normal breathing. If you or your spouse snore, learn about breathing and sleeping well beyond the snoring. Attend this lecture and learn about the causes, symptoms and treatment of sleep apnea.

Strategies For a Better Golf Game
Wednesday, March 16
7-9 p.m.
Jeff Smoltzen, ATC*, CSCS*

Jeff Smoltzen from The Sports Medicine Center will teach you first-hand... and strengthening exercises, and a local golf pro will provide tips to improve your game up to par or under it!

Tired of Counting Sheep? Treatments for Snoring & Sleep Apnea
Thursday, March 23
7-9 p.m.
Dr. Joseph Ojile, Pulmonologist

Snoring is no laughing matter. It could be a sign of sleep apnea, a serious breathing problem that can harm your health. Treatments not only with your own sleep, but... and your daily life. Come hear what treatments are available to help you to your snoring spouse are easy.

Lower Your Risk of Cancer Panel Discussion
Wednesday, April 13
7-9 p.m. — Cancer Prevention Health Fair
7-8 p.m. — Panel Discussion
Dr. Gerald Andriole, Urologist
Dr. Bruce Honghton, Otolaryngologist
Dr. Martha Schult, Surgical Oncologist
Dr. Erik Trpenen, Gastroenterologist

Join a team of cancer specialists for an informative discussion on evidence... your risk of cancer. Also hear about the Prostate, Lung, Colorectal and Ovarian (PLCO) Cancer Study currently being conducted at Barnes West County Hospital. 5-7 p.m., pick up information at our cancer prevention health fair.

Heel to Toe: Picking the Right Running Shoes
Wednesday, April 20
6:30-7 p.m. — Free shoe evaluations
7-8 p.m. — Lecture
John Motley, MS, ATC*, CSCS*

Running is an B.fitting shoe can indicate your finer fitness efforts. Learn how to pick the right running shoe to avoid discomfort and injury. Bring your current running shoes for a free evaluation of fit, comfort and wear pattern before the lecture.

Advances in Arthritis Treatments & Joint Replacements Panel Discussion
Wednesday, April 6
7-9 p.m.
Dr. Owen Kaeser, Rheumatologist
Dr. Lee Whiteside, Orthopedic Surgeon

Internationally renowned surgeon Dr. Lee Whiteside and Barnes-Jewish rheumatologist Dr. Owen Kaeser will lead this fascinating panel discussion. You'll be able to ask questions and learn about the latest trends in treating arthritis, including advanced replacements for hips and knees.

Knee & Joint Replacements
Thursday, March 10
7-9 p.m.
Dr. Robert Shively, Orthopedic Surgeon

Great strides have been made in replacements for the knee and other joints. Learn what they are doing to restore joint function today.

Sniffling & Sneezing: There Is Help
Wednesday, April 6
7-9 p.m.
Dr. Stanley Thawley, Otolaryngologist

Designed to help with one hand in the timely how? Get to the bottom of your sniffling and sneezing, and hear about treatments that can alleviate the possible symptoms of allergies or asthma.

Urological Problems As You Age
Thursday, May 5
7-9 p.m.
Dr. David Kartch, Urologist

As we age, many of us are affected by a loss of bladder control or urinary tract infections. Hear Dr. Kartch explain the causes of these problems and present remedies that can keep urinary problems from disrupting your lifestyle.

Midlife Women's Fan Club
Meet women only in the Private Dining Room of Barnes West County Hospital to learn about topics of interest to women. For more information or reservations, Dial DOC-TORS (362-8677).

Caring for Yourself While Caring for Your Aging Parent
Thursday, February 22
7-8:30 p.m.
Rose Mary, Licensed Clinical Social Worker

Menopause & Midlife, Women to Women
Thursday, March 29
7-8:30 p.m.
Open discussion among participants.

Barnes Plus Breakfast Series
Meet us in the cafeteria of Barnes West County Hospital for a light breakfast and presentation. We'll cover the latest medical news that often people age 55 and over. $3 fee at the door for all participants. Dial DOC-TORS (362-8677) or 1-800-392-0936.

Asthma News
Asthma Center Open House
Tuesdays, April 12
3-6:30 p.m.
Downtown Office Building
Suite 112

Adults with asthma and parents of children with asthma are invited to come and learn the facts about asthma and allergy treatment. An asthma specialist will be on hand to answer any questions. You can also register to win free prizes.

But since reservations or more information, Dial DOC-TORS (362-8677) or 1-800-392-0936.

New "In-HALE" Asthma Support Group
4-7:30 p.m., Thursdays
March 17 & May 19 — Barnes West County Hospital, Private Dining Room
February 24 & April 21 — Jewish Hospital, Brown Room

In-HALE (Having Asthma, Living Easier) is a free support group designed to educate and encourage healthy lifestyles and to optimize activity levels of people with asthma. Each session will include a free dinner. The earnest Center at 851-8670 or 1-800-243-LUNG.

Adult Asthma Education Classes
10 a.m.-1 p.m. Saturdays
March 11, April 15 & July 23
Private Dining Room, Barnes West County Hospital

To register or for more information, call The Asthma Center at 851-8670 or 1-800-243-LUNG.

Clinical Drug Studies
The Asthma Center is continually involved in new and exciting studies of asthma treatments, and is looking for people who would like to participate in this research. If you're interested, call 851-8988 or 1-800-962-7498.

Adult CPR Classes
8:30 a.m.-12:30 p.m. Saturdays
February 19, March 19, April 16 & June 18 Barnes West County Hospital

Call the American Red Cross at (314)658-2048 to register. Class fee of $23 per person.

Certified Athletic Trainer
Certified Strength & Conditioning Specialist

A subtle color palette

Here's another newsletter that creates a fresh look each month by using a different second color. It's a bit unusual, though, in that the designer chooses deep, muted colors rather than brilliant hues.

There's many other details worth noting in this design, including: a skillfully handled variety of typefaces; a town-of-the-month photo integrated into the banner; and unusual treatments for bylines, decks, kickers and department heads.

ReCareering Newsletter
Jan./Feb., March, & September, 1993
- Publisher: Publications Plus, Inc., Northbrook , IL
- Designer: Sharon B. Schuster
- Colors: Black and one spot color (shown here: PMS 4985, 5555, 5473)
- Type: VAG Rounded, Univers Condensed, Spring, New Baskerville
- Dimensions: 8½ by 11

Minimalist punch

This design gets a lot of bang out of a very restricted use of color: Blue is used in the nameplate, department heads, logo and the end-of-story markers. Period.

Those big solid blocks of color are hard to miss. They also add a strong sense of organization and unity to the page design—a nice complement to the type strategy, which is clean and straightforward.

Update
Spring, 1993
- Publisher: Executive Service Corps of Chicago, Chicago, IL
- Development: Marilyn Dawson, Continental Bank
- Designer: Jeff Stasik, Stasik Design Inc.
- Colors: Black and blue (PMS 2718)
- Type: Futura, Berthold Caslon Book
- Dimensions: 8½ by 14

Strictly business?

How colorful should a financial or business-oriented newsletter be? What's the most appropriate format? What about typography?

As these two examples show, it's partly a matter of taste, partly what needs to be communicated to what kind of audience. The example on this page uses a conservative type strategy and three-column design, but prints with four spot colors.

The example on the opposite page opts for a looser two-column design with a single vibrant color. The latter newsletter seems less demanding and perhaps targeted at a less technical audience.

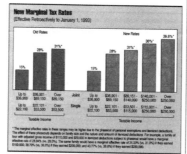

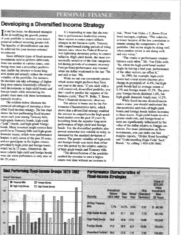

An in-depth look at issues facing

FAMILY BUSINESS *Today*

Challenges Facing Your Family Business

The challenges facing businesses as we approach the end of this century and prepare for a new millennium are overwhelming. There are several problems, however, that are unique to the family business that we would like to discuss. Essentially, we believe there are five predominant challenges facing a family business that, while they are not new, have become far more prevalent as more families try to grow more businesses.

OWNERSHIP SUCCESSION

Providing for an orderly family transition from one generation to the next has always been one of the major challenges facing family firms. Several factors appear to make succession more problematic now.

These include the increasing prevalence of non-family members serving in management roles and the complexities of businesses that require the CEO to have a broader knowledge of how to run a company than the founder once needed. Furthermore, many founders who are torn between the traditional transfer of the business to their son or sons, are considering daughters who now have the same opportunity to develop the necessary skills to take on leadership roles.

In order to plan for succession, founders now have to lean on their advisors, retain consultants for aid in selecting successors, and mold and develop the proper atmosphere so that the successor can help the company continue to grow.

EXPANDING FAMILY

As businesses continue to grow and second generations begin thinking about planning for their succession, one major challenge becomes obvious. There are more people to deal with. A business founder is fortunate to pass the business along to two or three children and feel there is some chance that there will be compatibility between the successors to develop a good working leadership team.

However, as time goes on there may be more people coming into the family business such as cousins, nieces, or nephews. This creates two obvious problems. First, there are more personality differences, along with a great diversity in technical skills, educational backgrounds, etc. Furthermore, there is no well-defined generation gap as you would have between parents and children.

What you have is an overlapping of generations with major age and experience differences that sometimes vary significantly from skill and ability differences. No business leader would employ and give responsibilities to outsiders who generate conflicts within the organization and do not get along with other executives. However, implementing the same policy when dealing with family members is not easy. Overcoming this will certainly be one of

Put your firm name, address, and logo on this marketing tool
from Practice Development Institute (PDI)
Call Today: 1-800-227-0498

Customize this area with a photo

Include a short 30-35 word biography here to accompany the photo of your firm's key family business advisor.

---

the major challenges for family businesses during the next few decades.

MAINTAINING PROFITABILITY

Many successful family enterprises were founded from a simple, well-promoted, well-executed idea. There was usually a unique product, service, or market niche that was exploited, allowing the business to flourish in a short period of time and create a significant amount of financial stability.

As a company matures, however, competitive pressures, changes in technology, and the buying habits of customers impact profit margins. Although more family members appear to take active roles in the company, this could result in fewer dollars spread among more people. Consequently, a challenge facing these businesses is to keep developing new ideas, products lines and avenues for the creation of wealth.

FAMILY VOLATILITY

The change in the general structure of families during the last generation creates another challenge for family businesses. Unlike the way family businesses used to be, it is no longer a natural career path for offspring to automatically join the family enterprise.

Furthermore, divorces are more prevalent and have a major impact on the family enterprise, even in these circumstances where the in-law was not part of the family business. Our society also has changed to the point where spouses who play no active role in the business still have advisory input. As you might expect, this input is not always consistent with keeping business activities harmonious.

Family businesses will have to face these problems to a greater extent in the future and how they are able to cope will certainly be a determining factor in the continuity of the business.

FINANCIAL DISENTANGLEMENT

Another challenge is the one faced by the founder who has properly trained and prepared his or her successors, has found ways to deal with all the other challenges discussed above, and is ready to retire and allow the next generation to take over. This individual must cope with his and other financial problems ahead. From a tax standpoint, the estate and gift tax considerations involved in transferring a family business, including the difficulty in "freezing" the value of the business so that future growth is not attributable to the older generation's equity in the business, is always a problem.

In addition to the tax considerations, however, the founder must cope with other financial issues. How to get the portion of wealth, sometimes representing the majority of an estate, out of the corporation for investment is a common dilemma. Another issue is how to get the founder's name off the loan guarantees at the bank.

Whatever challenges are faced by family businesses, one thing is for sure: The future of America depends on the creation and success of family owned businesses.

The Impact on the Family Of Businesses in the Home

When this country was very young, virtually all business activity was revolving. Blacksmithing, furniture-making, buggy-making, etc., started in or around the residence. As the industrial age developed, shops became factories and enterprises grew, urban centers developed and there was a rapid evolution continuing through current times, where most family businesses operate out of office buildings, shopping centers or industrial parks.

As we near the end of the 20th century, however, it seems there may be a noticeable shift back to consideration of running business operations out of the home. This article will discuss some of the factors that may be causing this change.

Budgetary Considerations. Many businesses have found it necessary to locate their corporate headquarters outside the hub of their retail, manufacturing or distribution concentration. With office space in urban center cities costing so much and offices located adjacent to principal production facilities being so inconvenient, establishing an office out of a residence or facility located adjacent to the principal residence seems like a beneficial financial move.

Convenience. As commuters get longer, the convenience of work being a few feet away has become very appealing.

Employee Accessibility. It used to be important to have your offices located on major bus lines and readily accessible to a pool of employees.

Today, the traffic, parking problems and inconvenience of public transportation seems to make it easier for someone to drive to a residential area. The pool of employees has also expanded, particularly among highly qualified working mothers who may want flexibility or the ability to go home for lunch, drop off and pick up their children on the way to or from work, and perform other chores

Lifestyle Changes. In addition to all the added time, either to work or to personal life by shortening the commute, the business-in-the-home option also creates an additional kind of flexibility. Many business owners would like to move farther out than the perimeter suburbs and acquire significant acreage for horses, recreational farming or other pastimes. This becomes impractical from a commuting standpoint, whereas if the business operations can be run out of the same geographical area, there can be additional significance.

Technology. With the use of computers, modems and fax machines, the need for more offices to be located near business districts has diminished. Many corporations have established work-at-home offices for these employees without creating any hardship for the business.

Family Involvement. If done properly, children growing up in a family business run out of the home certainly can have an opportunity to get a positive experience and even develop some real business awareness. Obviously, there is more time to spend with the family part of the family business when you live and work in the same location.

Contrary to some opinions, working with family members in a home environment, creates no additional stress or personal disruptions, than having the family members work together in a separate location. This has been verified in research done by Alma J. Owen and Mary Winter of Lincoln University and Iowa State University, respectively.

Of course, running a family business out of the home is not for every business. In fact, among laws, facility limitations and the lack of nearby amenities, such as restaurants and shopping, and sometimes just the size of the business, excludes trying the family business into the home. But, there is no question that the number of family businesses run out of the home will increase dramatically in the decades ahead.

> "...establishing an office out of a residence or facility located adjacent to the principal residence seems like a beneficial financial move."

Where the Time Goes

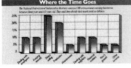

The T. Rowe Price Report
Fall, 1993

- Publisher: T. Rowe Price, Baltimore, MD
- Designer: Pam Gecan, Fresh Produce
- Colors: Black, blue, red and orange (PMS 286, 200, and 158 or 471)
- Type: Times and Helvetica
- Dimensions: 8¼ by 11

Family Business Today
1993

- Publisher: Practice Development Institute, Chicago, IL
- Designer: Practice Development Institute
- Colors: Black and purple (PMS 2593)
- Type: Cheltenham, Gill Sans
- Dimensions: 8½ by 11

Synergy

In terms of color and graphics, these designs sparkle with synergy—the end products appear more interesting than the simple sum of their parts.

The example on this page is, for the most part, a basic two-color design. But the colors are cleverly combined in the photos. A purple tint has been added behind the black ink—a simple but effective way to "colorize" black-and-white images. (Speaking of synergy: note how the nameplate doubles as a mailing panel!)

The health newsletter on the opposite page also uses two colors, but it almost appears to be a three-color design. That's because the body text, which is set in the deep blue, can be mistaken for black at first glance. The same blue appears quite colorful, however, where it's used in the nameplate, drop caps and accent graphics.

Animal Crackers
Fall, 1993

- Publisher: The Anti-Cruelty Society
- Designer: Scott Wills, Design Associates
- Colors: Black and purple (PMS 252)
- Type: Cheltenham, Franklin Gothic, Times Roman, Kabel
- Dimensions: 11 by 17

THE ANTI-CRUELTY SOCIETY
157 West Grand Avenue
Chicago IL 60610
ADDRESS CORRECTION REQUESTED

NON-PROFIT
ORGANIZATION
U. S. POSTAGE
PAID
ANTI-CRUELTY
SOCIETY

ANIMAL CRACKERS

FALL '93

Estate Planning Seminars at The Anti-Cruelty Society

Jane M. Stern, Executive Director

For the past year The Anti-Cruelty Society, as a service to its donors, has presented a number of estate planning seminars. The response has been great! These free workshops have explored different aspects of estate planning including the importance of having a Will, planning for retirement and most recently, the concept of a Living Trust. Our speakers lead the participants through the oftentimes confusing language associated with these financial vehicles in an easy to understand presentation.

Our next seminar will once again be the topic of the Living Trust and will be presented at The Anti-Cruelty Society on Saturday, October 30 at 11:00am. The program will run approximately one hour, followed by refreshments, a showing of our award-winning film, "Protecting the Web" and a tour of the shelter and low-income clinic.

We have enclosed a postcard so you can reserve a space at this seminar. We hope to see you there. If you have any questions about the seminar, please call me at (312)329-8725.

Flood Disasters

Everybody has heard news reports about the great flood tragedy in the midwest. The disaster affected thousands of people directly, and many more indirectly. We all know what a terrible hardship many people suffered, but what about the animals?

The Anti-Cruelty Society was ready to help. When we heard that the Davenport animal shelter was three feet under water we went to help. When we arrived, the Davenport crew was doing the best they could. They had moved the animals to a stable on the fair grounds on dry ground. We loaded two ambulances filled with dogs (we were filled to capacity at ACS with cats at the time) and drove them back to Chicago.

When the Saint Louis shelter called, we were ready. They were receiving thousands of animals more than they were expecting. Many animals were strays, displaced by the floods. We sent many vaccines to St. Louis so that all of these strays could be vaccinated. Although the flood was a terrible tragedy for everyone, we hope that we were able to do our small part by taking care of the animals.

The Fenced-Yard Mystique

Ah, yes, the fabulous fence! Everyone's perfect "solution" to the "problem" of owning a dog!

A fenced-in yard is indeed a wonderful convenience on those early mornings, or while house-training a puppy, and a super play area to have fun WITH your dog. But when a yard becomes a substitute for personal, playful, disciplined attention to a dog, it is no different than expecting a TV set to babysit a little child. And we all know the pitfalls of that reasoning!

To apartment dwellers who love their dogs and dream of the day when they will have a fenced-in yard, we say: APARTMENT DOGS ARE NOT BEING DEPRIVED OF A FULL AND WONDERFUL LIFE! Their special person is WITH them whenever they go out. Most of them have their own play group of canine pals. Many attend dog obedience classes and have fun practicing the exercises with their owners. Often, their minds and bodies get more exercise than dogs with yards.

There is no "magic" in a yard, fenced-in or otherwise. The true "magic" lies in the relationship between dog and owner. A fenced-in yard can be good, bad, or ugly. It depends entirely upon the circumstances.

GOOD: It's a secure play area. Your dog is safe from dogs who run loose. Your dog can't run loose. Your dog can't chase cars or bikes or other animals. Your dog can't frighten or intimidate children, joggers, delivery persons, etc. Your dog

has a place to "entertain" dog friends (and you).

BAD: A yard without you in it can be lonely and boring for your dog. In fact, without companionship, it is more like a prison. Yard dogs often "amuse" themselves by barking, running back and forth, digging under, or climbing over the fence. Barrier frustration often manifests itself in aggressiveness toward anyone (friend or foe) who approaches the fence. It is no substitute for training, or for the mental and physical benefits of long walks with you. Coprophagia (eating feces) is a behavior often seen among dogs who spend a lot of time alone in the yard. Nobody can be 100% certain that everyone will always remember to shut (or lock) the gate. Shyness, fearfulness, aggression, and territorial behaviors become worse as a dog who is alone in the yard. Neighbors have a right to complain if your dog barks non-stop!

UGLY: Very few fences can keep outsiders from teasing a dog or tossing food or objects into a yard. Dogs are STOLEN all the time—from yards that owners believed to be secure. Firecrackers, lighted cigarettes, and matches are dangerous missiles that can injure or seriously traumatize a dog. Many a fence-climbing dog has hung herself when her collar got caught. It takes ONLY ONE careless person to leave a gate ajar, and ONLY ONE escape, for a beloved dog to die under the wheels of a car.

Dog Meets Cat

Introducing a New Animal into the Household

The old tale that a cat and dog cannot live together peaceably is untrue. What is true, however is that it does take some skill and patience to make it work. It also takes a dog who is already well trained and an owner who has excellent control of his dog.

Successful introductions have much to do with each animal's previous experiences with other animals, if any at all, and how well their guardians introduce them. When choosing an animal (whether a cat or dog), be considerate of each animal's background, and in some cases, breed.

For instance, a dog who has been around bully cats may not be too keen on your idea of adding a cat to the family. Or a cat living in a household with a dog who has a nasty habit of chasing other animals may just decide to live the rest of her days perched in fear atop the refrigerator or dressers.

But let's say you go to great lengths to choose the right cat or dog to live with you and the rest of your animal family, do not ruin this by introducing them improperly. First impressions between cats and dogs are as important as they are between people.

Keep a positive attitude and don't apologize or agonize over your decision to bring another animal into your home. The stress it causes will reflect in how you interact with your companion animals. In other words, if you are nervous, you

will make your companion animals nervous too. This will certainly affect how they view the other animal and you may be sabotaging your efforts for a successful relationship.

Begin by keeping the new animal in a separate room or area for several days. Make sure he is kept comfortable with food, water, bedding and a litterbox for cats. The current pet(s) should have free roam of the rest of the home. Allow them to sniff and growl under the door. If you wish to let the new animal out of confinement for short periods, it should be done only when he can be supervised by an adult and the current pet is kept in another room or area.

Once the grumbling has slowed, allow the animals to see each other through a screen or slightly opened door. This allows each animal to work out defensiveness or aggression without really being able to harm each other physically. Do this exercise for several days until you feel comfortable enough to introduce them face to face.

When you can be home all day and are feeling quite relaxed, allow the new animal out of his confinement. Unless you are certain that the dog involved is very well trained and has been gentle with small animals in the past, introduce the dog on a very loose leash. Do not hold the dog tightly or close to you. Do not force them to be together! Doing so could make each animal feel out of control or threatened and a fight could easily break out. Instead, be

casual and let them encounter each other on their own.

It is perfectly normal and expected that these animals hiss, growl, chase, swat and bat at each other. This may go on for several days or several weeks. Do not consistently punish one animal and/or rescue the other. It could only complicate matters. Be patient. If your animals are well adjusted, they will work things out on their own time.

However, if there is severe fighting in which the animals are being injured, separate them by throwing water on them or making a loud noise. Do not try to separate them with your body. In the frenzy you could be bitten or scratched by accident. Keep the animals apart and after a few days try to introduce them again.

Do not expect your cats and dogs to become pals right away.

Friendships take time to develop. It is not wise to expect too much from your companion animals too soon. Have realistic expectations and goals. If problems persist, or if you have any questions, do not hesitate to call The Anti-Cruelty Society's animal behavior specialist at (312) 644-8338.

Focus On

HeaLTH

Spring/Summer 1993

Form/Function: Plastic Surgery Options

Features

Plastic Surgery
Options

Ergonomics at Work

Starting an
Exercise Program

Nutrition Test

Pre-Conception Advice

Hospital Programs

It was the Greeks who contributed the word "plastic" to plastic surgery. The term derives from "plassis," meaning "to mold or form." "That translation accurately refers to the work we do," says John Lease, M.D., plastic surgeon at Columbus Hospital. Plastic surgeons perform a wide variety of surgical procedures that address the patient's form and function.

The specialty includes many reconstructive techniques — not just the "aesthetic" options. Dr. Lease points out that the range of reconstructive procedures performed by the plastic surgeon is vast, including

● repair of facial injuries;

● burn care — acute and reconstructive;

● trauma and wound repair;

● hand surgery, including tendon repair and the treatment of carpal tunnel syndrome;

● breast surgery, including reconstruction and reduction;

● scar revision;

● treatment of skin cancers;

● reconstructive procedures for cancer of the head, neck and other areas;

● repair of congenital defects, such as cleft lip and palate; and

● treatment of chronic wounds, such as leg ulcers

Reconstructive surgery is covered by most insurance policies. Questions about this and other aspects of these procedures should be discussed with your surgeon.

Looking Better, Feeling Better

Many people seek the services of a plastic surgeon when they become unhappy with how nature or the aging process has affected their appearance. For these patients, the plastic surgeon's domain includes a variety of "cosmetic" techniques. The following is a brief guide to some of the more common plastic surgical options.

What Does It All Mean?

Abdominoplasty: During this procedure, also called a "tummy tuck," the surgeon removes excess skin and fat and tightens the abdominal wall to achieve a flat contour.

Facelift: Facelifts eliminate some of the effects of aging and gravity by mobilizing facial structures and removing excess skin and fat. Incisions are usually made at the top and back hairline and in front of the ear. A facelift is excellent for removing folds and banding in the neck.

Rhinoplasty: Commonly known as a "nose job," an incision is made inside the nose, from which the surgeon alters the structural framework of the nose in order to change the external appearance.

Blepharoplasty: In this procedure, the surgeon removes excess skin and puffiness from upper and/or lower eyelids.

Otoplasty: Protruding ears are tucked closer to the head through a procedure that involves several small incisions.

Liposuction: An increasingly popular technique, fat is "vacuumed" from such areas as the abdomen, thighs, hips and neck. While not a weight reduction option, liposuction helps to re-contour target areas.

Breast Augmentation: This procedure is currently performed with saline implants, through small, inconspicuous incisions.

Mastopexy: Commonly known as a "breast lift," the skin of the breast is tightened to correct sagging.

Collagen Injection: Small amounts of collagen, inserted with a syringe, can temporarily correct facial wrinkles. It also can be used to correct small contour defects.

Dermabrasion: In this technique, the skin is lightly abraded to correct contour deformity resulting from scarring due to trauma or acne.

Chemical Peel: Topical application of certain chemicals removes fine wrinkles such as those around the mouth.

Length of Procedures, Risks and Side Effects

"Most cosmetic procedures can be performed in from two to four hours," Dr. Lease explains. "And, many techniques can be done on an outpatient basis, with the patient under just local anesthesia, with some sedation. *continued on back cover*

"For many people, cosmetic surgery contributes greatly to heightened confidence and self esteem. This is most likely to happen when there's a good partnership between the surgeon and the patient."

Working Smart!

We used to call it a "desk." Now, it's known as "a work station." This change in office terminology reflects the many technological changes in the workplace faced by millions of Americans. And with these changes come some hazards. Whether your job is on the assembly line or in front of a computer terminal, there's a lot you should know about potential risk factors in the work environment.

Ergonomics is the field of study that helps sort out issues related to worksite health and safety. "The word 'ergonomics' can confuse people, but the concept is simple," says Elke Friedman, ergonomics coordinator, Columbus Hospital. "Ergonomics specialists help people adjust their work environment and work habits to ensure comfort and safety on the job." *continued on page 2*

*Healthful
Information
from
Columbus Hospital*

Focus on Health
Spring/Summer, 1993
- Publisher: Columbus-Cabrini Medical Center, Chicago, IL
- Designer: Mary Beth Bostrom-Sybul
- Colors: Deep blue and purple (PMS 3005 and 246)
- Type: Garamond and Futura, with a variety for the banner and drop caps
- Dimensions: 11 by 17

Simple does it

This design is a great example of simplicity hard at work. It's just a single tabloid sheet, but it packs plenty of news, thanks to a five-column format and an efficient, condensed typeface. The spot color strategy is also simple and unobtrusive.

The compressed typeface used in the banner is repeated in the drop caps—a nice touch.

FOCUS Family Service DuPage
Fall, 1993

- Publisher: Family Service DuPage, Wheaton, IL
- Designer: Anna M. Pugsley Graphic Design
- Colors: Black, purple (Pantone 266)
- Type: Willow, Helvetica Black and Condensed
- Dimensions: 11 by 17

FOCUS

FAMILY SERVICE DUPAGE

A United Charities Affiliate

FALL 1993

FSS program helps families find independence

Kathyanne, a 34-year-old single mother of two, glows with enthusiasm and pride when she talks about the Family Self-Sufficiency program.

"I can't even imagine where I'd be right now without FSS. I feel so good about myself now. It's going to work out and I'm going to be worth their investment. I'm sure of that."

Kathyanne left her husband of six years when the marriage turned abusive and fled to a shelter for abused women. The four years since then she describes as "stagnant: I was drinking. I just wasn't getting ahead and I was making some really unwise decisions."

It wasn't until she started a 12-step recovery program and later learned about FSS (through the DuPage County Housing Authority) that "everything came together," she says.

Family Self-Sufficiency is a program that offers low income families educational and job training opportunities so that they can become economically self-sufficient.

The program is providing counseling, support from case managers, and helping Kathyanne by paying tuition as well as assessing grants. In addition, FSS often pays for various related expenses such as child care and transportation. Last month Kathyanne completed her first year at College of DuPage preparing for its radiology technology program.

The majority of families in the FSS program are very low income; most are single heads of households who are usually women, according to Peggy Radke, of the DuPage County Housing Authority, program coordinator. There are now 62 families enrolled and 42 families in the application process.

Any family currently participating in the Section 8 Certificate Program, a federally funded rental assistance program, or who meets FSS's income guidelines, is eligible for the program.

FSS is administered by the DuPage County Housing Authority in partnership with United Charities Family Service

> "I can't even imagine where I'd be right now without FSS. . . It's going to work out and I'm going to be worth their investment. I'm sure of that."

DuPage, the DuPage County Human Services Division and the Job Training Partnership Act.

Funding is provided by the DuPage County Board and the DuPage County Housing Authority Board. Additional funding has been provided by the DuPage Community Foundation and, for fiscal year 1993, by The Alfred Bersted Foundation, a trust administered by Continental Bank.

The most obvious difference between FSS and other programs is that FSS is a comprehensive program that can last up to five years with families receiving supportive services every step of the way.

Kathyanne and her children, Jimmy, 8, and Jenny, 5, are one of many families becoming independent through the Family Self-Sufficiency program.

"Our involvement in this program is our way, in part, of addressing our mission to help families become self-sufficient," says Louise McCown, Family Service DuPage associate director.

"FSS identifies client strengths as well as obstacles that impede progress. We then deal with those obstacles through tangible services as well as counseling. The program is just starting its second year and we're already starting to hear success stories."

Kathyanne's story may well be one of these successes.

Kathyanne attended FSS counseling sessions and workshops geared to help her on topics such as budgeting, rentals, and family relationships.

Mike Hurst and Alan Bell, Family Service DuPage counselors, work with FSS participants. Hurst met with Kathyanne

and her case manager, Suzanne Wennig, of the Department of Human Services, and helped her decide on a career and guided her in utilizing her family's strengths.

"Mike has helped me work through a lot of problems and anxieties. Whenever there's a stressful situation, he's there to help me," she says.

Wennig meets with her monthly. They set goals and together see they're accomplished.

Kathyanne has made friends with other women in the program and they help support each other.

She also says she feels every FSS staff member really cares about her and truly wants her to succeed. That's very important to her, she says, "because a lot of us women don't have very high self-esteem to begin with and we need people who will care about us."

Things are wonderful now with her children, Jenny, 8, and Jimmy, 6, she says. "We're just so much more a family. And they're proud of me. They tell their friends, 'My mom's going to college.' " .

Because FSS is a five-year program, Kathyanne says this means "that ultimately I am going to be self-sufficient. I am not going to need to be on food stamps or any kind of assistance. I'm going to succeed and it's a wonderful feeling."

In memory of Edith Bruckner

Edith A. Bruckner, the founder of Family Service DuPage, died Feb. 18, 1993, at her home in Hinsdale. She was 111.

During the early days of the Depression this remarkable woman saw the need for a service organization whose mission would be to help families help themselves.

As a historian notes, "she put her heart and her hand to the task of convincing others of the need, driving ahead diligently, as a voluntary leader, crusader, and a community organizer." Mrs. Bruckner's vision became reality in 1930 when Family Service DuPage opened a one-room office in Glen Ellyn.

"Edith Bruckner's dedication to the needs of others is a legacy we at Family Service DuPage proudly continue today," says Roger Johnson, Family Service DuPage executive director.

Mrs. Bruckner is survived by a daughter, Charlotte Schmitt of Hinsdale, and a son, Herbert, of Florida.

Memorial contributions honoring Mrs. Bruckner have been received and acknowledged by Family Service DuPage.

Treasure House tallies $1,000,000 in contributions to DuPage families

The Treasure House Resale Shop is proudly announcing its contribution of more than $1,000,000 to Family Service DuPage since 1974.

"It's really more than that, but records before 1974 were not available," says Gerry Alvarez, president of the Treasure House board. "We're proud too that we've met our fiscal year 1993 goal of raising $100,000 for Family Service DuPage."

Through the years the volunteers who run the Treasure House have paid all the repair, remodeling and operating expenses of the resale shop, and have even managed to buy the building.

"All of this represents a lot of work on the part of lots and lots of dedicated people. For many of our volunteers, that enthusiasm

and devotion has lasted over a long period, going back 20 or 30 years," says Alvarez.

The Treasure House, founded in 1959, is located in a double-front brick store building at 497 Pennsylvania Avenue in Glen Ellyn. The shop is run by volunteers from the Leagues of Family Service DuPage. Leagues are located in Glen Ellyn, Wheaton, Naperville, Lombard, Downers Grove/Lisle and Hinsdale/ Clarendon Hills. Men and women who are not affiliated with the leagues also volunteer.

The present location is about the shop's fourth, recalls Charlotte Wempe, a Treasure House volunteer for 31 years. The first was in a barn at the corner of Glen Ellyn's Main Street and North Avenue.

"In the early days we were

Ann Shearburn, left, and Relia Spencer sort through items for sale at the Treasure House.

filled with the desire to help a struggling young agency because it offered so much. As the agency has grown, our volunteers still retain that feeling of accomplish-

ment," she says.

The Board of Directors of Family Service DuPage will celebrate this million-dollar milestone and honor the volunteers in a very special afternoon celebration at the annual meeting October 3 at The Lodge on the McDonald's office campus, 2815 Jorie Blvd., Oak Brook.

Says Don Ursin, president of the Board of Directors of Family Service DuPage, "We are indebted to our volunteers for the amount of time, effort and money that they have contributed to Family Service DuPage. We're also grateful for both the extended number of years and the number of people who have brought our agency not only an impressive dollar amount, but their support and dedication as well."

DuPage Children's MUSEUM

FALL 1993
CALENDAR OF ADVENTURES

OCTOBER IS "ALL ABOUT ME"

Who am I? What is my body like? How does my size compare to others? Who are my family, friends, pets, or classmates? Explore "all about me" in our arts, science and math activities.

Me and My Space
Thursday, October 7, 10:00 a.m.–noon
Use pictures from magazines and items from the surplus shop that describe all about you and your family. These items can be placed in your own cardboard box for display in the "My Own Space Display House". Free with museum admission.
Leader: *Jodi Stapleton, Museum Education Specialist*

Portrait Quilt
Part I – Sunday, October 10, Create a portrait square – 1:30, 2:00, 2:30, 3:00
Part II – Sunday, October 17, Tie squares into a quilt – 1:30, 2:00, 2:30, 3:00
Create your own portrait with fabric, yarn, buttons, lace, etc. Come back the following week and tie the three necessary quilting fabrics together to create a beautiful quilt square. Appropriate for children ages 4 and up. The program is designed so that children and their parents will work as a team. Advance registration required.
Leader: *Emilie Pollman, Fiber Artist*
Register for one half-hour session on each of these two days.
Fee: $4.00 per child for members
$6.00 per child for nonmembers (plus museum admission for the first session only)
The workshop fee covers the cost of materials for both sessions.

Hand and Foot Printing
Thursday, October 14, 10:00 a.m.–noon
Where else can you find such interesting designs and patterns as those found on your hands and feet? How do our prints compare to a squirrel, a rabbit, or a raccoon? Animal footprint stamps, borrowed from the Willowbrook Wildlife Haven, will be available for exploration. Free with museum admission.
Leader: *Dorothy Carpenter, Early Childhood Educator*

Body Beautiful
Thursday, October 21, 10:00 a.m.–noon
Trace your whole body outline, then color and cut it out. Take home a life-size rendition of your child or yourself! Free with museum admission.
Leader: *Suzanne Gierke, Teacher*

Face Painting
Thursday, October 28, and Saturday, October 30, 10:00 a.m.–noon
Water-soluble crayons will be available for you and your child to create marvelous works on your own face. Free with museum admission.

Friday Fun with Music
Fridays, 10:00 – 11:00 a.m.
Friday mornings will be filled with lively music, lyric voices, and rhythmic movement as we sing and move to songs about "me" in October with our talented, musical leaders. Free with museum admission.
Leaders: *Dee Christie, Early Childhood Educator; Nancy Culp, College of DuPage Instructor; Vickie Wills, Director of Kindernusik of Wheaton; and Marian Schulz, Recreation Specialist*

Saturday Stories
October 9 and 23, 10:30 – 11:30 a.m.
Join us for a storytime "all about me" with our talented and engaging storytellers. Free with museum admission.
Leaders: *Members of the Prairie State Story League*

A "FEAST FOR ALL" IN NOVEMBER

A feast for the eyes, a feast for the ears, and a feast for the tummy! Explore fanciful foods from many different aspects—food for our furry friends, food on fabric, and much more!

Foods That Kids Like
For the whole month of November, the museum will accept donations of non-perishable foods especially for kids and their families. These foods will be distributed to local shelters who work with children and families. Your children may enjoy the opportunity to grocery shop for other kids! You can bring the food to the museum during regular public hours or call the museum office for Monday, Tuesday, or Wednesday drop-off times. (Please, no sugar cereals or candy!)

This is for the Birds!
Thursday, November 4, 10:00 a.m.–noon
Help to feed the birds in your yard by creating a scrumptious bird feeder using peanut butter and bird seed! 50¢ materials fee. No advance registration required, however, space is limited.
Leader: *Jodi Stapleton, Museum Education Specialist*

Dough for Playing
Thursday, November 11, 10:00 a.m.–noon
Create your own edible play dough and enjoy hours of sculpturing fun! 50¢ materials fee. No advance registration required, however, space is limited.
Leader: *Suzanne Gierke, Teacher*

Saturday Stories
November 13, 10:30 – 11:30 a.m.
Sink your teeth into a feast of tales during our hour of stories. Free with museum admission.
Leaders: *Members of the Prairie State Story League*

Food Prints
Thursday, November 10:00 a.m.–noon
Enjoy another quilting activity, this time making prints with various foods. The prints will be sewn together to form a glorious feast on fabric! The program is designed so that children and their parents will work as a team. $1.00 materials fee. Space is limited.
Leader: *Emilie Pollman, Fiber Artist*

Plentiful Plates
Sunday, November 21, 1:00–3:00 p.m.
Use your imagination and create a collage of food-like objects on a paper plate. Careful, though, someone may try to eat your artwork! Free with museum admission.
Leader: *Debbie Harrison, Museum Program Coordinator*

A Feastful of Fun with Music
Fridays, 10:00 – 11:00 a.m.
How many songs can we sing about food, eating, drinking and being merry? Come and find out with our talented, musical leaders. Free with museum admission.
Leaders: *Dee Christie, Early Childhood Educator; Nancy Culp, College of DuPage Instructor; Vickie Wills, Director of Kindernusik of Wheaton; and Marian Schulz, Recreation Specialist*

★ WEEKEND GRANDPARENT COUPON ★

Free admission for a grandparent when an adult or child admission is purchased.
Valid any Saturday or Sunday in November and December, 1993.
(Not valid with any other discounts.)

A calendar-letter

A good many newsletters are like this one, two parts calendar, one part news and features. More typical newsletter-style stories are placed on the inside spread (not shown here), while event listings and calendar grids dominate the front and back. Tinted graphics are set in the background to keep things light and playful.

Calendar of Adventures
Fall, 1993
- Publisher: DuPage Children's Museum, Wheaton, IL
- Designers: Rebecca Lindsay, Regina Migacz
- Colors: Black and red (PMS 192)
- Type: Futura Condensed, Times
- Dimensions: 11 by 17

The big picture
Nothing makes an impression
quite like a huge graphic or
photo—especially when the
accompanying text is set in a
large, easy-to-read typeface.

If you have the space, flaunt it.

Gateway News
Fall, 1992
- Publisher: Charles R. Feldstein &
  Company for the Chicago Botanic
  Garden, Chicago, IL
- Designer: Lynn Martin Design
- Colors: Black, orange and green
  (PMS 151 and 443)
- Type: Serifa, Goudy, Berkeley
  Medium
- Dimensions: 11 by 17

Chicago Botanic Garden
Chicago Horticultural Society
Post Office Box 400
Glencoe, IL 60022–0400

Non-Profit Org.
U. S. Postage
P A I D
Northbrook, IL
Permit No. 1568

Gateway News

A Campaign

Newsletter from

the Chicago

Botanic Garden

Fall 1992, No. 2

Plant Resource Center Planned

While all Gateway to the Garden campaign
objectives will contribute significantly to the
progress of the Chicago Botanic Garden in
the years ahead, few are more pointedly addressed to the Garden's fundamental mission
than the $4 million to be raised for a new
Plant Resource Center and its programs.

"The center will be the Garden's first dedicated research facility," Society President
Roy L. Taylor, Ph.D., stated. "It has been criti-
cally needed for a long time and will have
meaning and impact for many years to come."

Funding and construction of the Plant
Resource Center will advance the Garden to
dramatically more productive levels of
investigation in such research areas as:

— Evaluating, selecting, and promoting the
use of disease-resistant plants, which in turn
will contribute to the reduced use of pesti-
cides, a major environmental concern.

— Evaluating new plants to enhance mid-
western gardens, which will not only increase
their beauty but contribute such environmental improvements as decreased noise and
air pollution and the softening of hard urban
landscapes.

— Testing and evaluating plants for qualities
such as low maintenance and utility in con-
trolling erosion.

— Collecting useful plants from other countries, encouraging use of overlooked native
plants, and creating new hybrid plants that
are well adapted to our climate and soils.

An Improved Capacity

Of the $4 million campaign objective, $3 million will be invested in the phase-one construction of the Plant
Resource Center itself.
The low-rise, 20,000-
square-foot center—
to be built at the
*(continued
on page 3)*

Gateway Center Rises Among the Willow Trees

With capital resources raised through the
Chicago Horticultural Society's Gateway to
the Garden campaign, the Chicago Botanic
Garden's $6.5 million Gateway Center has
begun to rise on its site across from the Garden's main island. Active fund raising is
continuing in order to secure all private support needed for the new orientation and
visitor-service complex.

A recent leadership commitment from Mr.
and Mrs. Marvin J. Herb and Coca-Cola has
funded the center's Orientation Theater. This
key facility will provide visitors with state-of-
the-art audio-visual information about the
Garden, including an overview of its mission,
the location of principal features and facilities, guidance on designing a personal visit,
and news about programs and activities.
Whether a person is a first-time or a frequent
visitor, the Orientation Theater will offer
(continued on page 3)

HYATT OVERSEAS

HOT PIGS?

I guess it just sounds stranger than roasting "hot dogs"... Leonard Berk, President of Epicurean Expeditions East, led six U.S. food and travel writers to Hong Kong at the end of February. Hyatt Regency Hong Kong's Chef Chow Chung showed Mr. Berk how to correctly prepare Cantonese roast pork at the hotel's Chinese Restaurant.

The tours offer North American and European diners on 11-day gastronomic journey to 12 of Hong Kong's finest Chinese restaurants.

The Chinese Restaurant at HR Hong Kong was selected as one of the tour's featured venues because of its reputation for blending traditional Chinese ingredients and flavors with a nouvelle-style of preparation and presentation. If you're interested in finding out more about Epicurean Expeditions or Hyatt Regency Hong Kong, call Denise or me for details.

YOU CAN'T BEAT IT WITH A STICK

(A great old saying ...) I'm referring to the Ambassador Grill's new Friday night "Seafood Extravaganza" which offers a four-course seafood dinner for $35.00 per person. Start with seasonal favorites from the seafood bar, and move on to a selection of salads and entrees that include Pan Seared Salmon with a Mushroom Crust or Roasted Monkfish on a Tortilla Crust. The Ambassador Grill is at the U.N. Plaza—Park Hyatt, 44th St. and First Ave. in New York City.

GOING TO THE CHAPEL

Want to elope somewhere unusual? How about Japan? Hyatt Regency Osaka will feature a Wedding Chapel and Shinto ceremonial hall for both Western and traditional wedding services. The 524-room hotel will also have two roof-top restaurants that offer views of Osaka Bay. And there's plenty of time to plan...it opens in mid 1994.

Hyatt Regency Coolum

A BEVY OF BARGAINS

For "Value for the Dollar," try one of our new packages: "Viva Mexico" at Hyatt Regency Cancun, "Refreshingly Hyatt" at Hyatt Coral Grand (Puerto Vallarta), "Sparkling Summer" at Hyatt Carlton tower (London), "Regal Weekend" at Hyatt Kingsgate Sydney, or "Deliciously Hyatt" at Grand Hyatt Melbourne.

Ambassador Grill, U.N. Plaza—Park Hyatt

WHERE CAN YOU SEE

Camels and whales? How about Australia's Sunshine Coast? Hyatt Regency Coolum is where you'd stay ...a bush and beach safari takes guests and their "steeds" along the sands of Noosa's north shore and into the bushland of Lake Cooroibah Park. If you visit mid-August to mid-October, you can take a drive to Hervey Bay for humpback whale watching.

DELHI-IGHTFUL

Hyatt Regency Delhi is renovating all guestrooms, restaurants, meeting facilities and public areas. New telecommunications technology is part of the revamp-all rooms will have two phone lines and provisions for the installation of fax machines. Completion is scheduled for late 1992.

APRIL 1992

Hyatt Overseas
April, 1992
- Previously published by: Hyatt International
- Designer: Sue Niggemann, Lee Hill, Inc.
- Colors: Deep blue and red (PMS 289 and 485)
- Type: Futura, Palatino
- Dimensions: 11 by 17

Non-stop color

This informational newsletter, published by a producer of baby formula, is a stunning example of what can be achieved with four-color process printing.

Not many newsletter publishers—or designers—would dare to try this level of color design. But there's plenty of fascinating ideas here worth considering, even for a standard one- or two-color newsletter.

The Welcome Edition
1991-1992
- Publisher: Ross Pediatrics, Columbus, OH
- Designer: Sue Niggemann, Lee Hill, Inc.
- Colors: Process
- Type: Futura, New Century Schoolbook
- Dimensions: 8¼ by 8¼

THE WELCOME EDITION

?? ?

CHOOSING

L a m a z e

THE "RIGHT"

B r a d l e y

CHILDBIRTH

G r a n t l y   D i c k - R e a d

CLASS

As many as 73% of expecting couples participate in childbirth classes. Taking childbirth classes can answer many of your questions and help prepare you for labor, delivery and caring for your new baby. Knowing the types of childbirth methods—and some of the guidelines to consider—will help you choose the class right for you.

The three most common childbirth preparation methods are Lamaze, Bradley and Grantly Dick-Read. These approaches are all based on the philosophy that much of the discomfort during childbirth is caused by fear and tension. Through a combination of education, support, relaxation, paced breathing and focusing and touch techniques, you can reduce the fear, tension— and the pain—of childbirth.

(Continued on next page.)

The Welcome Addition Club Newsletter from SIMILAC® Infant Formulas

---

"Once your baby arrives, the most important 'test' of the pediatrician you have selected is how [he or she] cares for your child and responds to your concerns."

The American Academy of Pediatrics, CARING FOR YOUR BABY AND YOUNG CHILD Birth to Age 5, Stewart P. Shelov, M.D., F.A.A.P., Robert E. Hannemann, M.D., F.A.A.P.

(Continued from previous page.)

■ **Pediatricians** are graduates of four-year medical schools with three additional years of residency training solely in pediatrics. The initials FAAP after a pediatrician's name mean that he or she is a Fellow of the American Academy of Pediatrics and certified by the American Board of Pediatrics. To earn the FAAP designation, pediatricians need to pass a tough qualifying exam in advanced principles and practices of pediatric care.

■ **Family Physicians**, called FPs, are also graduates of four-year medical schools and have completed three extra years of residency training in general family care. FPs who are certified by the American Board of Family Practice have also passed an advanced exam in family care.

Consider these additional tips to help you decide:

■ Ask your obstetrician or your friends who are parents—or call the accredited hospital near you for referrals.

■ Set up an interview with each doctor during the final months of your pregnancy...you and the dad-to-be should try to attend so you both fully understand the doctor's policies and philosophy of care.

Here are some questions to ask during the interview:

■ How soon after birth will the doctor see your baby?

■ What are the office hours? Are they compatible with your schedule?

■ How often will the doctor see your baby for checkups and immunizations?

■ When is the doctor available for routine telephone calls?

■ With what hospital is the doctor affiliated?

■ How are emergency calls handled during office hours? After office hours?

■ Who "covers" the practice when the doctor is unavailable? Practice partners? Other community doctors?

■ How much does care cost? What methods of payment are accepted?

DadDELIVERS

With your baby on the way, now's the time to:

■ Install smoke detectors throughout your home, check them monthly and change the batteries according to instructions. Develop and practice a fire escape plan—now and after the baby arrives.

■ Make sure carpeting, tile and other floor coverings are tacked down to prevent tripping or slipping.

■ Add night lights in the bathroom, kitchen and hallways.

WhatToEXPECT

Swelling, called **edema**

(e dē' mah), is normal for many pregnant women. Edema is caused by the retaining of fluid. It usually occurs in the legs, and gets worse as the day goes on, generally disappearing by morning. If your legs swell, follow these suggestions for relief:

■ Elevate your legs when possible.

■ Rest in bed on your side, preferably your left side, to improve circulation.

■ Don't wear binding tights, stockings or socks.

■ Wear support pantyhose or stockings.

■ Stick to your exercise program.

■ Notify your doctor if swelling becomes worse.

Word Wise

■ BEYOND JENNIFER & JASON An Enlightened Guide To Naming Your Baby By Linda Rosenkrantz & Pamela Redmond Satran. $10.95. St. Martin's Press.

■ THE BIRTH OF A FATHER An Invaluable Guide To Fatherhood By Martin Greenberg M.D. $4.95. Avon Books.

■ PLANNING FOR PREGNANCY, BIRTH AND BEYOND From the American College of Obstetricians and Gynecologists. Offers information and opinions on subjects related to women's health and reproduction. $10.95. Contact: The American College of Obstetricians and Gynecologists. (800) 762-ACOG.

Video Watch

BABY CARE BASICS A special collection of videotapes produced by Ross Laboratories. Please ask for your free tape during your prenatal visits to your obstetrician, prenatal instructor, hospital or baby's doctor. Features include:

■ ...To Make A Difference (Part IV) For You and Your Baby, featuring T. Berry Brazelton, M.D.

■ Either To Breastfeed Your Baby or To Formula Feed Your Baby

■ Seat Belts and the Family

ROSCO'S LIBRARY

2

3

November 1993

Ameritech
Dialogue
In Illinois

Give the Gift Both You and Your Teen Will Love

Every holiday season, you head to the malls to match the perfect gift to each person on your list. This year, why fight crowds and lug around heavy packages? If you have teenagers at home who tie up your phone, consider giving them their own phone line.

An extra phone line is less expensive than you might think. It's available for a low monthly fee, plus a one-time installation charge. Ameritech also offers a special billing option that allows you to spread the installation cost over several months.

An extra phone line will give you peace of mind as well, so that the phone is available when you need it.

Ordering an extra line is easy. To make holiday shopping more convenient, Ameritech offers expanded calling hours. You can call Ameritech toll-free, Monday through Saturday, 24 hours a day. To schedule installation by Dec. 25, call before Dec. 13, 1993. To order, call 1-800-650-LINK.

REMINDER
Save your phone bills! They may come in handy at tax time!

Know Who's Calling Before You Answer

Do you ever hesitate before answering your telephone, unsure of whether the caller is someone you want to speak to? Ameritech's Caller ID* or Caller ID with Name* service could be what you need.

When the phone rings, Caller ID displays the telephone number that call is being made from. Caller ID with Name also displays the caller's number and up to 15 characters of the caller's residential or business name.

Caller ID costs $6.50 a month. Caller ID with Name costs $2.50 more a month, plus a $15 installation fee (the display device is not included). A small price to pay for peace of mind. You can order from Ameritech by calling toll-free 1-800-428-2111, Dept. 35.

*Available in limited areas. Both parties must be in specially equipped areas.

Address comments/questions to:
Mary Shully, Editor, P.O. Box 2112, Warren, MI 48090-2112

Your Next Call May Be Worth $25,000

Intriguing? It's the Ameritech Pay Phone Payout, and you can win the grand prize of an Ameritech Complete™ MasterCard® worth $25,000 in pre-paid purchases! You'll also are a shot at — first prize: Your phone bill paid for 5 years, up to $4,500; second prizes (5): Your phone bill paid for one year, up to $900; third prizes (20): Your phone bill paid for six months, up to $450. And there are lots of bonus prizes, too — such as $10 in free phone calls.

Contest entry is automatic when you use your Ameritech Calling Card or HomeLink account or the calling card feature of your Ameritech Complete Card to place a call from an Ameritech pay phone — or any phone where you hear the Ameritech identification tone before your call is connected (until 12/31/93). Or use coins to call from any Ameritech pay phone (until 1/21/94). Enter as often as you like by calling between 7 a.m. and 7 p.m. The more calls you make, the better your chances of winning. Don't use a pay phone a lot? You can still play. Send your name, address, and phone number on a 3x5 card to Ameritech Pay Phone Payout, Box 8107, Grand Rapids, MN 55745-8107. Entries must be postmarked by 12/31/93, and you must be 18 years or older to enter. To get your Ameritech Calling Card or Complete Card, call 1-800-695-2273.

For complete rules, and 1-800-900-9914. Void where prohibited. Bonus prize winners will be selected periodically from ... calls between 10/24/93 and 1/21/94. Ameritech Pay Phone Payout is sponsored by Ameritech ... know how. 38 Maple Place. Marshland, MA 11030. From the selected brand (Ameritech's U.S. residence all other than the general public, the winner will be determined through insured by Ameritech ... "Surcharges apply to all calling card and HomeLink calls.

Holiday Helpers

Ameritech brings you some helpful ways to make it easier to say "Seasons Greetings" this holiday season.

First, the Greeting Call. What better way to let family and friends know you're thinking of them than to pick up the phone and call? It's the most personal way to brighten someone's holiday. Use it to add a special touch to cards and greetings you've sent, or to say thanks for those you've received.

Greeting Calls fit easily into your busy schedule, and they help you stay in touch during the holiday season. Make Ameritech Greeting Calls a new part of your holiday tradition.

Second, if you're sending cards to complement your Greeting Calls, you'll want to make sure your address book is up-to-date. Ameritech can help there, too.

Call 796-9600 from the 312 or 708 area code and give us the telephone number of a person whose address you are trying to locate. Ameritech Custom Name and Address will give you the name (including usage) and complete address (including ZIP code). You can check up to two listings for just 35 cents.

Or, dial 411, and give us a name, and an information operator will give you the telephone number and full address. Check up to two listings for just 30 cents.

No matter how you choose to say "Happy Holidays," Ameritech is here to help make your choices easier than ever.

Ameritech
YOUR LINK TO A BETTER LIFE

Dividing with color

Both of these examples take the unusual strategy of dividing the page into blocks of different colors. It's a device that's hard to ignore, but probably best suited for publications made up of short, easy-to-read articles set in fairly large type.

This large format newsletter on this page is sent to current and prospective patients of a large hospital. Each story is set in a separate color block, with captions reversed out of darker color blocks. The color background also allows for white bullet symbols—a striking detail.

This issue also features a perforated information request card.

Breakthroughs
Number 3, 1993
- Publisher: University of Chicago Hospitals, Chicago, IL
- Designer: Jeffrey Swoger, Swoger + Company
- Colors: Process
- Type: Clearface, Kabel, Times
- Dimensions: 11 by 17

A "newscard"

Is it a newsletter or a huge postcard? It's really both. These cards are sent out periodically by a benefits consulting firm as a way of updating their clients and promoting dialogue.

Each card usually centers on a single "story." Color blocks separate parts of the story and provide a column structure. In the darker color blocks, type is reversed.

The back of the card, which is the mailing panel, is shown in reduced size below each of the examples.

Health Care Reform

- Publisher: Towers Perrin, Chicago, IL
- Designers: Kathleen Aiken, Jeanmarie Powers, Annette Smaga, Elizabeth Alonzo
- Colors: Deep blue (PMS 286) and one or two other spot colors that change each issue
- Type: Univers Condensed, Galliard, Kuenstler Script
- Dimensions: 9 by 6

Experiments in color

This informational journal for desktop publishers is noted for its adventurous spirit. Each issue features a different color design and a new combination of typefaces for the articles inside. This is truly a case where the medium is a big part of the message—the idea is to share a new design plan with the readership each month, for better or for worse.

The compressed, numbered nameplate and the unusual page size are the only design elements that stay constant from issue to issue.

ThePage
Issues 57, 59, 61, 66 and 68, 1992–1993

- Publisher: The Cobb Group, Louisville, KY
- Designer: David Doty, PageWorks
- Colors: Process (issues 57 and 68); black, PMS 1788 and 279 (issue 59); black and PMS 360 (issue 61); PMS 226 and 329 (issue 66)
- Type: Helvetica Condensed and Ultra Compressed (nameplate), with various combinations of faces inside
- Dimensions: 7 by 11

Section 6

Resources

Design & Printing Checklist

Concept

Goal analysis

❑ Describe audience

❑ Describe objectives of newsletter

❑ Describe strategy for achieving those objectives

❑ Describe in general terms the overall look of the newsletter

❑ Set publication schedule

Budget analysis

❑ Determine initial design costs

❑ Determine production costs for each issue, including proofing, high-resolution printing and mass printing

❑ Determine mailing costs

❑ Determine promotional costs

❑ Determine clerical costs, such as fulfillment and mailing list maintenence

Content analysis

❑ List regular departments and columns

❑ Estimate typical number and length of news stories per issue

❑ Estimate space reserved for display or classified advertisements

General design issues

Page size

Pages per issue

Paper weight, color and finish

Number of columns

Width of margins

Space between columns

Number of colors

Nameplate: Size and position

              Styling

Photos: Frequency per issue

          ❑ Scan for printing   ❑ Scan for position only

          ❑ To be inserted at the print shop

Contents block position

Masthead position

Folio position

Header text, if any

Footer text, in any

Type styles: Face, size, leading, alignment

Body text

Major heads

Second level heads

Subheads

Department heads

Column heads

Captions

Bylines

Eyebrows

Decks

Pullquotes

Masthead

Credit block

Jump lines

Prototype & template development

❑ Discuss project with print shop and get estimates

❑ Modify design if necessary to satisfy budget constraints or print shop requirements

❑ Set up page design in software (size, margins, columns)

❑ Design nameplate

❑ Set up master page/header/footer items

❑ Lay out and typeset dummy articles

❑ Check word counts against anticipated story lengths

❑ Define paragraph styles

❑ Review and refine

❑ Save prototype as template

Production

- ❑ Compile story inventory
- ❑ Sketch article placement
- ❑ Scan photos
- ❑ Open template and save with issue name
- ❑ Change issue number or date on cover in headers or footers
- ❑ Place stories
- ❑ Apply paragraph styles
- ❑ Apply local formatting where necessary
- ❑ Place scans and other artwork
- ❑ Adjust story flow
- ❑ Print proofs
- ❑ Proofread and edit text
- ❑ Print final pages
- ❑ If using color, print laser spot color separations for proofing and/ or for reproduction; if further approval is required, print color proofs
- ❑ If higher resolution is required, copy all required files to disk and send to service bureau or disk-to-print shop; check imagesetter output before sending to press
- ❑ Send to print shop
- ❑ Review printer's proofs before approving press run

Further Reading

Books

Beach, Mark. *Editing Your Newsletter.* Portland, OR: Coast to Coast Books, 1988. Distributed to the trade by Writer's Digest/Northlight Books, Cincinatti, OH.

Nitty-gritty details of proofreading, production and printing.

Beach, Mark. *Graphically Speaking: An Illustrated Guide to the Working Language of Design and Printing.* Portland, OR: Coast to Coast Books, 1992.

If you have a question about any technical aspect of getting your newsletter produced, look it up here. Includes nearly 3,000 definitions and over 200 illustrations.

Beach, Mark. *Newsletter Sourcebook.* Cincinatti, OH: Northlight Books, 1993.

Perfect for brainstorming. A good collection of real-world newsletters annotated with comments on design strategy and plenty of tips.

Beach, Mark and Russon, Ken. *Papers for Printing: How to Choose the Right Paper at the Right Price for Any Printing Job.* Portland, OR: Coast to Coast Books, 1990.

The title says it all.

Bivins, Thomas H. *Fundamentals of Successful Newsletters.* Lincolnwood, IL: NTC Business Books: 1992.

A closer look at goals, strategy and effective writing and editing.

Floyd, Elaine. *Marketing With Newsletters.* St. Louis MO: EF Communications, 1991. 800/264-6305; 314/647-6788.

An in-depth resource for writers and publishers of promotional newsletters. Includes discussion of strategy and distribution.

Hudson, Howard Penn. *Publishing Newsletters: A Complete Guide to Markets, Editorial Content, Design, Printing, Subscriptions, and Much More..., Revised Edition.* New York: Charles Scribner's Sons, 1988.

A good guide for thinking through the many details involved in launching, producing and promoting a new newsletter.

Parker, Roger C. *Looking Good in Print, Third Edition.* Chapel Hill, NC: Ventana Press, 1993.

A great reference for layout ideas, typographic principles and makeovers.

Parker, Roger C. *The Makeover Book.* Chapel Hill, NC: Ventana Press, 1989.

Over one hundred before-and-after examples. An inside look at how professional designers solve problems and generate new solutions.

Pattison, Polly; Pretzer, Mary; and Beach, Mark. *Outstanding Newsletter Designs.* Portland, OR: Coast to Coast Books, 1990.

A beautiful collection of real-world newsletters from around the world with comments by three experts in the field.

Roth, Steve and Blatner, David. *Real World Scanning and Halftones.* Berkeley, CA: Peachpit Press, 1993.

If you plan on putting in your own photos, and you haven't had much experience in the area, pick up this book for some invaluable tips.

White, Jan V. *Graphic Design for the Electronic Age.* New York: Watson-Guptill, 1988.

A general guide to desktop typography, layout and illustration with emphasis on principles of good graphic design.

White, Jan V. *Graphic Idea Notebook, Revised Edition.* Rockport MA: Rockport Publisher, 1991.

Having trouble coming up with an idea for a graphic, logo or illustration? Need some ideas for photo layouts? Turn to this book for fresh ideas.

Periodicals

Before&After
PageLab
1830 Sierra Gardens Drive, #30
Roseville, CA 95661-2912
916/784-3880

Subtitled "How to design cool stuff," this beautiful full-color bimonthly inspires and instructs. It's heavy on illustration techniques, but most issues feature page design or typography lessons as well. Once you subscribe, you'll want to buy all the back issues as well.

Step-by-Step Electronic Design
Dynamic Graphics
6000 North Forest Park Drive
P.O. Box 1901
Peoria, IL 61656

The premiere how-to-do-it journal for graphic designers and illustrators. Every issue provides a detailed analysis of how a design was conceived, modified and executed on computer. Regular columns discuss current technical issues.

ThePage
The Cobb Group
9420 Bunsen Parkway, Suite 300
Louisville, KY 40232
800/223-8720

An information-filled monthly targeted at both novice and experienced desktop publishers. Every issue is a little different: Some emphasize design ideas, others focus on software techniques; the best issues provide a synergistic mix of these areas. Each issue is printed with a new color scheme and a new combination of typefaces to provide readers with fresh ideas.

For more information

ADEPT
(Association for the Development of Electronic Publishing Technique)
National Computer Graphics Association
2722 Merrilee Drive 200
Fairfax, VA 22031
800/233-7811

Call this national association for news about chapter meetings and other activities in your area.

Newsletters in Print
Gale Research
835 Penobscot Building
Detroit, MI 48226
800/347-GALE

An annual directory of newsletters in publication. A good reference for investigating the marketplace and scouting out your competition.

Tools of the Trade
3148-B Duke Street
Alexandria, VA 22314
800/827-8665

A one-stop shop for just about every worthwhile graphic design book published in the past ten years. If you can't find the title you're looking for at your local store, call Tools of the Trade.

Glossary

A

Align left

To set a paragraph so all lines of text begin at the left edge of the column, but end at different points on the right side of the column. *Also known as* Flush left *or* Ragged right.

Ascender

A tall stroke in a letter, such as the vertical stroke in a "d."

B

Bad break

A word hyphenated at an awkward point. What's considered "awkward" is often a judgment call, but most designers consider the following to be bad breaks: a hyphen following the first two letters of a word; a hypen in a proper noun, such as a person's name; a hyphen at the end of a page.

Balance

A desirable design quality. Roughly speaking, a layout is considered balanced when blocks of text and graphics are distributed evenly around the center of the page or spread. For example, one large photo on the left side of a spread may balance two small photos on the right side.

Banner

See Nameplate.

Baseline

The invisible horizontal line on which letters without descenders sit.

Bitmap

A computer graphic, often a scan, which is stored as a collection of colored pixels. Can be created or edited with a paint or image processing program. Common file formats are MacPaint or PICT on the Mac; .BMP, .PCX, .CGM and .TGA on the PC; and TIFF on both.

Bleed

n. An element, such as a graphic, bar or background tint, that prints to the edge of the page.
v. To position an element so that it extends past the edge of the page.

Blend

A series of shades or objects that create the impression of a gradual transition.

Blueline

A monochrome printer's proof created from film negatives.

Blueprint

See Blueline.

Binding
The joining of pages into a book. Common methods include saddle stitch (staples), plastic comb, wire and perfect binding (glue).

Box
A container that can be outlined or hold text, graphics, tints, color fills or blends.

Bubblejet
A low-cost printer that deposits liquid ink, usually from 300–400 dots per inch.

Bullet
1. One of a series of short phrases or paragraphs that are preceded by a symbol; often indented. 2. The symbol used in such a series. Some common bullet symbols are •, ■ and ◆.

Byline
The short paragraph that provides the author's name. Usually appears immediately below a headline or as the first line in an article.

C

Camera-ready art
Positive prints, such as complete laser or imagesetter prints, that include type, graphics and photos, and are fully ready for the print shop to shoot with a camera to create film negatives.

Caption
A short paragraph that accompanies a photo, chart or illustration.

Caption head
An introductory line preceding a caption, usually set in a bold version of the caption style.

CD-ROM
A compact disc that can hold 660 MB of computer data. Often used to deliver large libraries of fonts, clip art or photos.

Centered
Text set so that each line of a paragraph is positioned in the middle of a column.

Clip art
Generic illustrations that can be purchased for unlimited reproduction in publications of your choice; may be available in printed or electronic forms or both.

CMYK
Cyan, **M**agenta, **Y**ellow, **B**lack: The four process colors used in full-color printing.

Colorize
To print a monochrome (i.e., grayscale) scan in a non-black ink, or to apply various color tints or fills to a monochrome scan.

Color proofs
1. Desktop color proofs: Pages printed in full-color directly from a computer to a digital printer. 2. Printers' color proofs: Simulations of final printed pages created by the print shop from film negative separations; brand names include Color Key, Cromalin and MatchPrint.

Color separations
A series of pages, each of which contains only those elements that should be printed in a particular color of ink. There are two types of color separations: spot color and process color.

Color xerographic
Refers to a color proofing technology in which a desktop computer is connected to a color copier.

Column
1. Imaginary vertical boundaries for a block of text. 2. A space in a newsletter consistently devoted to the opinions of one writer.

Column depth
The number of words that will fit in a column or partial column.

Column guides
Nonprinting vertical lines indicating the edges of a column.

Compress
To reduce a file's size by creating a specially encoded version. This may be done with scanning software, an image processor or a special file utility program. The compressed file must first be expanded, or decoded, before it can be used.

Contents block
Table or list that identifies major stories in each issue. Best used in a newsletter that has several long, feature-type stories. "Inside" and "In this issue" are common variations for the heading.

Continued line
See Jump-to line, Jump-from line.

Copy
1. A duplicate of a file or of an item on a page. 2. Text to be used in a publication. Usually refers to a file that has not yet been extensively styled.

Copy fitting
To fit articles to the available space. Common tactics include: providing a maximum word count to writers and editors; deleting text when an article exceeds the maximum word count; or, when an article runs over just a bit, changing hyphenation manually or reducing type width slightly to make more words fit on each line.

Credit block
Short paragraph, usually at the end of a story, containing information about the author.

Cromalin
A type of color proof created by the print shop from film negatives at the request of the customer. Most often used for process color separations. Also known as a *DuPont Cromalin*.

Crop
1. To trim the edges of a scan or graphic in a graphics or page layout program. 2. To have the print shop reproduce a portion of a photo.

Crop marks
Short lines added to the borders of a photographic print or transparency to indicate to the print shop what portion of a photo should be reproduced.

 D

Dateline
Line of text, indicating date or number of issue. Usually appears as part of the nameplate.

Deck
A brief paragraph introducing the theme of a story. It usually appears between the headline and first paragraph, or hung to the left of an article.

Decompress
To decode, or expand, a file that has been compressed.

Deep
See Depth.

Default
An option or setting that a program uses automatically unless you specify otherwise.

Demand publishing
Printing copies of a newsletter as you need them, as from a desktop laser printer or an office copier.

Department
Space in a newsletter set aside for a particular type of news, information or advice. A department usually is identified by a consistent department head, often set in a special style. May contain more than one article.

Depth
1. A way of describing how many words will fit in a column or partial column. 2. A color attribute similar to "darkness." Deep colors provide enough contrast against white paper that you can use them for printing small type or as backgrounds for reversed type.

Descender
A stroke in a letter that drops below the baseline, such as the vertical stroke in a "p" or the curled stroke in a "g."

Desktop printer
Any computer printer, though the term most often refers to printers priced inexpensively enough for business users.

Design device
A graphic, typesetting or layout technique used to unify elements on a page or direct the eyes of a reader.

Dialog box
A box that appears onscreen that presents you with controls or numeric settings.

Dingbat
Graphic symbol, such as ☞ or ✔. Usually part of a typeface, such as Zapf Dingbats.

Disk-to-print
A printing service that accepts files on disk and turns them into finished, printed newsletters.

Dither
A method of simulating tones in an image by creating fine patterns of dots, where the dots are the same size but the patterns vary in density. Dithering may be used to simulate grays on black-and-white monitors and printers, or to simulate additional colors on a low-resolution color device.

dpi
dots-**p**er-**i**nch. A measure of resolution for a printer or a printout. The higher the dpi, the sharper type and images tend to appear.

Draw software
A program that allows you to combine geometric shapes, lines, arcs and text. Files are saved as object files (such as PICT or EPS on the Mac, Metafiles or EPS in Windows).

Drop cap
First letter of a story or a new section of a story, enlarged and positioned in the indented area of the first few lines of a paragraph. Draws reader to that location.

Drop shadow
A duplicate of a box or headline, usually set in gray or black, placed behind and slightly offset from the original.

Dummy text
A text file made up of nonsense words. Used for designing prototypes of a newsletter before the actual articles are available.

Duotone
A grayscale photo printed in two colors, usually black and a Pantone spot color. An easy and generally inexpensive way to add a touch of color to photos in a two-color publication.

Dye sublimation
A type of color proof printing technology. Dye sublimation printers can reproduce color photos with great fidelity and little or no dot pattern.

Dylux
A monochrome printer's proof created from film negatives.

E

EPS
Encapsulated **P**ostScript **F**ile. An illustration, image or piece of type that has been saved in PostScript format for importing into a program.

Eyebrow
Line of text that appears above headline. Usually in smaller type and italic. Sometimes called kicker or teaser.

F

Family
A group of related typefaces, usually including Roman, Italic, Bold and Bold Italic variations. Extended families may include additional weights and their italic counterparts.

Feature
Story that may mix news, analysis, profiles, interviews and criticism.

File
Electronic version of a document.

Fill
The gray, patterned or color interior of an object.

Film negative
Transparency with clear ("white") image on black background, either produced directly from an imagesetter or created by a print shop with a camera from positives. Used to make print plates.

Filter
1. A special effect command in an image processing program. 2. A companion file to a publishing program that allows the program to import or export a particular file format.

First-line indent
A paragraph format setting. Positive first-line indents are often used to signal a new paragraph; negative first line indents are usually used for bulleted paragraphs; and "zero" indents are used for the first paragraph following a head or for paragraphs separated by a space.

Flow
The manner in which text is placed and juxtaposed on a page.

Flush left
To set a paragraph so all lines of text begin at the left edge of the column, but end at different points on the right side of the column. *Also known as* Align left *or* Ragged right.

Flush right
To set a paragraph so all lines of text end at the right edge of the column, but begin at different points on the left side of the column. *Also known as* Align right.

FocolTone
One of several color matching systems.

Folio
A page number.

Font
1. Shorthand term for a family of typefaces, such as "Times" for Times Roman, Italic, Bold and Bold Italic. 2. Traditionally, a typeface in a particular size, such as Times Roman 10.

Footer
An item, such as a page number or date or both, that appears near the bottom of every or every other page.

Format
1. A particular page size and column structure. 2. Common term for size, style or alignment of type. 3. A language used to create a particular kind of file.

Four-color
Most often refers to full-color reproduction techniques using CMYK printing. May also refer to the use of four spot colors.

FPO
For **P**osition **O**nly. Placeholder for a photo or piece of art to be inserted by the print shop. A low-res scan or an outlined box labeled FPO.

G

Gradient
A seamless blend of shades or colors, usually in a rectangular or circular shape.

Graphic
General term for illustration, photo, chart, cartoon, rule or any geometric shape. The more specific terms are generally preferred.

Graphic device
Elements on the page, such as bars or colored shapes, positioned to add visual flair, direction or coherency.

Grayscale
Used to describe anything—art, photos, monitors or scanners—in which the color range consists of white, black and intermediate grays.

Grid
See Layout grid.

Grid line

A vertical or horizontal line in a chart or graph placed to indicate an axis value.

Guide

A nonprinting line that can be moved around on the screen to help you align objects or text on the page.

Gutter

In general, refers to space between live areas on facing pages. In some programs, gutter refers to space between columns.

H

Hairline

A very thin line, usually around a quarter-point thick (roughly $1/300$ of an inch).

Halftone

Picture with gradations of tone, formed by spots of varying sizes. The frequency of the spots is given in lines-per-inch.

Head shot

A portrait photo.

Header

An item, such as a page number or date or both, that appears near the top of every or every other page.

Headline

Large type that introduces a story. The most dominant element on the page aside from illustrations or photographs. Sizes typically range from 18 to 36 points, but may be smaller when boldface is used.

Hue

The property of color usually associated with color names, such as "red," "orange," "yellow," "blue" or "green"—as opposed to properties such as lightness, darkness, saturation or brilliance.

I

Illustration software

A program that allows you to draw using paths and other PostScript effects. Files are usually exported as EPS files.

Image processor

A program that allows you to modify high-resolution scanned art or photos. Files are usually exported as TIFF files.

Imagesetter

Professional-quality printing device that produces highly detailed type and photos on special paper or on film negatives. Typical resolutions are 1270 and 2540 dpi with screen frequencies over 100 lpi. Usually owned and operated by a service bureau.

Import

To insert a file from one program into the file of another program.

Indicia

A mark representing a postal permit.

Inkjet

A low-cost printer that sprays liquid ink onto a sheet of paper, usually from 300–400 dpi. Both black and color models are available.

Interlocking flow
A way of juxtapositioning stories on a page as though they were tiles of varying sizes and shapes.

J

Jaggies
Rough edges in a computer image or scan that appear when the pixels in the image are as large or larger than the spots created by the printer.

JPEG
Joint **P**hotographic **E**xperts **G**roup. A compressed file format for scanned images that uses lossy compression. Tends to discard color variation rather than brightness variation.

Jump
To continue a story on another page.

Jump-from line
A line added to tell the reader which page a story started on.

Jump-to line
A line added to tell the reader which page a story is continued on.

Justify
To align the beginning of each text line to the left edge of a column and the end of each full line to the right edge. This is accomplished by altering the letter and word spacing in each line.

K

KB
See Kilobyte.

Kerning
Removing space from between letters.

Keyline
A box drawn to indicate to the print shop where art or type should be placed.

Kicker
See Eyebrow.

Kilobyte
A measure of data consumption or capacity. 1024 bytes. (A typical page of text, without any formatting commands or graphics, takes up about 4 KB.)

Knockout
An area within a color background where the background color will not be printed because an item in a different color ink is set to print there. Prevents overprinting of two colors.

L

Laser printer
A desktop printer that deposits tiny particles of toner on a page, much like a copier. Resolutions range from 300–1200 dpi.

Layout grid
An arrangement of guides or imaginary lines used as an underlying structure for columns and page elements.

Leading
Space between lines of type; also known as *line spacing*. Pronounced "ledding."

Legend
A list of colors, patterns or symbols used in an accompanying chart, along with explanations of what each signifies.

Ligature
A single type character in which two letters are joined; substituted for two single letters which touch. For example, **fi** for **fi**, and **fl** for **fl**.

Line art
A graphic composed of black-and-white areas, lines or dots.

Link
The connection between text or a graphic on the page and the original file from which it was imported.

Live area
The area of the page that contains type and graphics.

Local formatting
Type style settings applied to a range of text; often refers to a *style override.*

Logo
1. The primary design element in a nameplate. 2. A graphic or typographic symbol representing an organization.

lpi
lines **p**er **i**nch. A measure of halftone detail, or "screen frequency." With a higher lpi, smaller halftone spots are packed more densely to simulate a shade of gray.

M

Mailing panel
Section of front or back cover devoted to addresses and postage or postal permits. Only required if newsletter is a *self-mailer.*

Margin
The area between the edge of a page and the live area. Often set for one-half inch, but may be much larger or a bit smaller.

Master item
Type or graphic placed on a master page or in the repeating header or footer areas of your document. Typical master items include automatic page numbers and repeating graphics.

Master page
Special background page where items and guides may be placed to repeat continuously throughout a publication.

MatchPrint
A type of color proof created by the print shop from film negatives at the request of the customer. Most often used for process color separations. Also known as a *3M MatchPrint.*

MB
See Megabyte.

Masthead
Block of text identifying the publication, including staff, address, copyright information and so on. Sometimes used incorrectly to refer to the *nameplate* or *banner.*

Megabyte
A measure of data consumption or capacity. 1024 kilobytes. (A typical scan of a 3x5 color photo consumes 1–2 MB.)

Midtone
Middle shades in a photo. In a black-and-white photo, midtones are medium grays.

Mirror
To use identical but opposite grids on facing pages. An example is a spread where two columns are used on each page but set the same distance from the inner edges, leaving a wide margin on opposite sides of the spread.

Mixed format
A design in which two or more column structures are used, each for a different purpose.

Monitor
Display screen.

N

Nameplate
Design on front cover that includes the name of the newsletter and usually items such as an issue date, a tagline or a logo.

New line
A command or keystroke that forces a line of text to break at a certain point and wrap to the following line without creating a new paragraph.

O

One-color
A design to be printed with a single color of ink—often, but not necessarily, black.

Orphan
Last line of a paragraph appearing alone at the top of a column. Sometimes also used to refer to a single word or partial word appearing alone on the last line of a paragraph.

Outline
1. A style of type in which characters are white with a black outline. 2. To remove background detail surrounding the main subject of a photo; the background is often replaced with white or a solid color.

Overlay
A spot color printing plate.

Overprint
To print an element in one color over a background element in a different color.

Overset text
Text at the end of a story that has not yet been placed on any page.

P

Page number (automatic)
Special symbol placed on a master page or in a header or footer that automatically sets correct page numbers throughout a document.

Paint software
A program that allows you to change the color of individual pixels using brushes, pencils, erasers and selection tools. Files are saved as bitmaps.

Palette
A small window, containing tools or settings, that floats in front of a document window.

Pantone
The most commonly used color matching system.

Paper positive
A page printed in black on white paper. Usually refers to a page printed on an imagesetter on RC paper.

Paragraph rule
A paragraph format setting that automatically inserts a rule of a specified weight, color and length above or below the selected paragraph.

Paragraph space
A paragraph format setting that automatically inserts a specified space above or below the selected paragraph.

Paragraph style
A collection of type styling and formatting commands that can be instantly applied to a paragraph or range of paragraphs by choosing a name from a menu or palette.

Pica
Unit of measurement used in graphic design and typesetting. Equal to $\frac{1}{6}$ of an inch or 12 points.

Pixel
One of the tiny dots that make up a screen display or a scan.

Place
To import and position a story or graphic.

Plate
A thin sheet of material (usually metal) that carries the printing image.

PMS
Pantone **M**atching **S**ystem. Usually used as a prefix to a Pantone number for a specific color (e.g., PMS 286).

Point
Unit of measurement used in graphic design and typesetting. Equal to $\frac{1}{12}$ of a pica or $\frac{1}{72}$ of an inch.

Postal permit indicia
A mark, usually an outlined box of type, included on a mailing panel to indicate that the newsletter's postage is paid with a post office permit.

PostScript
A programming language for describing typefaces, graphics and page layout.

ppi
pixels **p**er **i**nch. Measure of resolution in a scanned image or of a monitor.

Printer spread
A pair of pages that face each other before all the sheets in a newsletter are assembled, bound and folded.

Process
1. Printing technology for reproducing full-color art and photos based on the use of four primary inks. 2. A primary ink, such as cyan, magenta, yellow or black.

Process simulation
Approximate reproduction of a special-formula color, such as a Pantone color, using a combination of process inks instead of the specific ink.

Proof
An intermediate print produced for proofreading or for checking colors.

Prototype
Experimental version of a publication created to investigate design issues or problems.

Pullquote
A text block containing an important or provocative quote from a story. Usually set in larger type with some sort of graphic device, such as a background tint or rules above and below.

R

Rag
An irregular edge in a type design.

Ragged bottom
A page or spread where columns end at a variety of points.

Ragged right
A paragraph set so all lines of text begin at the left edge of the column, but end at different points on the right side of the column. *Also known as* Align left *or* Flush left.

RC paper
Resin **C**oated paper. Photographic paper used for output from imagesetters.

Reader spread
A pair of pages that face each other after all the sheets in a newsletter are assembled, bound and folded.

Register
To align two or more color plates perfectly during printing.

Registration mark
A target symbol with crosshairs printed in the trim area of the page. Used by the print shop to precisely align color plates during printing.

Resolution
Any of several measures of detail and visual quality. Screen and printer resolution are typically measured in dots-per-inch, though the resolution of printed images is usually measured in lines-per-inch. In general, printers with a higher dpi can more ably produce images with a higher lpi.

Reverse
An item printed in white over a darker tint or color.

River
Large spaces in three or more successive lines of text that fall along a line. Usually caused by justified paragraph alignment.

RGB
Red, **G**reen, **B**lue. The three primary colors of scanners and monitors.

Rough
A crude drawing or block layout of a page.

Rule
Straight line used as a graphic device or divider, usually between a quarter-point and 12 points in thickness (weight).

Ruler guides
Nonprinting guides pulled out from onscreen rulers to aid alignment.

Runaround
See Text wrap.

Run-in subhead
Lower level headline that appears as the beginning of a body paragraph. Usually bold, sometimes in a different typeface or size.

Running foot or **head**
See Footer *or* Header.

S

Scan
1. Photograph or artwork converted to an electronic image that can be modified on the computer and placed in a publication. 2. To create such an electronic image with a scanner.

Scanner
Device that can "read" artwork or a photo into an electronic format, such as TIFF.

Screen
Tint, or lighter shade of a color, produced by printing an ink as closely placed spots or lines. The darkness of a screen is specified as a percentage, such as "10%."

Screen frequency
See lpi.

Self-mailer
A newsletter that is mailed without an envelope. Requires the addition of a mailing panel on the front or back cover.

Separate
To print color separations.

Separations
Two or more printing plates that are combined during printing to create a multi-color page.

Serif
1. Typeface that includes short perpendicular lines at the end of many letter strokes. 2. The short line itself.

Service bureau
A company that offers high-resolution printing services.

Sidebar
Text related to a story but handled as a separate element.

Signature
A group of pages prepared as a large composite sheet for book printing on commercial presses. Usually 4, 8 or 16 pages per side.

Smart quotes
A software feature that automatically converts typewriter quotes to typographer's quotes as you type.

Snaking flow
Arrangement of text where each story flows down column after column, and stories follow each other one after the other in the same manner.

Snap to guide
Software feature that helps you align elements to nonprinting guides as you move the elements onscreen.

Space after, space before
See Paragraph space.

Spot color
A color applied to certain elements in a page design but not others. Usually specified as a Pantone color.

Spread
Two facing pages. *See* Printer spread *and* Reader spread.

Stick-up cap
The first letter of a story or section that has been enlarged relative to the rest of the body text. Serves same purpose as drop cap.

Story list
An inventory of the stories that are available or scheduled for an up-coming issue, usually with approximate word counts.

Stripping
Assembling film negatives, including type, photos and artwork, into a single page that will be used to make a printing plate. Done by the print shop.

Style
1. A collection of styling and formatting commands that can be instantly applied to a paragraph or range of paragraphs by choosing a name from a menu or palette. Also called "style sheet." 2. A variation of a typeface, such as plain (roman), bold or italic.

Style definition
The specific settings in a paragraph style.

Style override
Type style settings applied to a range of text after a paragraph style has been applied.

Subhead
Lower level headline that appears within body of text. Usually bold, sometimes larger. May have additional space before or after.

T

Tabloid
Oversized newsletter. Technically, the term refers to an 11 x 17 inch page size, but smaller custom sizes may also be used.

Tagline
Line of text in nameplate that mentions publisher, audience or purpose of newsletter.

Template
A blank or empty publication set up with page specifications (margins, text columns, standing items, etc.). Opening a template file produces a new, untitled copy that can be filled and saved under a specific issue name.

Text block or **box**
A rectangular area that holds text. May be changed in length or width, or connected to other blocks to continue story flow.

Text wrap
Software feature that automatically arranges text around a graphic.

Threaded text
Single story running through two or more connected text blocks.

Thumbnail
A miniature print of a page or pages.

TIFF
Tag **I**mage **F**ile **F**ormat. A file format for bitmaps of any resolution or color range. Usually used for scans.

Tile
To print an oversized document on standard sheets by dividing the printed image among several sheets that can then be assembled for proofing.

Tint
See Screen.

Tombstone
The visual effect created when several headlines appear at the top of adjacent columns.

Track
A typesetting control in page layout software that adjusts letter spacing in proportion to type size.

Trim
To cut away the edges of a publication prior to binding.

TruMatch
One of several color matching systems.

Two-color
A design to be printed with two colors of ink, usually black and a Pantone spot color.

Two-up
A printing technique in which two pages, such as a spread, appear adjacent on a single sheet.

Type ornaments
Small graphics that are part of a typeface.

Type solution or **treatment**
A design approach that relies solely on the positioning and manipulation of type without any graphics.

Type width
Software control that allows you to condense type.

Typeface
Letterforms of a specific design, such as Helvetica or Times.

Typeset
To apply styling and formatting commands to text.

Typographer's quotes
Curly quotes.

W

Weight
1. The thickness of a line, usually specified in points. 2. A variation of a typeface based on the thickness of letter strokes, specified with terms like Light, Roman, Book, Bold, ExtraBold or Heavy (though occasionally specified by number).

White space
Open areas around the page that provide relief from—or act as a counterpoint to—the text areas.

Widow
First line of a paragraph appearing alone at the bottom of a column. Sometimes also used to refer to a single word or partial word appearing alone on the last line of a paragraph.

Word count
1. The number of words in a story. 2. The number of average-length words that will fit in a given space.

Wrap
The movement of text from one line to the next.

Index

A

Address labels   135
Alignment   120–21
   to grids   18
   justification   60, 120–21
   left   61
   nameplate elements   84–85
Ascenders   108
Audience   10–11, 44–45
   typeface choice   106–7

B

Banners
   See Nameplates
Baseline   108
Bibliography   331–33
Bitmapped drawings   168
Bleeds   87, 142–43, 289–90
   defined   143
   printing   252–53, 257
Books resource list   331–32
Boxes   86
Brochures   292
Budget checklist   325
Bullets   31
Bylines   127

C

Calendars   314
Camera–ready graphics   260
Captions   127
   defined   9
Charts   176–79
   customizing   177–79
   page layout program   232

Clip art   168–74
        background   169
        buying   168
        enhancing   172–73
        problems   170–71
        sources   174–75
        types   168–69
Color separations   189, 191
        process color   207, 209
        proofing   249, 254–55
Colors
        balancing   201
        bleeds   87, 142–43, 252–53, 257
                See also Bleeds
        counting   182–83
        dividing pages   319
        gallery   297–321
        headlines   146
        nameplates   86–87, 89
        Pantone   194–97
        paper   21
        photographs   185
        printers   256–57
        printing costs   186
        proofing   256–57
        tints   22, 141, 197, 242–43
        type   185, 196–97
        See also Process color; Spot color
Column space   54
Columns
        balancing   27
        five   313
        four   284–88
        separating   120–21
        single   16–17, 60–63
                successful   60–61
        three   17, 25, 68–69
                disadvantages   68
                gallery   277–82
        two   64–67
                centered   269
                gallery   269–76
                set to right   271
                symmetrically inside   270

     wide 67
     wide apart 273
   width 122
Credit blocks 127, 235
Cropping photographs 158–59

D

Decks 131
Descenders 108
Design
   attention–getting 142–49
   audience considerations 10–11, 44–45
   checklist 325–29
   determining limitations 42–43
   evaluating 15
   experimental 321
   getting ideas 39–41
   layout 18–19, 227, 231–33
      simplicity 267–68
   prototype 216–23
      checklist 328
   revising 20–21
   rules 8
   strategy 45
   templates 224–25
   See also Specific items to be designed
Dingbats 128, 132–33, 148, 167
Disk–to–print shops 250
Dithering 175
Dpi (printers) 243, 245
Drop caps 132–33
Duotones 175, 192–93

E

Encapsulated PostScript files 169
Eyebrows 30, 128

F

Film negatives 250, 258–59
First impressions 40
Folds, paper 240

Fonts
    See Typefaces
Footers 130
Formats
    brochure 292
    centered 65
    choosing 54–59
    defined 53
    five–column 313
    four–column 284–88
    legal–size 74–75, 295–96
    letter–size 72–73
    magazine–style 270, 274–76, 287, 291
    mixed 17, 283, 288
    offset 65, 70–71
    one–column 16–17, 60–63
        successful 60–61
    post–card 320
    sketching on paper 58–59, 214
    tabloid–size 76–77, 272
    three–column 17, 25, 68–69
        disadvantages 68
        gallery 277–82
    two–column 64–67
        centered 269
        gallery 269–76
        set to right 271
        symmetrically inside 270
        wide 67
        wide apart 273
    type settings 61
    types 58–59
    unusual 305–6
Four–color design 202–3
FPO 22

G

Glossary 335–49
Gradients 22, 192
Graphics 165–80
    basic tools 166–67
    camera–ready 260

charts   176–79
clip art   168–74
color   299
conceptualizing   180
defined   165
dithering   175
duotoning   175
large–format   315–16
lightening tone   300
nameplates   90–91
printing   241
See also Charts; Clip art; Photographs
Graphs
    See Charts
Grayscale   22
Grids   18
Guides   18
Gutter   54

H

Halftones   242–45
    printing methods compared   244
Hanging heads   16, 63, 65
Headers   130
Headlines
    color   146
    defined   9
    designing   218–19
    line spacing   103
    in margins   16, 63, 65
    tombstoning   71
    type size   100–101
    wide   67
    wrapping   76–77
Hyphenation   123

I

Imagesetters
    See Service bureaus
Indents   118–19
Initial caps   132–33
Interlocking articles   69, 71, 280

J

Jumps   29, 129
        defined   9
Justification   60, 120–21

K

Kerning   108
Kickers
        See Eyebrows

L

Layout   18–19, 227, 231–33
        simplicity   267–68
Leading   102–3, 108, 122
Letter spacing   108
Line spacing   102–3, 108, 122
Logos   82, 167
Lpi   242–43, 245

M

Magazine resource list   333
Mailing panels   135
Margins
        equal   62
        headlines in   16, 63, 65
        inner pages   70–71
        ragged bottom   77
        setting   63
        wide left   61
        wide right   60
Mastheads   79, 134–35
Measuring space   19
Mirror pages   71

N

Nameplates   20, 79–96, 167, 215
        aligning elements   84–85
        characteristics   80–81
        color   86–87, 89

defined   9
elements   82–83
gallery   263–65
graphics   90–91
problem–solving   92–96
separating elements   86–87
table of contents   83
typefaces   88
vertical   266, 292
Newsletters
audience   44–45, 106–7
business   309–10
characteristics   6–7
creating   213–36
checklist   328
prototype   216–23
templates   224–25
defined   7
elements   9
goal   44
production   226–36, 329
types
informational   46–47
membership   48–49
promotional   50–51
See also Design

O

One–color design   182
Orphans   119
Overlapping elements   147

P

Pages
dividing with color   319
inner   70–71, 220–21
mirrored   71
number   6
numbering, folded format   75
unusual shapes   291
Paint files   168
Pantone colors   194–97

Paper
  color   21
  folds   240
  legal–size   74–75, 295–96
  letter–size   72–73
  printing options   241
  tabloid–size   76–77
Paper positives   250, 258–59
Paragraph styles   118, 222–23
  overriding   234
Paragraphs
  separating   118–19
  stragglers   119
PCX files   168
Periodicals resource list   333
Photographs   151–64
  award shots   160
  choosing   152–53
  color   185
  contrast   153
  cropping   158–59
  duotones   192–93
  large–format   293–94
  outlining   161
  placement   23, 154–57
    non–news articles   156–57
  portrait shots   159, 234, 295–96
  preparing for printer   162
  problems   160–61
  product shots   161
  resembling illustrations   161
  scanning and enhancing   163
  space from text   163
Pi symbols   148
Picas   19
Pixels   246
Points   19
Print shops   22–23
  graphics   241
  quote checklist   239
  talking with   238–39
Printer spreads   23
Printers (machines)
  color   256–57

      desktop   252–53
      dpi   243, 245
Printer's proof   251
Printing
      bleeds   252–53, 257
      color pricing   186
      graphics   241
      halftones   244
      paper options   241
      preparing newsletter for   237–60
      process   251
      quality comparisons   33
      summary   260
      See also Print shops; Service bureaus
Process color   203–5, 317–18
      color separations   207, 209
      defined   204
      vs. spot color   206–7
Proofreading   248–57
      color separations   249, 254–55
      colors   256–57
Pullquotes   130–31

Q

Quotation marks   125

R

Reader spreads   23
Reference resources   334
Resolution
      printers   243–45
      scans   163, 246–47
      screen   245
Resources
      books   331–32
      periodicals   333
      reference information   334
Reverses   88, 128, 144–45
Rivers of white   120–21
Rotated type   146
Rules   61
      defined   16

separating nameplates   86–87
separating stories   133, 141
styles   144
Runarounds   149

S

Sans–serif typefaces   108
    vs. serif   98
Scanning
    drawings   168
    matching printer resolutions   247
    photographs   163
    pixels per inch   246
    real objects   175
Screens   141, 242–43
Separating
    columns   120–21
    nameplate elements   86–87
    paragraphs   118–19
    photographs from text   163
    stories   61, 65, 133, 140–41
Serif typefaces   108
    vs. sans–serif   98
Service bureaus   32, 34–35, 258–59
Sidebars   30, 131
Snaking text   68–69, 279
Spaces after periods   125
Spot color
    bold design   303–4
    casual design   302
    choosing   27, 194–99
        legible type   196–97
    combined   311–12
    conservative design   301
    defined   183
    design guidelines   184–85
    four   202–3
    graphics   299
    limited   308
    muted   307
    one   182
    overlapping   190–91

preprinting   187
simple design   188–89
special effects   192–93
three   200–201, 303–4
two   183, 192–93
vs. four   297–98
vs. process color   206–7
Spreads   15, 23
Stick–up caps   132–33
Story lists   226
Strokes   108
Styles
See Paragraph styles
Subheads   30–31
defined   9
Symbols   148
See also Dingbats

T

Table of contents   83, 236
Taglines   83
defined   9
Templates   224–25
checklist   328
saving   229
Text
snaking   68–69, 279
wrapping   149
Three–color design   200–201, 303–4
TIFF files   168
Tints   22, 141, 197
defined   242–43
Tombstoning   71
Two–color design   183, 192–93
Type
checklist   327
colors   185, 196–97
rotating   146
size   100–101, 122
Typefaces   26, 28
choosing   106–7, 217
combining   110–16
extended families   112–13

        mixed families 114–15
        single–family 110–11
    families 109
    nameplates 88
    reversing 88, 128, 144–45
    sans–serif 108
        vs. serif 98
    serif 108
        vs. sans–serif 98
    terminology 108
    types of 109
    unusual 289–90
Typography 98–105
    guidelines 104–5
    professional look 124–25
    special characters 124

W

White space 66, 142–43
    defined 16
    separating stories 65
Widows 119

X

X–height 108

Z

Zapf dingbats 148, 167

Colophon

This book was developed on a Macintosh Centris 650 and a Macintosh IIcx. Planning and project management were handled with Microsoft Word 5.0 and Claris FileMaker Pro 2.0. Illustrations were produced with QuarkXPress 3.2, H-P DeskScan 2.0, Photoshop 2.5, FreeHand 3.1 and 4.0, DeltaGraph 1.5 and Aldus PageMaker 5.0. Headlines, body text and captions are set in various weights of Futura and ITC Century Condensed. Pages were composed in Aldus PageMaker 5.0 and proofed on a RealTech Laser 960, a Hewlett-Packard LaserJet 4-M, an Apple LaserWriter IIg and an Apple LaserWriter Pro. Film negative separations were created on an Orbotech Sprint 110. Two-color pages were printed at 2540 dpi with a screen frequency of 110 lpi; four-color pages were printed at 2540 dpi with a screen frequency of 133 lpi.

Design and

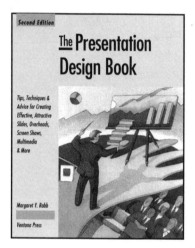

Advertising From the Desktop
$24.95
427 pages, illustrated
ISBN: 1-56604-064-7
Advertising From the Desktop offers unmatched design advice and helpful how-to instructions for creating persuasive ads. With tips on how to choose fonts, select illustrations, apply special effects and more, this book is an idea-packed resource for improving the looks and effects of your ads.

The Presentation Design Book, Second Edition
$24.95
320 pages, illustrated
ISBN: 1-56604-014-0
The Presentation Design Book is filled with thoughtful advice and instructive examples for creating business presentation visuals, including charts, overheads, type, etc., that help you communicate and persuade. The *Second Edition* adds advice on the use of multimedia. For use with any software or hardware.

The Gray Book, Second Edition
$24.95
262 pages, illustrated
ISBN: 1-56604-073-6
This "idea gallery" for desktop publishers offers a lavish variety of the most interesting black, white and gray graphic effects that can be achieved with laser printers, scanners and high-resolution output devices. The *Second Edition* features new illustrations, synopses and steps, added tips and an updated appendix.

Conquer

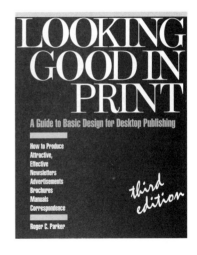

Looking Good in Print, Third Edition

$24.95
412 pages, illustrated
ISBN: 1-56604-047-7

For use with any software or hardware, this desktop design bible has become the standard among novice and experienced desktop publishers alike. With over 200,000 copies in print, *Looking Good in Print* is even better, with new sections on photography and scanning.

The Makeover Book: 101 Design Solutions for Desktop Publishing

$17.95
282 pages, illustrated
ISBN: 0-940087-20-0

Transform your work from average to outstanding! Seeing original "before-and-after" desktop publishing examples, you'll learn how basic design principles can dramatically improve your ads, brochures, flyers and more.

Newsletters From the Desktop, Second Edition

$24.95
306 pages, illustrated
ISBN: 1-56604-133-3

Now the millions of desktop publishers who produce newsletters can learn how to improve the design of their publications. Filled with helpful design tips and illustrations.

Can't wait? Call toll-free:
800/743-5369 (U.S. only)

Ventana Companions

Windows, Word & Excel
Office Companion, Second Edition
$21.95
544 pages, illustrated
ISBN: 1-56604-083-3
Your Microsoft business bible. This three-in-one reference is organized as a quick course in each program. Chapters contain valuable information on basic commands and features, plus helpful tutorials, tips and shortcuts.

Voodoo Windows
$19.95
282 pages, illustrated
ISBN: 1-56604-005-1
A unique resource, *Voodoo Windows* bypasses the technical information found in many Windows books to bring you an abundance of never-before-published tips, tricks and shortcuts for maximum Windows productivity. A one-of-a-kind reference for beginners and experienced users alike.

The Windows Shareware 500
$39.95
417 pages, illustrated, 4 disks
ISBN: 1-56604-045-0
This value-packed book/disk set introduces the world of affordable software. Comes with 4 disks, including America Online membership disks and 10 hours of free online time.

To order any Ventana Press title, use the form in the back of this book or contact your local bookstore or computer store.

For Creative Computing

Mac, Word & Excel Office Companion
$21.95
370 pages, illustrated
ISBN: 1-56604-065-5
The only 3-in-1 guide to the hottest Mac software on the market. Three easy-reference sections highlight key commands, tools and features of each program. The step-by-step tutorials offer tips on System 7, Word 5.1, Excel 4.0 and Interprogram rapport.

Voodoo Mac
$21.95
307 pages, illustrated
ISBN: 1-56604-028-0

Computer veteran Kay Nelson has compiled hundreds of invaluable tips, tricks, hints and shortcuts that simplify your Macintosh tasks and save time, including disk and drive magic, font and printing tips, alias alchemy and more!

Mac Shareware 500, Second Edition
$34.95
504 pages, illustrated
ISBN: 1-56604-076-0
The only comprehensive guide to the best Mac shareware programs, this two-disk, 504-page set offers users program overviews, instructions and tips on shareware. PLUS! free hours of America Online time (new members only).

Immediate shipment guaranteed
Full money-back guarantee

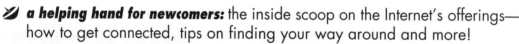

To order any Ventana Press title, fill out this order form and mail it to us with payment for quick shipment.

	Quantity		Price		Total
Advertising From the Desktop	_____	x	$24.95	=	$ _____
The Official America Online for Windows Membership Kit & Tour Guide	_____	x	34.95	=	$ _____
The Official America Online for Mac Membership Kit & Tour Guide	_____	x	$34.95	=	$ _____
The Gray Book, 2nd Edition	_____	x	$24.95	=	$ _____
Looking Good in Print, 3rd Edition	_____	x	$24.95	=	$ _____
The Mac Internet Tour Guide	_____	x	$27.95	=	$ _____
The Mac Shareware 500, 2nd Edition	_____	x	$34.95	=	$ _____
Mac, Word & Excel Desktop Companion	_____	x	$21.95	=	$ _____
The Makeover Book	_____	x	$17.95	=	$ _____
Newsletters From the Desktop, 2nd Edition	_____	x	$24.95	=	$ _____
The PC Internet Tour Guide	_____	x	$24.95	=	$ _____
The Presentation Design Book, 2nd Edition	_____	x	$24.95	=	$ _____
Voodoo Mac	_____	x	$21.95	=	$ _____
Voodoo Windows	_____	x	$19.95	=	$ _____
The Windows Internet Tour Guide	_____	x	$24.95	=	$ _____
The Windows Shareware 500	_____	x	$39.95	=	$ _____
Windows, Word & Excel Office Companion, 2nd Edition	_____	x	$21.95	=	$ _____
			Subtotal	=	$ _____

SHIPPING:
For all regular orders, please <u>add</u> $4.50/first book, $1.35/each additional.	=	$ _____
For "two-day air," <u>add</u> $8.25/first book, $2.25/each additional.	=	$ _____
For orders to Canada, <u>add</u> $6.50/book.	=	$ _____
For orders sent C.O.D., <u>add</u> $4.50 to your shipping rate.	=	$ _____
North Carolina residents must <u>add</u> 6% sales tax.	=	$ _____
	TOTAL =	$ _____

Name_____ Company_____

Address (No PO Box)_____

City_____ State_____ Zip _____

Daytime Telephone _____ ___ Payment enclosed ___VISA ___MC

Acc't # _____ Expiration Date_____

Signature _____

Mail or fax to: Ventana Press, PO Box 2468, Chapel Hill, NC 27515 ☎ 919/942-0220 Fax 919/942-1140
International Customers: Write or fax us at above address for information on our distributors worldwide.

CAN'T WAIT? CALL TOLL-FREE ☎ 800/743-5369 (U.S. only)

A Gi...

Begin exploring America Online
and watch the world open up.

**The Official America Online
Membership Kit & Tour Guides
put the most versatile commercial
online service at your fingertips.**

- Get your news from dozens of online wire services and magazines.

- Download tens of thousands of software files for your Macintosh or PC.

- Get expert computing advice from top hardware and software companies.

- Access stock quotes, buy and sell stocks online and track your investments with an online portfolio management system.

- Exchange e-mail with friends on the other side of the world.

- Explore the Internet through America Online's new Internet service.

- Discuss politics and current affairs in AOL's convention halls. AND MORE!

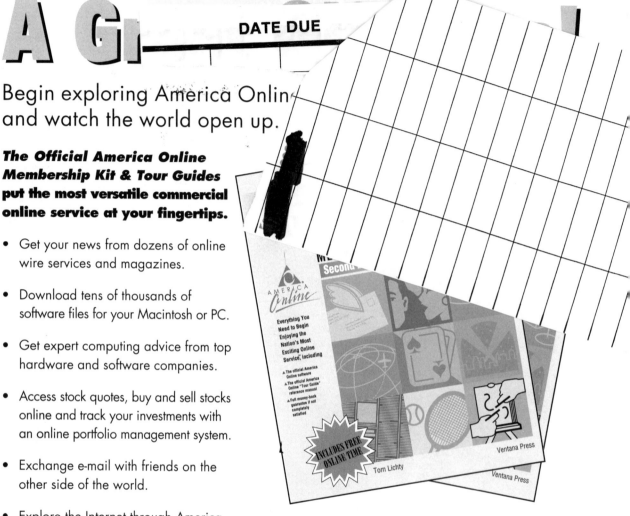

INCLUDES:

☞ The America Online starter disk.

☞ 10 FREE hours of online time.

☞ A readable, richly illustrated "traveling companion" to help you get the most from your time online.

Let **The Official America Online Membership Kit & Tour Guides** help you find your place in the emerging digital global village. While you're at it, buy a friend a copy—a great gift for novice and experienced online users alike!

Kits also available for Macintosh and DOS.

To order *The Official America Online for Windows Membership Kit & Tour Guides*, use the form in the back of this book or contact your local bookstore or computer store.